THE LIMITS OF LOYALTY

THE LIMITS OF LOYALTY

ORDINARY PEOPLE IN CIVIL WAR MISSISSIPPI

JARRET RUMINSKI

University Press of Mississippi / Jackson

www.upress.state.ms.us

Designed by Peter D. Halverson

The University Press of Mississippi is a member of the Association of
American University Presses.

A version of chapter three first appeared in the *Journal of the Civil War Era*,
vol. 2, no. 4, December 2012, 511–53.

First printing 2017

∞

Library of Congress Cataloging-in-Publication Data

Names: Ruminski, Jarret, author.
Title: The limits of loyalty : ordinary people in Civil War Mississippi /
Jarret Ruminski.
Description: Jackson : University Press of Mississippi, [2017] | Includes
bibliographical references and index. |
Identifiers: LCCN 2017017860 (print) | LCCN 2017019089 (ebook) | ISBN
9781496813978 (epub single) | ISBN 9781496813985 (epub institutional) |
ISBN 9781496813992 (pdf single) | ISBN 9781496814005 (pdf institutional)
| ISBN 9781496813961 (cloth : alk. paper)
Subjects: LCSH: Mississippi—History—Civil War, 1861–1865. |
Mississippi—Politics and government—1861–1865. | Group
identity—Mississippi—History—19th century. | Nationalism—Confederate
States of America.
Classification: LCC F341 (ebook) | LCC F341 .R89 2017 (print) | DDC
976.2/05—dc23
LC record available at https://lccn.loc.gov/2017017860

British Library Cataloging-in-Publication Data available

For Edith and Abbey

Loyalty wants the cause in its unity; it seeks, therefore, something essentially superhuman.

JOSIAH ROYCE, *The Philosophy of Loyalty*

CONTENTS

ACKNOWLEDGMENTS

AS A KID WHO GREW UP IN A NORTHERN RUST BELT TOWN, I WAS ALWAYS fascinated by the South. It seemed so distant and different, but also as American as any Ohio farmstead or factory. It was only natural that I write about the South in some fashion, and now I can finally present the results. It has been a long, often arduous journey, turning what began as a graduate school idea into a book, and I had plenty of help along the way. First, my wife Abbey put up with way more than she bargained for as I researched this book over the years, and she deserves the utmost thanks for sticking with me through the whole process. Thanks also to my parents, Vicki and Jerry Ruminski, for encouraging me to pursue this type of work, although now they will have to read a whole book. To Clay Ruminski: I am sorry there are no furnaces in this study.

As for developing the ideas and conducting the research for this study, I had valuable help from beginning to end. Frank Towers and Jewel Spangler provided constant support and aid from the moment I decided to study Civil War Mississippi. Their guidance made this book immensely better than it ever would have been without them. The University of Calgary's Department of Graduate Studies provided the research and travel grants that helped me research this book, as did the Faculty of Social Sciences and the Department of History.

While researching this project, I had help from the excellent staff at all of the institutions I visited over the course of several years. Clinton Bagley and the entire staff at the Mississippi Department of Archives and History were incredibly welcoming and helped me locate everything I needed during the weeks I spent in Jackson. I also want to thank Jennifer Ford at the University of Mississippi's Department of Archives and Special Collections for aiding me during my research stint at 'Ole Miss. Moreover, I am indebted to Ben Gilstrap for generously providing me with lodging in Oxford and for taking me to a heck of a Drive-By Truckers show. The staff at the University of North Carolina at Chapel Hill were awesome, and I especially want to thank them for allowing me to listen to my iPod while researching. Special thanks also to the staff at the Louisiana State University Special Collections Department and the staff at the National Archives in Washington, DC, and College Park, Maryland. Further, thanks to all of the archivists and historians hard at work digitizing primary sources; you are making historical research easier and more affordable.

Many colleagues provided valuable commentary and suggestions on this project. Thanks to Victoria Bynum for reading the manuscript and for writing a book that was adapted into a great movie. Thanks also to Lynn Kennedy, Elizabeth Jameson, Hendrik Kraay, Faye Halpern, Aaron Sheehan-Dean, Andy Slap, William Blair, Paul Quigley, and Timothy B. Smith for the helpful commentary. Finally, thanks to the staff at the University Press of Mississippi for giving me the opportunity to publish this work and for being so accommodating throughout the process.

THE LIMITS OF LOYALTY

INTRODUCTION

AT NOON ON DECEMBER 26, 1862, AN OVERFLOW CROWD PACKED INTO the legislative house in downtown Jackson, Mississippi, to hear a speech by native son Jefferson Davis, the president of the Confederate States of America. Davis took the opportunity to assure the crowd that the recently enacted—and unpopular—Conscription and Exemption Acts were necessary to ensure the Confederacy's survival against the North. Omitting mention of the May and October battles at Corinth, Davis stated that "you in Mississippi, have but little experienced as yet the horrors of the war. You have seen but little of the savage manner in which it is waged by your barbarous enemies." He emphasized that "the great aim of the government is to make our struggle successful" and asked the audience if they were willing to lose their rights and their property to Yankee rule should the Confederacy fall in defeat. "I feel that in addressing Mississippians the answer will be that their interests, even life itself, should be willingly laid down on the altar of their country," he concluded.[1] As Davis earlier noted, Mississippi in general had yet to experience the war's worst hardships, but in suggesting that Mississippians should willingly sacrifice *everything* to the goal of Confederate independence, he fused their interests with those of the nation. In doing so, Davis tried to instill in them the devotion needed to ensure Southern victory.

How Mississippians responded to Davis's exhortation is the subject of this study. I use Mississippi from 1860 to 1865 as a case study of Confederate loyalty during the Civil War. This Deep South state should have been rabidly pro-Confederate: in 1860, slaves made up 55 percent of the state's population, and their labor made it the country's leading cotton exporter. It was also a hotbed of secession and was the second state to leave the Union.[2] Yet, Mississippi was also an early militarily divided state that faced Union army occupation through most of the conflict, making it fertile ground for exploring the influence of different allegiances.

Rather than trying to discern whether Mississippians' allegiance to the Confederacy was weak or strong, this study enters the scholarly debate over the nature of Confederate nationalism by viewing Mississippians through the lens of different, overlapping loyalties that indicated neither popular support for, nor rejection of, the Confederacy. It draws on manuscript sources that illuminate how a wide range of Mississippians—rich and poor, white and black, female and male—navigated the complex maze of wartime loyalties that characterized the Civil War. In contrast to scholars who view Confederate nationalism from a "weak or strong" binary, I argue that loyalty during the Civil War can seldom be understood in absolute terms. My approach suggests that the often contradictory evidence regarding Confederate allegiance in Mississippi can better explain the limitations of modern nationalism in terms of the state's influence on its subjects.

Take one example. Confederate nationalists labeled Mississippians who traded across Union lines—in defiance of Confederate law prohibiting such exchanges—as treasonous, claiming that such trade fed supplies to the Union war effort and undermined Confederate economic independence. Many citizens, however, claimed that they traded simply to procure goods with little regard for nationalist stances. Others claimed that they traded in order to smuggle goods to Confederate soldiers, insisting that their patriotic intentions overrode their illegal actions.

These competing interpretations of trade across the lines raise broader questions about what types of obligations modern nationalism placed on citizens via their relationship to the state, and what citizens expected from the state in return. Paul Quigley defines nationalism as "the conviction that each nation—a group of people with a distinctive identity, typically based on some combination of language, descent, history, cultural values, or interest— ought to be aligned with an independent unit of governance in the modern institution of a *nation-state*." The central component of modern nationalism is its totality, its status as "the supreme form of legal allegiance and cultural identity in the modern world," both "unitary and indivisible."[3] This totality was particularly salient for Confederate nationalists who sought to define their nation-state while simultaneously warring for its very survival.

Faced with a Northern government that denied the legitimacy of the Confederacy's existence, Confederate boosters sought to prove their Southern nation to the North and to the world. To achieve this goal, they promoted what scholars have termed protective nationalism, in which the Confederacy would be economically self-sufficient and its citizens would work toward the singular goal of winning independence from the North.

Achieving economic self-sufficiency entailed the promotion of Southern industry, a national currency, and prohibition of trade with the North in favor of homespun and domestic production. Because Confederate nationalists forged their nation in war, they argued that citizens should be willing to endure any amount of suffering, mortal or otherwise, to achieve Confederate autonomy. The war, however, created an environment ill suited to protective nationalist ideals. In different circumstances, Mississippians acted on multiple, coexistent loyalties that influenced their actions in ways that did not always correspond to national allegiance. In doing so, they demonstrated that the reach of the nineteenth-century nation-state was more limited than historians have concluded.

This study, then, is not a complete, chronological history of Mississippi during the Civil War. Recent works by Ben Wynne, Timothy Smith, and Michael Ballard are excellent examples of the former.[4] Instead, it focuses on the relationship between Mississippians and the rival Union and Confederate governments, both of which adopted protective nationalism and therefore made demands on citizens' daily lives in order to elicit their total national allegiance. Both governments required citizens to swear oaths of allegiance, restricted commerce with the other side, intervened in the relationship between masters and slaves, encouraged espionage, forbade desertion, and approved of military exemptions only in cases where doing so was deemed to be of equal or greater national benefit than soldiering. These impositions by the two warring states demanded that individuals abandon established habits shaped by multiple loyalties to self, family, and neighborhood and instead act to reflect a total fidelity to one nation or the other.

As Andre Fleche notes, patriotic thinkers of the Civil War era judged governments "by their ability to command the allegiance of their citizens and marshal the resources of the entire state." They considered these abilities to be the hallmarks of a "modern, unified state."[5] By attempting to use all facets of daily life as a gauge of national allegiance, both states disrupted the interplay of Mississippians' loyalty layers. In the process, they tested the limits of protective nationalism and exposed the importance of multiple allegiances in guiding human actions.

The problem of multiple allegiances complicates scholarship on Confederate nationalism, which attempts to measure the extent of Southerners' commitment to the nascent slaveholding republic. Historians who argue for strong Confederate loyalty emphasize how white supremacy, conflation of home with nation, and the construction of a separate, functioning government with new national borders united Southerners across class lines to fight for the Confederacy.[6] Others contend that martial pride fueled Confederate nationalism, as civilians rallied around the military and the soldiers' forged camaraderie that fueled their desire to keep fighting.[7]

Looking beyond the army, some scholars invoke Benedict Anderson's concept of nationalism, arguing that common cultures of print and symbolism promoted Southern values and created a united Confederate identity among white Southerners.[8] While these historians identify different motives for white allegiance to the Confederacy, they are nonetheless in agreement that such support was real and widespread.

By contrast, other historians emphasize the South's regional, political, and economic divisions, especially class conflict between slaveholders and non-slaveholders, which carried into the war and internally crippled the Confederate effort.[9] Somewhat in the middle are historians of Southern unionism and of the Border/Mountain South, who acknowledge Southerners' multiple allegiances but still view them as deriving from national loyalties that determined wartime behavior. Although they highlight the complexity of wartime allegiances, these studies still emphasize an either/or spectrum of weak to strong Confederates at the margins with a larger group in the middle whose national allegiance waxed and waned, rather than demonstrating how nationalism could be unconnected to other allegiances that exercised a significant influence.[10]

This study of loyalty in wartime Mississippi takes up Gary Gallagher's suggestion that scholars "move beyond a binary approach to questions of disaffection, commitment to the nascent nation, and the like."[11] Understanding how Mississippians acted on allegiances beyond nationalism can explain why the Confederacy can seem both united and divided, why some historians think it should have lasted longer, and why others marvel that it lasted so long against such steep odds.

THE NATURE OF LOYALTY

Loyalty is an influence on human action, prone to varying levels of intensity and directed at multiple targets. Whereas "nationalism" is a fidelity to a political state, "loyalty," as Eric Hobsbawm wrote, "is always combined with identifications of another kind, even when it is felt to be superior to them." Philosopher Simon Keller defines loyalty as "the attitude and associated pattern of conduct that is constituted by an individual's taking something's side, and doing so with a certain sort of motive." Loyalty is "tied in with the contingent psychologies, needs and interests of humans," and humans can express loyalty to multiple things.[12]

Complementing Keller, sociologist James Connor argues that people express loyalty toward different "micro" and "macro" targets via a process called "loyalty layers," or the "multiple targets of loyalty that operate on individuals, spanning the micro to the macro levels of social structure." Macro loyalties are allegiances an individual has in association with a very large group of people toward broader spatial collectives like religion, ethnicity, and nation. The larger social and spatial geographies of these macro targets (not to mention their abstract nature) means that they do not always directly affect a person's life at the micro level. For example, some people may be loyal to a particular religion without applying that religion's every stringent rule to their daily life, especially if those rules create uncomfortable monetary or familial problems. Yet those persons would scarcely deny their still firm religious beliefs.[13]

Micro loyalties are the fidelities people hold toward smaller, more localized individuals and groupings like self, family, friends, and neighborhood, which exist in more compact spatial geographies within the macro space. Micro loyalties often have a greater influence on an individual's actions and more commonly guide a person's daily life. For example, some persons may hold strong macro loyalty to a national political party, but their micro loyalties to self and family may lead them to vote against that party's local candidates or policies, which they may view as harmful to their personal interests. Such an action does not prevent such persons from retaining their allegiance to the national party. Connor explains that the existence of loyalty layers means that "there are multiple loyalty influences being placed upon the actor." This fluctuating hierarchy of fidelities ensures that no single loyalty can exclusively shape a person's identity. Those who express a seemingly unconditional loyalty to a single cause, individual, or institution at the expense of all other allegiances are often derisively labeled fanatics, zealots, or fundamentalists precisely because they are the rare exceptions to the former rule.[14]

In light of circumstances, an individual will act on one particular loyalty without abandoning others. Social psychologists call this phenomenon "loyalty without conformity," in which loyalty "might occasionally require people to place the interests of the group ahead of their self-interest" without abandoning their independence. This phenomenon is especially prevalent in highly individualistic societies like the United States that have fluid and dynamic sociopolitical cultures. Multiple loyalties exist concurrently within the human actor because loyalties are also the building blocks of identity.

To identify with something or someone, a person must be loyal by siding with and supporting that thing, person, or cause. During the Civil War, if Mississippians were not on some level loyal to the Confederacy, then they could not identify as Confederates. Exactly *how much* loyalty Mississippians should profess to the Confederacy, and what they should *do* to demonstrate their allegiance, however, proved a major point of contention between citizens and the Confederate state.[15]

PROTECTIVE NATIONALISM

Specific wartime circumstances motivated Mississippians to act in ways that others considered disloyal to the Confederacy. These acts included swearing the Union oath, allegedly spying for the Union army, illegally trading at federal lines, deserting from the Confederate army, claiming exemption from military service, and other actions that made perpetrators vulnerable to charges of disloyalty. Mississippi's wartime and postwar histories, however, belie the existence of a large, anti-Confederate faction. While the state did have unionists, there was no large unionist uprising, and those Mississippians accused of treason who left firsthand accounts rarely professed loyalty to the Union or the Republican Party, or support for federal war goals such as emancipation. Finally, the existence of many apostate Mississippians does not correlate with their hostility to occupying federal forces during Reconstruction.[16]

By considering what national allegiance meant to Mississippians who were inclined toward alleged "disloyal" behavior, the concept of multiple loyalties addresses the gap between secondhand sources that charged Mississippians with disloyalty despite an absence of corroborating proof. To get at their motivations, historians can look at what people *did* in addition to what others *said*. They can read against the grain of secondhand accounts to consider how the "hidden transcripts" in peoples' daily actions might contradict the "public transcripts" of secondhand reports. These hidden transcripts suggest that Confederate patriotism was merely one component in Mississippians' social interactions, in which other allegiances also guided their behavior.[17]

Recognizing the role of multiple loyalties in driving human behavior in Civil War Mississippi also reveals much about the nature of the nineteenth-century nation-state and the impact it had on its subjects. Confederate partisans promoted what Nicholas and Peter Onuf call protective nationalism, the idea of nation as "a corporate entity, with a life that transcended the lives of its present citizens and a purpose that transcended their purposes." Since

secessionists espoused the vision of a politically and economically independent South, achieving a Southern nation "depended on domesticating national
power" by "aligning economy and society" via a multifronted mobilization
against Union forces as well as a concerted effort to shore up internal dedication to the Confederate cause. This type of nationalism intended to *protect*
Confederate strength and identity at every possible level.[18]

For ardent Confederates, protective nationalism was both a means to
achieving independence and an end in itself. Certainly, the Confederacy fell
into the category of a full-fledged state, an entity Ernest Gellner defined as an
"institution or set of institutions specifically concerned with the enforcement
of order." Whether or not the Confederacy was a nation, however—whether
it embodied "the artifacts of men's convictions and loyalties and solidarities"
that coalesce into a shared culture—had yet to be demonstrated in 1861.[19]
For protective nationalists, constructing the Confederate state was merely
the means by which they tried to create a nation that united Southerners'
convictions and loyalties through an intangible shared culture.

To make the Confederate nation a reality, protective nationalists advocated
a total devotion to the state by its component parts through the mustering of
all human and material resources to work toward the singular goal of achieving Confederate economic, social, and cultural independence.[20] As Quigley
observes, the demands of modern wartime mobilization "have caused national
governments to demand even greater commitment from their citizens." In the
Confederacy, war-induced suffering injected the "ideal of national sacrifice"
into all aspects of daily life.[21] Thus, planters should prioritize staples over commercial crops to feed the army and civilians. Civilians should wear homespun
rather than purchase clothing from the North to avoid funding the Union
war machine. Above all else, Confederate soldiers had to be willing to die for
their country's independence. In a very real sense, total dedication to the cause
meant exactly what Jefferson Davis said it meant: that Mississippians should
be "willing to sacrifice everything, even their lives, to the goal of Confederate
independence."[22]

THE POWER OF THE MODERN NATION-STATE

When the Union army brought war to Mississippi in 1862, it also unleashed
all of war's hardships. In light of wartime circumstances, many Confederate
authorities feared that Mississippians would waver in their dedication to
the cause. In response, they expanded the state's police powers in order to

enforce national loyalty. The US government also desired a total commitment
to its cause, and similarly expanded its state apparatuses to enforce it.[23] These
wartime attempts to weld the people to the nation, often through coercive
means like conscription and arrest, have led historians to conclude that the
Civil War effectively created the modern American nation-state. Scholars
view the Confederate state as especially powerful, with the infrastructural
capacity to reach "inside every household."[24] Such a conclusion, however,
does not distinguish means from ends. Historians should instead investigate
whether the Confederacy's infrastructural capacity (the means) actually
facilitated increased national loyalty among its citizenry (the ends). This was,
after all, protective nationalists' stated goal.[25]

Consider Mississippi senator Albert Gallatin Brown—a "Fire-Eater's Fire
Eater"—who ruminated on the necessary steps required to enforce national
loyalty during wartime before the Confederate Congress in 1863. "When the
States, composing this Confederacy, delegated to this central government the
exclusive right and power to make war, they necessarily gave with it all the
rights and powers incidentally necessary to make the war grant efficient and
effective."[26] For the Confederate government, enforcement of total national
loyalty was both the means and the end. To win the war, the people had to
be loyal, and if they were not voluntarily loyal, the state had to be tasked
with using its entire available infrastructure to *make* the people loyal. In
Mississippi, however, the influence of citizens' multiple loyalties stymied
the Confederate state's attempts to enforce total loyalty. This revealed that
the strong Confederate nation-state was not that strong because it could
not achieve the paramount goal of loyalty enforcement, which was the very
justification for its expanded powers.

This study, then, is less concerned with the war's outcome than with the
process by which it unfolded. It focuses on what the experiences of the
war's participants reveal about the influence of the nation-state in the great
era of nationalism.[27] To better understand how the Civil War affected those
who lived through it and how it shaped the trajectory of American history,
historians would do well to reject nineteenth-century nationalists' claims
that nationalism is "the supreme form of legal allegiance and cultural identity
in the modern world."[28] For Mississippians during the Civil War, even the
lived experience of wartime did not color all of their actions with nationalist
hues, as multiple loyalties that were separate from nationalism continued to
guide their behavior. Understanding the influence of loyalty layers allows for
a more skeptical approach to contemporary claims of nationalist supremacy,

which, in turn, explains the nation-state's limited ability to command total allegiance from its citizens.

Gaining a better understanding of nationalism's influence, or lack thereof, on Civil War–era Mississippians specifically and Southerners in general will also clarify the often perplexing mix of change and continuity that defined the war and its contentious aftermath. This approach to nationalism explains why the war created two distinct nation-states but could not sever their established socioeconomic ties. This theoretical approach also helps to make sense of how nationalism spawned national armies whose members were still susceptible to the influence of localized allegiances. Finally, an approach that considers nationalism as one of many coexisting loyalties illuminates why racial conflict continued to rage in the war's aftermath and shaped the course of Reconstruction.

Each chapter highlights a different way that Mississippians' multiple loyalties complicated protective nationalists' attempts to foster and enforce total allegiance to the Confederacy during the Civil War. Chapter 1 focuses on Mississippians' reaction to Abraham Lincoln's election, and it explains how overly zealous Fire-Eaters planted the seeds of protective nationalism, which fueled the state's enthusiastic mobilization for war in 1860 and 1861. Rather than argue that Mississippians were overwhelmingly supportive of secession, this chapter contends that secession and the prospect of war with the North created a heightened patriotic environment that made many Mississippians temporarily embrace protective nationalism. Its influence, however, was ultimately fleeting: as war became reality, other loyalties reasserted their influence alongside a nationalism that could not totally overtake them.

Looking at the years 1862–1865, chapter 2 explores how the war and Union occupation led Mississippians to act on multiple loyalties, even as Confederate partisans in the military and at all levels of government used nationalist language to judge people's behavior. This chapter examines situations such as swearing the Union oath, life under Union military rule, and the conflict between securing personal property and donating it to the Confederate war effort, especially among planters. Confederate authorities further complicated civilians' relationship to Union occupiers by accusing citizens of treason and espionage. These day-to-day conflicts over national allegiance reveal that the tidy ideals of protective nationalism proved difficult to enforce at the messy ground level of everyday life.

Chapter 3 focuses on the contraband trade between Mississippians and the Union army from 1862 to 1865 and the effect that it had on conceptions of national loyalty. Initially, the Confederate government banned trade with the North, claiming that it stifled Southern economic independence. Yet when key Southern commercial cities like Memphis and Vicksburg fell to the Union, Mississippians immediately began exchanging goods at Union lines for manufactured articles and raw commodities. Confederate authorities debated among themselves over whether the trade was treasonous and to be squelched, or whether it could be beneficial by supplying Mississippians with much-needed goods. Far from simply denoting treason or loyalty, the contraband trade demonstrated how multiple allegiances informed Mississippians' behavior, and it also revealed a crucial thread of continuity during the Civil War through the maintenance of long-established market ties between North and South.

Chapter 4 examines deserters and absentees, who unleashed waves of crime and violence in Mississippi, as well as soldiers and civilians who requested military exemptions under the pretense that they could better serve the Confederacy in a civilian capacity. Despite scholarly claims that Confederates deserted to protect hearth and home, Mississippians clearly distinguished home from nation. Moreover, this chapter connects desertion to a form of banditry that harked back to the Revolutionary War, when wartime chaos drove detached military units to commit criminal acts. The collapse of Mississippi's social order spurred Confederate deserters to engage in opportunistic collective violence sustained by preexisting group loyalties. Yet the war also created new gang loyalties, which expanded outside of partisan boxes. Soldiers also demonstrated the importance of prewar attachments through shirking, absenteeism, and exemptions, which civilians encouraged and supported.

Differing notions of loyalty among slaves and slaveholders from 1860 to 1865 are the subject of Chapter 5. This chapter highlights how the internal war between Mississippi slaves and slaveholders, which had simmered during the antebellum era, exploded during the Civil War. Slaveholders insisted that their slaves should only express an unconditional servile loyalty to their masters, the basis of the master-slave relationship. Slaves, however, rejected this forced servility and embraced multiple conceptions of freedom by acting on loyalties that they had forged while in bondage. These loyalties, in turn, enabled them to envision the lived experience of freedom during and after the war. Although black Mississippians shared a collective desire to escape from the forced servility of white mastery, once emancipated they embraced different views that associated freedom with land ownership, property rights, wage labor, and military service.

The book ends with a conclusion that discusses Mississippi's immediate postwar period from mid- to late 1865. In particular, it focuses on the Christmas rebellion of that year in order to demonstrate how white Mississippians continued their attempts to uphold the racial hierarchy against freed people's continued rejection of white dominance. This struggle dominated Mississippi's sociopolitical landscape through Reconstruction and beyond. Union forces won the war, but they could not suppress the continued influence of racial loyalties, which exerted a powerful influence over defeated Confederate soldiers and Southern civilians.

CHAPTER ONE

"A CONTEST OF PASSION, NOT REASON"

Secession, War, and the Roots of Protective Nationalism

IN DECEMBER 1860, WEST POINT, MISSISSIPPI, RESIDENT ROXANA GERDINE told her sister, Emily, about the secessionist fires that burned throughout the Magnolia State. "The people in this section of country are all of one idea. Secession is the talk in the streets, houses, pulpits, and everywhere, and I have not the least doubt but the time will do it," she wrote. By May 1861, Mississippi governor John Pettus requested that President Jefferson Davis send federal payments to fund Mississippi troops' demand for camp supplies. "Suffice it to say," Pettus wrote, "all Mississippi is in a fever to get to the field, and hail an order to march as the greatest favor you can bestow on them, and if you take the field they could not be restrained."[1] Both Gerdine, a civilian, and Pettus, a state official, recognized how Mississippians were swept up in a protective nationalist atmosphere—stoked by secession and war—that advocated a total collective devotion of resources and energy toward winning independence for the new Confederacy. This all-consuming nationalism left little space for other loyalties, and its goal of molding citizens into wholly dedicated patriots defined Mississippi's Civil War.

This chapter focuses on Mississippians' reaction to Abraham Lincoln's election and how protective nationalism fueled the state's mobilization for war from 1860 to 1862. Promoted by Fire-Eaters like Albert Gallatin Brown and John Pettus, a pro-secession atmosphere gripped the populace. In this nationalistic maelstrom, militant secessionists equated dissent from their position with treason. Residents who questioned the wisdom of immediate secession found themselves in the minority. Voting booths became sites of pro-secessionist intimidation, and bullying pro-secessionist vigilance committees patrolled counties intimidating unionists. Mississippians, however, were not so much overwhelmingly supportive of secession and the Confederacy as they were swept up in a heightened nationalist atmosphere.

Independence and the prospect of war led them to embrace, temporarily, a new national loyalty above other allegiances, especially before the real hardships of war hit Mississippi soil.

Even before hostilities broke out, the prospect of civil war demanded a new and total form of dedication to the national cause. This nationalist fervor, however, was fleeting. By mid-1862, the Union army had invaded, and, in light of war-induced hardships, micro loyalties reasserted their influence. Mississippians continued to act on prewar attachments that were often unrelated to national loyalties, even as ardent protective nationalists interpreted Mississippians' micro loyalties as potentially treasonous behavior.

Admitted to the Union as a slave state in 1817, Mississippi's frontier beginnings spawned a political culture characterized by a preference for individual independence, personal honor within tight-knit communities, and a reactionary stance toward outside threats. Following the United States' southwestern victories during the War of 1812 and the attendant free navigation of the lower Mississippi River, a flood of new migrants came to the territory. Most of the population centered in the southwestern Natchez District along the Mississippi River, where wealthy planters dominated state politics and expanded their trade connections with the North. The acquisition of millions of acres of Indian lands in the 1820s and 1830s added thousands more migrants from other Southern states, as well as the Atlantic Seaboard. These migrants settled in newly formed counties throughout the state and brought with them the Jeffersonian ideal of the independent yeoman. Responding to this shift in population, in 1832 the state adopted a more democratic constitution, embracing the Jacksonian concept of universal white male suffrage, even as planters continued to control state politics. At the same time, the Second Party System took hold on the heels of rapid immigration and economic development. The large population of small farmers and laborers continued to identify as Jacksonian Democrats, while many bankers, merchants, and planters sided with the Whig Party, supporting Henry Clay's American System of federally subsidized internal improvements, a national bank, and the promotion of American industry.[2]

Slavery was woven into the fabric of Mississippi's foundation as a state. The territory out of which the state emerged had been essentially donated to planters through the promotion of the Jeffersonian Land System, which encouraged the rapid cultivation of western lands into commercial agricultural property tilled by virtuous yeomen. The Land Ordinance of 1785, however, set the stage for the transformation of the Deep South into a region dominated by slaveholding planters. Enacted by the Continental Congress, the ordinance imposed a rectangular survey of valuable western lands to be divided for purchase and settlement by private citizens. By 1812, the federal government had sold nearly a half a million acres of public land in the Mississippi Territory, mostly to wealthy planters who could afford to place money on land before actual settlement. Thus, as Adam Rothman writes, the Public Land System "facilitated the spread of the plantation system in the Deep South just as a burgeoning cotton economy increased the value of the land and the profits to be earned from slave labor." At Mississippi's 1817 Constitutional Convention, wealthy representatives from the established plantation districts held sway over the proceedings, and they enacted a state constitution that firmly protected slavery. The democratizing Constitution of 1832 further upheld the latter measure. Cotton emerged as Mississippi's major crop by the early nineteenth century, and its growth and influence, in turn, increased white farmers' reliance on slave labor to harvest the valuable crop.[3]

Slavery became intimately entwined with Mississippi politics, as politicians asserted the right to own slaves as central to their state's economic and social fabric. Within the consensus of proslavery politics emerged a vocal minority of extreme states' rights proponents, or Fire-Eaters. These radicals flexed their political muscles during the Nullification Crisis of 1832–1833, during which South Carolina's political leaders protested several national tariffs that they believed were excessive. Led by US senator John C. Calhoun, South Carolina's legislature claimed the right to nullify any federal law it deemed unconstitutional or harmful to the state's interests. Should the federal government not accept this stance, Calhoun argued that a state had the right to secede from the Union. Even as many Mississippians sympathized with Calhoun's position, they admired President Andrew Jackson—who opposed nullification—as a rugged frontiersman who had cleared the state's Indian lands for white settlement and stood for the common man's democracy. Thus, Mississippi, along with the rest of the South, backed the federal government over South Carolina, but a loud minority within Mississippi politics supported Calhoun, denouncing the tariff as an affront to Southern interests and asserting the inalienable right of secession. These Mississippi nullifiers, led by two-term governor and states' rights ideologue John Quitman, specialized in using slavery as a wedge issue, claiming that any outside influences threatened the South's peculiar institution.[4]

The supposed threats to slavery proved an effective political tool for states' rights radicals to unite white Mississippians through a common interest. Liberty and slavery had a symbiotic relationship in the antebellum South via the concept of Herrenvolk democracy, which held that, despite their inequality in property and status, all white men were equal in their shared domination over blacks. This concept offered a clear contrast between the free and the unfree, as slaveholding and non-slaveholding whites alike measured their liberty against the millions of slaves who surrounded them. Poor and yeoman whites recognized a common kinship with Mississippi's planters and feared competing with blacks for land and labor in the event of slavery's abolition. Thus, Herrenvolk democracy made white Mississippians susceptible to "us versus them" styles of political demagoguery. By 1850, Mississippi had more enslaved black people than it did whites, an imbalance that remained in place on the eve of the Civil War. States' rights radicals exploited the fear of slavery's imperiled status to rally Mississippians around their goal of securing protection for, and expansion of, the institution even if doing so meant disunion.[5]

Mississippi first flirted with secession in 1850, following US victory in the Mexican-American War. In 1846, Pennsylvania congressman David Wilmot introduced an amendment to an appropriations bill banning slavery from territories won from Mexico. Mississippi governor Joseph Matthews labeled the so-called Wilmot Proviso, and any other attempts to ban slavery from new states or territories, as unconstitutional and possible grounds for secession. The Wilmot Proviso never became law, but in conjunction with the Compromise of 1850—which admitted California to the Union as a free state—it emboldened Southern states' rights extremists like Calhoun, who called for a united Southern resistance to Northern threats to slavery's expansion.[6]

In May 1849, the Mississippi legislature responded to Calhoun's call by appointing delegates to a slave-state convention in Nashville, Tennessee, ultimately held in June 1850, to frame a united response to Northern belligerence. In the meantime, sectional issues dominated Mississippi's 1849 elections: states' rights Democrat John Quitman eventually sailed to the governorship, replacing the retiring Matthews, and Democrats won control of both state houses. The new legislature enacted resolutions opposing congressional antislavery bills and appropriated $200,000 for additional domestic defense. When the Nashville convention convened in June 1850, however, moderates led by Mississippi judge William Sharkey outnumbered the Fire-Eaters and rejected secession. Following the Nashville decision, Quitman organized a state convention to vote on secession in the fall of 1851, only to be defeated by a unionist coalition led by Democratic US senator Henry Foote. When Quitman withdrew from the gubernatorial race, states' rights Democrats replaced him with Jefferson Davis, also a federal senator, who lost to Foote by a slim margin. Unionists also won control of the state legislatures. In November, at the request of governor-elect Foote, the state convention rejected calls for secession.[7]

Despite the unionist victory in the 1850–1851 secession crisis, the events of the decade continued to fuel Mississippi Fire-Eaters' claims that abolitionist conspirators were working tirelessly to eradicate slavery. James Buchanan's narrow victory in the 1856 presidential election was little solace to radicals who viewed the new Republican Party's strong performance as further evidence of slavery's imperiled status in the old Union. Mississippi's radicals also pointed to the bloody clashes between pro- and antislavery forces in Kansas between 1854 and 1858 as proof of the supposed determination of abolitionists to destroy the institution with either the saber or the ballot. In 1859, John Brown, one of the antislavery Kansas fighters, raided Harper's Ferry, Virginia, in an attempt to incite a slave insurrection. His raid terrified whites across the South, helped Mississippi's states' rights Democrats to consolidate their hold on the state party, and swept uncompromising Fire-Eater John Pettus to the governorship.[8]

Mississippi entered 1860 steeped in a climate of fear and paranoia. With Pettus's full support, states' rights Democrats rallied behind John Breckinridge, vice president under Buchanan but running for president with the southern wing of the Democratic Party, which emerged after the party split into factions at its 1860 Baltimore convention over the question of how best to protect slavery. Breckenridge riled up large crowds by stoking fears of abolitionist infiltration, slave insurrection conspiracies, and the supposed destruction of Southern culture that would follow black Republican rule. These radicals embraced the ideological underpinnings of what soon became Confederate protective nationalism. They insisted on total devotion to one party or group as the vehicle for promoting the South's perceived best interests, and they fostered fear, intimidation, and group-think to achieve and enforce this goal. The vehicle shifted rapidly, transitioning from the southern wing of the Democratic Party, which was staunchly proslavery, to the Fire-Eaters, who were proslavery and pro-secession, to finally the new Southern Confederacy, but the goal of uniting all Mississippians behind supposed Southern interests remained the same.[9]

First Breckinridge supporters, then secessionists relied on self-organized Minute Men and vigilance committees that traversed the state pressuring citizens, often through threats of violence, to vote for the southern Democratic candidate and to support immediate secession. In September 1860, while canvassing for Breckinridge in Corinth, Mississippi, Jefferson Davis described what this type of total devotion to the party line meant for ordinary citizens. When a spectator inquired if a state's secession rendered treasonous any continued fealty to the Union, Davis answered that "the neck of the author of such an inquiry was in danger of hemp," and that respecting federal law after secession would be "treason against the sovereignty to whom he owned his first allegiance." Davis further reminded the questioner that the Democratic Party espoused "the right of a State to judge in the last resort of its wrongs and the remedies to be applied," and those who disagreed repudiated the notion of state sovereignty.[10] Although the vehicle soon shifted from the Democratic Party to the Confederacy, Davis nonetheless described the modus operandi of protective nationalism: a total dedication to goals of the state. This vision of national loyalty left no room for other allegiances and aimed to squelch any perceived dissent.

Breckenridge won Mississippi handily, but Lincoln's victory in the 1860 presidential election was the last straw for the Fire-Eaters, who called for the state's immediate withdrawal from the Union. "If we falter now," Pettus warned the state legislature, "we and our sons must pay the penalty in future years" and be "cursed with Black Republican politics and free negro morals." The legislature printed over ten thousand copies of Pettus's address and distributed them throughout the state.[11]

Pettus and other radicals successfully infused a sense of urgency into the populace, and Mississippians embraced an atmosphere crackling with excitement over the birth of a new nation. The *Daily Evening Citizen* noted "a general commotion throughout the land" and told citizens that "we of Mississippi have a great ... state to defend, and now is the time to defend it. ... [A] disruption of the Union is inevitable." Madison County resident Edward Terry wrote his sister that "there has been and is still a great deal of excitement in this part of the country on count [sic] of the election of *Lincoln*." A self-identified "strong *disunionist*," Terry felt that there was "no doubt but Mississippi will go out of the Union." Thomas Bailey of Columbus told his mother in North Carolina: "[W]e are in the midst of great excitement—the State will secede and unless you all go with us we will belong to different nations in a short time." Greenville, Mississippi, resident William Nugent informed his wife that there was "a decided tendency to Secession everywhere. Almost everyone I meet has come to the determination to vindicate the rights of our outraged section if need be at the point of bayonet." From Lauderdale County, A. F. Burton told his North Carolina relatives that "the secession movement is all the go in this country. ... [S]eparate state secession is the only mode." For many Mississippians, Lincoln's election signaled the beginning of an exciting—if uncertain—new era of independence. They felt in the political atmosphere the thrill that came from living in a clearly historical moment.[12]

Just as some Mississippians caught secession fever, however, others questioned the wisdom of such excitement. The largest slaveholding planters, who lived in the state's Mississippi and Yazoo Delta counties, were among the strongest proponents of compromise. This makes sense, given that they had the most to lose materially in the event of a disruptive war. One such planter was Natchez's George Sargent, who despaired that "a very large number in even this, the most conservative county in the state[,] advocate immediate, unconditional secession." A conditional unionist who voted for John Bell (the Constitutional Union Party candidate in the 1860 presidential election), Sargent feared that rushing to secession left the state "no hope for moderation" and that "we the moderate try to hold her back but one might as well with a twine string toy [try] to hold an enraged elephant." He blamed political radicals for arousing "the worst passions of the human beast" and worried that "the people naturally are slow of comprehension, and the leaders are taking care not to give them time for reflection."[13]

Plenty of others echoed Sargent's feelings. Washington County resident L. L. Walton chastised rash politicians. "The young men of the present day deem themselves wiser than our forefathers; our proud country is now disgraced," he wrote; "party feelings & politics have done this." Jackson native Ruffin Thomson criticized the failure of political moderation. The masses, he told his father, "were half mad everywhere," as "prudence and discretion" fell by the wayside "under intense excitement." Thomson concluded that "it seems to me a contest of *passion*, not *reason*."[14] Thomson and others thought that the pro-secessionist atmosphere thrived on inflamed passions, while relegating reasonable discussion to the sidelines. Such cautious feelings also echoed in the state's editorial pages, which lambasted secessionists' bloodlust. A letter to the editor of the conservative *Daily Vicksburg Whig* described a speech by disunionist Attorney General Thomas Wharton as epitomizing the secessionists' foolish rush into war. "He unsheathed his sword, threw away the scabbard and like the panting of a war steed . . . he snuffed the smell of battle afar off and was eager for the fray," the writer grumbled. A few days later, the *Whig* reported on a pro-secession rally in Jackson at which Fire-Eating senator Albert Gallatin Brown proclaimed the Union "dead" and "in a process of mortification." The editorial decried Brown and other "would-be leaders of the public sentiment" as advocates of "extreme measures" who were driven by "fanaticism." Mississippians skeptical of hastily embracing immediate secession believed that the Fire-Eaters' feverish desire for independence had blinded them to the potentially dire consequences of such an action.[15]

In the midst of this heated environment, the state legislature called for a secession convention to be held in January 1861, with delegates to be elected from each county according to the number of representatives it had in the lower state legislature. Although the candidates did not run on uniform platforms, they generally cast themselves as either secessionists or cooperationists. These titles were somewhat misleading, however, since both groups generally believed in the constitutional right of secession. Therefore, the real debate centered not on *if*, but *when*, the state should secede. Secessionists favored immediate, separate state separation with no prerequisite agreement between other states on the matter. Cooperationists were conditional unionists who believed that secession should happen only in conjunction with other Southern states, since they faced a uniform threat. They argued that because Lincoln's election was not in itself grounds for secession, all alternatives within the Union ought to first be exhausted.[16]

Proponents of both views canvassed the state. Prominent conservatives like planter/politician James Lusk Alcorn and attorney William Sharkey campaigned for the preservation of the Union under the cooperationist banner, but their efforts met with little enthusiasm. "I am beginning to believe this 'Co operation Party' a sham & that our only salvation is in separate-state action & *then* cooperation," wrote Vicksburg resident T. W. Compton.[17] Certainly, the Fire-Eaters advocated the more succinct and proactive message: secession versus the cooperationists' indeterminate delay. They also propelled their campaign in the state with an intense combination of fear-stoking urgency and peer pressure in an effort to garner total dedication to "Southern interests" from the populace.

Those interests were, of course, slavery. The central goal of the southern Democratic Party, and then the secessionists, was securing protection for the South's slave property. Conditional unionists shared this goal but claimed that slavery was still safer in the Union. Lincoln, they noted, vowed to not interfere with the institution in states where it already existed. The secessionists, then, held the more radical stance, and to advance it they relied on time-tested methods of intimidation. Rooting out real and imagined threats to slavery by keeping slaves, and wayward whites who might question the institution, in line had long been a focus of the Deep South's violence-prone social landscape. Southern mob violence was a tool for enforcing the ideal of mastery, a by-product of a slave society that dictated that whites who owned slaves held absolute authority over them at the most personal, domestic level. Because Southern mastery stemmed from racial hierarchy, it also presupposed that all Southern whites, regardless of whether they personally owned slaves, nonetheless held the right to mastery over blacks through their shared white racial solidarity and thus their superiority. Southern mastery, then, gave one group total dominance over another, and so great was the need to uphold this dominance that it sanctioned mastery's would-be enforcers with the right to attack and silence anyone who might be critical of slavery and the racial hierarchy that bolstered it.[18]

Extralegal violence flowed out of the perceived need to stifle anyone who questioned the slave system and, by extension, the ideal of mastery upon which it rested. This was symptomatic of what William Freehling calls the "dictatorship" of Herrenvolk democracy. Slaveholders could easily label any dissenting opinions incendiary. They accused poor whites, Northerners, and foreigners believed to harbor antislavery feelings of inciting slave insurrection and threatening the Southern social order. The planters' social influence within communities ensured that a steady supply of Southern whites, slaveholding or not, were willing to physically defend the slave system against internal or external threats. Neighborhood slave patrols kept an eye on unruly slaves and hunted down runaways, and they tried to root out whites suspected of aiding slave resistance. Thus, the cultural and institutional apparatuses through which to coerce and threaten perceived dissidents already existed in the South. In a natural extension of slave patrols, pro-secessionist vigilance committees intimidated all possible "incendiary" people who might thwart immediate secession and thereby threaten what disunionists considered the South's best interests. They created a hypernationalist atmosphere that swept up much of the state's population into an independence-minded fury.[19]

Mississippi had a history of extralegal mob violence that coexisted with formal law. In the antebellum era, the majority of the state consisted of countryside dotted with small towns and neighborhoods dominated by planter families. Law enforcement was available in the form of the sheriff or justice of the peace but was usually a second resort in any fundamental exercise of justice that involved disciplining slaves. The centrality of slavery within the state's social and economic structures drove Mississippians to embrace extralegal violence as a necessary means of upholding white mastery, a process that legitimized vigilantism as a means of law enforcement.[20]

British-born storekeeper Betty Beaumont faced this intimidation in Wilkinson County, Mississippi. Although she and her husband were agnostic on slavery, locals took her indifference as evidence of secret abolitionism. Especially among planters, Beaumont noted that "there seemed to be a strong prejudice . . . against those who did not own slaves . . . and a disposition to persecute and prosecute them on every occasion." She described the 1860 presidential election as "a season of special political excitement" during which "being foreigners and non-slaveholders, we were watched unceasingly" by spies who made their "most innocent words and actions subject to miscon-struction." Town officials forbade Beaumont from interacting with slaves without a permit. Other foreigners, Northerners, and anyone else deemed suspicious endured insults and occasionally physical attacks. In one instance, a group of mechanics left their plantation jobs to escape the abuse.[21]

Similar incidents occurred around the state. In December 1860, a local committee charged Batesville resident Tom West with selling whiskey to slaves and sharing his "filthy abolitionist sentiment." As punishment, they "administered to him a severe flagellation," scrawled the words "nigger wor-shipper" alongside a north-pointing hand on his back, and shipped him north via an express company. That same month, the Newton County vigi-lance committee arrested longtime resident John Blissett, an English-born schoolteacher, on charges of "expressing abolition sentiments" and "being too familiar with slaves." The committee decided against hanging Blissett "in consideration of his infirmities" and instead drove him out of the state. In Jefferson County, locals arrested an Ohio-born "lady Abolitionist" teacher for supposedly informing slaves about Lincoln's election and "telling them that they would soon all be free." The mob forced the woman onto a river steamer headed north. In Coahoma County, along the Mississippi River, one planter reported that eighty armed men waited along the river's edge, determined to "sink every Abolition city boat that floated by the banks of the great Southern river." After all, he added, "the secession excitement is intensely raging throughout the country parts." Secessionists employed the tactics of the slave patrol to identify alleged abolitionist subversives. In so doing, they operated under what became the framework of Confederate protective nationalism: the requirement of total dedication to Southern in-terests. When those interests became, in Fire-Eaters' eyes, synonymous with secession, vigilance committees and mobs enforced allegiance at any cost.[22]

Vigilance committees or Minute Men (the labels were used interchange-ably) were private citizens who formed volunteer groups in order to squelch any perceived threats to "Southern interests," namely slavery. These groups played a major role in securing support for immediate secession in South Carolina. In addition to inflicting waves of proslavery vigilantism on accused abolitionists, the South Carolina Minute Men served as armed visual reminders of the supposed imminent threat the North posed to the South. Stephen West notes how they "contributed to a political climate in which dissent constituted not a difference of opinion but an act of treason." Their actions successfully persuaded opponents of secession to disengage from the debate and often kept them from voting. Breckinridge supporters, with the help of the states' rights press, called for vigilance committees to be formed in every Southern community.[23]

Mississippi vigilance committees worked tirelessly to promote secession. The Jackson Minute Men, organized on November 13, 1860, distributed ten thousand copies of an abolitionist article printed in the *Chicago Democrat* as a means of alerting the populace to the threats such ideas posed to the South. Two members of the Jackson committee, Wiley P. Harris and W. P. Anderson, became candidates for the separate state secessionist ticket, chosen by their fellow members who controlled the committee on resolutions at the Hinds County nominating convention. Attala County secession convention delegate John W. Wood, one of the few to ultimately cast a unionist vote, noted how, immediately following Lincoln's election, secessionists "went to work calling county meetings, haranguing the people, forming companies of 'minute men,' and using all of those artful appliances . . . to get up a great political excitement." Part of the process of ginning up "political excitement" involved intimidation through violent threats—sometimes followed by violent acts.[24]

John Aughey, an evangelical minister and unconditional unionist from central Mississippi, witnessed firsthand the intimidation wrought by pro-secessionist groups. Days before Lincoln's election, Aughey heard a secessionist speaker intone that "[c]ompromise with the Yankees, after the election of Lincoln, is treason against the South." The speaker then bragged about vigilance committees hanging seven "tory-submissionists" in northern Mississippi. Following this execution, the local unionist candidates, "having the wholesome dread of hemp before their eyes," stopped canvassing the county. Beaumont reported similar intimidation in Wilkinson County. "Some few people among us were opposed to secession," she wrote; "a number of these, knowing their danger, hurried away; those who remained were closely watched and even accused of thinking much more than they expressed or even felt." Randolph Roth notes that "vigilante violence effectively and emphatically marked the bounds of dissent" via "indiscriminate fanaticism." The vigilance groups "intimidated racial moderates and antisecessionists and gave militant whites the upper hand in shaping the Confederacy."[25] These groups' presence during Mississippi's campaign for the secession convention made the general atmosphere deeply hostile to those against immediate secession.

In addition to the proliferation of violent threats as a voter deterrent during the secession campaign, voting itself proved logistically problematic and necessitated fortitude in the face of hostility. The logistical problem arose because few counties even had a unionist candidate on their ballots, forcing voters of that inclination to back "cooperationist" tickets offering fusion candidates with murky stances on secession. As a result, many voters simply stayed home. Forty percent of Mississippi's eligible voters did not vote in the secession convention election, about thirty-eight thousand, compared to the 60 percent—or sixty-eight thousand—who voted in the presidential election. This low turnout benefited the secessionists, as those counties with the sharpest decline in voter participation also went solidly for secession. Many polling places did not even stock cooperationist ballots. The *Daily Vicksburg Whig* noted that, despite indications of secessionist triumph, "we hardly think more than two-thirds of the vote of the State has been cast in this election," pointing out that "in a majority of the counties but one ticket was in running," while in others the candidates' positions were "jumbled up," thereby skewing the results in the radicals' favor.[26]

Beyond logistical issues, peer pressure was deeply intimidating, especially given the localized and public nature of Southern elections in which everyone knew everyone else. As Christopher Olsen writes, neighborhoods were the "sine qua non of Mississippi politics," making elections highly ritualized social and cultural events in which individuals, in keeping with the Southern desire for community-validated honor, submitted their reputations to peer approval. Wood noted, regarding Southern elections, that "a very few individuals are often enabled to control the people of a State." Party leaders in the state capital kept county leaders "posted" and never missed the chance to harangue people at court days, barbecues, and other occasions where they could be "conveniently assembled together." Such environments encouraged conformity to the dominant group.[27]

Pontotoc County resident R. F. Crenshaw witnessed this conformity, telling his cousin that "we are so convulsed here now in Miss. With Secession, that the man who does not give, not only *one day* but *all his time* to his Country is regarded at best but a lukewarm patriot." The *Daily Vicksburg Whig* described such haranguing in Rankin County. "You never saw such means used as were employed by the seceders of this county," the paper noted; "whiskey was freely given; promises of corn and meat made. Threats were made; in fact, all means used, and the lowest, meanest and dirtiest tricks resorted to." Although Rankin went cooperationist by a 119-vote margin, the secessionists nearly won a conservative county. John Aughey was forced to write out his own unionist ticket in his precinct "amidst the frowns, murmurs, and threats of the judges and bystanders." He claimed that many other pro-unionist residents were so intimidated that they abstained from voting, period.[28] Although secessionists used a number of tactics to browbeat voters into their column, violence or the threat of violence proved especially effective.

Ohio-born John Goss attested to the latter point when he told fellow Attala County resident Jason Niles that, during the vote, "drunken rowdies" had whipped several men in his neighborhood on account of their "unsoundness on the secession question." Noting that "party feeling" was "very high" in Adams County, George Sargent advised a fellow cooperationist to "give your vote and try and get back as soon as you can . . . there is no need of anyone knowing who you vote for."[29] By enforcing conformity to disunion, secessionists created a fear-laden atmosphere that discouraged any deviations from their party line. Such tactics proved successful in roping some of the state's fence riders into the disunionist fold, but those who abstained from voting further aided the radicals' goal. Ultimately, these tactics, driven by a desire to achieve dedication to a singular cause, undergirded Confederate protective nationalism after Mississippi seceded from the Union.

When the state convention assembled on January 7, 1861, the Fire-Eaters had the wind at their backs. The few cooperationists, however, refused to sit quietly while the secessionists raged. John Wood warned the delegates that secession meant war. "Let us pause and reflect, before we plunge into the dark abyss now opening at our feet," he pleaded; "if Secession is carried out, there will be nothing but ruin and desolation follow in its course . . . war, pestilence and famine will spread over the land." Other conservatives proposed amendments to at least stave off the disunionist fury. Washington County delegate Jacob Yerger proposed that Mississippi continue to seek redress for grievances within the Union. James Alcorn advanced an amendment permitting secession only in concert with other states, while Warren County delegate Walter Brooke proposed that an ordinance of secession be submitted to a statewide popular vote before its passage. The delegation soundly rejected these proposals.[30]

Ultimately, recognizing the futility of further resistance, much of the Union minority voted with the radicals to secede. Calhoun County cooperationist delegate M. D. L. Stephens, for example, ultimately could not resist the secessionist tide. When the vote had been narrowed down to "submission or secession," Stephens said, "I am for secession." Other cooperationists followed suite. On January 9, 1861, the convention passed Mississippi's Ordinance of Secession with eighty-four votes in favor and fifteen dissenting. Following the vote, the state's congressional delegation in Washington resigned and headed home. A month later, Jefferson Davis took the oath of office as the first, and only, Confederate president. The secession convention also published a document outlining its raison d'être. As if there were any lingering doubts regarding the main issue at hand, the document stated that "our position is thoroughly identified with the institution of slavery—the greatest material interest of the world." And how to protect slavery? "There was no choice left to us but submission to the mandates of abolition, or a dissolution of the Union, whose principles had been subverted to work out our ruin," the convention concluded.[31] The declaration's insistence that there was no choice but to secede foreshadowed Confederate boosters: there was now only *one* nation to which Southerners owed their allegiance.

In the wake of secession, John Pettus prepped the state for war even before the firing on Fort Sumter, sending cannon and a militia to guard the Vicksburg bluffs overlooking the Mississippi River. The militia ended up firing on an innocent commercial vessel, although no one was injured. In addition to fortifying Vicksburg, seven volunteer companies went to reinforce Fort Pickens, Florida, and a militia unit planted the state flag on tiny Ship Island, off Mississippi's Gulf Coast. By late January, the convention had authorized the formation of a volunteer infantry division, to be mustered for one year of service and managed by a military board led by the governor and the major general of the militia. Pettus also ordered seven Mississippi companies to assist Alabama and Florida troops in securing the navy yards at Pensacola, Florida. On January 23, the convention organized the new state regiments into the formal Army of Mississippi, commanded by Jefferson Davis until he formally took the oath of the presidency. In April, President Davis called for thirty thousand Mississippi troops to be mustered as a reserve corps at Corinth, a crucial railroad junction in northwestern Mississippi that could transport troops to Virginia.[32]

To fund this military buildup, the convention issued a military tax of 50 percent on state taxes and 0.3 percent on capital invested out of state. Further, in a controversial move, prominent politician James Z. George proposed that taxes on slaves be increased from seventy-five cents per slave to a dollar twenty-five, while another delegate, S. J. Gholson, raised the proposal to two dollars. Outraged slaveholding delegates moved to stifle this proposal, offering instead an ad valorem amendment, taxing slaves on total value rather than on quantity. Although this offered a loophole to undervalue, the slaveholders won out, indicating a concern for property that emerged again later in the war. Yet, despite some funding controversies, by late 1861 Mississippi was armed for war. Pettus reported to the legislature that the state had twenty-three thousand troops, including infantry, cavalry, and artillery companies, plus an additional twelve thousand who had already been sent west to Albert Sidney Johnston's army. The buildup to war, in turn, encouraged a heightened nationalist excitement within the state's populace, as many welcomed the coming conflict.[33]

Through 1861 and early 1862, Mississippians reacted enthusiastically to their state's secession from the Union, even though the Jackson delegation never submitted the issue to a statewide referendum. Many, former cooperationists and conditional unionists included, embraced protective nationalism and claimed that they were ready to sacrifice all to the new cause. They began the war confident that Mississippi would survive—even thrive—in the Confederacy more than it ever could in the old Union.

In February 1861, Columbus resident Thomas Bailey told his mother in North Carolina that her state would be better off joining the young Confederacy. "How can you hesitate?" he asked; "we offer all that the old government did, & more besides—protection to your greatest interest and dearest right." *Protection* was key here, for only an independent South could provide it, and Bailey's confidence in the "gallant sons of Mississippi" only grew with the passing months. Louisa Lovell, the wife of a Natchez planter, assured her husband that Mississippi would survive any turmoil unscathed. "Our property will be more valuable than ever, and there will never be anything like the suffering here, that there will be in the North," she reasoned. John Kirkland of Attala County echoed Lovell's assertion that the North would suffer deeply from any conflict. "Our subjugation seems to be determined by the north," he wrote, "and the south will never submit, of course it must be a war of extermination of one party or the other." Indeed, many Mississippians outright embraced the prospect of a "war of extermination," and they were confident that the South would win.[34]

War talk often dominated conversations in the months after secession. Writing to his cousin from Jackson, N. H. Boyd described how Mississippi was now "one of the nations of the earth" and that "every appearance of war surrounds us." By April, he noted, citizens continued to rejoice over "every prospect of war" as the firing on Fort Sumter sent Mississippi military companies en masse to Pensacola. Eliza Patterson of Tunica County also noted the militarized environment. "All we hear is War! War!! War!!! But if

we southerns can only subdue those villainous republicans 'all will be well,'"
she wrote. University of Mississippi law student Henry Garrett seconded
Patterson when he observed how Oxford's normally calm streets were "filled
with men in whose mien we read 'war, war, war!!!'" Lincoln had better listen
to cooler heads, Garrett warned; "we all know the Southern heart and how
it rebels at anything like oppression. . . . [I]f one blow is struck or one drop
of Southern blood spilled, we may look for dreadful consequences." In May
1861, William Nelson expressed similarly enthusiastic sentiments and chided
his sister for doubting "the judiciousness of the move [secession]." The South,
he assured her, teemed with men "armed in the holy cause of liberty," and
such men were "invincible against any force the enemy may send against
them."[35] Mississippians' display of such bravado characterized the wave of
nationalist sentiment that swept the state in the months after secession. In
the early phase of the war, national allegiance often eclipsed, but did not
dispel, other loyalties in a highly militarized environment.

Because the Confederacy was born in the midst of war against the North,
its nationalist boosters framed their declarations of independence in terms
of separation from it. Such nationalistic fervor, therefore, brought about
an enthusiasm for self-sufficiency, as Mississippians expressed the need to
devote all of the state's human and material resources to the cause of independence. Early on, many boosters promoted Confederate self-sufficiency
by the severing of all economic ties with the North, which would open the
Confederacy to the rest of the world as an independent nation. Even before
the vote to secede, some Mississippians embraced this protective nationalist
stance.

In November 1860, the *Vicksburg Sun* declared the South "a separate
nationality" and proclaimed that king cotton would ensure Southern self-
sufficiency. "The civilized world depends on the cotton of the South," the
paper's editor stated; "in case of secession we shall have more than half the
crop on hand, and all the world clamoring for it. Again we say we are independent of the world and can take care of ourselves." The *Natchez Daily Free
Trader* similarly recommended urgent secession to create a self-sustaining
Southern republic that was already "a vast territory, rich in natural wealth."
A Southern nation, the *Trader* opined, "might rival Rome in its palmy days."
Even beyond the editorial pages, however, the idea of an independent South
flourished. In October 1860, Will Kirkland of Attala County suggested that
the South should "cut short the cotton crop for one year" so that the North
would recognize its dependence on the Southern commodity. Meanwhile,
the South could "raise everything we need in the way of living except what

we can get from the West [I]ndies. Improve the farm stock and the south can live better and happier." Still, some questioned such optimistic assumptions. The *Daily Vicksburg Whig* reminded readers that "the South, through its merchants, is largely indebted to the North." Mississippians gambled in choosing "to rely upon our own resources," however abundant they were. "We should remember we have never stood alone and will be in a condition of infancy when called upon to help ourselves," the *Whig* argued.[36] After secession, however, the calls for national independence drowned out the already minority appeals to caution, as Mississippians pledged total devotion to an independent and economically self-sufficient Confederacy.

Now it was time to turn rhetoric into action, and first came the practical issue of raising enough money to fight a war. In January 1861, the *Weekly Panola Star* proclaimed that the duty to raise funds through more taxation for "the defense of the State" was imperative. Although admitting that the tax burden would "fall heavily on the people," the *Star* believed that most would pay "without grumbling" to supply "the necessaries of war." After all, as Wiley Harris boasted in January 1861, Mississippians were now inextricably bound to their state. "In making it [Mississippi] independent . . . we have made it stronger," Harris blustered, "because it is now the object of our undivided devotion." Jackson resident Howel Hobbs echoed Harris's sentiments, touting to his daughter the need for total devotion to the state. Mississippi was now an "Independent Republic," he wrote, and "war or no war, we all will have to be Taxed high to raise money to Arm the State & pay the ordinary expenses of the government." He even intended to cancel his subscription to the Northern-published *Lady's Home Journal*, lest he funnel any further Southern dollars into Yankee coffers. Hobbs embraced Confederate self-sufficiency on a personal level to the point of rejecting Northern periodicals. By doing so, he tried to demonstrate, per Harris's statement, that the state was now the focus of his "undivided devotion."[37]

Other Mississippians made similar calls for citizens to sacrifice to the cause via material and spiritual unity. Believing that it was Mississippians' duty "to sustain the State with all of their means," Tippah County planter Francis Leak bought state bonds and donated cotton to the new government, and encouraged others to do the same. By contrast, Louisa Lovell thought that unity to the cause would ensure victory in war. "If the South will unite, be true, firm and brave and act nobly, we *will* succeed and be more prosperous than ever before," she wrote to her husband. Similarly, Albert H. Clark of the Forty-Second Mississippi Infantry contended that it was "the firm resolution of every true Southerner never to be whipped." As long as Southerners remained true to this resolution, they could "never be conquered." Thomas Burton of Kemper County informed his brother that "our people are all ready to fight old & young," adding that "if Linkin's [*sic*] boys ever gets on the soil of Mississippi they will have hot work as every man & boy is ready to fight them."[38] Early in the war, proponents of protective nationalism enthusiastically rallied to the Confederacy's defense. Many of them were certain that maintaining this enthusiasm would, in and of itself, bring about Southern victory.

Nationalist-minded Mississippians also emphasized that suffering should not be an impediment to sacrificing for the Confederacy. In doing so, they embraced a key component of protective nationalism: other loyalties—self-interest included—should be subservient to the national loyalty. Jefferson Davis expressed this view in his inaugural address. "To increase the power, develop the resources, and promote the happiness of a Confederacy," he stated, "it is requisite that there should be so much of homogeneity that the welfare of every portion shall be the aim of the whole." Here, Davis elucidated a key protective nationalist point, that citizens should express a "homogeneity" of individual devotion to benefit the "aim of the whole," the nation. In this view, loyal Southerners should embrace the chance to suffer for their country.[39]

Davis's exhortation quickly diffused through the populace. In August 1861, Okolona, Mississippi, resident C. A. Howe explained to his daughter that "individual suffering must not be considered for a moment when such vast interests are at stake." These "vast interests" were, of course, those of the Confederate nation, and failure to link mind, body, and soul to the nation spelled doom for all: "Defeat is death," Howe concluded. Robert and Willie Hughes, of Pike County, similarly invoked corporeal sacrifice, telling their cousin that even in the face of "war with all its horrors," the South's "one resolve" should be "a perfect willingness, to give all, & our lives too, to secure our independence."[40] Even if giving all to the Confederacy necessitated a loss of personal property, suffering physical deprivations, or outright death, many Mississippians argued that the cause of independence was worth the steep cost.

This cost was acceptable to Betty Beaumont's secessionist neighbors, whom she described as "eager to do everything possible for the cause, willing to sacrifice property and ready to send their sons to fight and to die . . . in defense of Southern institutions." They were not the only ones. In August 1861, William Nugent told his wife that "a man must do something, in such times as we are having, for his country & state, and if he doesn't fight he ought to work in other ways." Nugent believed that suffering should not impede support for the cause. "The people at home must not complain, if they are called upon to suffer inconveniences," he wrote; "privations are ennobling to any people if willingly endured for the sake of the public good." Copiah County native J. J. Little, stationed in Fort McRee, Florida, agreed with Nugent. "Man, Woman & Child should be armed and equipped with the implements of warfare," he wrote his parents. Little also warned that "such things as the people have been in the habit of buying they must now learn to do without," and he even welcomed the opportunity "to fall at the post of duty, in the service of my country."[41] Mississippians embraced protective nationalism as the only means of winning Southern independence. In the process, they relegated themselves into mere component parts in service to the greater whole of the nation. Such an all-consuming approach to nationalism left no room for dissent.

The hypernationalist climate that characterized the secession campaign continued after the state legislature voted to secede. Vigilance committees and local mobs, operating on the paranoia that drove them to intimidate unionist and cooperationist voters, now intensified their efforts to root out "traitors" who threatened to destroy the new Confederacy from within. Protective nationalism required unbending national loyalty. In this atmosphere, extremes begat extremes, and any slight against the state, real or imaginary, had to be suppressed and loyalty enforced. The vigilance committees attempted to enforce Confederate nationalism through threats and physical intimidation. They had to, because national loyalty was all that mattered. John Wood and John Aughey were examples of the dissenters who lurked in Mississippi, and their very existence threatened the protective nationalist ideal. Whatever the dissenters' actual numbers, the fury with which the vigilance committees sought to root them out demonstrated that, to achieve total devotion to the Confederacy, protective nationalists needed to enforce that devotion with the same measure of totality. These decentralized attempts at organized loyalty enforcement foreshadowed the Confederacy's more centralized attempts at policing allegiance that came into full effect in Mississippi by 1862.

Mississippi's nationalist vigilantes targeted any perceived seditious behavior as grounds for punishment. In April 1861, Bunker Hill resident B. A. Terry informed Governor Pettus that he and some locals had formed a band for "keeping down Toryism among the people." Terry sought to bypass local peace officers by gaining the authority to indefinitely detain anyone found "hostile to the institutions, and the interests of our common country." In July 1861, Louisa Lovell relayed rumors that her neighbor, Mr. Marshal, had

returned from a northern trip where he supposedly took "the Black Republican oath." When word spread of this "cowardly submission," locals ran
him and his family out of Natchez. Marshal fled to Vicksburg "to save his
life," only to be met by a "furious mob" brandishing a noose. He survived
because friends intervened and placed him on a steamboat. In May 1861,
John Dickerson, leader of a Fair River, Mississippi, vigilance committee,
was "determined to ferret out all disloyal persons in our bounds." He asked
Pettus what should be done with Jasper Coon, a neighbor whom Dickerson
labeled as "dangerous" and "opposed to our southern movement." Coon allegedly identified as a "Free Soiler" and openly praised Lincoln. Dickerson
considered him "an enemy to our Country" who would "injure our Cause
in any way that he could."[42] The vigilance committees and makeshift mobs
believed that all subversives who threatened Confederate interests had to
be dealt with. For these early Confederate protective nationalists, the actual
number of supposed "disloyal persons" mattered little. The existence of even
one traitor implicitly impeded the goal of ensuring that all Mississippians
were loyal to the Confederate cause.

With this protective nationalist goal in mind, the vigilance committees
fervently targeted alleged traitors for conspiring against the new Southern
nation. Such was the intensity with which protective nationalists sought to
enforce loyalty to a country still in its infancy. Writing to his friend Julia
Southall, Columbus native and Union sympathizer Henry Barnes described
how the hypernationalist atmosphere in Mississippi was pervasive to the
point of rendering speech against the Confederacy treasonous, and contrasted it with that of the Northern states, where he was visiting friends. "I
stopped at Chicago over Sunday," he wrote; "in that church I prayed for the
President of the U.S. *in public for the first time in months* and it gladdened
my heart to be able to do so." Barnes believed that the Southern people
were "laboring under a grievous mistake," having been "precipitated into
revolution" by "designing men," a process that turned public speech into a
treasonable offence. In January 1862, John Goss, the Ohio native who had
escaped a whipping by secessionists in Attala County a year earlier, ran afoul
of the local vigilance committee when they discovered a letter Goss had
written to his brother in Ohio describing "the troubled state of the times" in
Mississippi. The committee arraigned Goss, but he escaped physical punishment through a friend's intervention. Goss then moved to Holmes County,
but when another individual got wind of his political views, Goss again
"deemed it prudent to migrate."[43] Whether or not vigilance groups' targets
were true abolitionists and/or unionists was less important than the fact that

the hypernationalist climate rendered any antisecessionist behavior, including mere speech, grounds for suspicion. Those looking for subversives were bound to find them.

Treasonous speech alone could even be grounds for execution, as Chickasaw County planter Levi Naron, who eventually worked as a spy for the Union army under the name "Chickasaw," soon discovered. In 1861, the vigilance committee admonished him to "desist from speaking against the Confederacy." They had severely beaten one local Union man and hanged two others, and Naron's unionist sentiments were well known. A few weeks later, armed men ambushed him at dusk and took him to a tree, where they interrogated him and threatened the noose. When Naron refused to join the Confederate army, the men prepared to hang him, arguing that "we have all got to fight, and he who will not fight is against us." Naron escaped by eliciting the sympathies of some clergymen in the committee, but the threats eventually became too much, and he fled the county. Like Naron, John Aughey avoided being lynched when a sympathetic layperson argued that he had uttered treasonous words but had not committed treasonous actions, and that the committee was not operating with the proper civil or military authority. Others were not as lucky. Mobs hanged a Presbyterian unionist pastor from Macon, Mississippi, and murdered a friend of Aughey, and two friends of Aughey's former pupils simply disappeared. Aughey himself spent the rest of the war on the run and endured time in a Confederate prison before finally reaching Union lines.[44] Naron's and Aughey's experiences underscored how even public speech could be interpreted as dissent in an atmosphere in which the Confederacy's unquestioned authority had already been established by mob rule.

The fact that the vigilance committees deemed many suspicious persons "abolitionists," or at least suggested that their alleged dissent against the Confederacy stemmed from their sympathizing with antislavery views, was no coincidence. These vigilance mobs owed much in terms of tactics and ideology to the antebellum slave patrols. Although slave patrols existed before the Confederacy, vigilance committees patterned themselves after these patrols because they, too, sought to counter threats to slavery, though in a different form. Slave patrols worked to control the behavior not only of seditious slaves but also of suspicious whites who might aid slaves. In the antebellum period, supposed abolitionist infiltrators threatened slavery as an institution. After secession, nationalist-minded Confederates insisted that abolitionists, who had seized power in the North through the election of antislavery "black Republicans," now threatened the Confederacy itself.[45]

In mid-January 1861, the Woodville Vigilance Committee drove two men out of town, one for using two names, the other for being a "suspected" abolitionist from Illinois. In Pike County, John Simmons asked Governor Pettus if the home guards had permission to detain "suspicious characters." Simmons claimed that these "characters" had been "instructing Negroes in military discipline and claiming themselves as abolitionists," while also boasting that if drafted into the army they would "take their first shot at Jef. Davis." He was especially concerned about secret abolitionists infiltrating close-knit neighborhoods where everyone knew everyone else. In June 1861, Greene County resident O. J. Hood complained to Pettus about four members of the McLeod family, who for years had been expressing "abolition sentiments." In response, the vigilance committee arraigned them and held a public trial. Allen McLeod allegedly called Jefferson Davis a "Murderer, Scamp and Traitor," while his brother, Peter, compared the slaves to the "children of Iseral [*sic*]" who would soon be freed. The committee gave Peter a choice between swearing the Confederate oath or leaving the county. When he refused to do either, Hood confessed to "feeling a *little* delicacy in resorting to extreme measures however great the crime might be without some higher authority."[46] That Hood even viewed antislavery speech as worthy of "extreme measures" on residents of his own neighborhood demonstrated the desire among Confederate nationalists for everyone to toe the party line.

Confederate nationalists viewed any supposed threat to slavery as worthy of immediate suppression. Suspicious persons did not have to be labeled "abolitionists" to be considered a threat. In early 1862, Roxana Gerdine told her sister that "the country here has a patrol every night to see that no suspicious person is around to incite the negroes," adding that "a suspicious looking woman" had recently been hanged in nearby Columbus. The woman's executioners found strychnine, along with "papers" and "books," on her person. "Have to look out these days what they do," Gerdine cautioned. Later that summer, a Jefferson County provost marshal jailed an Ohio man for labeling Mississippi's planters "a set of G D thieves," wishing that the Union gunboats would "shell every God Dam plantation on the river," and calling for a slave insurrection.[47] In these incidents, threats to slavery became threats to the nation. Following Mississippi's secession and the formation of the Confederacy, the fact that individuals within the state itself might incite a slave insurrection designated them enemies of the Confederate cause. Rooting out dissidents who threatened slavery was the only way for protective nationalists to ensure that every Mississippian was loyal to the nation and its foundational institution.

In 1860 and 1861, the methods for enforcing protective nationalism in Mississippi were already in place. This type of nationalism envisioned individual citizens as component parts in service to the greater national whole, and it demanded a total devotion of bodies and resources to the goal of Confederate independence. Relying on a long tradition of public and institutional acquiescence to extralegal mob violence, secessionists and then Confederates created a deeply partisan atmosphere hostile to any dissenters who might question the wisdom of disunion or the authority of the new Confederacy. They threatened violence against unionist and cooperationist voters during the secession campaign and left few options on the ballot for those wishing to support anything but immediate disunion. Following Mississippi's vote to secede, these same hypernationalist groups continued their campaign of rooting out supposed abolitionists and Union sympathizers. In 1861, however, these attempts at organized loyalty enforcement were still decentralized. The fact that many vigilance committee members questioned Governor Pettus about what to do with alleged dissidents reveals that, although they functioned as extensions of Mississippi's extralegal mobs, they lacked the type of centralized system for loyalty enforcement that the Confederate government had enacted by mid-1862. This centralized system was a product of the expanded nation-state that emerged in both the North and the South during the Civil War.

The vigilance committees and other extralegal groups, however, did not emerge in a vacuum, nor did they by force alone compel Mississippians into disunion. Rather, these groups were the extreme product of an already extreme concept: protective nationalism. They did not create this nationalist fervor, they embodied it, and they flourished in the wake of Lincoln's election with the support of a majority of Mississippians. Across the state, people rejoiced at the idea of an independent Confederacy and vowed to devote themselves to its cause. Mississippians were overtaken by militaristic fervor, and protective nationalism seemed tenable when it did not require material sacrifice. In these circumstances, declarations of loyalty and the prioritization of micro and macro allegiances were more clear cut. This all-consuming nationalism, however, was built on sandy foundations that ultimately made it difficult to uphold. Its attempts to completely negate the influence of other loyalties proved unworkable in practice.

The vigilance committees' and later the Confederate government's attempts to use force as a means of squelching dissent revealed the impossibility of enacting a concept at odds with the reality of human loyalty layers. When the Union army arrived in the summer of 1862, the shifting circumstances of the war forced Mississippians to reexamine what Confederate loyalty meant in practice. They did not abandon the Confederate cause in the wake of war-induced hardships, nor did they suddenly embrace unionism. Rather, wartime hardships diminished protective nationalism's appeal. These hardships were trenchant reminders to Mississippians that living up to the protective nationalist ideal meant neglecting other loyalties, which did not cease to influence human behavior merely to accommodate the demands of überpatriots.

CHAPTER TWO

"WELL CALCULATED TO TEST THE LOYALTY OF HER CITIZENS"

Property, Principle, and the Oath of Allegiance

AUGUST 1862. THE CANTON *AMERICAN CITIZEN* PROCLAIMED THE INDE-
fatigable resolve of Mississippi in the face of a Union army onslaught. "So far
as Mississippi is concerned," the paper boasted, "the Yankees will have bitter
and unrelenting foes to fight for one hundred years, if they choose to continue the contest so long." The paper described the state's soldiers as "furious
devils in battle" and assured readers that its women "offered everything upon
the shrine of liberty" much like Cornelia of ancient Rome, whose steadfast
devotion to her sons Tiberius and Gaius Gracchus, the "Gracchi," and tireless
commitment to the Roman republic made her the model matron in classical
literature. "Even our slaves despise the Yankees," the *Citizen* claimed.[1]

In a stark contrast to the *Citizen*'s confidence, however, the June 1863
issue of the Macon *Beacon* cast doubt on Mississippians' commitment to
Confederate independence. As General Ulysses S. Grant's troops marched
toward Vicksburg, the *Beacon* warned that if the city fell, "the whole State
will be subjected to hostile institutions, and then the spirit of our people
will be subjected to a test of fidelity to principle for which they have been ill
prepared." The paper claimed that Mississippians would "disgrace themselves"
by caving to federal rule "when the love of property and of principle operate
in different directions" and disparaged "the base wretch who swears a lie, to
save his property" by taking the Union oath. The *Beacon* found this behavior
especially galling in the face of a hostile foe, asserting that only "unwavering
courage and unyielding resistance under all circumstances" would ensure
Confederate victory.[2] In encouraging resistance to Union invasion, the *Beacon* hoped to make Mississippians live up to the nationalist ideal that the
American Citizen had promoted a year earlier.

By suggesting that white Southerners should be, per the *Citizen's* description, resolutely patriotic and decrying them as traitors when they fell short, the *Beacon* and other proponents of protective nationalism did not consider how individuals negotiated between multiple loyalties. Consider the case of Tishomingo County resident James B. Wells. In November 1863, the federal army arrested Wells for bushwhacking in northern Mississippi but released him after he swore the Union oath. Soon after, Confederate officials charged him with treason. He claimed to be a poor wagon maker exempted from Confederate service due to "rheumatisms" and "that he might work on his trade." Wells insisted that he was a "true southern man" who took the federal oath out of a desire to return home and help feed his starving family, and he "bitterly regretted" taking the Union oath out of necessity. Wells offered to join the Confederate army but preferred to tend to work and family. Ultimately, the Confederates deemed him "honest & truthful" and recommended that the conscript bureau release him.[3]

When considering people like Wells, historians often ask whether they were loyal Confederates, but this question rests on the assumption that national allegiance guided their actions. Certainly, Union and Confederate authorities operated on this theoretical framework. Depending on the proclivities of the observer, the Confederates' judgment of Wells as "honest & truthful" might render him a patriot of "brilliant colors." On the other hand, his oath swearing might make him a "base wretch" who swore a lie to protect his self-interest. Wells's assertion that he swore the oath in order to go home to his family suggests that, patriotic feelings aside, micro loyalties were on his mind. Wells's level of devotion to the Confederacy was, in this circumstance, beside the point. Rather than try to measure his national loyalty, historians should ask what other fidelities beyond nationalism motivated him. Doing so leads to a clearer understanding of how multiple loyalties guided Southerners' behavior during the Civil War. The influence of multiple allegiances, in turn, reveals that the reach of the nineteenth-century nation-state was more limited than historians have concluded, despite the Civil War's imbuing it with expanded apparatuses for loyalty enforcement.

This chapter examines how Confederate and Union forces tried to police and enforce loyalty among Mississippians by judging them according to the standard of protective nationalism. Although Mississippians had largely embraced a protective nationalist fervor during the buildup to secession and throughout the first year of the war, such enthusiasm came easy when the conflict's hardships had yet to come to their doorsteps. As the second year of the war arrived, however, military events tested Mississippians' ability to devote themselves entirely to the Rebel cause. Their multiple allegiances made loyalty enforcement problematic for two warring governments seeking to put citizens into dichotomized "loyal" and "disloyal" camps. The ideals of protective nationalism proved elusive when faced with the harsh reality of its practical implications on the ground.

When Union forces came to Mississippi in the summer of 1862, they attempted to enforce Mississippians' loyalty to the United States through mechanisms like the oath of allegiance. Confederate forces responded by enforcing the protective nationalist model that had emerged during the secession crisis, labeling treasonous any citizens who allegedly kowtowed to federal demands. As Elizabeth Duquette notes, the Civil War's two factions believed that security was only guaranteed "if friend was systematically and reliably distinguished from foe." With this point in mind, "war takes . . . the opposition of friend and enemy," strips away "all potential nuance," and "demands the clear categorization of all persons and actions."[4] In Mississippi, Confederate forces needed to distinguish friend from foe. Thus, they rejected the nuance of human loyalty layers and attempted to enforce total loyalty to the cause. This contributed to an already heated climate that turned everyday actions into potential tests of an individual's fealty to one side or the other. Union forces operated under the same concept.

For ordinary Mississippians, however, the situation was far more complex. They continued to act on allegiances separate from nationalism in the face of Confederate partisans' attempts to spot treason at every turn. Others embraced a more limited national vision that conflicted with that of the Confederate government. In these situations, the model of protective nationalism led civil and military authorities to extend the state's apparatuses into people's lives in an effort to enforce allegiance, an effort stymied by Mississippians' multiple loyalties. Mississippi's experience demonstrates how the newly empowered nation-state emerged during the Civil War, a model that subsequently arose during succeeding American conflicts.[5] Paradoxically, however, the war created a "strong" state that was simply not that strong. Despite its expanded powers, it could not enforce total loyalty among its subjects, which was the very justification for its increased powers in the first place.

Mississippi hosted several major campaigns of the Civil War's western theater, ensuring that Mississippians would be in close contact with the Union army through most of the conflict. Following defeat at the Battle of Shiloh, Tennessee, April 6–7, 1862, Confederate forces retreated south to Corinth, Mississippi, with the battered Union forces in slow pursuit. In the meantime, the Confederates realized their untenable position against a numerically superior foe and evacuated the city. The Federals marched into Corinth unopposed on May 30, establishing a foothold in Mississippi that, in tandem with the success of Union naval operations on the Mississippi River, they retained from that point on. The Union thrust into the state culminated on July 4, 1863, when General John Pemberton's Army of Vicksburg surrendered to Ulysses S. Grant after a prolonged siege. Confederate military fortunes in Mississippi never recovered after Vicksburg's fall. Capturing the city gave the Federals a base from which they could raid throughout the state. In mid-July 1863, Pontotoc County resident M. J. Blackwell recognized this fact immediately, telling his sister-in-law that "since the fall of Vicksburg I suppose we may look for the whole state to be overrun."[6] Union occupation posed numerous challenges for Mississippians, especially in regard to the ethical quandaries around swearing the oath.

Historian Anne Rubin notes that many Confederates considered an oath taken under coercion inherently nonbinding. They therefore swore it pragmatically, allowing them to violate it with a clean conscience as a means to achieving other ends like securing housing, food, and protection while still remaining loyal Confederates.[7] However, on closer inspection, the line between "practical" and "ideological" behavior blurs considerably. Rubin concedes that oath swearing did not necessarily indicate disloyalty, but her assertion that oath takers were de facto Confederates implies that nationalism remained the bedrock standard by which Southerners operated. This assumption fails to consider the constrained circumstances under which people swore oaths.

Mississippians took the oath as a means to get something they wanted, such as trading passes, protection from Confederate conscription, or permission to move behind the lines. In order to achieve these desired ends, they had to profess Union loyalty. In so doing, however, they took part in a nationalist discourse in which partisans tried to ascertain peoples' loyalties to one side or the other. This environment rendered all claims of allegiance inherently suspect. To explain how oath taking undermined the effectiveness of protective nationalism, this chapter examines the reasons some Mississippians gave for criticizing oath takers, and how oath takers defended their actions. Critics considered the oath a reliable mechanism for determining a person's loyalty. By contrast, rather than demonstrating pragmatism, oath takers invoked multiple loyalties to self and family that had little to do with nationalist feelings.

America's relatively unstructured and unhierarchical society made a poor backdrop for Old World–style nationalist pageantry such as oath swearing. Moreover, its Protestant suspicion of ritualistic pomp and circumstance (which reeked of Catholic idolatry) meant that oaths never entailed the same level of ceremonial reverence there that they did in other societies. Nevertheless, the use of oaths as a mechanism for identifying allegiance had been established in the United States well before the outbreak of the Civil War. Upon their arrival in New England, the Puritans instituted an oath to identify those loyal to the new commonwealth. The first item produced by the English colonies' new printing press in 1639 was the loyalty oath. Americans during the Revolutionary era also embraced the oath, and George Washington viewed it as a reliable "test act" for distinguishing friends from enemies.[8]

Oaths played an important role in affirming human relationships and demonstrating honor in eighteenth- and nineteenth-century America, especially in the South. In many aspects of southern life, including courteous agreements, university formalities, and demonstrations of honor between political rivals, the oath served as a binding contract, respected by those within the circle of honor who swore it. Moreover, southern honor served both individual and communal functions. A person's individual worth was in part measured by his or her status within the community, and Southerners looked to peer approval on public and private matters.[9]

From 1861 through the end of Reconstruction, the Northern government relied on the oath as the chief mechanism for enforcing loyalty to the United States. The federal army in Mississippi made the oath a prerequisite for Mississippians wishing to travel through the state or trade at Union lines. As William Blair writes, "coerced patriotism based on provisions was becoming one of the bases for creating the reunion of the country." Federal authorities' conception of loyalty to the Union specifically referred to the Union that formed as the war progressed, embracing emancipation and reconstruction of the seceded states. This new conception contrasted with many Mississippians' vision of the Union as constituting the old antebellum political order with slavery intact.[10]

Mississippians held varying opinions about taking the oath. Some wrestled over the ethical dilemma inherent in the act, but others viewed the oath's implications for loyalty as irrelevant because they swore the oath out of allegiances altogether distinct from nationalism.

One Mississippian who considered the oath a serious matter was Vicksburg Episcopal minister William Wilberforce Lord. In a lengthy 1863 treatise,

Lord ruminated over "whether a man owing true allegiance to one government" could in good faith "take an insincere oath to support a hostile government." An oath taken under any kind of duress, Lord reasoned, was void by law since the nature of its administering was itself a breach of law. Nonetheless, Lord viewed the oath as still morally binding, especially when one's life did not hang in the balance. Distressed that many Mississippians evidenced a "strong temptation" to take the oath, Lord insisted that they refrain from doing so, even if the alternative involved "serious loss and detriment to personal interests." He maintained that any Mississippian who swore it was "governed by no higher motive than self-interest."[11] Lord's view of oath swearing fit squarely within the protective nationalist model. For him there could be no compromise between loyalty to the state and personal interests. Mississippians should be wholly devoted to the Confederacy. Anything less than total commitment to the national cause was unacceptable.

Other Mississippians agreed with Lord that oath swearing evidenced the moral weakness of insufficient patriotism. Writing to his son in the army in April 1863, Jackson resident William Thomson noted that, in Lauderdale County, "all within their [Union] lines have taken the oath of allegiance." The Federals were a "fiendish" and "hellish . . . horde," Thomson wrote, but oath takers were "more abhorrent to me than the vile Yankees themselves." Eliza Sively of Hinds County echoed Thomson's sentiment, telling her daughter, "I am sorry to say many of the citizens of Hinds are very much demoralized and have taken the oath," including one individual who had been a "hot secesh." In February 1863, a Hinds County police board member complained to the governor that nearly all other board members had "taken the Oath of Allegiance to the Lincoln Government." William Dameron, writing to his wife from Meridian in the fall of that year, commented that an acquaintance, Kershaw, had gone to occupied Memphis, where he swore the Union oath. "[M]oney, money, money, what will it not make a man do & become."[12] Oath takers often elicited such criticisms from fellow citizens, who considered swearing the oath to the Union to be an unforgivably treasonous offence.

Confederate patriots found it especially galling that their fellow Southerners were willing to dishonor themselves in the eyes of their peers by shamelessly taking the Yankee oath. Mississippi soldier Edwin Miller, stationed in Virginia in 1863, bristled at the "wretches in North Mississippi" who would "reap the harvest which they are now sowing" by swearing the Union oath. "[I]t is my most devout wish," Miller wrote, "that they should have their heads shaved on one side and be branded, as deserters are, with a red hot iron, as traitors, and then banished forever from our country." W. C. Taylor, of Panola County, also considered oath takers to be traitors and chafed at rumors that he was among them. Following the Union occupation of Oxford, Mississippi, in March 1863, a local doctor named Phipps accused Taylor and two acquaintances, Thomas Wendal and Peter Slate, of appearing in a Chicago newspaper's list of Mississippians who had caved and sworn the oath. Whether this was true is unknown, but Taylor vehemently denied this accusation. "[N]either your name or that of Mr. Slate's were ever alluded to other than as true & loyal southerners," Taylor told Wendal; "highway robbery & assassination are respectable crimes compared to these malicious assaults against the integrity of a man's honor and integrity of southern principle." Like other Mississippians, Taylor embraced the protective nationalist stance that placed national loyalty above all other concerns. In keeping with the Southern tradition that linked patriotism to the upholding of personal and communal honor, he believed that those who violated this ideal had committed a dishonorable offense.[13]

Oath swearing was of such concern that Governor John Pettus spoke to the Mississippi legislature about it in November 1863. Although he admitted that the war in his state had been "well calculated to test the loyalty of her citizens," Pettus downplayed talk of mass oath taking. "[I]t is perhaps true that some individuals . . . have taken the oath of allegiance to and sought the protection of the Government of the United States," Pettus said. Yet he insisted that "the great heart of the people of Mississippi remains as true to the cause . . . as when the contest first began."[14] In claiming that most remained "true" to the cause, Pettus implied that oath takers, by implication, *did not* remain true. He believed that swearing the Union oath and remaining loyal to the Confederacy were two diametrically opposed actions. The demands of protective nationalism were such that mushy displays of weak patriotism evidenced clear-cut treason.

Despite the limits that such an ideal placed on human behavior, some Mississippians nonetheless struggled to live up to it by remaining "true to the cause" and refusing to take the oath. In October 1862, a *Chicago Times* report from General Grant's headquarters in Oxford noted that while "a considerable number" who desired "protection in person and property" swore the oath, others were "silently refusing to take it." In Warren County, Jane Gibson, the widowed owner of Deer Creek Plantation, wrote to Jefferson Davis that even though her neighbor had taken the oath to sell cotton to the Federals at Vicksburg, she refused to do the same. "I can't do it unless starvation drives me to it," she wrote, even as she admitted that "our situation here is a bad one." Another Warren County resident, Emilie Riley McKinley, also refused to swear the oath despite the omnipresence of Union forces. One of her neighbors, local physician Daniel Nailor, agreed, claiming that his bones would "bleach on this hill before I take it." Others, such as plantation owners on the Big Black River, did take the oath under the pretense of "protection," much to the disgust of McKinley and her friends.[15] Many Mississippians swore the oath under the premise that doing so secured protection for their property or permission to travel, excuses that infuriated loyal Confederates.

Caroline Seabury, a schoolteacher living in Columbus, Mississippi, was one of those Confederates who did not buy the "protection" excuse. In August 1863, she criticized Delta planters "whose only ambition" was to "'make a big crop'—no matter by what means." The planters brandished the "protection papers" that they had scored after taking the Union oath in Memphis, and Seabury found this behavior hypocritical. "I soon saw that there was very little devotion to the Confederacy," she wrote, "perhaps because a Yankee market was too accessible." Indeed, Confederate nationalists were shocked at the seeming ease with which heretofore red-blooded Rebels turned into Yankee milksops. In May 1865, for example, Wayne County resident Anna Pickens complained that locals had become "dear lovers of the Union and haters of secession" after the fall of Mobile. A local planter named Goodman epitomized such alleged treason when he "hurried off to take the oath of allegiance for the purpose of saving his property in Mobile." In August 1863, Amite County, Mississippi, native Samuel Moore told his wife that a neighbor, whom Moore thought "would be the last man that would take the oath," had done just that. That same month, former state representative James Alcorn regretted that "many of our people" took the oath in order to visit Helena, Arkansas.[16] Imbued with the protective nationalist ideal that rendered any collusion with Union forces evidence of treason against the Confederacy, critics of Mississippians who swore the oath insisted that safeguarding personal property was insufficient grounds for betraying their loyalty to the Southern cause. Doing so placed self-interest above Confederate independence.

Other Mississippians, however, demonstrated why this conclusion was too simplistic. Many touted their Confederate loyalty but nonetheless indicated that micro loyalties were legitimate motivations behind taking the oath. Their actions revealed how multiple allegiances undermined protective nationalists' attempts to interpret "treasonous" wartime behavior on its face as evidence of disloyalty to the Confederate cause. Trying to enforce a simplistic patriotic ideal in the complicated real world was bound to hit some roadblocks, but the presence of so many critics of oath taking indicates that protective nationalism functioned as an ideal toward which people still strove. Much to the dismay of protective nationalists, however, no mechanism—oaths or otherwise—could compel total allegiance.

Take, for example, the experience of Louisa Lovell, daughter of former Mississippi governor, John Quitman. Amid rumors of a Yankee invasion of Natchez in May 1862, she feared that Union forces would "try to compel us to take the oath, which I will *never* do." By February 1864, with the Federals established in Natchez, Lovell told her husband, Joseph, that if she did not swear "that horrible oath," the Yankees would confiscate her plantation, Palmyra:

> What to do I do not know. I feel as if I would submit to every privation rather than go against my conscience & yet here is the fearful alternative of that or starvation & beggaring. I believe that should we persist in our present feeling as regards this diabolical oath, that the next move would be to order us out of the lines & away from our home. Would not this be awful!

Still, Lovell refused to submit, complaining that "none but a base, groveling, covetous Yankee" would "place helpless women" in such a position. "Many advise taking the oath as one would submit to the torture of the rack," she noted; "such indeed it would be to me. I don't believe I could *ever* do it." In March 1864, however, after nearly two years of resisting, Lovell did it. "*I will tell* we were compelled to take the *oath*. Think of that, Joe!" she exclaimed. "However it is the *oath* of *amnesty*," she added; "it was this or starvation & beggary."[17] Self-interest, driven by the fear of material discomfort, drove Lovell to swear the oath. These separate attachments conflicted with her national feelings. Had the influence of protective nationalism won out in this instance, Lovell would have risked losing her home and endured banishment from the lines. That she ultimately caved to federal demands demonstrated protective nationalism's limited influence on even self-identified die-hard Confederates.

Just like Lovell, other Mississippians claimed that taking the oath out of self-interest did not reflect their true national feelings. In June 1862, Chickasaw County unionist Levi Naron was initially surprised to see Mississippians "flock" to swear the amnesty oath at Union-occupied Corinth. He soon discovered, however, that the citizens had done so "not out of any pure motive, but for the purpose of selling their cotton." Indeed, these oath takers "all had arms, which they kept concealed," waiting to help the Confederates "clean out" the Yankees from the area. Naron separated the "pure motive" of national loyalty from the base behavior of selling to the enemy. Had he examined the matter a bit more closely, however, he might have recognized how the oath takers kept their self-interest distinct from their true national loyalties, especially since they were ready to take potshots at the same Yankees to whom they sold cotton.

Confederate cavalry scout Charles Allen came to this conclusion—albeit from a limited perspective—when addressing the wave of oath swearing after the fall of Vicksburg: "[N]early all here have taken [the oath] . . . it would be easier to name the true ones," he wrote. In response, he intended to "take every horse from the spotted men of Warren & turn them over to the [Confederate] government." Yet, even as he railed against other oath takers, Allen noted that his cousin, Will, had sworn the oath after the Federals threatened to arrest him and confiscate his property. "[I]t was a forced oath," Allen reasoned; "he could not leave his children[;] he told them he would take the oath but would not consider it still binding." Here Allen acknowledged that his cousin's attachments to property and family were separate from national feelings and thus warranted no punishment—a courtesy he would not extend to other allegedly traitorous oath takers in Warren County.[18]

Other Mississippians faced the same dilemma when the oath pitted national interests against personal interests. In early June 1863, Claiborne County resident Elizabeth Ingraham, the sister of Union general George Meade, criticized neighbors who swore the oath from federal raiders. One in particular, she noted, "calls himself a 'Union man'; property saved; only still point." Although Ingraham chided her neighbors, she and her husband, Alfred, wrestled with the same conflicts. "I do pray to God he [Alfred] will withstand the oath," she wrote; "we can't lose much more, in a worldly view." She prayed for the strength to "resist that despotism . . . until the whole country succumbs, and there is no Confederate government."[19] The willingness to sacrifice all material possessions for the good of the cause was an ideal that Ingraham struggled to live up to, but self-interest was a constant motivator. Her determination to "resist" the "despotism" imposed by the Union oath suggests that even as she remained resolutely patriotic, the mere thought of committing what others might construe as a treasonous act ate away at her conscience. Such fear resulted from the unrealistic level of devotion that protective nationalism demanded from even self-identified loyal Rebels.

For a good many Mississippians who swore the Union oath, however, accusations of treason stung hard, especially when oath swearing was so rampant. Planter James Dick Hill, for example, became irate when the Confederate army refused to return his slaves whom he had sent to Alabama for safekeeping in 1863. Describing the treason charge as "an infamous falsehood," Hill protested to Jefferson Davis that "we were all compelled to apply for protection and there is no one in this place who did not do it." Hill was not alone in swearing the oath in exchange for something in return.[20]

In September 1863, a Confederate cavalryman in northern Mississippi informed Governor Pettus that people "all along the Rail Road, had taken the 'oath,'" so that they could trade at Union lines. "The scarcity of salt & meat is the alleged excuse for this illicit trade," the officer noted. Following a Union raid through Attala County, Will Kirkland told his cousin, Bettie, that, with few exceptions, "nearly all the men in the neighborhood" had taken the oath. He assured Bettie, however, that, "the sympathies of nearly all are with the south," and they had sworn the oath "to get pay for property which the Yanks had taken" and "to buy supplies for their families." A group of Yazoo County planters and one laborer likely had similar incentives for swearing the oath in July 1863. Although their oaths included no personal statements, all save the laborer, H. B. Watson, had substantial holdings in property and real estate liable to federal confiscation. Watson likely worked on the local plantations and therefore had an interest in protecting planters' property.[21] These examples indicate that even as Confederate nationalists conflated oath swearing with treason, such a charge did not prevent Mississippians from swearing it out of micro loyalties unrelated to nationalism. When it came to the Yankee oath, the Confederate state simply did not have the power to enforce the protective nationalist ideal.

Securing protection for property was a prime motivation for Mississippians to swear the Union oath, but there were other reasons as well. Federal officials tended to view oath swearing as a declaration of loyalty to the Union, but Mississippians' reasons for taking the oath were often far more nuanced than a sudden soft spot for Lincoln. Some took the oath to avoid Confederate conscription, others to continue commercial activity, and others to visit family and friends living beyond Confederate lines. These Mississippians swore the oath under constrained circumstances, in which pledging Union allegiance was a necessary means for achieving their desired ends. This fact suggests that historians should be wary—federal officials' conclusions notwithstanding—of equating oath swearing with Union loyalty. Such a conclusion conflates Mississippians' ends with their means, shifting the focus away from the micro loyalties that they indicated were important influences on their behavior. This is not to deny the possibility that some Mississippians who took the oath were indeed unionists, but it *is* to say that the oath was not a reliable gauge with which to make such a judgment.

In December 1863, Rankin County farmer Archibald St. Clair escaped to Union-occupied New Orleans to take the oath to avoid being "again forced into Rebel service." Similarly, Jasper County residents Joseph Byrd and Marion, Martin, and Obadiah Parker came to New Orleans claiming that they had "always been loyal." After being conscripted in 1862, they escaped to Union lines, where they desired to take the oath. The federal commission judged the men to be "honest and sincerely loyal," having deserted "from aversion to fight against the government and flag of the United States." Franklin County residents Beer Gardner and Barnet Brodnintza fled to federal lines "to escape conscription in rebel service." Both took the oath, and the Federals deemed them "not suspicious persons." In October 1863, Biloxi natives George Andrews and William Norberg came to Ship Island "to avoid conscription." From there, Union officials sent them to New Orleans, where they took the oath to "go to work in the city." Local resident Louisa Frederick vouched for the men, noting that both had relatives in the Union army, reinforcing their standing as "good Union Men." Taking federal officials' word that these Mississippians were loyal unionists neglects the fact that all of them swore the oath to avoid Confederate conscription. Maybe they were loyal to the Union, maybe not, but their self-interested desire to avoid conscription indicates that swearing the oath had little to do with proclaiming allegiance to either North or South.[22]

The convoluted case of Thomas Sheppard of Pontotoc County further illustrates this point. Sheppard was working as a US government clerk in Kansas before the war but came to Holly Springs, Mississippi, in late 1862. There, Confederate forces arrested him and shuffled him between prisons, where he gave conflicting loyalty statements. Initially, Sheppard said that he had returned to Mississippi "to seek his relatives in the south and join the Conf. Army," claiming that he had never fought for the United States nor taken the Union oath. Once moved to Columbus, Mississippi, Sheppard explained that after leaving Holly Springs he went to Illinois to continue working for the US government but reiterated that he came back to Mississippi "to seek his relatives South, and join the Confederate service." In a *third* statement, however, Sheppard contradicted his previous testimonies, claiming that he could not join the Confederate army due to a "case of the kidneys." He also said that he had "taken the oath of allegiance to the U.S. govt." and was "unwilling to violate it," preferring instead to remain in prison. Ultimately, the Confederate authorities recommended that Sheppard be sent to Salisbury

Prison in North Carolina "to be confined as an alien enemy."[23] Sheppard's emphasis on visiting family within Confederate lines, and his desire to avoid military service, suggest that these issues, rather than nationalism, guided his behavior. This may explain why he gave otherwise contradictory loyalty statements: he used nationalist language as the means to other ends.

Perhaps the nationalist claims of Sheppard and others who swore the Union oath to avoid Confederate military service were sincere, but these men also had personal motives for doing so. Thus, their oath taking should be viewed as part of the greater nationalist discourse within Civil War Mississippi, a response to partisans who demanded that people take sides, rather than as statements of absolute truth. Their desire to avoid service reflected self-interest that was distinct from patriotism, and this micro loyalty clearly drove them, at least in part, to swear the oath. Certainly, some federal authorities recognized the unreliability of oaths. Union General Order no. 6 from Vicksburg stated that "in deciding upon the class of persons who are to be assessed, it should not be forgotten that the oath of allegiance is not an infallible test of loyalty.... [M]en must be judged by their acts and not by the oaths they have taken."[24] This realization did not stop Union and Confederate officials, however, from continuing to use the oath to elicit declarations of loyalty from Mississippians. The binary framework of protective nationalism demanded that friend be distinguished from foe, and the oath, however flawed, was the primary mechanism available for this task.

The continued use of the oath by both sides underscored a primary goal of the modern nation-state: to elicit the allegiance of its citizens. With this goal in mind, Union and Confederate authorities continued to require Mississippians whose motives seemed unrelated to patriotism to affirm their allegiance through oath taking. For some Mississippians, close proximity to federal lines ensured relatively smooth traveling per their willingness to swear it. Those living on the Gulf Coast and river waterways had easier access to these lines than those in the state's interior. In April 1862, the Union navy captured Biloxi and Pass Christian, the Gulf region's two major cities, and established a Confederate prisoner of war camp on Ship Island, off the coast of Pascagoula. In addition to housing prisoners, Ship Island attracted Mississippi civilians who wanted to get passage beyond Confederate lines. When Union forces captured New Orleans, Natchez, Vicksburg, and Memphis, they gained control of the Mississippi River and all of its ports.[25]

In February 1865, eight Mississippians took the federal oath on steamers off of landings at Vicksburg, Olive Branch, Natchez, Eggs Point, Hannet, and Skepwith. In November 1863, eleven more, most from the Gulf, took the oath at Ship Island, citing the scarcity of provisions and fear of conscription as their reasons for doing so. Of the eleven, three Pascagoula residents refused to take it, having already sworn the Confederate oath, but still wanted to stay in Union lines. When federal boats prevented Jackson County timber mill operator Henry Kirkwood from shipping turpentine from Mobile to Pascagoula, he told Union authorities that he had "always been loyal" and wanted to take the oath "to obtain [a] permit to bring in turpentine again." Judging Kirkwood to be "a loyal man," federal authorities acquiesced. Harrison County business owners Mr. and Mrs. Charles Gumbell took the oath and received a pass to run their Pascagoula hotel and travel along the Gulf to visit friends. In December 1863, Biloxi resident Camelia Gerard arrived in New Orleans, where she swore the oath in order to "visit relatives" after Union authorities deemed her "not a suspicious person." Likewise, Biloxi native Louisa Lafaure, along with several family members, swore the oath at New Orleans to "reside with relatives." The federal provost marshal considered them to be an "inoffensive creole family" and allowed them to stay in Union lines, even though they "had a friend in rebel service."[26]

Mississippi's Gulf Coast contained a large number of foreign-born residents, and ethnicity was one of many factors that informed non–native born Americans' decisions to support either side during the war. In general, however, foreign-born whites were no more or less inclined to support the Confederacy than native-born whites.[27] These Gulf Coast residents cited self-interest in the form of avoiding conscription and privation, maintaining commercial activity, and desiring to visit friends and relatives beyond Confederate lines as undergirding their decision to take the oath. These allegiances were powerful motivators regardless of peoples' national sympathies, and they revealed that the US government, which used its expanded wartime resources and manpower to gauge the loyalty of Southerners, was weak where it mattered most: in obtaining Mississippians' unquestioned allegiance. Its resources were still insufficient in light of the influence of loyalty layers.

Just as Union forces relied on the oath to measure Mississippians' allegiance, Confederates continued to view actions like oath swearing as evidence of citizens' alleged faltering patriotism. While the ideal of protective nationalism loomed large over controversies regarding oath swearing, the Civil War in Mississippi created other instances that, according to ardent Confederate nationalists, challenged people's devotion to the cause. Although Mississippians' multiple loyalties revealed the inherent difficulty of enforcing protective nationalism among the populace, Confederates responded by doubling down on their attempts to do so. This was the illogically logical next step in trying to make an unrealistic ideal into a reality. If Confederate victory required unyielding loyalty, then enforcement of loyalty had to be unyielding as well. This circular logic ultimately contributed to the modern wartime state's embracing of loyalty enforcement as an end unto itself.

Those within the Rebel government who believed that only a total dedication to the war effort could win Southern independence continued to balk at any perceived departure from their nationalist ideal. Mississippi senator Albert Gallatin Brown epitomized this stance in a blustery Christmas Eve 1863 congressional speech, and his core argument is worth quoting in full:

> If I were asked, Mr. President, what the country most needs in this hour of peril, I would say patriotism; an all pervading and universal patriotism; not the babbling, noisy patriotism, that prates of what it is about to do or has done, but the earnest, heartfelt, quiet, but bounding, patriotism that does all things and dares all things, and wholy [sic] oblivious as to self, lives only for the cause. Such patriotism will strengthen our army and improve our currency. Will fill up the ranks, convert paper into gold, put shoes on the feet of our soldiers and shirts on their backs. It will nerve the arms and quiet the hearts of, husbands and fathers in the field, by feeding and clothing their loved ones at home. Then, Mr. President, let us all, high and low, rich and poor, from this day forth cultivate a more earnest and ardent patriotism.

Here, Brown encapsulated the essence of protective nationalism, defined by an "all pervading," "earnest and ardent patriotism" that was "wholy oblivious to self" within citizens who lived "only for the cause." This type of nationalism had no room for dissent, real or perceived. Echoing Brown, in 1862 the *Weekly Panola Star* stated that all those who "either directly or indirectly" expressed Union sentiments were "enemies of the South" who were "daily trying to injure our cause." Many other Mississippians seized upon Brown's and the *Star*'s vision of total dedication to the cause as the only viable path to Confederate victory.[28]

In late 1862, Carroll County native W. Cothran told Governor Pettus that, in light of the Union invasion of the country, "it is the duty of every citizen to contribute all he possesses, of mind, body and muscle, as well as property, to its defense." Yet Cothran was dismayed when he saw citizens, including "strong, able bodied men," leaving the state with their property, and reiterated that "if every man" would stand and fight, the state could "drive out the invaders far hence." That same month, Kemper County citizens complained to Pettus that people were fleeing in order to save their property from Yankee confiscation and demanded that the state legislature pass laws to prevent such behavior. In early 1863, a recruiting officer in Greenwood, Mississippi, told Pettus that the "principal cause" of men shirking military duty was "the lack of patriotism." Sometimes, even the heretofore "loudest mouthed Secessionists" preferred to "recline at home" and wait out the end of the war. A year later, a Mississippi cavalry officer wrote that citizens must "consecrate everything to their country," adding that "until a people . . . determine to make all considerations subservient to the grand end in view, . . . little hope can be entertained for their success." He noted that each Mississippian was "a component part of the people, and that his actions, good, bad, or indifferent, tend to govern the final results."[29] Protective nationalists believed that Confederate victory could only be achieved if Mississippians acted as "component" parts in service to the greater collective cause. Any deviation, such as favoring self-interest at the nation's expense, would stymie this goal.

Few groups raised protective nationalists' ire like alleged speculators and extortionists, whom they believed epitomized the loathsome triumph of selfishness over patriotic duty. The Jackson *Weekly Mississippian*, for example, called out speculators in late 1862. "Mississippians!" the paper proclaimed, "why are so many men left in our cities, who, like vultures, feed on the vitals of the country?" Similarly, the Natchez *Weekly Courier* complained of skyrocketing prices for basics like butter. "What can we do, with such extortion bringing us to ruin, and our households to distress?" A Monroe County resident told Pettus that "all along the railroad you can see men Speculating in everything that will sell," while an ordinance officer informed the governor that "traitorous, cowardly, yankee spirited note-shaving, money grasping" extortionists were hoarding lead and charging prices "which the state cannot afford to pay." The Paulding *Eastern Clarion* accused merchants of reducing the population "to the condition of paupers" by overcharging for necessities. The situation became so dire that the Confederate Commissary Office in Mississippi issued a September 1864 circular ordering state commissioners to arrest people caught speculating in army subsistence. Anyone caught selling off excess produce or otherwise engaging in "business prejudicial to the interests of the Government" was to be reported at once.[30] The message was straightforward: sacrifice everything or risk punishment.

Critics targeted planters in particular for growing commodity crops when the population needed food. The Canton *American Citizen* called planters "the main . . . cause of the high prices now crossing the country, demoralizing the consciences of our citizens and paralyzing the arms and the hearts of our gallant soldiers." In May 1862, Tippah County resident Francis Leak informed Pettus that northern Mississippi planters, who had "heretofore done least for the cause of Independence," were pursuing "so unpatriotic a course" by planting cotton instead of food. As punishment, Leak thought that they should endure "heavy taxes" to fund the war debt and support soldiers' families. The *Weekly Mississippian* sarcastically noted how planters "have often declared their readiness to 'sacrifice the last dollar' for honor and independence," adding that "when they have sacrificed the *first* dollar, we will listen to them." Similarly, a Macon *Beacon* editorial stated that collusion between planters and speculators "almost partakes of the nature of a conspiracy." A Mississippi militiaman believed that greed had overtaken the state, telling Pettus that "the calamities of the war have developed every selfish feeling—men now only do for themselves." A Pontotoc County woman echoed this sentiment, noting that "a spirit of selfishness & greed pervades the whole country."[31] These critics thought that those who allegedly profited at the Confederacy's expense were traitors. Every dollar these traitors earned was one less dollar in the nation's coffers, one less shirt on a soldier's back.

Some Mississippians, however, balked at the notion that making money equaled disloyalty. An editorial in the *American Citizen*, for example, asserted that the laws of supply and demand drove market sales based on scarcity and currency depreciation. "All who trade are speculators;—every one who has any article to sell, will take the biggest market price." The *Citizen* asserted that individuals had a right to consider their own personal interests and claimed that the government made matters worse by trying to regulate trade rather than protect it as a basic right. Adams County planter Charles Whitmore agreed, claiming that it was the nation's duty to protect citizens' personal interests, not the reverse. The English-born Whitmore earned his US citizenship in 1832, but as the war drained his slave property, he pined for his birth citizenship because the American government was "not actively protecting" his interest. Whitmore felt that any nation, Union or Confederate, that failed to secure personal property did not deserve his allegiance.[32]

At the heart of the controversy over speculation, extortion, and property rights was a basic question with no easy answer, which presupposed conflict between macro and micro loyalties: how much should Mississippians do for themselves and how much should they do for their country? This controversy was one facet of a much broader debate within the Confederacy over the meaning of nationalism itself and how far the state could go—*should* go—to try to make protective nationalism a reality. In addition to the role it played in the argument over free markets in wartime, this issue also emerged when Mississippians protested the military's authority to impress personal property in the name of the cause. Some contended that such a justification directly conflicted with *their* concept of nationalism, based as it was on a state that respected individual freedom by defending property rights.

In late 1862, Arnoldus Brumby of Holmes County complained to his sister about Confederate authorities violating individual rights by impressing leather makers into government service. Calling this policy a "high handed usurpation of power," he lamented that citizens were "being denied the privilege of controlling their own private property" and warned that *"such military necessities* as they are egregiously called will crush the spirit upon which the foundation of all republics are built—namely *goodwill.*" Likewise, Oxford resident William Delay claimed to speak for many "prominent citizens" when he complained to Governor Charles Clark, who succeeded John Pettus in November 1863, that Confederate troops were confiscating citizens' wagons and salt. Citizens had petitioned to recover the property but were "overruled and disregarded by the military authority." State agent I. W. Watson also conceded to Clark that impressment was to some extent "necessary," but wondered "by what authority is confiscation of . . . property added to the penalty of the statute, and enforced against citizens by a military ex-parte tribunal?" He believed that this policy was "demoralizing" the citizenry. Brumby and Watson were not alone in their critiques of excessive state power as a means of ensuring Confederate victory. The excuse of military necessity, and its attendant vision of protective nationalism as a justification to impress private property, was a contentious issue in the Confederacy throughout the war.[33]

In July 1862, for example, Joshua and Thomas Green, bankers who owned the Pearl River Mills in Jackson, protested military necessity in a memorial to Jefferson Davis. Since the start of the war, the Confederate quartermaster had required the Greens to manufacture clothing for the government, and in the process they neglected their private customers in order to sell to the state at fixed rates below the market price. The Greens objected, however, when the Confederate provost marshal, under orders from General Earl Van Dorn, took possession of the mill and demanded that the Greens work for the state "on penalty of being regarded as 'disloyal to the government.'" The Greens considered Van Dorn's invocation of martial law to justify the seizure unconstitutional and demanded recompense for all losses incurred. They touted their patriotism, reminding Davis that they had "always been willing to supply the government with goods," but argued that their opposition to martial law stemmed from a desire to conform to "a free government,

founded on written constitutions & written laws." The Greens invoked constitutionalism to defend a nationalist vision based on respect for private
property and limits on military authority. This vision stood in contrast to
the kind of protective nationalism that authorized the army to flout citizens'
rights to meet the needs of the state.[34]

Confederate provost marshals, authorized by the March 1861 Articles of
War, played a key role in policing loyalty on behalf of protective nationalists
within the Rebel government. As Kenneth Radley writes, for Confederate
provost marshals, "the suppression of disloyalty and subversion . . . entailed
the imposition of ever wider and more stringent controls over many civilian
activities."[35] Yalobusha County lawyer Samuel Hawkins found this out the
hard way. As with the Greens, Hawkins's troubles sprang from the increasingly rigorous methods of loyalty enforcement—over soldier and civilian
alike—adopted by Confederate provost guards. During the summer of 1862,
Provost Marshal R. L. Forrester arrested Hawkins and fined him fifty dollars
after Hawkins refused to accept Confederate notes as payment for hired-out
slaves. Forrester warned Brigadier General John Villepigue that Hawkins and
other "selfish and unpatriotic men" were devaluing Confederate currency, and
recommended a "stern check upon the further progress of the evil." Villepigue
agreed, telling Secretary of War George Randolph that Van Dorn's general
order to sustain government credit justified Hawkins's arrest. Enforcing the
order had to be done "at some personal and pecuniary inconvenience to a
few citizens," but Villepigue deemed these citizens "at least indifferent to
the success of the Confederacy's fighting men, if not positively disloyal to
their Government." In his own defense, Hawkins claimed that his arrest was
unconstitutional on the grounds that true patriotism respected individual
rights. "I love my country," he wrote, but he wondered "what barriers exist
against the worst of tyranny, if Martial Law . . . without any rules or limitations, [is] to be carried into effect in Mississippi." Former state judge E. S.
Fisher seconded Hawkins, arguing that army regulations did not apply to civilians and that the constitution should protect them against "acts of tyranny."
War Department clerk Robert G. H. Kean conceded that "the *law* is with
Hawkins" and that protecting government credit was beyond the provost
marshal's duty, leaving "no other grounds to question Hawkins' loyalty."[36]
As Hawkins's case demonstrated, protective nationalism turned mundane
acts like refusing money into full-on sedition against the state and stirred
controversy between different branches of the Confederate government.

Protective nationalists like Van Dorn, Forrester, and Villepigue believed
that to protect the Confederacy meant to protect its currency to secure

economic self-sufficiency. Their position was not without support. An 1863 *Weekly Mississippian* editorial stated that anyone with a "heart truly in the Confederate cause . . . will be conscious of . . . the duty to uphold the credit of the currency which is the life-blood of that cause." A letter to the editor of the Canton *American Citizen* stated that those refusing Confederate money were bringing "discredit on our Government." "How small must be the spark of patriotism in that man's breast who would not do all in his power to save and help his country in this her hour of greatest peril?" the writer asked.[37] Hawkins, Fisher, and others did not agree with such all-or-nothing assessments. They rejected a nationalism that advocated the sacrifice of personal interests to the whim of the state and saw a nation concerned only with its own perpetuation as both unworkable and undesirable. For its part, the Confederate government demonstrated how, even with an expanded arsenal of powers that enabled a provost marshal to identify treason in the vagaries of a personal loan, it could not circumvent the influence of other allegiances in citizens like Samuel Hawkins.

Pitting personal interests against the needs of the state also pitted Confederate officials against planters in a dispute over the state's right to appropriate slaves for the war effort.[38] Historians have pounced on this dispute as evidence of the fleeting nature of planter loyalty—that they "were more concerned with property than nation."[39] This interpretation assumes that the totality of protective nationalism could be—*should* be—embraced by citizens and that the influence of other attachments necessarily indicated disloyalty. Further, the issue of slave impressments put the newly empowered state in the ironic position of seizing slave property, the protection of which being the Confederacy's raison d'être, to help perpetuate its own existence.

Mississippi planters, however, claimed that concern for property did not indicate a lack of patriotism. As was the case in other states, many willingly leased slaves to work on fortifications. They opposed further impressments when they deemed their contributions sufficient or when the needs of the harvest demanded slave labor. Mississippi offered slave owners thirty dollars per month compensation plus rations and clothing for each leased hand. Planters sending more than thirty slaves could provide their own overseer, with the state paying his salary. Congress passed a general slave impressment act in March 1863, empowering the military to impress in accordance with state laws. In 1864, a second act authorized the collection of twenty thousand more slaves. Many planters donated hands but protested when the state failed to uphold its promise to maintain slaves' health and when they perceived the act as having not impressed equally among slaveholders.[40]

In early 1863, several Holmes County planters voluntarily sent slaves to work on the Vicksburg fortifications but were dismayed to learn that the slaves were placed under military overseers who "treated them badly & roughly using cuggels [sic] or sticks in chastisement." When several slaves fled, the planters demanded compensation and exemption from further impressment. "We think we have patriotism enough to send all our hands," they wrote, but contended that "this extra & continued" impressment had "retarded" their planting. The same issues concerned Gallatin resident Benjamin King, who told Pettus that slaves taken for fortification work were poorly sheltered, neglected when sick, and not permitted to go home. "The people," he wrote, were willing to lend slaves to the cause provided they were well treated and "worked for the public good," but he noted that planters would not have their property neglected.[41] While slave owners voluntarily contributed hands to the war effort, they demanded that the state uphold its end of the bargain by maintaining their property's value.

Issues regarding equal contribution also irked planters who felt that the number of slaves sent to the fortifications should be in proportion to the number owned. In March 1863, for example, Colonel John Humphreys endeavored "to take from those owning the largest number of able bodied men ... discriminating in favor of those who had sent freely and liberally." Planters protested deviations from this policy. State judge Robert Hudson was among Mississippi's most blustery Confederates, but he chafed at further impressments of his slaves after he had voluntarily sent some to Vicksburg: "I have ever responded to all calls for such help and stood ready to do so still ... but they choose to impress ... and I know of no authority they had for doing so." Copiah County planter F. Dillard owned twenty-eight slaves and sent several to work at Vicksburg, but complained of "great injustice" by singling out three fellow planters who each owned between forty and fifty slaves but only sent one or two to the fortifications. "[We] don't complain at sending our Negroes to Vicksburg but we do complain at injustice," he wrote. Dillard's reasoning was straightforward, if arbitrary: those who owned more slaves should contribute more slaves. Yet, his arbitrariness reflected that of the government, which did not give specific numbers regarding slave impressment beyond prohibiting it on premises with fewer than four slaves aged eighteen or older and setting a 5 percent quota per county.[42]

Planters themselves often decided when they had given enough hands. Adams County resident Thomas McCowen, for example, wrote to Pettus that he had already "sent some men to Port Hudson" and requested that the sheriff exempt his force from impressment. That McCowen had already sent "some men" was sufficient for him. Rather than prioritize self over country, planters invoked micro and macro loyalties in an attempt to serve both. They cited their willingness to send slaves to the army as evidence of their patriotism, but complained when slaves were mistreated or when the state became overzealous in its impressment. Planters argued that self-interest necessitated limiting property confiscation in the name of the cause. In doing so, they demonstrated how self and national interest need not conflict, at least to a point. The fact that micro loyalties influenced their behavior did not necessarily evidence a weakened devotion to a total nationalist model that many Mississippians found undesirable anyway. Although the state had the power to impress slaves, it could not enforce total compliance among planters.[43]

While businesspeople and planters objected to accusations of treason simply because they would not subordinate profits to cause, there were other Mississippians for whom Confederates' accusation of treason was justified. These were the state's minority number of unionists, those who openly expressed Union sentiments or actively resisted Confederate authority and worked to sabotage the Southern war effort. Their existence only fueled many Confederate partisans' zeal to identify traitors at every turn.[44]

One such individual was Presbyterian minister James Lyon, whose anti-slavery views were a rarity among even Mississippi unionists. In his journal, Lyon considered secession "a great political heresy," maintaining that war would bring "ruin upon the land." He also criticized Confederate protective nationalists who "commenced the thousand efforts & appeals and devices . . . to . . . create the war spirit and keep it up." Lyon thought that protective nationalism stifled individual rights in the name of exultation of the state and in the process installed an "absolute despotism." He eventually ran afoul of the state in 1863 when a friend asked him to endorse a circulating letter naming him as the head of a pro-Union "Reconstruction party." Citing ministerial nonpartisanship, Lyon declined to sign, but his son, Theodric, a Confederate soldier who nonetheless shared his father's politics, answered the letter, which was read publicly and printed in a local newspaper. The provost marshal deemed the letter a "disloyal treasonable document" and arrested the two Lyons. Theodric was court-martialed, relieved of his command, and banished to Virginia. The authorities released James Lyon, but Confederate partisans continued to hound him.[45]

Lyon's case was similar to that of other unionists whom Confederates targeted for treason. In April 1864, the Macon *Beacon* reported that Confederate soldiers arrested Ben Hawkins, who had gone to Illinois in 1861 to be honored as "a Union man from Mississippi." Confederates confiscated a "United States flag" from his house, and, when William T. Sherman's troops marched through Mississippi in 1863, Hawkins allegedly "spoke to Union meetings" and told citizens to "fight the rebel soldiers like the devil." His four sons also deserted from the Sixth, Sixteenth, and Thirty-Seventh Mississippi Infantries. In the fall of 1863, the *Beacon* reported on a Reconstruction meeting in Canton that nominated planter Moses Jordon to run for the governorship on a Union platform. Jefferson Davis received reports describing other Mississippi "traitors" who plotted reconstruction. They included Vicksburg attorney James Shirley, who communicated with federal officers during the Vicksburg siege and whose son, Quincy, even joined the Union army. The report also named Sunflower County physician and state senator W. Q. Poindexter and former state congressman and state Supreme Court judge William L. Sharkey, a longtime Whig who opposed secession and became Mississippi's first Reconstruction governor in June 1865. The presence of a small number of unionists in the state confirmed Confederates' suspicion that traitors in their midst had to be rooted out and that the state should use all of its power to do so before these enemies subverted the cause from within.[46]

Confederates' fears about internal enemies were not entirely unfounded. Some Mississippians did collude with the Union army, although Confederates exaggerated their strength and numbers. Perhaps the state's most well-known unionist spy was Chickasaw County planter Levi Naron, known as Chickasaw. When the Federals reached Mississippi, he spied for them in the northern part of the state, even establishing a clandestine newspaper service through which other unionists supplied information to the Federals. Two other Mississippi federal spies were John F. Riley and J. J. Williams. Being "well acquainted with the country" in northern Mississippi, they rooted out Confederate guerrillas and smugglers. On one mission, they arrested a citizen who harbored guerrillas. In another instance, they led Union troops to a Confederate smuggling party's stash of stolen goods outside of Holly Springs, which included "silk, calicos, hats, socks, boots, shoes, thread, sardines & varieties hid in a pit beneath the floor." Riley and Williams wore Confederate uniforms to enable them to move freely through hostile territory. While some acted as federal spies, an additional five hundred to nine hundred white Mississippians fought in the Union army as members of the First Battalion, Mississippi Mounted Rifles, and the First Alabama Cavalry Regiment, known as the Alabama Tories.[47]

In addition to those who colluded with Union forces, a number of Mississippians fled as refugees to federal lines, and there were likely Union sympathizers among them. In September 1863, for example, the Federals arrested fourteen citizens outside Corinth who eventually took the oath and went north. Twenty-three Mississippi refugees came to Union lines at Jackson, Tennessee, in the spring of 1863, while others entered the lines at Ship Island, Natchez, Vicksburg, Pass Christian, New Orleans, and points along the Mississippi River during 1863–1864. Amallus Douthet of Tishomingo County, Mississippi, arrived at Union lines without her husband, William Douthet, who had enlisted in Company C of the Alabama Tories in 1863. Historians, however, should exercise caution when too closely associating Southern refugees with unionism. In one instance, federal authorities reported that a group of Pascagoula and Biloxi refugees were living in the "most desperate condition imaginable" and "being conscripted without regard to age or nationality." Some deserters among them were "being hunted with hounds and shot down or torn to pieces." Self-preservation likely influenced their flight to Ship Island, whatever their patriotic inclinations. Poor whites in particular came to Union lines to procure food and supplies or to find work, suggesting that personal motivations often guided their actions.[48]

The fact that Mississippians might act on multiple allegiances, however, did not stop Confederate partisans from judging all behavior as potentially treasonous. Operating on a nationalist model that consigned individuals to one side or the other, Confederates dealt with allegedly suspicious people in the same way they dealt with the state's minority of unionists. They therefore pushed charges of "unionism" on people whose national sympathies were often unclear—and possibly even irrelevant to—the situations at hand. Confederates justified the state's increased policing of the citizenry by invoking the threat supposedly posed by seditious Mississippi unionists.

In November 1863, Confederates arrested Tishomingo County Baptist preacher W. Cranford Whooten on charges that he was a "Union man" and a "fanatic" who spied for the Federals and encouraged Confederate desertion. Whooten confessed to taking the Union oath out of "destitute circumstances" but hoped that Confederate authorities would not force him to "violate said oath by taking it again to your Confederacy." He requested release from Richmond's Castle Thunder Prison, stating that he had lost property to both armies even though he had sheltered Confederate soldiers. Several Tishomingo neighbors vouched for his loyalty, claiming that he had a family to support and posed no danger to the Confederacy. That same month, Confederates charged Pontotoc County farmer Eli Botts with being a "Tory." Botts's arrest papers stated that he "was a Union man as long as it existed, but is now a southern man." He claimed that he was "forced to go" with the

Yankee enemy but would not swear the Confederate oath because he had already sworn the Union oath. While Botts and Whooten were imprisoned, William Morris fared better when arrested for allegedly aiding deserters. Morris claimed ignorance regarding his arrest, and Confederate officials concluded that he was "not a Union man," discharging him after he swore the Confederate oath. Morris may have won release after claiming, truthfully, that he had a son in the Forty-Fourth Mississippi Regiment, which perhaps convinced Confederates that he showed sufficient patriotism.[49]

Confederates labeled Whooten and Botts unionists despite the men's contradictory testimonies. Whooten claimed to have sworn the Union oath out of destitution and to have aided Confederate soldiers, but would not take the Confederate oath. Botts's testimony described a Union man turned pro-Southern, a man forced to associate with the Federals but unwilling to swear loyalty to the Confederacy. Finally, Morris, arrested under circumstances similar to those of Whooten and Botts, was nonetheless deemed loyal and released. Historians trying to ascertain these men's loyalty based on their often conflicting statements risk arbitrarily judging them loyal or disloyal according to the idea that people had to be one or the other, just as Confederates did. These men's true national sympathies cannot be known, but the ideology of protective nationalism demanded the identification of friend and foe, justifying the state's policing of citizens' loyalty even when said loyalty proved difficult to nail down. Citizens' loyalty layers only further demonstrated the shortcomings of this dualistic conception of national allegiance.

Such was the case with Jackson businessman Solomon Tift, whom Confederates arrested in 1863 after witnesses testified that he had called secession a "damned farce," waved a US flag, and colluded with federal troops. Based on these statements, Confederate general W. H. Jackson concluded that Tift was a "secret agent" for the North. Tift's personal letters purportedly revealed his unionism but actually told a more nuanced story. He wanted to "see the Federals enter this place" and complained that a "Secesh" had taken his property. Yet, he noted how both armies had ruined him financially and that General Sherman deemed him "worse than a secesh," leading Tift to conclude that he had "no friends on either side." Tift promised to flee north if released, but he feared that Confederates would "disturb" his slaves, and, after telling a friend to rent out his house, said that he would soon return to Jackson. Paradoxically, Tift was also "determined" to "stand strictly to the promise made" and "not forfeit [his] word" to flee north. Regarding these contradictory claims, the Confederate provost marshal stated that "the two statements are so inconsistent, as to warrant the conclusion that he intends to evade his promise," and recommended that Tift be imprisoned "as a traitorous Mississippian."[50]

Confederates bent on rooting out traitors considered people like Tift guilty until proven innocent. Tift indicated some Union sympathies, as his name appears on a list of unionists kept by the Federals in Vicksburg, but whereas Confederates viewed his meeting with Sherman as evidence of treason, he seemed more concerned with saving his personal property. Nonetheless, Confederate nationalists sought to put individuals with complicated motives into simplistic partisan boxes. People like Tift, who acted on multiple loyalties and whose national allegiances were "inconsistent" at best, revealed the state's inability, despite its empowered military apparatuses, to accomplish this goal. But the state never stopped trying.[51]

During the Civil War, especially in territories with occupying forces, a refusal to demonstrate loyalty could lead to presumptions of disloyalty.[52] Relying on this dualistic conception of allegiance, Confederate forces inevitably punished likely innocent people. This was the case when Confederates in Tishomingo County charged Martha Emmaline Maness with spying for the Union and imprisoned her without trial in Castle Thunder, Richmond—even though a friend contended that she had been arrested while merely visiting family. Brigadier General Daniel Ruggles claimed to have "no doubt" that she was a spy but admitted to lacking "direct evidence" for this assertion. By contrast, Brigadier General W. M. Pardner admitted that there were "no definite charges" against her and "no prospect of a prosecution." In prison, Maness complained of "awful conditions" but did not mention her charges. The Confederates released her in July 1864. That same summer, Confederates arrested Kemper County native July Clark for trying to "pass through" the Mobile lines with "dangerous documents upon her person," but soon paroled her as well. These cases demonstrate how Confederates who only appeared to be in the wrong place at the wrong time were accused as treasonous people. They were the collateral damage of a suspicion-ridden atmosphere in which protective nationalists demanded that everyone take sides. The occasional mistake, however, was never enough to make authorities cease their attempt to enforce Confederate allegiance.[53]

Even when suspected spies' actions seems to be guided by nationalism *and* self-interest, Confederates described them as switching sides as opposed to acting on coexisting loyalties. When a scout in Charles Allen's company questioned a traveling black man wearing a federal uniform about his status and destination, the man claimed to have left Union lines to work for a Dr.

Jones of Holmes County. When Jones refused to surrender the man, a gun-
fight erupted, killing the scout. "Jones was a Yankee spy . . . as was his wife,"
Allen wrote, adding that the couple had "made largest fortune" by trading
cotton in Vicksburg. Despite this behavior, Allen revealed that Mrs. Jones
had sent the scout, stating that "she is a good secesh here and a good Yankee
over there." What Allen described as switching sides was more likely the
influence of micro and macro loyalties. If Dr. Jones was indeed a "Yankee
spy," then he may have given information to federal troops while also trading cotton for a profit. What Allen identified as Mrs. Jones's dual Union/
Confederate allegiances was more likely a combination of self-interest, via
her trading, and Confederate loyalty, which led her to send the scout. The
Joneses appeared to act on different—but concurrent—loyalties to self and
country. Allen, however, viewed this behavior through the binary lenses of
"secesh" and "Yankee."[54]

Just as Mississippi's Confederate forces tried to ascertain allegiances in accordance to this dualistic framework, so too did Union authorities. Like their
Confederate counterparts, the Union military tried to use its expanded power
and reach to enforce Mississippians' loyalty to their side. This position was,
in large part, a response to the enormous task of trying to police the widely
dispersed population in a vast amount of Confederate territory. William
Blair observes that "virtually any kind of goods or information that could
provide the South with human, material, and intellectual resources became a
threat to a government fighting to hold itself together."[55] Union forces relied
on flawed mechanisms like the oath to enforce allegiance, but individuals'
multiple loyalties rendered such attempts futile. Although the federal military
eventually succeeded in subduing Confederate forces, controlling Mississippians' hearts and minds was beyond its otherwise substantial powers.

In December 1863, Captain Franklin Fisk of the Fourth Illinois Cavalry
ran into planter W. B. Partee and two associates; all were carrying Union
passes permitting them to carry out goods from Vicksburg. The men denied
knowing the whereabouts of Confederate scouts, and the Union officers
relied on their passes as "assurance of their good character." However, the
cavalrymen later captured two Rebel scouts who admitted that Partee had
been sheltering Confederates, leading Fisk to conclude that Partee and his
acquaintances had "received permits and protection papers through false
statements." In November 1864, Union authorities at Vicksburg expelled
Elizabeth Eggleston from the city on charges of being "a general busybody
with rebel interests." Her daughter, Mahala Roach, insisted that Eggleston
"gave no 'aid or comfort' to the rebels." This claim notwithstanding, the

women ran a hospital and smuggled supplies to Confederate soldiers during the Vicksburg siege. Eggleston's soldier nephew, O. S. Holland, thanked his aunt for her service but warned her to keep her "noble patriotism and sympathy for soldiers" in check.[56] Partee and his cohorts claimed Union loyalty as a means of aiding Confederate soldiers, taking advantage of federal rules that allowed residents of the surrounding areas to sell excess produce in Vicksburg. Eggleston likewise declared Union loyalty to aid Confederate troops. In these cases, Union authorities found that oath swearing was a poor indication of peoples' allegiance.

Union authorities in Mississippi's garrisoned districts faced the difficult task of identifying clandestine Confederates from among all manner of individuals, including unionists, criminals, ne'er-do-wells, and businesspeople. A Union list of civilian prisoners in Natchez, for example, detailed a range of charges, including "selling contraband goods . . . Entering lines . . . disloyalty . . . Selling whiskey," while a similar sheet from Vicksburg included charges of "swindling soldiers . . . Forgery . . . Theft . . . Rebel Spy." Lodged between petty crimes were charges of "disloyalty," demonstrating how protective nationalism facilitated a surveillance state. Union forces had to be alert in a wartime environment where any behavior could potentially mask treasonous intent. They extended this alertness to gauge the intentions of Mississippians who declared Union loyalty as a prerequisite to doing business in occupied areas.[57]

Plenty of Mississippians had ulterior motives for declaring loyalty, whether they were sympathetic to the Union or not. In August 1864, for example, Tippah County mechanic W. E. Rogers told federal officials in Memphis that he had been forced into the Confederate army to avoid losing his "political status & influential friends." After being mustered out of service, he insisted that he had come to Memphis "willing to cast my lot with the Union until the last" and that he would be "pleased to do business in Memphis" if permitted to do so. In another instance, a prominent Natchez resident lobbied treasury agent R. S. Hart to approve an application by Mina Concke to keep her trade store open. Concke, he pleaded, was a struggling widow with a son working for the Union army in New Orleans, and she "has been always a loyal Union familie [sic]." For federal authorities, however, weeding out the truly loyal was difficult when individuals had personal interests at stake in swearing Union allegiance.[58]

This was especially true in Vicksburg. A major commercial hub strategically located on high bluffs overlooking a Mississippi River bend, the city was occupied by the Union army from July 1863 to the war's end. By the 1850s, the city had attracted Americans from all over the country as well as European immigrants, who gave the city economic diversity and a cosmopolitan air. Conservative Whigs had long maintained a majority in city politics, and the Whig influence continued during the secession crisis of 1860–1861. The city's merchants feared that secession and war would disrupt business transactions, and pro-Union voters beat out secessionists 561 to 173. After Mississippi seceded, however, Vicksburg cautiously went with the Confederate tide. But when the city fell to Grant, residents had to reckon with an occupying force that demanded allegiance in exchange for permission to go about daily business.[59]

The city's merchant classes knew that war threatened their livelihoods. Watchmaker Edwin Sabin recalled "the utter ruination brought upon us Southern businessmen," as the war left him with just $1,220 out of a $56,000 fortune. Sabin received Grant's permission to open another shop to try to recuperate his finances. Other Vicksburg residents did the same. Federal forces outlawed commercial activity by avowed Confederates, so individuals wishing to do business had to swear the oath and promise not to aid known Rebels. Use of the military courts also incentivized peoples like Cornelius Ryan, Thomas Purcell, Alexander Jeffrey, and other Vicksburg residents who identified as "loyal citizen[s] of the United States" in order to resolve common property and land disputes.[60]

With these incentives in mind, 230 Vicksburg residents added their names to a list of "Union men in and around Vicksburg believed to be undoubted!" kept by federal forces. The occupations of the 152 listed men (see appendix A for the list) who appear in the census include professionals, proprietors, artisans, and unskilled laborers, consistent with the general makeup of nineteenth-century American cities.[61] Profession of Union loyalty, as represented on the list, was not limited to a specific occupational group. All but nine were Vicksburg residents. The rest lived in other parts of Mississippi, while one merchant came from Texas. Finally, the men represented the city's diverse backgrounds: thirty-nine were born in cotton and Southern border states, thirty-five were born in Northern states, and seventy-eight were born in Europe or Canada, or their place of birth is unknown.[62] In 1863 and 1864, at least twenty-four of these men paid a fee and applied to federal treasury agents for permission to establish stores in Vicksburg. Their applications were among hundreds that Mississippians submitted to Union authorities from 1863 onward, when prewar trade patterns on the Mississippi River, no longer hindered by Confederate blockades, picked up again. In addition to giving out trade store permits, Union authorities issued permits to people wishing to open supply stores and ship products from within Union lines to Northern markets. The Federals also kept track of vessels moving in and out of river ports.[63]

Some Union authorities, demanding that friend and foe be identified, remained suspicious of professed unionists. A Union officer noted on the list of Vicksburg loyalists that some were "pretty good Union Men," others were "somewhat compromised," and still others would "not take the oath up to the present time." This officer's doubts regarding some of the men's loyalty indicated the cautious approach Union authorities took toward declarations of allegiance made in conjunction with business interests. In a petition to treasury agent William Mellen, one of the listed men, recently naturalized merchant Solomon Rothchild, boasted that he risked "life and liberty" by refusing to fight against the United States, to which "he had but recently before sworn allegiance." When the Federals captured Vicksburg, Rothchild "cheerfully" took the Union oath and wanted to continue his family's proprietorship. Another listed man, clergyman Alston Mygatt, applied to open a trade store and won permission to lease an abandoned Warren County plantation. He and Rothchild may well have been honest unionists, but the fact that they declared loyalty in the pursuit of business interests necessarily made them targets of suspicion to Union forces.[64]

The case of Vicksburg jeweler Max Kuner demonstrated why this suspicion was often warranted. Kuner applied for a trade store permit in 1863, swore the oath, served as a surety on a plantation lease, and was among the listed Vicksburg loyalists. Nonetheless, his former apprentice, Valentine Vogh, claimed that in 1861 Kuner raised a Rebel company, flew a Confederate flag, and housed Rebel soldiers. Another person on the list, self-described "truly loyal Union man" Charles Francis, called Kuner "one of the leading rebels of Vicksburg." Kuner denied most of the charges but admitted to housing Rebel soldiers out of sympathy for their hunger. He dismissed Vogh as a disgruntled former employee and contended that a dispute with former business partner turned Confederate captain D. N. Moody led Moody to raise the Rebel flag over Kuner's store, making the incident "[a] declaration of the Dissolution of Partnership" as opposed to an indication of Kuner's Confederate sympathies. In light of these allegations, the treasury agent threatened to close Kuner's supply store. Kuner's accusers knew that Union authorities were scouting for traitors, so maybe he was truthful in claiming that their accusations stemmed from personal grievances. Owning $50,000 in real estate and a home worth $5,000, he had much to lose from not cooperating with the Federals. Yet additional motives by Kuner and his accusers mattered little to Union officials charged with enforcing loyalty. When presented with claims that Kuner's case involved more than just Union or Confederate stances, they were only concerned with where his national loyalties lay.[65]

Kuner's case demonstrates how Mississippians could use charges of disloyalty to gain the upper hand in personal disputes that might be only tangentially related to nationalism. Nevertheless, nationalist discourse was the only way to curry favor with Union authorities. In June 1864, Murray Carter and M. Levy appeared before federal authorities in Vicksburg to dispute the ownership of six bales of cotton. Both accused the other of disloyalty, and both produced witnesses who testified to each man's Union loyalty. Carter claimed that Levy had stolen the cotton and dismissed Levy's oath swearing, noting that "the Oath of Allegiance is not always a test of loyalty." In his own defense, Levy assured the probate court that he was "a loyal citizen" with "well known Union Sentiments," and called Carter a "cotton speculator." The court ultimately ruled in Carter's favor, noting that Levy's witness, a Mr. E. Unger, resided "outside of our lines" and that "*his* loyalty *aught* not be above suspicion." Even if Unger took the oath, the court reasoned, such an action would "complicate him with his Confederate friends & allies."[66] The national sympathies of both men are unclear and were, from their angle, beside the point: they argued over property, using patriotic language in the service of self-interest. To the federal court, however, nationalism trumped lawful issues pertaining to property theft. Its singular focus on policing allegiance led it to judge Levy guilty not because it believed him guilty of theft but because it considered him disloyal, which in turn rendered all of his behavior suspicious.

The nation-state's need to compel total allegiance from its citizens survived the war and became the central factor in the US government's decisions to reject Reconstruction-era property claims by residents of former Confederate Mississippi. During the war, planter John Vick appeared on the Vicksburg unionist list and swore the amnesty oath. In 1872, he filed with the Southern Claims Commission to get back $4,550 in confiscated property. When receipts revealed that he had sold supplies to the Confederate army, however, he admitted to doing so "for the sole and only purpose" of supporting his family. Yet, Vick also admitted to being unable to "consciously declare" that he "constantly" backed the Union. Vick believed that the Emancipation Proclamation betrayed Southern unionists who had been promised that "rights of property should not be disturbed." His vision of an effective nation was predicated on the protection of these rights. As a result, Vick "ceased to sympathize with the Union cause," since doing so cost him $200,000 worth of "slave property." The commission rejected Vick's claim, unconvinced of his loyalty.[67] Vick's Union loyalty hinged on whether the US government would protect his slave property. The Union government, however, believed that loyalty during the war must come without strings attached. In this regard, the commission found Vick lacking.

The federal government denied claims by other listed Vicksburg unionists on similar grounds. Planter James Cathell submitted a claim for $6,550, but the commission denied it when witnesses testified that Cathell publicly favored the South and receipts showed that he had sold fodder to Confederates in 1862. Stating that he had "always been a truly loyal man," farmer Aquilla Bowie filed an 1871 claim for $489, which the commission barred without explanation even though Bowie's name had appeared on the list of wartime unionists.[68] The US government doubted Vick's, Cathell's, and Bowie's loyalty because each case involved no small measure of economic self-interest. The United States emerged from the war with the bureaucratic capacity to gauge Mississippians' allegiance via property claims. The government was convinced that it could do so effectively, when, in fact, it was ill prepared to deal with the reality of multiple human loyalties. The complex nature of these claimants' allegiances notwithstanding, when personal interests appeared to contradict patriotism, Union partisans cut them little slack.

This was also the case regarding claimants from Natchez. During the war, druggist George Fox swore the Union oath and claimed that he would face "considerable loss & inconvenience" if not permitted to keep his store open. In 1871, however, Fox found his loyalty questioned when he filed a claim for $900. He stated that he had always been a unionist and that had "circumstances" been more favorable, he would have aided the United States "by all means in my power." Two witnesses described Fox as a "Union man," and one of them, William Henderson, Fox's former slave who joined the Union army in 1863, said that Fox did not directly aid the Union but did give Henderson free supplies from his store. The commission rejected Fox's claim, noting that Fox's behavior "rather proves ... neutrality than loyalty." A similar case involved a Natchez merchant, Matthias D. Marks, who applied for trade store permits in April and June 1864. In 1872, he filed a claim for $370, arguing that he was a Mexican-American War veteran who would never raise a hand against the United States. A friend testified that Marks "would have gone into the Union Army" if forced, although he suggested that Marks remained functionally neutral. Unconvinced, the commission rejected Marks's claim.[69] To a Northern government that demanded an all-or-nothing show of allegiance from Mississippians, neutrality was tantamount to disloyalty. To *be* loyal, one had to *act* loyal. Imbued with the power to judge (however arbitrarily) Mississippians' devotion to the Union cause, the federal government demanded a total show of patriotic devotion. Those claimants who fell short of the protective nationalist ideal were out of luck.

This unbending conception of national allegiance, however, proved problematic when individuals acted both loyal and disloyal at different times. Such was the case with Natchez merchant Casey Mallory, a self-proclaimed "bone fide Union man" who swore the oath in January 1864, applied for a trade store permit, and, in 1872, claimed $7,950 worth of confiscated bricks. Witness Abraham Scofield considered Mallory "disloyal" but admitted that others did not. Malory's former slave said that his master started as a "Union man" but "changed soon after the war commenced." Another witness similarly claimed that Mallory was a former "Union man" who turned Confederate when "things did not blow right" financially. Yet another witness said that Mallory voiced both Union and Confederate sympathies, while another considered him "rather neutral." On his own behalf, Mallory touted his Massachusetts birth, noted his thrice swearing the Union oath, claimed that he had threatened to disown his Confederate soldier son, and added that he boarded and supplied Union soldiers. Nonetheless, he admitted that, while he was "hot" for Union victory when the war started, he leaned Confederate "towards the last" after federal troops took his bricks. The commission rejected Mallory's claim, citing his admission of Rebel sympathy and his inflating the number of stolen bricks as evidence of his unreliability.[70]

As with other Mississippi claimants, interested partisans employed nationalist discourse to interpret Mallory's concerns over property as evidence of his "support" for one side or the other. Mallory himself used this nationalist language even when discussing a separate issue by equivocating anger over federal confiscation of his property with a desire for Confederate victory. Seeking to root out traitors, the federal government took "admissions" of Confederate sympathy as reason to reject Mallory's claim, even though Mallory appeared to be more concerned with protecting his property than he was with choosing sides. Although the US government had the capacity to police Southerners' loyalty even after the war, Mississippians' loyalty layers rendered it incapable of compelling total allegiance.

When the federal army invaded Mississippi in 1862, Confederate and Union partisans operated according to a protective nationalist ideal that made devotion to one side or the other necessary to achieving victory. In the process, they turned everyday actions into suspicious acts, resulting in a heightened climate of surveillance in which both sides attempted to categorize Mississippians as either patriots or traitors. Turning the protective nationalist ideal into an on-the-ground reality, however, proved impossible. The Union army tried to elicit proof of loyalty via the oath of allegiance. Mississippians, however, swore the oath under constrained circumstances as a prerequisite for getting protection for property, avoiding Confederate conscription, doing business under federal occupation, and traveling beyond Union lines. Rather than being de facto Confederates who pragmatically swore what they considered a nonbinding oath in exchange for security, housing, and protection, Mississippians acted on separate micro loyalties to self and family. In some instances, oath takers privately professed Confederate loyalty, but in other instances their national allegiances were unclear because they swore the Union oath as a means to ends that were distinct from nationalism.

Meanwhile, Confederate partisans interpreted any perceived capitulation to the Union side as evidence of clear-cut treason. Ardent Confederates charged alleged speculators and extortionists with inhibiting Southern independence, and they arrested individuals for colluding with the Union on the shakiest of grounds. Many Mississippians, however, continued to act on multiple loyalties that were altogether distinct from nationalism. Others envisioned a Confederate state defined by respect for individual rights, an ideal that conflicted with that of protective nationalists, who made Southern independence into an uncompromising end unto itself. The war's ever-shifting exigencies, as well as Mississippians' loyalty layers, made defining Confederate nationalism a contested and fluid process. This process, in turn, demonstrated how the Civil War created a powerful Southern nation-state armed with the bureaucratic apparatuses with which to enforce loyalty in the populace. In an ironic turn, however, the state was not strong enough to succeed in this, the primary justification for its expanded powers.

Like its Confederate counterpart, the Union state's infrastructural capacity grew during the Civil War, but it also failed to compel total loyalty to its cause. Federal authorities struggled to enforce Mississippians' allegiance to the Union, especially in occupied cities where multiple loyalties informed peoples' everyday actions. By couching their allegiance in requests to do business behind the lines and to claim lost property after the war, Mississippians demonstrated how self-interest often intersected with patriotism to muddy the waters of loyalty enforcement. With this fact in mind, federal authorities viewed all declarations of allegiance with inherent suspicion. The demands of protective nationalism were simply too stringent, human loyalty layers too complex.

The exigencies of wartime commerce further challenged both Union and Confederate attempts to gauge peoples' patriotism. An extensive contraband trade between the lines developed as soon as Union forces arrived in Mississippi, and it grew as the war progressed. This trade undermined protective nationalists' dreams of creating a self-sustained Confederate nation whose citizens lived only to serve the cause.

CHAPTER THREE

"TRADYVILLE"

The Contraband Trade and the Problem of Loyalty

IN 1863, AN UNNAMED CONFEDERATE OFFICER CASTIGATED OSTENSIBLY loyal Confederates who traded with Union forces in Natchez, a key commercial port north of the officer's base of operations in southeastern Louisiana. A year earlier, Confederate field commanders had ordered planters to burn their cotton to keep it out of federal hands. "[Y]et strange to say," the officer wrote, "some 6,000 bales were kept not long distance from the city. Was it suppineness [*sic*] on the part of the planter or was it saved in order to present to the enemy and thereby assist in subjugating the southern people?" This trade with Union-occupied Natchez prompted the officer to criticize the "out-and-out immeasurable, uncompromising secessionists ... who in '61 were for 'War to the Knife' and 'Knife to the hilt,'" who now "gave and drank the toast at 'Tradyville'; in the presence of Federal Officers."[1] Confederate and federal officers alike called Natchez "Tradyville," recognizing its role as a center of commerce in "contraband" goods. While better known as a term for fugitive slaves, contraband in this case referred to the goods that Mississippians illegally exchanged across Union lines. The officer commenting on Natchez viewed the trade as a test of citizens' Confederate loyalty, labeling those engaged in it as traitors.

Not all Confederates went this far. Writing from Oxford, Mississippi, Inspector General Jacob Thompson explained to President Jefferson Davis that the government's policy of forbidding trade with the Union was a "cause of exasperation" because it prevented residents of the state's northern region from procuring supplies at Union-held Memphis. "In this state of things," he argued, "you cannot consider it strange or peculiar or disloyal that the distressed people should endeavor to procure ... actual necessaries which could be obtained in no other way than from those who resided near Memphis where their location, of course, facilitates their trade with the enemy."

Unlike the Natchez observer, who regarded contraband trade as treasonous, Thompson thought that trade with the Union benefited the Southern war effort. "To admit the people to buy in way of barter and exchange what is absolutely necessary, will enliven our people and greatly aid our army," he argued; "[m]ore than half of what is brought in, finds its way to the army in one way or another."[2]

Central to these conflicting interpretations of the trade was an important question: could Mississippians be loyal Confederates while trading with the enemy? This bartering across the lines was epidemic. Although the term "Tradyville" referred specifically to Natchez, it accurately describes the trade's impact throughout Mississippi. The Confederate government officially prohibited citizens from trading all privately held goods at federal-occupied territories. Nonetheless, Mississippians, including many women, continually swapped cotton and federal greenback notes at Union lines in exchange for an abundance of goods normally sold in the regular marketplace but made scarce by the Union blockade and general wartime privation. These included raw commodities like tobacco, sugar, rice, foodstuffs, and molasses, as well as other supplies like clothing, guns and ammunition, cotton and wool cards, whiskey, wines and brandies, calico, coffee, shoes, and medical supplies.[3] Trade helped the Confederacy by supplying Southern troops and bolstering local economies, but it also undermined the war effort by depreciating Confederate currency, funneling valuable cotton to the Union, and compromising many Confederate nationalists' ideal of self-sufficiency.

The contraband trade, then, holds wider implications for understanding Confederate nationalism because it reveals how Mississippians negotiated among multiple loyalties to self, family, neighborhood, and nation. In these cases, acting on ties other than patriotism did not necessarily mean that a person was a disloyal Confederate, even if by trading they appeared to be acting against the Confederacy. This chapter focuses on white Mississippians because they were the core constituency from which the Confederate government sought support, and many contemporary observers believed that white Mississippians' engagement in the trade reflected the influence of Confederate allegiance in the state.[4]

The problem of multiple allegiances also adds new dimensions to the scholarship on the contraband trade and women's wartime experiences. Despite the trade's implications for expanding the historical understanding of how Confederate nationalism influenced people on the ground, historians of the topic have approached it as a framework for evaluating the effectiveness of each side's war effort. As with the weak-strong debate over Confederate nationalism, these scholars have been more concerned with outcome than process. They apply to both sides a cost-benefit analysis of the trade, concluding that it aided the Confederacy more than the Union. When Confederates' belief in "King Cotton" diplomacy proved unfounded, the trade provided an outlet for cotton sales to the North and brought food and supplies to Southern civilians and soldiers, helping the Confederacy prolong its war effort.[5] Historians studying the North write that the influence of Northern textile owners and the threat of European intervention on the Confederacy's behalf led Lincoln to retain the trade to the Confederacy's advantage. The Union blockade boosted cotton prices, and goods exchanged between the lines negated the blockade's effects.[6] Thus, historians have emphasized how the trade affected the war's outcome rather than how it influenced citizens' allegiances as the war unfolded.

Examining women's participation in the trade also adds to the historical understanding of their wartime experiences by emphasizing the continuity of those experiences. This approach contrasts with scholarship that casts the Civil War as an entrance point for women's participation in the public spheres of politics and the marketplace, making it a departure from the past in which they were primarily relegated to the private household.[7] The contraband trade demonstrates how Mississippi women continued antebellum commercial activity during the war. Their trading highlighted a familiarity with the marketplace that contradicts scholarly claims that the Civil War itself brought women into traditionally male-dominated public arenas.

Because trading with the Union did not necessarily indicate disloyalty to the Confederacy, examining the contraband trade offers a way of getting around dichotomized approaches to Confederate nationalism, women's experiences, and the war's outcome. In some circumstances, micro loyalties to self or family fulfilled traders' needs and assumed precedence over, but did not necessarily dispel macro devotion to, the Confederacy. Different allegiances overlapped, and trading could serve each of them. Simply labeling traders "strong" or "weak" Confederates does not address these complex motivations. Confederate patriotism was one component in traders' social interactions, in which more immediate ties also informed their behavior. Considering the influence of these loyalty layers explains why Mississippians viewed the trade as simultaneously treasonous, patriotic, or of little nationalist consequence altogether.

The divide over traders' motivations also further illuminates the internal political debate about the nature of Confederate nationalism in Mississippi. Although there was no consistent pattern regarding the types of goods that flowed through the lines, critics accused traders of purchasing "luxuries" over "necessities," thereby putting their own prosperity above that of the Confederacy.[8] Yet, what constituted a "luxury" and a "necessity" was often a matter of perception. Whiskey, for example, could be seen as the latter when used to calm patients before surgery in a field hospital, the former when consumed by an army shirker. Contained within the language of "luxury" and "necessity" were larger debates between those who favored protective nationalism, characterized by a self-sufficient Confederate state, and the traders, whose actions suggested the impossibility of that vision. Protective nationalists promoted domestic manufacturing and agricultural diversification in order to supply Confederate armies and lessen economic dependence on the North. They truly wanted to *protect* the Confederacy from Northern economic and cultural influence, but the contraband trade proved to be their undoing.[9]

The contraband trade followed antebellum routes and culminated at established centers of commerce such as Memphis, Vicksburg, New Orleans, and Natchez that fell under Union control. The trade demonstrated that while the Civil War created two theoretically separate political states, it could not sever what was a historically connected economic unit. The Confederate government maintained stronger control of its territories in the East, but Union occupation in the West fostered a continued economic exchange despite the altered political circumstances. This pattern fits with James Cobb's critique of "change" as a theme in southern history. Cobb argues that "[t]he history of southern identity is not a story of continuity *versus* change but continuity *within* it." Those who criticized traders for purchasing "luxuries" from the Union by extension denounced this pattern of continued economic relations as contradicting their ideal of an autonomous Confederacy. The contraband trade therefore complicates efforts to define the Confederacy either as a "revolutionary experience" or as the South's attempt to continue its pursuit of proslavery "Americanism."[10]

The presence of continuity within change helps explain the contraband trade's inherent contradictions. In Mississippi, where both governments controlled territory, the process by which different fidelities motivated human actions helps explain why the Confederacy can seem both united and divided, why some historians think it should have lasted longer, and why others marvel at its staying power against such steep odds. The Confederacy represented a break from antebellum political connections, but secession and war could not destroy stronger regional connections. The contraband trade demonstrated a form of continuity amid the changes caused by the Civil War.

The difficulty of stopping interregional trade bothered both Union and Confederate policy makers who wanted to prohibit trade between the lines but could not ignore its practical benefits. With this in mind, they settled on regulation, not prohibition, the enforcement of which changed frequently as different officials weighed in on the issue. In August 1861, President Abraham Lincoln banned all commerce with the seceded states unless it was done with special executive permission through the secretary of the treasury. Total prohibition did not last, however, as Lincoln and his advisers came to recognize that the trade could supply cotton to New England textile mills and encourage latent unionism in the seceded states through economic ties. In 1862, Lincoln authorized trade with inhabitants of Union-controlled Confederate territory, to be conducted under the authority of treasury agents, but forbade trade with Southern states still in Confederate hands. Lincoln therefore permitted a regulated trade while trying to maintain the illegality of commerce with the enemy. In addition to allowing trade by authorized treasury and military personnel, Lincoln also permitted loyal citizens, North or South, to trade on condition that federal authorities validate an individual's Union loyalty and claims to Southern cotton.[11]

The contraband trade in Mississippi began shortly after the Federals captured Memphis in June 1862 and gradually increased in volume as the Union army advanced southward. The trade increased when Federals gained a major base in Mississippi via the fall of Vicksburg, a fact reflected in the primary sources on the trade, which were mostly written from late 1863 through the end of the war. Union control of Memphis and Vicksburg, combined with the capture of New Orleans, meant that Mississippians wishing to transact business at these major Mississippi river commercial hubs had to deal with Union authorities. Despite government rules, Union field commanders had the power to regulate the trade. With a few exceptions, they remained hostile to a trade that fueled corruption and supplied Confederate armies, especially since a loophole in the law allowed treasury agents to prevent the transfer of goods outside of Union lines but not to stop goods from coming into the lines from Confederate territory.[12]

Reflecting the Lincoln government's policies, Confederate policy makers essentially decreed the trade simultaneously legal and illegal. As in the North, the Confederate stance grew out of an initial distaste for trading with the enemy that was soon tempered by reality. Although worried about undermining public confidence in Southern financial independence, Confederate officials facilitated a regular trade across the lines because Union occupation of Southern lands, destruction of Confederate railroads, and the coastal blockade stymied other means of moving domestic and foreign supplies. In addition to supplying Confederate soldiers and civilians, the trade also brought in higher-valued US currency.[13]

Confederate congressional acts in May and August 1861 confined the export of raw materials like cotton to Rebel seaports and Mexican territory. Congress prohibited exports to Union-blockaded ports but was unwilling to prohibit Northern imports, which continued to flow south. Beyond congressional measures, President Davis paid little attention to the trade, delegating the matter to the War Department and commanding generals in the field, whose policies varied from total prohibition to outright facilitation. Secretary of War James Seddon permitted trade by licensed private contractors and government agents to supply Confederate troops and civilians but prohibited it among all private citizens. Aware of the futility of stopping all private trade, however, Seddon limited arrests of traders to those suspected of espionage and restricted impressments of their goods to supplies deemed of military necessity. Thus, despite the restrictive laws, the War Department tacitly made itself a partner in an officially illegal trade.[14]

Nonetheless, even limited restrictions irked Mississippians like lawyer E. S. Fisher, who thought they unduly punished citizens who traded only to procure "articles of prime necessity."[15] Fisher directed his frustrations at state and national policy. Like Richmond's approach, the Mississippi government practiced a confusing combination of official prohibition and tacit permission. At first, the task of stopping the trade fell to military commanders, who initially responded with harsh punishments, including the destruction or confiscation of goods, imprisonment, and the occasional execution of traders. These penalties notwithstanding, state authorities could not quell the trade, and they soon realized that it could benefit the Confederacy. Acting on Seddon's recommendations, Department of Mississippi commanders James Chalmers and John Pemberton confiscated traders' goods that were useful to the army and returned the rest to their owners. In late 1863, however, state judge Alexander Clayton transferred confiscating authority from the military to state civil officers. He then declared private trade legal in all districts exposed to the Union army, since the government could not stop it anyway. Still, army confiscations did not stop, resulting in claim disputes over confiscated goods between civil and military authorities. Governor Charles Clark sided with the civil courts and denounced what he thought to be Richmond's overly prohibitive policy. He permitted licensed private contractors to exchange cotton at Union lines for supplies like wool cards and medicine that could aid his war-torn state.[16]

These contradictory policies regarding the trade created endless confusion, prompting one Union officer in Mississippi to exclaim: "War and commerce with the same people! What a Utopian dream!"[17] Such sentiments echoed those of policy makers in both governments who simply could not characterize the trade as wholly treasonous. Instead, they wanted to have it both ways and therefore could neither fully outlaw it nor fully embrace it. Such wavering tacitly acknowledged the inherent contradiction of both trading with, and fighting against, the enemy.

Despite governments' wavering policies, many Mississippians criticized the trade, claiming that it corrupted the citizenry and made the Confederacy dependent on the Yankees. In the winter of 1863, a scout in northern Mississippi told General Daniel Ruggles that "our own currency in this portion of Miss. . . . is being rapidly supplanted by U.S. Treasury notes, mostly I suppose the proceeds of the sale of cotton." The scout warned that people who obtained Union currency contributed to "the depreciation of our own currency," which "alienates the people from our Government and binds them to the enemy." Robert Read, a resident of Holly Springs, the center of northern Mississippi's cotton economy due to its Memphis railroad connection, also felt that the Memphis cotton trade was undermining Confederate independence. He fumed that the Union commander in Memphis, William T. Sherman, "could not desire a more potent agency in our midst for the benefit of the Federal cause than this rapidly increasing seduction of this entire range of country from the loyalty due to our government." State judge Robert Hudson echoed Read's sentiments in a letter to Governor Clark. "The idea of any of our people trading with the Yankees, while they are waging this unholy war, slaying our best & dearest flesh & blood, destroying our property, burning our homes, violating the persons of our women, [and] setting our negroes up in arms . . . is at once disgraceful and unpardonable," he wrote. Hudson demanded that traders suffer the "rigid and prompt infliction" of "the severest penalties."[18] Such criticism framed the trade as a phenomenon that undermined Confederate independence and ingratiated Mississippians to Union authority.

Mississippi Confederates frequently asserted that the contraband trade promoted treason by undermining all attempts to protect the Confederacy and its people from Yankee influence. After observing "disloyal persons" who were "actively engaged in endeavoring to supply the Federals with cotton," a Confederate officer in southwestern Mississippi ordered all commanders to squelch the "nefarious" and "treasonable" traffic. When Rebel soldiers caught two Mississippians in the act of smuggling cotton into Memphis, the *Weekly*

Panola Star opined that "our military authorities cannot be too rigid with the black-hearted and avaricious traitors engaged in the base work of selling their country." The Meridian *Daily Clarion* similarly proclaimed that "the cravings of the 'trading traitors' are rapidly on the increase" and berated traders for "besoiling their souls with Yankee oaths, bedizening their bodies with Yankee gew-gaws, gratifying their palates with Yankee viands, and destroying their senses with Yankee whiskey." The *Clarion*'s editorial voiced a common complaint that traders bought luxury items at Union lines and thereby sacrificed Confederate independence on the altar of personal pleasure.[19]

It was a common refrain, especially from editorials, that the lust for luxury outweighed patriotic devotion. The *Daily Mississippian* decried the "petty contrabandist and smuggler" involved in the "illicit, clandestine trade with the enemy" who "takes all chances and runs all risks, with no other object in view but the making of money."[20] Such charges accused traders of engaging in the supposedly treasonous quest for money and material goods even as the Confederacy wanted for even basic food and supplies. Consider the following 1863 poem by Holly Springs resident P. A. Willis, who echoed the *Mississippian*'s claims that traders prioritized the pursuit of profits over the Confederate cause:

> *Veal, beef, pork, and sheep*
> *Wheat more plenty, corn more cheap*
> *Men more honest, true, and bold*
> *Less inclined to lie for gold*
> *More disposed our cause to aid*
> *By cutting short this Yankee trade*
> *Feed the widow and the wife*
> *Of him who daily risks his life*
> *In battle, or in the tented field*
> *And from all harm his children shield*
> *When this is done, the war will cease*
> *And heaven help a prosperous peace*
> —"Cokespeare"

Like many Mississippians, Willis decried the allegedly greedy contraband traders who fueled the speculation that robbed food from the mouths of the wives and children of Confederate soldiers. Willis claimed that, by valuing profits and failing to make sacrifices for soldiers' families, traders were undermining the Confederate cause.[21]

Other patriotic Confederates extended these criticisms to the soldiers themselves. Men who ostensibly embodied Rebel loyalty displayed a reprehensible fall from grace when they succumbed to the trade. Stationed in Columbus in 1863, Colonel Frank Powers reported a "regular system of trade carried on between citizens, Confederate soldiers, and the enemy" and emphasized that "[l]arge quantities of cotton have found their way into the enemy's lines, guarded by Confederate soldiers." Brigadier General George Hodge similarly complained about having to punish officers "for taking bribes to pass cotton at the very points I had placed them to guard." Stationed in Jackson, Captain Sam Harris lamented to General Braxton Bragg that "few persons . . . have not sold cotton to the enemy." He disparaged government-sanctioned traders for depositing cotton at prearranged Union raiding points, and he singled out Confederate cavalry for taking bribes to ignore such collusion. "'A pair of boots and a bottle of whiskey' will scarcely ever fail . . . to secure a passage for a load of cotton through the lines," Harris noted. In light of these facts, he wanted to prohibit the trade completely. These officers considered the trade exceptionally demoralizing because it corrupted Confederate soldiers. More than anyone else, these men should have been unwaveringly devoted to the Southern cause.[22]

Worse yet, at least according to Confederate nationalists, cotton-smuggling soldiers corrupted ordinary citizens. Cavalry scout R. H. Bowers claimed that "at first citizens are afraid to engage in the trade except within the lines, thinking it [cotton] would be burnt, but after some of our soldiers got to buying & selling cotton many of the citizens engaged in it also." In 1863, teacher Caroline Seabury described the trade and its effects on Confederate soldiers on a trip through the state's northern tier. "All along the roadside were stray fleeces of cotton—the remains of what had been sent clandestinely to Memphis," she wrote. "Even some army officers, who in the beginning of the war, 'would give their last dollar on the altar of their country,' had it was said received gold from the hands of the detested Yankees—though their touch was thought such defilement—except through that incorruptible medium."[23] Such reports led many Confederate officials to demand that the trade be crushed, lest it inspire soldier and civilian alike to place self over country. Moreover, it made Mississippi dependent on the Yankee foe.

Like newspaper editorials that pointed to contraband traders' supposed lust for luxuries as proof of their prioritizing self over nation, some Rebel officers advocated total nationalist devotion, predicated on the idea that an independent Confederacy should be economically self-sufficient—that it ought to be protected from Union influence. For example, Captain W. E.

Montgomery, stationed along the Mississippi River in 1863, argued that the only way to stop the trade was by "burning all the cotton in the country except enough for spinning purposes." Montgomery explicitly advocated an autonomous Confederacy subsisting entirely on homespun. Governor Charles Clark echoed this view in his 1863 inaugural address. Among the most loyal Mississippi women, he claimed, "the spinning wheel is preferred to the harp, and the loom makes a music of loftier patriotism and inspiration than the keys of the piano."[24] Clark emphasized that *living* loyalty on a daily basis, through the wearing of homespun, was superior to merely *voicing* loyalty through patriotic songs. Contraband traders, by contrast, purchased alleged luxuries like whiskey and "gew-gaws" at Union lines. They therefore placed self-interest above what should have been a resolute devotion to the Confederacy. Protective nationalists believed that only prohibiting illicit trade would preserve the Confederacy's economic and cultural independence.

Other Confederates, however, couched criticisms of the trade in more qualified terms. They were willing to tolerate it to the extent that it allowed Mississippians to acquire perceived basic necessities but decried as disloyal those who traded for supposed luxuries. One such instance involved Holly Springs resident William Crump, who regularly sent trainloads of cotton to federal lines at Memphis and, in turn, imported what Inspector General Harvey Walter called "luxuries not essential to the public welfare," including large shipments of whiskey. Walter accused Crump of making "merchandise of treason," distinguishing what he perceived to be Crump's disloyal profiteering from other Holly Springs residents, "whose wants compel him to send his bale of cotton to Memphis to procure the food necessary for existence."[25] Walter tried to distinguish the greedy Crump from others who traded with the Union in the name of survival, but Mississippians often complicated such distinctions by trading under the mantle of necessity.

An observer in Brandon, Mississippi, noted as much. "I am not opposed to people being permitted to haul cotton to Tennse. [sic] and exchanging it for needed supplies," he told Clark, "but there is a regular traffic of speculation going on. . . . If they per chance to have anything of use, they will not sell it for money, but will exchange it for more cotton." Another Mississippian echoed this point, stating that "the excuse for this traffic with the enemy was the necessity for procuring food and clothing for family use and for relatives in the Confederate army." While conceding that "in some instances it was true," he added that "in very many cases it was for the purpose of speculation and extortion, and to carry into Memphis such information as would be of use to the Yankees in their future raids." The Reverend Samuel Agnew noted that while many traders bought corn, a scarcity in northern Mississippi, "cotton seemed to be in considerable demand by persons who wish to go to Memphis to get groceries and finery." Another concerned citizen informed Secretary Seddon that traders exchanged cotton for "brandies, wines, and flimsy gewgaws that bring exorbitant prices" but brought back "little in articles that produce substantial good."[26] In many cases, ardent Confederates struggled to differentiate between traders whom they believed operated out of self-interest, and others who seemed to be loyal Confederates but for whom ties to self and family needed addressing through permission to trade.

Whether or not authorities should accommodate Mississippians' multiple loyalties by permitting a limited trade proved an impossible conundrum. "Trade with the enemy is universal. The temptations to fraud are overwhelming," stated an 1864 Confederate Treasury report. "Do you have any blockade runners in your county?" northern Mississippi resident M. Hairston asked her niece. "There is a good deal of it done in this [region] & occasionally they get caught," she added, describing a Dr. Means who "started with a load of cotton toward Memphis" but who "was stopped at Oxford, team and wagon confiscated & himself ordered to the army."[27] There was indeed "a good deal" of trading among civilians despite Confederate officials' threats to arrest such transgressors.

Occasionally, authorities caught traders in the act, but enforcement was never sufficient. Some Confederate officials thought that the temptation to trade corrupted individuals like Lowndes County minister T. C. Teasdale. According to General Ruggles, Teasdale went to Memphis in late 1862, "preached there, brought articles through our lines, and sold them without the cognizance of the proper authorities." In addition, the reverend also obtained a trading pass for Lowndes County merchant Lewis Rawitch, for which Rawitch paid Teasdale $1,000. "This clergyman," Ruggles noted, "is reported employed as a traveling missionary . . . having access to headquarters of our armies and moving to and fro, while circumstances indicate his doubtful loyalty." In a similar incident, Confederate scouts caught Carroll County physician H. P. Atkins at a Mississippi River point using suspected forged government documents to exchange bales of cotton for gold and greenbacks. "I am almost satisfied that his papers are not genuine," the scout leader reported. Laws permitting a regulated trade attempted to benefit the Confederacy while hedging against personal pocket lining. Judge advocate R. J. Morgan reiterated this point to General Leonidas Polk. "This permission [to trade] is to be granted for the benefit of the army and not for personal advantage or private speculation and can not therefore be given to individuals for procuring their own or neighborhood supplies," he wrote.[28] In restricting the trade for military purposes, Morgan wrestled with a variation of the same necessity argument that challenged commanders on the ground. Demarcating local loyalties from national ones was as difficult as banning the trade altogether.

Local loyalties often drove Mississippi's planters to trade with the Federals, especially those living in the Delta region with easy access to the Mississippi River. Most were wealthy people who, in theory, could not believably claim the mantle of necessity. These planters' behavior irked military authorities, who suspected profiteering at the Confederacy's expense. In April 1862, General Dabney Maury proclaimed that "the [Mississippi] river is now open to the enemy, and . . . the interests of our country demand that they [planters] shall at once destroy all of their cotton." Those who failed to comply were to have their cotton confiscated and burned. Despite this policy, reports circulated that "planters along the Mississippi hesitate to burn cotton" and that the Federals were "sugar-coating the planters, offering them ample protection to all private property." In February 1863, a Panola County partisan ranger reported widespread cotton trading with the Union, while Lieutenant Colonel S. W. Ferguson reported that whole communities in the northern portions of Bolivar and Coahoma Counties were "engaged in this disgraceful traffic." That same month, troops confiscated wagons and mules hauling cotton to the Mississippi River, which they deemed "an act that cannot be interpreted otherwise than for trade with the Yankee boats." The wagons belonged to Bolivar County planter Reuben Starke, who, previous to this incident, "had already sent off one boat load of cotton." Military authorities issued a warrant for Starke's arrest but were unable to locate him. Starke also traded alongside fellow Bolivar County residents D. W. Davis and a Mr. Hammond. In late February 1863, Confederate military personnel found "four mule wagons and teams loaded with 12 bales of cotton" at Bolivar County's Concordia Bayou landing, which they quickly learned belonged to the three men.[29]

By trading with the Union, many Mississippi planters protested the Confederate government's policies of burning cotton and, by extension, its policy of protective nationalism. After observing planter activity in the Delta, quartermaster A. M. Paxton told Davis that "the citizens of this section of country," fed up with the government's "extortion and inhospitality," planned to "raise cotton and open a trade with the enemy along the river." The planters' reasons for this were straightforward. In exchange for keeping guerrillas at bay, Union forces gave them "written protection for their persons and property" and allowed them to "exchange goods for cotton on the river-bank."[30] These planters were concerned about their property and financial well-being, and wanted to keep business going at any cost.

James Lusk Alcorn was one such planter who flouted the dictates of sacrifice-obsessed Confederate nationalists. One of Mississippi's most influential politicos and a vociferous critic of Jefferson Davis and the Confederate experiment, Alcorn brazenly refused to give up "every comfort at home" and spoke plainly about his plans to reap personal profits by trading at Union lines. An active Whig in antebellum politics, Alcorn fought to preserve the Union during the 1850 secession crisis, a position he maintained during the crisis of 1860–1861 until the futility of further resistance drove him to begrudgingly cast a secession vote. Afterward, he was elected a brigadier general of Mississippi state troops, whom he led into Kentucky in 1862 without seeing action. When state troops became part of the Confederate army, however, Davis, doubting Alcorn's loyalty, revoked his generalship. Alcorn spent much of the war trading with the Union on his Coahoma County plantation and criticizing Davis's actions at every turn.[31]

In November 1862, Alcorn told his wife that he was "so flush of funds" after selling eighty bales of cotton and netting over $12,000. He hoped to sell "a hundred bales more" in exchange for greenbacks that were far more valuable than Confederate currency, which he could buy "by the sacks full." Alcorn smuggled his cotton at night, when he waited on the river shores for the Yankees to arrive with payment. Nor was he alone. "The smuggling business has now become popular and people are beginning openly to trade," he wrote, noting that Company B of the Eighteenth Mississippi Cavalry Partisan Rangers temporarily disbanded for two weeks and "went into a regular trade with the Yankees" to get salt. "I was at Delta a few nights since when near four hundred bales of cotton were openly sold and full fifty men were on the bank participating. There is scarcely an exception in the county," he continued. Among these men were Coahoma County residents James Pettit, B. A. Simms, Isaac Hull, John Miller, John Jones, and William Atkinson, all of whom were planters with extensive land and slaveholdings, except Pettit, a farmer who owned four slaves. "You remember how they once talked," Alcorn exclaimed, referencing the planters' former zeal for secession; "[t]he [Confederate] authorities out on the hills, I am told, are furious."[32]

For all his braggadocio, however, Alcorn made no such reversals of opinion and blamed his political enemies for bringing destruction to the South. "I sought to avoid this terrible war, but the wild mania had seized upon the passions of the southern people, when I would point them to the coming danger they would laugh in derision," he wrote in his diary. He had stronger words for Jefferson Davis, whom he labeled a "miserable, stupid, one-eyed, dyspeptic, arrogant tyrant" who "should be sunk into the lowest hell." Nonetheless, Alcorn had little love for the invading Federals. He wanted to preserve the Old South's social order, including his personal wealth and his family's well-being. Doing so meant keeping business going, war be damned.[33]

When contemplating if he should flee Mississippi to join his wife in Alabama, Alcorn told her: "I think I can save many thousands by remaining. Duty to yourself and to our children requires that I should save from the wreck what I can." He avoided a wreck and more, increasing the price paid for his cotton and procuring fineries for his daughters. In 1864, his two older daughters shopped for themselves in occupied Memphis. "I will send you everything I can and should I dispose of my cotton in time will come myself," he told his wife; "I wish, however, to fill my pocket—and should the war continue, we will spend our summer in New York—and leave them to fight who made the fight."[34] Alcorn's disdain for the Confederacy meant that he had no qualms about trading with the Federals, but personal and family interests primarily motivated him to keep the cotton business going. To Confederates, Alcorn's actions fell under the definition of treason, but Alcorn himself traded with a clear conscience, refusing to abide by the laws of what he considered an illegitimate government.

Alcorn's deep anti-Confederate sentiments allowed him to justify trading with the Union, but self-proclaimed Confederate citizens such as Samuel Agnew struggled to maintain a pure, nationalist devotion in light of the trade's temptations. In 1863, Agnew criticized his neighbor, Martha Hannah, for trading in federal lines at Corinth and Memphis. To get through the lines, Hannah swore that she was from Tennessee rather than Mississippi, prompting Agnew to scoff, "I do not know that much dependence is to be placed in her statements, for anybody who would go to Memphis and swear a lie will with as little compunction come home and tell a lie." Notwithstanding his disapproval over Hannah's actions, Agnew noted at one point that she "gave me some items from the Federal lines." Indeed, Agnew and his relatives visited the Hannahs on more than one occasion "to see if they could not get anything or rather something out [of] their Memphis stocks which they needed." On another occasion, he had a neighbor bring him sugar, coffee, and French calico from Memphis.[35] The conflict between Agnew's patriotism and his desire to get goods from Union lines reveals how loyalties to self and family were strong motivators even among nationalist-minded Mississippians.

This was also the case with Augustus Vaughn, a pro-Confederate resident of Holmes County who called the Federals "scoundrels" yet still wanted to shop at their lines. In September 1864, Vaughn wrote to his brother-in-law, Louisiana businessman Richard Simpson, instructing him to buy a host of items in federally occupied New Orleans. These included "a nice suit of dark Cassimere clothes, a dark heavy frock overcoat . . . [a] doz. fine white shirts" and three dresses "of dark Calico" for his daughter. To smuggle these items, Vaughn told Simpson to "get a permit from the Provost Marshal at Amite City—taking up those goods to exchange for flour *for your own family use.*" Despite his Confederate sympathies, Vaughn bluntly admitted that "*my taste is fastidious.* I want nice goods."[36] The war's circumstances drove people like Agnew and Vaughn to engage in what even they understood as disloyal behavior in order to continue participating in the market economy and procure "nice goods."

Other Mississippians displayed the same contradictions when it came to the trade. Eliza Sively of Raymond, Mississippi, complained about contraband traders to her daughter, Jane, a schoolchild in Alabama. In one instance, a local girl failed to procure a new wedding dress from Vicksburg in order to marry a man whom Sively considered a "dissipated scamp." "Poor girl," Sively wrote, "it appears that [marriage] is all the girls think of (and fine dresses). They are as crazy about Yankee goods as they are to marry, [they] don't appear to think of their Brothers that are enduring all kinds of hardships, nor the condition of the country." Sively invoked protective nationalism to criticize women who succumbed to the lure of Yankee fineries and therefore failed to make hard sacrifices in the name of Confederate independence.[37]

Despite her criticisms of others, however, Sively also traded with the Federals. In a January 1864 letter to Jane, she explained, "we can't get anything from Memphis *now*, I will try and get some greenbacks and get you some muslins from Vicksburg, you ought not to wear all your clothes and have them all ruined." Her refusal to let her daughter go without nice clothes contrasted sharply with her chiding of other women who traded for the very same reason. Sively even enlisted friends and relatives to bring her all manner of goods from behind Union lines. In one instance, Sively's sister brought her "two calico dress patterns, two pair shoes, two corsets, and the bulk goods for the [horse] riding suit" from Memphis. Later that month, Sively told her daughter to expect gifts from their neighbor Sallie. "Sallie got you a rite pretty pink muslin when she went to the Yankee City, [and] decked herself out in grand stile [*sic*], had her a beautiful dress made there."[38] Her Confederate loyalty notwithstanding, Sively's desire for life's finer things led her to engage in activity she considered treasonous when done by other people.

As with Sively, the contraband trade lured in plenty of other Mississippians even as they espoused Confederate sympathies. In response to several pro-Union Northern newspaper editorials, Amanda Worthington, a Washington County plantation mistress, doubled down on protective nationalism. "Rather than go back into a union with such people I would have *every man, woman and child* in the Confederacy killed," she wrote. In this passionate moment, Worthington preferred death to Rebel defeat, but such rhetoric had little sway in reality. In January 1865, Worthington was enthralled when her sister brought her a copy of *David Copperfield*, photographs, linen dresses, two pairs of shoes, handkerchiefs, stockings, perfume, jewelry, fancy hats, and two custom-made silk dresses—all from Union-occupied New Orleans. Worthington even praised her sister's tactful behavior among the Federals: "She just spent 1,000 dollars, got everything we wanted and didn't have to take the oath!"[39] Although Worthington claimed to prefer death to reunion with the Yankees, she was still willing to trade with them.

Other plantation mistresses followed Worthington's suite by simultaneously bad-mouthing, and trading with, the Union. Like Eliza Sively, Louisa Lovell, a resident of Monmouth Plantation outside of Natchez, criticized fellow Mississippians for trading at Union lines. "All day long miscellaneous trains of wagons . . . have been passing by this place," she wrote to her husband, Joseph. "I saw about 50 return a short time ago loaded with cotton & fodder. Why don't the people burn the cotton? It seems as if cowardice has taken possession of the whole state." Yet in the same letter, Lovell admitted, "I have been seriously thinking of selling some of that linen for greenbacks & also sending what few vegetables we have left to the Yankee camp to sell." Her thoughts turned to action in March 1864. "Doubtless you will wonder what I am doing at Vicksburg, will you not?" she wrote to her sister-in-law, explaining that "Joe has told you what I expect of the cotton business. Well, dear Paris [a friend] and myself are now up here to barter with the hated Yankees." That July, Lovell similarly found herself in New Orleans, ostensibly to see a doctor, but she took the opportunity to do "a good deal of shopping as our wardrobes needed replacing very badly."[40]

Each of these individuals continued to express Confederate allegiance even as they traded at Union lines. They were well aware that, from a legal standpoint, such behavior could be interpreted as act of treason, and they were quick to single out others for the very same behavior. Nonetheless, self-interest via the desire for market goods led them to trade. This micro loyalty was likely separate in their minds from the protective nationalism that the Confederate government promoted and that they openly embraced.

That they still traded with the "hated" Yankees underscores how protective nationalism simply could not be sustained on a practical level in a wartime environment in which loyalty layers continued to guide human behavior.

Numerous Mississippi contraband traders faced similar circumstances, but, unlike outspoken Confederates who appeared hypocritical for willingly participating in the trade, many traders kept silent, suggesting that the question of national allegiance was a secondary concern. Their own experiences reveal the influence of multiple loyalties that belied contemporaries' charges that trading at Union lines indicated treasonous motives. Narcissa Black, a planter's wife living just outside of Corinth, Mississippi, in McNairy County, Tennessee, traded to meet economic needs and satisfy local ties. Black's diary contains several instances when "northern gentlemen" stayed overnight, and she sold butter, onions, and cotton to Union soldiers.[41] When the Federals reached Corinth in 1862, Black and a bevy of her neighbors repeatedly visited Union lines to buy and sell. "Took the wagon in the morning and went to the northern camps and got a good many things. . . . I sold one bushel of onions, three pots of eggs and two pounds of butter," reads a typical entry. Confederate law forbade this kind of commercial exchange with the Union, but Black's actions suggested no particular national favoritism. Although she traded with the Federals, she also on more than one occasion fed and housed Confederate soldiers who came through the area.[42] Further, nowhere in her over one-hundred-page diary did Black express support for either government; instead she focused on local duties like tending to crops and purchasing plantation supplies. Her diary's matter-of-fact tone, its uninterrupted detailing of daily routines, and her lack of commentary about national loyalties suggest that the needs of her family and plantation were her top priorities.

In contrast to Black, other female traders made explicit connections between micro loyalties and trading at Union lines. Woodville, Mississippi, resident and British expatriate Betty Beaumont exchanged cotton and other goods for supplies at Union lines in Natchez and New Orleans. She then resold these supplies at her Woodville store. To some contemporary observers, Beaumont might have appeared to demonstrate Confederate allegiance when she made caps to sell to Rebel soldiers and named her tenth child "Jefferson Davis." In an 1887 memoir, however, she claimed that she did not understand why the war came and consequently "cared nothing about it."[43] Devotion to self and family drove most of Beaumont's actions, including her illicit trading. Her ultimate goal during the war was "to preserve the means of life and to procure a way of providing for the education of my family." Rather than align with one side over the other, she sold supplies to Confederate soldiers and traded with the Federals because both acts earned income. "My little store of goods bought at such risk were of great profit," she wrote of trading at Union lines; "I found I could arrive at pecuniary gain in this way, I gladly seized the opportunity."[44] National loyalties were less important to Beaumont than were self and family interests. Thus, she held no qualms about trading with the Union and ultimately did not care about the war.

Writing from England in 1887 allowed Beaumont to be frank about prioritizing micro loyalties over patriotism without fear of reprisal from the Confederacy. Such openness was rarer among women caught trading during the war who, faced with legal pressures, had to disavow treasonous intent. When Confederate authorities confiscated Martha Craigin's wagons bound for Yankee lines, she explained to Governor Clark: "I never would have attempted it if necessity had not have drove me to it." Craigin claimed that she traded in order to care for "a large and helpless family of girls with no husband or son to assist in making them a support."[45] Echoing Craigin, Harriet Spencer, a Pontotoc County native caught returning from Union lines with contraband goods, convinced Colonel William Falkner to petition Governor Pettus on her behalf. "She is the daughter of a widow woman, in very indignant circumstances, with no male persons connected with the family. She has been to Memphis, and purchased a few necessary articles all for family use," Falkner explained. He concluded that "although no man is more opposed to a traffic with the enemy than I am . . . I feel it is my duty to ask your Excellency to order her goods returned to her."[46] Spencer could also claim that her trading actually helped the war effort. While in Memphis, she bought shoe pegs for her neighbor, William Bell, a boot maker. Bell in turn vouched for Spencer when he explained that the shoe pegs were "necessary to carrying on my trade" so that he might "keep the soldiers shoed."[47] Like Black's private diary and Beaumont's postwar memoir, Craigin's and Spencer's letters to Confederate officials indicate that self and family fidelities drove them to trade. They invoked necessity to dispel possible treasonous charges laid at them by Confederate officials who often prioritized nationalism without considering how loyalty layers influenced people even in wartime.

Despite providing different justifications, the experiences of Black, Beaumont, Craigin, and Spencer share a key commonality: they were continuing their antebellum sectional commerce into the war. Commenting on the trade from Corinth after the fall of Memphis, Sherman told Major General Henry Halleck to "assure all country people that they will be permitted to take their cotton freely to market and that the ordinary channels of trade will be immediately reopened."[48] This connection to prewar market activity, through the "ordinary channels of trade," helps explain women's prominent role in the contraband trade beyond the obvious loss of men to the armies. Staunch Confederates who criticized female contraband traders failed to see this continuity. Instead, they criticized female traders as disloyal.

Take Judge Robert Hudson, who stated that "our women are the chief instruments and agents in this business" of "trading with the Yankees at Natches [sic], Vicksburg, Memphis & other points." In a scathing critique of the trade, the Meridian *Daily Clarion* declared that "amongst the women—we say it with shame—are the greatest transgressors." These women were "making frequent visits to Vicksburg or Memphis—the Meccas of their degradation" from which they returned with "quantities of everything calculated to demoralize the neighborhoods in which they live—including the political opinions of the Yankees." A Jackson-based Confederate colonel complained that "the women are losing their real faith and patriotism through this intercourse and traffic with the enemy." After the fall of Vicksburg, the *Clarion* warned of "the female cotton speculators from Vicksburg and Warren County" who became omens of federal presence. "Whenever you see ladies coming from the enemy's lines to buy cotton, commence moving your valuables away to a place of safety, for the Yankees will soon be along." By 1864, Mississippi women had made a regular business out of the trade. A. M. Paxton, stationed west of Vicksburg, reported that "ladies residing in this region, eminent for wealth, respectability, intelligence and beauty, make nothing of taking government cotton without authority and traveling in the night to the enemy's lines." These women bribed Confederate pickets and smuggled out goods like whiskey and calico, which they sold to others for a profit.[49]

Confederate observers took particular offense at female traders, who they believed flouted patriotism in exchange for what these observers viewed as material luxuries. "She is liable to perjure herself by taking the oath," a *Daily Clarion* editorial said of female traders, emphasizing how failure to swear the oath prevented the acquisition of goods. "How many come home without the much courted goods?" the editorial asked. "Let the rustling of fresh silk, the snowy handkerchiefs, the love of a bonnet, the light tap of prunella boot heels on our pavements, answer."[50] Others, such as Julia Bowman of Columbus, complained about the trade's popularity among local ladies. "The Memphis fever is still raging," she wrote her sister; "[n]umbers of ladies . . . are risking dangers and insults for a little finery. To our shame be it said . . . I would rather wrap in bear skin then sacrifice independence at this rate. They are the people that are going to have nothing to do with the Yankees when the war is over."[51] Staunch Confederates levied such criticisms at male and female traders alike, accusing them of abdicating their Confederate duties in their selfish quest for "finery." By claiming to prefer "bear skin" to clothing bought at Union lines, Bowman voiced a preference for homespun, thereby invoking the protective nationalist ideal that the Confederacy should be economically independent from the North. Traders who purchased goods from Union lines allegedly violated this ideal by demonstrating an unwillingness to sacrifice all material comforts in the name of national loyalty, thereby thwarting many Mississippians' goal of creating a self-sustained Confederate nation.

Critics who labeled female traders as apostates usually did not recognize how other loyalties could coexist with patriotism. Instead, they elevated patriotism as the most important allegiance that women should embrace, and they measured women's actions accordingly. Historians have taken a similar approach by tending to view Confederate women's actions through the lens of national devotion. This approach correlates with the rhetoric of paternalism that secessionists, and later Confederate officials, used to theorize women's relationship to the state. Southern paternalism emphasized a system of male-dominated household governance in which women and other dependents accepted their subordinated status in exchange for protection from outside threats. Paternalism accorded social and financial privileges to white women of slaveholding households, elevated them above dependent slaves, and praised them as the keepers of the natural virtue associated with the nineteenth century's cult of domesticity. In associating the home with femininity, however, Southern paternalism frowned on women's participation in the supposed masculine public spheres of politics and the marketplace.[52]

During the Civil War, Confederate officials appealed to this paternalism by suggesting that in exchange for women's support for the war, the Confederacy was to preserve women's dependent yet privileged status. Consequently, historians argue that women either withdrew their support for the Confederacy based on its failure to protect their privilege, or steadfastly supported the breakaway nation as "respectable" Southern women who feared the loss of privilege that would follow Confederate defeat.[53] Despite their differing conclusions, historians measure women's wartime actions as indicative of their degree of support for the Confederacy.

In addition, much of this scholarship has focused on elite plantation mistresses. As a result, historians tend to associate the elites' wartime experiences, defined by a sharp break from antebellum social patterns, with that of the mass of women from yeoman and non-slaveholding households. Stephanie

McCurry has made important distinctions between elite and nonelite women's wartime politics, arguing that the Civil War spurred lower-class women's entrance into the political sphere as a constituency of "soldiers' wives" who demanded that the Confederate state afford them protection from hardships as recompense for their husbands' military service. In contrast to planter women, who invoked paternalist language in their pleas to state officials, poor and yeoman women approached the state as a new and distinct political group.[54] Although they differ in emphasizing women's motivations and methods for approaching the state, historians of elite and nonelite Southern women share an interpretation that casts the Civil War as a starting point when white Southern women entered the political sphere as claimants to the state's protective power. This emphasis on a break from the past tends to overlook important elements of continuity that shaped how Mississippi's female contraband traders reacted to the war. Understanding the influence of established habits on these women puts their political relationship to the state in a different light. Rather than demand its protection, they wanted the state to leave them alone.

Many traders were poor and yeoman women who owned few or no slaves. Their participation in the trade indicates a familiarity with market commerce forged in the prewar years. Federal Treasury Department reports listing the names of hundreds of Southerners who traded at Memphis in 1863 and 1864 include at least thirty Mississippi women, many of whom traded on multiple occasions. Adams County planter Charles Whitmore described how "the [Union-run] supply stores are full everyday by country ladies and by getting permits they buy at reasonable rates." Speaking on behalf of five widows who came to the city to trade, a Memphis businessman told a federal officer that "these poor women" were "very much in need of the small parcels of goods for which they ask permits" and that they belonged "to that humble class of poor people in Mississippi, whose hearts have never been in the Rebel cause." Of the two women in the group who appear in the census, Lafayette County native Tabitha Ward had ten children and was married to a non-slaveholding farmer who owned $10,000 in personal property and $6,000 in real estate and who may have died by 1864. Susan Ward, also from Lafayette, was unmarried with two young children, owned no property, and lived with another family. Although only Susan Ward could be considered poor, neither of the two women came from the planter class.[55]

In May 1864, Eliza Sively described two Hinds County women, S. Simons and M. Florin, who were "bringing out a good many goods from Vicksburg" to "sell them very high and for Greenbacks or gold." They were opportunistic capitalists who also took both Union and Confederate currencies. Simons was married to a non-slaveholding brickmason who owned only $200 in real estate. Florin was the wife of a shoemaker who owned $200 in real estate and two slaves. Like the female Memphis traders, these women were far removed from the planter elite yet demonstrated a clear knowledge of market relations.[56]

Like Simons and Florin, Mississippian Eliza Herbert also did business at Union lines. In May 1863, federal officials at Memphis arrested Herbert for "smuggling contraband goods over the lines" in three large trunks labeled with seals on which she allegedly forged the signature of federal provost marshal A. J. Enlow and adopted the alias "Mrs. Steele." According to the military commission, Herbert admitted that she lived "in Mississippi, that her husband [was] a merchant there, and that she was taking these goods to Mississippi for his benefit," but she claimed that someone else had forged the seals and affixed them to her trunks. The commission eventually found her not guilty, asserting that her husband had paid a Mr. P. P. Schlicher $500 to obtain the forged passes for her. Herbert's husband could not be located, but Schlicher agreed to pay a $500 fine and leave Memphis for his actions. Federal authorities suspected Herbert of being disloyal in asserting that she attempted to bypass legal US trade regulations by forging passes in order to smuggle unspecified "contraband" into Mississippi, but they made no issue of the fact that she was a woman who traded with her merchant husband.[57] Like their Confederate counterparts, Union officials were concerned with women's national allegiance, not their engagement in the marketplace. Such omissions suggest that they were familiar with the sight of women involved in commercial activity.

As many historians have noted, poor and yeoman women often sold household-produced foods and goods in public marketplaces throughout the South from Appalachia to the Carolinas to Mississippi.[58] During the Civil War, Mississippi's female contraband traders maintained old commercial patterns adjusted to the war's circumstances. In the process, they echoed similar conditions during the American Revolution, when women engaged in illicit trade across army lines to get desired goods.[59] Betty Beaumont, for example, opened her Woodville general store six years before the war began.[60] These women did not demand that the Confederate state provide for them; rather, they requested that it not interfere with their providing for themselves. Micro as opposed to macro allegiances motivated many Mississippi women to trade at Union lines. Through their actions, they demonstrated the difficulty of maintaining many Confederates' ideal of a protective nationalism.

Particular silences in the sources from critics of female traders suggest that these detractors were most concerned with women violating the protective nationalist ideal, not paternalist gender conventions. Contemporaries called female traders "unpatriotic," "female cotton speculators," and "glittering snakes" in the Confederacy's bosom, accusing women of treason for buying so-called luxuries and allegedly placing their own comforts over their country's survival. Yet, women were no more likely to be accused of buying "luxuries" than were men, and critics did not mention or express concern for the fact that these women were operating outside of the domestic sphere.[61]

Confederate observers also framed their criticisms of female traders in class terms, often suggesting that poor white women were more prone to disloyalty. In a letter to his wife, for example, cavalry captain William Nugent described a group of poor Mississippi women who traded with the Federals at Memphis. "We had up yesterday some half-dozen trading wagons and a whole batch of women, whose goods had been confiscated," he wrote; "[s]ome of these women had traveled one hundred miles to trade, carrying a bale of cotton with them." To Nugent, these women's uncouth behavior comported with the stereotype of "white trash" used to denote class boundaries in the Old South. "They all brought back a full supply of *Scotch Snuff* and were as busy as bees with their rubbers," he told his wife. He then went on to describe the women's less-than-elegant appearance:

> Think of a female with the dirty colored tobacco streak around her mouth & on her lips, squirting discolored spittle all around her, and you have a fair sample of the "Buncombe Gals"—You must, though, add to the pitiable picture, a *tousled* head, unwashed face, drabbled dress, (no corsets), heavy shoes, a guffaw laugh and a sidelong leer. A dirty baby, too, is no unfrequent [sic] addition to the scene.

Despite his disgust with the female traders' unpolished appearances, Nugent did not criticize them for acting outside of the home sphere. To the contrary, he casually described how they would "take up their line of march hence to Memphis, preceeded [sic] by a small wagon drawn by a pair of mules in reference to whom there are several Bills of foreclosure filed by the undisciplined flocks of Buzzards hereabouts, with as much nonchalance as they would to go to the Cross-roads Meeting House." Clearly, Nugent was used to seeing poor women engage in commerce. Despite his blatant classism, Nugent's real ire stemmed from the women's supposed disloyalty. "We have two of these women in the Guard House for practicing their tory principles and keeping our people in dread," he concluded. Nugent found the women's "tory" principles offensive, not their engagement in the marketplace.[62]

Nevertheless, Nugent discovered that his own sister, Evie, had traded at Memphis, and worried that it was "very 'demoralizing' for gentle girls to be brought into Contact with the traffickers in Memphis & elsewhere." Although he claimed to have "every confidence in Evie's purity and modesty," Nugent felt uneasy about his sister being "thrown among" the poor white trash. Referring to the often seedy behavior that accompanied river traffic, he opined that "southern ladies are not regarded very highly by the miserable stuff that ... floats up and down the Mississippi" and worried that trading had driven "our best & most polished girls ... from the high ground of modest demeanor." Nugent thought that "polished" women's trading was a threat to moral character and worried about "nice ladies" who would travel alone to Memphis without a male attendant and expose themselves to the "bestial soldiery" therein. Indeed, rumors about rampant "illegitimacy" between Mississippi women and Yankees were just one more reason for Nugent to worry about the "demoralizing influence" of the contraband trade, although he was unconcerned about the fate of Mississippi's poorer "Buncombe Gals."[63]

This notion, that illicit commerce with the Union sullied Southern women's respectability, became a common refrain among male Confederate patriots as the war raged on. Mississippi attorney general Thomas Wharton made such remarks about female traders in Hinds County. "[W]omen (I cannot call them *ladies*, however respectable they may have been before) mount their horses, and ride over the neighborhood, buying up cotton, to sell to the Yankees, & invest the proceeds in merchandize, such as coffee, clothing, &, in some instances, in any kind of luxuries," he told Jefferson Davis. Like Nugent, who warned that the contraband trade corrupted genteel Southern womanhood, Wharton used nationalistic language to demote former "ladies" into mere "women." He castigated them not for trading but for *trading with the enemy* to procure "luxuries" through treasonous traffic.[64]

Both men framed their criticisms of "polished" female traders around what Barbara Cutter calls the idea of "redemptive womanhood," characterized by female espousals of morality, selflessness, and love in the midst of a nineteenth-century economic expansion that engulfed people into a public marketplace rife with greed, competition, and vice. This immoral marketplace particularly threatened middle-class women, the presumed keepers of moral virtue. Drawn into the increasingly public marketplace, they were expected to use redemptive womanhood to fight the sinfulness therein. Those "fallen women" who succumbed to the market's vices lost their sexual purity and moral character. Nugent and Wharton recognized that the wartime marketplace added treason to the vices with which women had to contend. They expected such corruption from "white trash" women but worried when the contraband trade threatened to corrupt "ladies" like Nugent's sister. For these men, collusion with the Union was a particular vice born out of a wartime environment during which commerce endured. The trade turned poor women into traitors and threatened the moral purity of middle-class ladies.[65]

Nugent and Wharton might have considered their charges of womanly corruption bolstered by the fact that many female contraband traders were wives of Confederate soldiers. Federal picket reports from outside of Memphis listed over a hundred traders who came into the city during the winter of 1863–1864, roughly twenty of whom were women. While the reports often lacked full names, at least nine of the names matched those of individuals who lived in northern Mississippi. They included Nancy Wiggins of Lafayette County, who made two trips to Memphis in December 1863, Martha Griffis of DeSoto County, Lucinda Herring and Mary Baily of Itawamba County, and Sarah Gossett and Sarah Boyd of Tippah County. Also on the list was Sallie Winn, a single woman from Panola County, and Susie Duke, the daughter of a Pontotoc County planter. Four of these women were soldiers' wives. Sarah Gossett's husband, John, and Mary Baily's husband, James, served in Companies B and L of the Second Mississippi Infantry. Lucinda Herring's husband, Alexander, served in Company I, First Mississippi Infantry, while Nancy Wiggins's husband, William, served in Company A, Twenty-Ninth Mississippi Infantry. The federal picket guards included these women's names alongside the male traders, and most of them had Memphis-based cosigners for their bales of cotton. These women's actions, however, need not imply, per Nugent's and Wharton's suggestions, that women traded out of moral weakness and its attendant treasonous baggage.[66]

Female traders claimed "necessity" to deflect protective nationalist critics' accusations of treason. These claims, in turn, helped mask women's desire to access a variety of goods at established trade centers for themselves and their families. By trading at Union-occupied depots like Memphis and Vicksburg, Mississippi women reacted to familiar market incentives like consumer choice and product availability that, alongside domestic production, defined even rural non-slaveholding household organization by the 1860s. Vicksburg resident Sara Couper, like many others, casually took advantage of this product availability, telling her soldier husband how her friend Mollie "had an opportunity to send to Memphis for her trousseau by a lady friend. I sent with her $30.00 to get a mantle, shoes & gloves."[67] Through their trading, women demonstrated an unwillingness to endure an arduous, wartime-induced state of pure domestic production that market capitalism had already alleviated. For all of its breaks with the past, the Civil War in Mississippi could not sever established market relations, and the Confederate state was not strong enough to make protective nationalism a reality by stopping the contraband trade.

So intact were prewar commercial ties that, contrary to their critics, some Mississippians claimed that trading with the Union *helped* the Confederacy by supplying their state with provisions. Citizens flooded the governor's office with conditional offers to furnish Mississippi with supplies obtained at Union lines. Their conditions were personal benefit.

Typical were proposals like that of W. M. Deason, who promised Governor Clark that he would distribute goods from Union lines to Mississippians. "I am poor and would like to do something for myself and also for my state," he wrote. Following his discharge from the Fifteenth Mississippi Infantry, private Simon Hartley similarly proposed to Clark a plan for "procuring supplies from the enemy's lines for the use and consumption of the people," but he also noted that he was "compelled to earn a living." Upon hearing about Clark's attempts at "procuring supplies for the Government," Holly Springs resident F. L. Martin informed Clark, "if you will give me a permit to carry the cotton through our lines, I will furnish my own cotton to buy the supplies with." Macon, Mississippi, resident Dr. J. R. Christian similarly promised, "I will turn over to the state of Miss. one half of the proceeds of any cotton you may allow me to transport into a Federal market, in such army supplies as I may be able to get out." Charles Newman told Clark that he could supply cotton cards on the condition that for every thousand pairs of cards delivered, he be permitted to "purchase and ship beyond our lines (150) . . . bales of cotton," which he would purchase in areas of Mississippi "most liable to the raids of the enemy."[68]

Mississippians with existing business connections in Memphis were particularly apt to trade there. Writing from Grenada, Mississippi, Captain J. S. Reid described the volume of "*illicit* trade now being carried out between this place and the City of Memphis" as being "entirely too great," adding that "merchants are almost daily offering new goods" that were manufactured outside of the South. DeSoto County farmer F. T. Paine claimed that his "old Merchants in Memphis" could supply Mississippi with cotton cards under condition that he be allowed to "take cotton to any market I may find most convenient to pay for them." Conveniently, Paine lived "near the [federal] lines," although he swore that he would only patronize the enemy in exchange for supplies beneficial to Mississippians. Like Paine, B. B. Wilkinson recommended himself as an agent to "open a correspondence" with parties in Memphis who could help Wilkinson funnel supplies into Mississippi. Writing from Grenada, E. C. Cabell told Secretary Seddon that "many of the supplies now so much needed by the Army can be obtained from Memphis, if the government will authorize it." Cabell was acquainted with Memphis businesspeople who would "furnish supplies" for "either a percentage in the cost, or a stipulated sum." William A. Strong, mayor of Greenwood, Mississippi, boasted that he had an acquaintance in Memphis "who can get a boat to anywhere he desires, and to be laden with whatever he may wish," from the city. Strong's connection was Choctaw County resident Robert Kirk, who wrote to Governor Clark from Mobile, proposing at Strong's suggestion to furnish cotton and wool cards to Mississippi in exchange for permission to ship cotton beyond Rebel lines. As the conduit for goods Kirk shipped from Memphis, Strong would gain a cut of the profits.[69]

Each of these prospective traders acted on multiple loyalties, trying to make a profit for themselves while also helping their country. Following his parole from a Mississippi cavalry company, Albert Q. Withers proposed that Clark appoint him as his "agent to controll [*sic*] the cotton trade to Memphis." Withers had "many true friends in the city" whom he knew from before the war and suggested reestablishing these connections, with himself as the goods' conduit from Memphis. Mississippian turned Memphis-based cotton broker W. L. Dogan likewise touted his commercial prowess, telling Governor Pettus in 1863 that he could supply Pontotoc County citizens with "the wants of the country." While Dogan knew of other Mississippians trading with the Union "in opposition to the wishes of all true Southerners," he pledged his "word of honor" to "avoid all trade and intercourse with the enemy." Yet Dogan's honor had seemed less binding a year earlier when he asked Jefferson Davis for permission to trade cotton at Memphis in exchange for "necessities." Dogan claimed that he could score big with Union authorities in Memphis, since he understood "the channels through which favors are obtained."[70] Such skills would be expected from a cotton broker who worked in the city, and, given Dogan's willingness to trade with the Federals in 1862, it seems unlikely that, his promise notwithstanding, he would harbor any qualms about continuing such business in 1863.

The actions of Dogan and other merchants, however, were not unprecedented: they paralleled those of merchants during the French and Indian War and the American Revolution who traded with their ostensible enemies in the name of continuing commerce.[71] Even in war, some Mississippians found old habits hard to break. It mattered little that their trade connections were now the enemy in Yankee blue, because they operated out of the same places, especially Memphis, that hosted such exchanges before 1861.[72] After all, commerce with the enemy was legal if done under Confederate government contract. It made sense to look out for one's self *and* one's country, especially when both actions could be done together.

Plenty of contraband traders admitted as much in their petitions to Rebel authorities. J. D. Burch of Bolivar County, for example, disputed charges that he and some acquaintances traded at Memphis merely to gain a profit. "Necessity is said to have no law, we were compelled to save life," Burch wrote. "We all have large families white and black to support," he continued; "any other course ... would have brought destitution." M. D. Shelly, a cosigner of Burch's petition, defended commerce with the Union as a patriotic act. Cotton was the only source of income, cash or otherwise, he said, and that income came from the Yankees. "How are we to pay our taxes—we can't do it unless we are permitted to sell cotton to the enemy," Shelly argued, justifying what was technically a "disloyal" act if the end goal was to support the Confederacy. "We are willing and anxious to pay our taxes," he stated, "and do all we can to assist both State & Confederate govts." Living south of federally occupied Natchez, planter J. Alexander Ventress similarly defended the trade as patriotic. "National wealth," he wrote to Clark, "is naught else than the sum of the wealth of the individual citizens of the nation—In a word, destroy our cotton and you stress the tendon Achilles of the war." Like other traders, Ventress claimed that the trade would bring "the most needful necessaries of life ... within our lines."[73] Like Burch and Shelly, Ventress argued that a protective nationalist policy that forbade trading with the enemy neglected Mississippians' multiple loyalties and harmed the Confederate cause.

State officials like Governor Clark eventually came to the same conclusion and supported a limited trade with the Union. Drawing on appeals from citizens, Clark permitted trade by state-sanctioned individuals, citing the need to bring goods "of prime and immediate necessity" into Mississippi. By invoking necessity, Clark embraced trade as a way of strengthening the Confederacy by materially strengthening its people. Other Confederate officials agreed. Responding to complaints by Vicksburg commander John Pemberton, Secretary Seddon explained that while the trade may have produced a "demoralization of the people," the War Department sanctioned trade contracts out of a "strong conviction" to adequately supply the citizens and soldiers. Seddon found it impracticable for Pemberton to oppose a trade that people were bound to "indulge in to a considerable extent."[74] Seddon's admission that Mississippians were "bound" to trade underscores just how impotent the otherwise expanded Confederate military apparatus was when it came to loyalty enforcement. It could not stop individuals from *wanting* to trade, nor could it stop them from *acting* on those wants.

Recognizing that the government was not strong enough to stop the trade, some Mississippians insisted that trading should be used as a means of fighting the Federals. In an appeal to the Confederate Congress in October 1863, Louisianan F. D. Conrad argued that although the contraband trade in Mississippi and Louisiana might appear treasonous to some, wartime circumstances demanded more nuanced approaches. "Can the introduction through the enemy's lines . . . of these necessaries . . . be injurious to the Confederacy?" Conrad asked. "If so," he continued, "it is strange that the enemy has deemed it so important to prevent their introduction, so important as to consider the prohibition of their introduction one of their most reliable means for our destruction and subjugation." If the Yankees believed that the trade hurt their own cause, Conrad reasoned, the Confederacy should embrace it.[75]

None other than Brigadier General James Chalmers eventually came to this same conclusion. Chalmers initially opposed the trade, but in late 1863 he reconsidered. "When I came to this district I thought any man was a traitor who would sell cotton to the enemy for any purpose," he explained from Oxford. "I now believe that our people on the border who have been compelled to trade with the enemy for subsistence are more patriotic and more liberal to our soldiers than those in the interior, and that they have been greatly misrepresented by those who did not understand their condition." Chalmers offered a straightforward reasoning for his turnaround. Since the fall of Memphis, the people in northern Mississippi had been left "to live within themselves," and "under these circumstances they traded with the enemy, and the husbands, sons and fathers in our army of the women in North Mississippi were supplied with many articles of clothing and comfort that came from the enemy's lines." The trade's benefits, Chalmers believed, outweighed its downsides, and he felt that history justified this conclusion. "Frederick the great was the wisest of military rulers, and he did not hesitate to trade with his enemy[;] . . . [and] British gold was one of England's most effective weapons in Revolutionary days and came near taking West Point, and I believe that southern cotton could have saved Vicksburg when southern arms were powerless to do so."[76]

Some Union officers shared Chalmers's assessment that the trade benefited the Confederate cause. When native Mississippian and federal scout John
Riley got word that "a certain widow Hildebrand had been keeping smuggled
goods for sale" outside of Holly Springs, Riley went to Hildebrand's residence
disguised in Butternut garb, where he found a stash of goods "worth of about
$2,000." Hildebrand was nowhere to be found, but she was likely the same
"Mrs. E. J. Hildebrand" whom federal pickets reported traded in Memphis
on at least four different occasions in the winter of 1863–1864. She ultimately
sent goods acquired at Yankee lines to supply Confederate soldiers. Examples
like Hildebrand irked Union general Dan Sickles, who complained to Lincoln
that "in the way it has been conducted [the trade,] immense supplies go to
the enemy." He concluded that the trade was a "concession which benefits
a hundred rebels where it relieves one Union man." Another federal officer
in Memphis noted that "the practical operation of commercial intercourse
from this city with the States in Rebellion has been to help largely to feed,
clothe, arm and equip our enemies."[77]

In June 1863, Brigadier General Alfred Ellet found what he considered
to be proof that corroborated Sickles's claims when Union naval personnel
raided the town of Austin in Tunica County and discovered "ample evidence
that a large smuggling trade has been successfully carried on at this point."
The evidence included barrels stuffed with "molasses and sugar, salt, whiskey,
fish, pieces of dry goods, and large quantities of medicines in the original
packages." After burning the town, Ellet met two trading boats that arrived
at the riverbank from Memphis boasting permits to bring out hefty amounts
of cotton. "[T]here were many suspicious circumstances that induced the
impression upon my mind that the arrival of these boats and this command
of the enemy so near the same time was occasioned by pre-concerted arrangement," Ellet noted. The Federals often found Mississippi civilians to be
less than trustworthy when it came to their engagement in the trade.[78]

Just as Union forces found it difficult to discern whether Mississippians
who swore the oath were truly "loyal," they could never be sure if contraband
traders were merely buying "necessities" or smuggling goods to Confederate
troops. Such was the case when Union officers learned from a female spy that
Hinds County dentist A. H. Hardenstein, sporting a permit from General
M. L. Smith, was working with other secret Confederates to smuggle "arms,
boots, shoes, and other contraband goods marked as something else" out of
the Vicksburg lines to Rebel troops on the Big Black River. "Under the guise
of a trader, Dr. Hardenstein was also acting the spy for the Confederates,
being thoroughly in their confidence," wrote Union major A. M. Jackson.[79]

Hardenstein was not the only one to use the veneer of trade to spy for the Rebels. After Union troops captured Confederate corporal Thomas Swan in October 1863, he revealed the names of several traders who had been assisting Rebel troops. According to Swan's statement, DeSoto County resident George Barley, acting in concert with his mother, had been exchanging cotton at Memphis for supplies that "he sells to citizens or soldiers." Marshall County native John Williams, a soldier in the Third Mississippi Cavalry Battalion, "regularly" engaged in bringing cotton to Memphis, "sometimes twice a week." Williams, the report noted, "does Chalmers more good than harm by bringing cotton in. [He] has often been arrested & taken before Chalmers who always releases him." Williams also apparently operated as Chalmers's spy. J. A. Blair, another Marshall County resident who lived near Holly Springs, traded cotton at Memphis for boots and calico, which he then sold to Confederate soldiers. Marshall County civilian William Wonson had evidently "passed into Memphis nearly every week during the last summer." Although he denied selling goods to Rebel troops, he would not "hesitate to do so if he had time to spare." Such individuals were problematic for the Federals because their national loyalties were always under suspicion, and many seemed to be actively working for the Confederates. "These men all profess to be loyal to the South with their neighbors and profess loyalty to the Federal Government when in the presence of our troops," a federal officer concluded about the individuals Swan identified as contraband traders.[80] The Union government, like its Confederate counterpart, lacked the power to prevent Mississippians from trading. Even when federal authorities tried to limit trading to "loyal" Mississippians, verifying that loyalty was a task simply beyond the government's infrastructural capacity.

Well aware that they could feign loyalty to Union forces, some Mississippians traded as a way to resist the Northern occupation of the South. Yet even for them, the trade elicited conflicting emotions. One such individual was Mississippi native Belle Edmondson, who spent most of the war on a farm in Shelby County, Tennessee. From this location, she funneled supplies and funds from Memphis to Confederate soldiers and friends back in Mississippi. She gained such notoriety that Union commander Stephen Hurlbut issued a warrant for her arrest in 1864. In her diary, Edmondson detailed how she smuggled goods across the lines. "We made a balmoral of the Grey cloth for uniform, pin'd the Hats to the inside of my hoops, tied the boots with a strong list, letting them fall directly in front, the cloth having monopolized the back & the Hats the side. All my letters, brass buttons, money, &c in my bosom," she wrote. Edmondson justified trading with the enemy by invoking her patriotic duty. "God bless the Rebels," she wrote; "I would risk my life a dozen times a day to serve them." On one trip however, federal pickets confiscated hats she intended as gifts. "Oh! how I hate them," she fumed, resenting having to deal with the enemy on a daily basis. When Edmondson went back to Mississippi to collect cotton in October 1863, cavalry captain Thomas Henderson entreated her not to feel guilty taking cotton to Federal lines. "The proceeds of the cotton will surely do us more good than the cotton will do them."[81]

Loyalty issues nagged at other ardent Confederates who dreamed of an independent Southern nation but knew that trading with the Union mean *dependence on* the Union, a tacit admission of subjugation. Such an arrangement inevitably spawned confusion over who was trading for what purpose. Depending on the observer, a trader might be a true Confederate or a loathsome speculator. Mississippi partisan ranger C. Shermin ran into this problem when his troops arrested Patrick Doyle, whom Shermin had contracted to exchange cotton at Memphis for clothes and boots. Petitioning General Earl Van Dorn for Doyle's release, Shermin insisted that Doyle was "a good citizen and was not speculating, for he was under the contract with me, and [I] think that his service has been for the good of the [Confederate] service."[82] Shermin's case demonstrates the confusion that trading created. Doyle's actions could be interpreted as loyal or treasonous depending on the proclivities of the observer.

The experiences of cavalry scout Charles Allen, stationed around Vicksburg and its surrounding counties, revealed similar problems. Allen traded at Union lines to supply his unit and to acquire goods like coffee for his family. "If you all want anything out of V.B. send or come over to Jackson or down here & I can get you anything you want," he wrote his parents in October 1863. Exclaiming that he had "a good mind to go to work running the blockade," he detailed how his slave, Lige, bought goods at Vicksburg and hid them "in his rations of rice & passes the pickets in that way." Allen was particularly adamant about scoring coffee for his parents—a true luxury item in wartime—on multiple occasions. Yet Allen's scouting activity cast a cloak of irony over his trading. In one incident, his company's major duties involved "picketing all the fords and crossings on Big Black trying to keep people from crossing cotton and trading with the Yankees." If the irony of this situation was lost on Allen, it was not lost on his colonel, who arrested Allen's fellow cavalryman, Henry Hyland, for buying salt at Union lines. "Col. Wood intends to confiscate the salt for illegal trade with the enemy," Allen wrote; "I tried to get Col. Wood to let him have the salt—but he refused."[83]

Allen was therefore a Confederate soldier who, along with others in his unit, traded with the Union, an act that his superiors deemed treasonous and ordered him to prevent other Mississippians from doing. This contradiction eventually led Allen to defend a fellow soldier when his own colonel reprimanded that soldier for trading with the enemy. The issue of trading with the enemy was always cloudy because of this contradiction: dependence on the Union in the name of Confederate *independence*. The war's circumstances challenged binary concepts of allegiance, and some Mississippians adopted an unpalatable means to serve desirable ends.

The contraband trade in Mississippi reveals how the Civil War's circumstances drove Mississippians to negotiate between loyalties to self, family, community, and nation. Proponents of a self-sufficient Confederacy viewed trading with the Federals as a disloyal act because it made the Confederacy dependent on the Union. It also depreciated Confederate currency, boosted federal greenbacks, and supplied cotton that funded the Union's production of war materials. Still, others considered it a patriotic act because it brought food and supplies to Mississippi civilians and soldiers. Advocates of the latter position implicitly preferred free trade with the Union in place of the impracticable self-sufficiency of protective nationalism. Viewing contraband traders as "weak" or "strong" Confederates does not recognize that Mississippians themselves disputed the trade's impact on the slaveholding republic, nor does it consider how multiple allegiances influenced their behavior. Acting on specific circumstances, contraband traders accommodated different loyalties, at the micro and macro level. Confederate patriotism existed alongside more immediate attachments to self, family, and community, which did not and could not simply vanish when the war came. Mississippians traded to benefit themselves while simultaneously helping or hindering the Confederate cause.

In addition, the contraband trade shows that, despite its many transformational aspects, the Civil War did not destroy established economic patterns. Mississippi traders shuffled their goods along traditional commercial routes and traded at established depots like Memphis, Vicksburg, and Natchez. Goods from these cities then went to ports in St. Louis and New Orleans before shipment to New York and eventually Europe. In this sense, Mississippians continued their economic relationship with the North even as they fought to sever themselves from that relationship. The Confederate state's inability to stop the trade between the lines underscored the concrete limitations of its expanded infrastructural powers, which were justified by the need to make protective nationalism a reality. Although historians have viewed the wartime Confederate state as exceedingly strong to the point where it reached up to citizens' very doorsteps, the state was not strong enough to stop its own citizens from acting on their loyalty layers in order to continue commercial activity in wartime.

Recognizing how multiple loyalties drove Mississippians to trade with the Union, and understanding how the trade reinforced established antebellum ties between North and South even amid conflict, helps explain why the Civil War seems so transformational and yet so continuous; why Confederates can seem concurrently loyal and disloyal. Human loyalties are multidirected, multilayered, and influenced by circumstances. These circumstances drove Mississippi contraband traders to act on different allegiances, which at different times and for different reasons could both help and hinder the Confederate war effort.

Although Confederate protective nationalists were frustrated at how Mississippians' prewar loyalties stymied their attempts to establish Southern economic independence, they did not stop trying to weld Mississippians' interests to those of the Confederacy in their bid for Southern victory. To many ardent Confederates, the military stood as the preeminent nationalist institution through which Southerners should literally give their lives to their country on the battlefield. Yet, even when it came to army service, Mississippians' multiple loyalties continued to influence how they viewed their relationship to the state. Moreover, the war's circumstances imbued old allegiances with new meanings, as Confederate deserters broke free from the war's partisan confines and took wartime conflict into illicit new directions.

CHAPTER FOUR

"PREY TO THIEVES AND ROBBERS"

Desertion, Exemption, and the Limits of Military Loyalty Enforcement

JUNE 1863. CLAIBORNE COUNTY PLANTER RICHARD ARCHER BEGGED GOV-
ernor John Pettus to send reinforcements into the Delta region to apprehend
a gang of ruffians wreaking havoc in the area. "Sir, this county is a prey
to thieves and robbers as infamous as the 'Cowboys' and 'Skinners' of the
Revolutionary war," Archer wrote. His invoking of "Cowboys" and "Skinners"
referred to roaming groups of bandits during the American Revolution who
claimed patriot or loyalist allegiances but robbed and pillaged citizens on
both sides. Such was the case, Archer claimed, with the "armed organizations
of men" who had been stealing Claiborne residents' mules, horses, and oxen
after federal raiders had turned the animals loose. "This country is full of
deserters from our army, most of them it is believed officers and many of
them engaged in these robberies," Archer explained. In contrast to the Yankees, who "robb [*sic*] our people only," the deserters pillaged "both enemies
and friends." Such wanton anarchism depleted civilian morale. "The demoralization is so great that no power can arrest it unless the executioner can
do so," Archer noted.[1] Archer understood Yankee pillaging, but when Rebel
soldiers—the supposed defenders of Southern hearths and homes—abused
Southern civilians, it was hard to take.

Deserters, however, were not the only problem plaguing Mississippi's
Confederate army ranks. In February 1863, Confederate militia general Ab-
salom West informed Pettus about the antics of Tillman Lomax, a Holmes
County farmer and army conscript. Lomax claimed to have permission from
Pettus to impress wagons and animals from his neighbors under the pretense
of using them to collect salt. This was apparently a scam. West noted that
Lomax was "a man devoid of moral principle," who "from the beginning
of the war shirked responsibilities." West and Lomax were both Holmes
County natives and knew each other before the war. Upon being conscripted,

Lomax tried to join West's brigade, hoping to become a field officer. When this failed, he faked illness and convinced a surgeon to give him a discharge certificate, but he was soon placed back into service. Finally, Lomax asked West for a discharge, citing his support for West's past state senate campaign as grounds for favoritism. "Lomax is ignorant, vicious and utterly wanting in those attributes necessary to constitute an honorable man," West wrote; "he will never serve his country as a soldier, if fraud or deception will enable him to avoid it." While it is unclear why Lomax dodged military service, he did own $2,500 in real estate and $2,140 in personal property, including sixteen slaves. Such ample holdings might be threatened were he to remain in the army. In addition to shirking duty, Lomax also took advantage of wartime conditions to impress property from his neighbors under false authority.[2]

Tillman Lomax's draft dodging and the Claiborne County deserters' plundering do not fit easily within the scholarly paradigms that identify military service and protection of hearth and home as foundations of Confederate nationalism. Many historians argue that because Confederate soldiers tended to fight near their homes, they conflated home and nation into a single entity, which they defended from federal intrusion. Aaron Sheehan-Dean, for example, contends that "because Confederate soldiers participated fully in both the battlefield and the home front, they did not distinguish the political nation from the domestic nation." While conceding that "at times obligations of family and nation conflicted," Sheehan-Dean ultimately concludes that Rebel soldiers "saw a harmony of interests between their dual responsibilities" to home and nation, and fought for both accordingly.[3]

Although some scholars contend that the Confederate defense of hearth and home bolstered the Southern cause, other historians claim that this type of localized nationalism fractured Confederate unity. In his study of Confederate desertion, Mark Weitz argues that most Confederate soldiers saw the South less as a unified nation than as a patchwork of localities. They deserted to defend their homes, which they prioritized over a young, abstract nation. Paul Escott attributes a steady decline in support for the Confederacy to the Davis government's failure to respond to soldiers' complaints over exemption and impressment laws that seemed to favor the rich and caused men to give "higher priority to the needs of their families than to the requirements of Confederate nationalism."[4]

Connected to the hearth and home thesis is an emphasis on the military as another source of loyalty to the slaveholding republic. Gary Gallagher, perhaps the most enthusiastic proponent of this view, contends that Robert E. Lee and the Army of Northern Virginia "served as an engine propelling national loyalty among civilians and soldiers throughout the Confederacy." Gallagher and other scholars cite high enlistment rates—in some cases 90 percent of military-age men—to argue that the armies played a central role in forging Confederate nationalism.[5]

Claiborne County's marauding deserters and Tillman Lomax's draft dodging, however, reveal key limitations of the hearth-and-home thesis. Such examples also indicate that the Confederate military was limited in its ability to instill and enforce loyalty in its civilian soldiers. The Claiborne deserters were among thousands who pillaged their fellow citizens throughout Civil War Mississippi. Their antisocial behavior indicated little reverence for the home front as a sacred symbol of the nation as a whole. After all, Tillman Lomax served in the army, but his military stint did not make him a stereotypically "loyal" Confederate. In fact, he seemed more concerned with self-enrichment than he was with national allegiance. Rampaging deserters and army shirkers were numerous in Mississippi. Their existence requires explanations that do not fit neatly into the established scholarly narrative.

Each Confederate state experienced the war in different ways, and historians should be cautious when attempting to universalize these disparate experiences. Scholars who connect strong Confederate nationalism to the military have largely focused on Virginia. Since Lee's army won many victories, it makes sense, they argue, that Confederates viewed that army as a symbol of national pride. While there is truth to this conclusion, it runs the risk of inflating the influence of Lee's army in particular and the Confederate military in general. Far from the Virginia front, loyalties separate from nationalism influenced Mississippians' behavior. Their cases are important because not only do they reveal important geographical distinctions in the Confederate war but they also demonstrate how the war affected military and domestic spheres beyond national issues.

The collapse of Mississippi's social order fueled an explosion of opportunistic collective violence among Confederate deserters. Group loyalties that preceded the war continued to influence these men during the conflict and sustained their destructive behavior, which expanded beyond nationalist affiliations. Even those soldiers who did not desert demonstrated the continued importance of prewar attachments through shirking, absenteeism, and exemptions, actions that civilians encouraged and supported. Soldiers and civilians clearly distinguished the local from the national but nonetheless used nationalist language to equate the two spheres in order to appeal to authorities, who expected citizens to embrace protective nationalism. While loyalties that predated the war influenced Mississippians, wartime conditions shaped how they acted on these allegiances in ways that did not always reflect patriotic feelings. This process, in turn, reveals the limited reach and influence of the nineteenth-century nation-state on people who were paradoxically caught up in a war to define that state's very existence.

As is the case with other subjects pertaining to the Civil War, the scholarship on desertion has attempted to assess its impact on the war's outcome, but it has not considered what desertion reveals about the Confederate state's conception of nationalism. Ella Lonn noted that Confederates deserted for numerous reasons, which, when combined, demonstrated "the ultimate failure of the effort at disunion." Similarly, recent studies by Mark Weitz and Robert Sandow emphasize how local loyalties combined with opposition to Union and Confederate policies to fuel desertion and weaken both sides' war efforts.[6] This chapter, by contrast, examines desertion as a process. Rather than focusing on the outcome of desertion, I emphasize how wartime circumstances and established local ties combined to influence deserters' behavior regardless of their patriotic inclinations.

Mississippians began deserting as early as 1862, but the bulk of the source dating indicates that desertion reached its highest levels from late 1863 through the end of the war, coinciding with the general socioeconomic collapse of the state. The Union army gained a foothold in northern Mississippi in 1862 following the battles at Corinth and soon began its destruction of the state's infrastructure and agricultural production. The loss of the railroad limited the state government's ability to transport needed supplies to both the Confederate armies and civilians. Upon capturing Memphis in June 1862, the Federals also gained a key port from which to raid plantations and farms via the Mississippi River's tributaries. These raids, in tandem with the two armies' destruction of land, crops, and supply trains, put the state in dire straits. The 1861 federal blockade closed seaports, leaving planters unable to sell their cotton abroad and merchants unable to import European goods. In addition, destruction from the two armies left the state's already limited domestic production facilities for clothing and war materials in ruins. The result was a shortage of supplies for soldiers and civilians.[7]

The food situation was no better. With thousands of yeoman farmers either serving in the army or already killed, crops went unharvested, and their families suffered. Slaves also fled to Union lines, depriving the Confederacy of much-needed labor. Efforts to diversify the state's agriculture to include more food production were successful at first but fell prey to a series of droughts and floods in 1861, 1862, and 1864. The presence of two armies on Mississippi soil further depleted crop and livestock surpluses, and salt shortages stalled meat production. Even when the state managed to successfully collect food, the destruction of the railroads inhibited its transport. These circumstances brought on economic collapse. Shortages in every type of goods fueled speculation, and the state legislature's printing of notes and bonds spurred inflation. Compounding an already bad situation, the government impressed civilians' supplies and compensated them with worthless Confederate currency. In light of food scarcity and high prices, Mississippians who lived outside of the Union-occupied cities faced destitution.[8]

The Mississippi state government evacuated the capital of Jackson two weeks before it fell to General Ulysses S. Grant's Union army on May 14, 1863, and, aside from a brief return, evacuated permanently in July 1863 when the Federals came back through the city. The capping of this downward spiral came with the fall of the river fortress city of Vicksburg on July 4, 1863, which effectively ended major military operations in Mississippi. The city's capture gave the Federals complete control of the Mississippi River and provided another base from which to march at will through the state. Vicksburg's fall accelerated the process of economic collapse, social dissolution, and military defeat that began in 1862. Fleeing the federal army, the Confederate state government established temporary capitals in Enterprise, Meridian, and ultimately Macon. While in exile, it passed, but could not carry out, relief legislation for civilians and soldiers. In 1863 the state judiciary began to break down, and civil courts largely came to a standstill by 1864. Under Union control and with an exiled state government, conditions in Mississippi outside of the occupied cities teetered on the brink of anarchy.[9]

Much of the chaos spurred by the Civil War in Mississippi came from Confederate deserters. Grant's 1863 decision to parole the twenty-nine thousand rank-and-file soldiers who made up General John Pemberton's Army of Vicksburg significantly added to the problem. While some of these men, especially those from outside of Mississippi, did return to military service in the Army of Tennessee, thousands of Mississippi deserters scattered throughout their state, augmenting a significant number of soldiers already roaming the countryside. In July 1863, for example, Attala County resident Jason Niles noted that "[a] crowd of 29 soldiers, with guns, passed through town, deserters from Gen. Jo Johnston's army." In 1864, Colonel Richard Taylor informed Secretary of War James Seddon that "the highest military crime, desertion, is committed almost with impunity. There does not appear on the part of a deserter to be any difficulty in obtaining shelter in any section of the country." Taylor concluded that "such a condition of disorganization and derangement cannot long exist without producing the most mischievous consequences." He was right. In his August 1864 address, after boosting the number of sheriffs throughout the state, Governor Charles Clark noted that "life and property in many parts of the State were insecure. The courts were seldom holden [sic], and the civil law was almost a dead letter. Deserters, thieves and robbers, banded together, [and] overawed the citizens." Spurred on by Mississippi's precarious conditions, deserters unleashed waves of crime and violence in their home state with seemingly little regard for national feelings.[10]

Focusing primarily on the Border and Mountain South, historians have highlighted the Civil War's anarchic underbelly of lawlessness and have generally linked it to the broader guerrilla war between irregular Union and Confederate partisans that raged in tandem with the war between the formal armies.[11] Noel Fisher demarks East Tennessee's partisan conflict into military, political, and criminal spheres, identifying a post-1862 "epidemic of crime" fueled by social dissolution and only sporadically partisan in nature. Daniel Sutherland covers the whole Confederacy, arguing that crime and violence was an outgrowth of the internal guerrilla war in which "[c]ommon outlaws, deserters and other misfits were exploiting the chaos of war for personal gain."[12] This scholarship has helped advance historical understanding of the interrelation between the battlefields and the home front during the Civil War. Yet the carnage caused by deserters in Deep South Mississippi was less an outgrowth of guerrilla conflict than it was the result of organized collective violence spurred by social collapse.

A breakdown in social order is a key element in the development of violence. Social order results from "the way societies craft institutions that support the existence of specific forms of human organization," and these characteristics are "intimately related to how societies limit and control violence."[13] Warfare can disrupt the social order by severely limiting the functional capacity of institutions like state government, courts, militia, and police. Such was the case in wartime Mississippi. While the Union army occupied major garrison towns, vast areas beyond these points and the Confederate frontier became what Stephen Ash calls "no-man's land," territory that existed in a "vacuum of authority, a twilight zone neither Union nor Confederate" where criminality flourished.[14]

Under these conditions, Confederate deserters engaged in "opportunistic collective violence." According to Charles Tilly, this form of deviance happens "when, as a consequence of shielding from routine surveillance and repression, individuals or clusters of individuals use immediately damaging means to pursue ends that would be unavailable or forbidden to them under other circumstances." These damaging means include "violent interactions that often take place during or in the immediate aftermath of major conflicts." Such violent reactions to conflict are integral parts of the human cultural process that occur when the normal channels for conflict resolution are destroyed. Historian Randolph Roth argues that violent crime increases during civil wars because, in such conflicts, governments' ability to compel law and order substantially weakens, causing crimes like homicides directed at political rivals to occur alongside other homicides that appear apolitical but "correlate just as strongly with the lack of political stability." In such conditions, Roth writes, "some men become predatory killers, raping, robbing, and murdering as individuals or members of gangs," and although they may initially act as political partisans, when they end up on the losing side in opposition to a new political order, they turn to preying indiscriminately on allies and noncombatants alike.[15] Wartime conditions in Mississippi fostered this type of deviant behavior.

Protective nationalists interpreted human actions as reflections of either Union or Confederate allegiance and judged marauding deserters according to this paradigm. This labeling also stemmed from a tendency to imbue positive attributes to the concept of loyalty. Yet deserters who wreaked havoc in Mississippi acted on self- and gang loyalties that promoted material rewards and freedom from social restraints. As Simon Keller notes, "loyalty is not an intrinsically evaluative concept. Without some substantive argument, there is no guarantee that if something counts as loyal then it counts as something good." The ties that bind gang activity fuel pillaging, and criminal gangs thrive on activities that outsiders may consider deviant. Deserters' destructive behavior likely had an antecedent in the antebellum culture of "jolly fellowship," in which men collectively engaged in borderline deviant—sometimes illegal—public behavior like drinking, fighting, and gambling in order to gain validation of manliness from their peers. The line between jolly fellowship and gang criminality could be thin, as the former could easily lead to the latter, especially in wartime conditions that fostered both.[16]

Confederate partisans often connected deserters' deviant behavior to their supposed disloyalty. Historians, in turn, have followed suit by categorizing crime and violence in the Confederacy as both an offshoot of the guerrilla war and as evidence of anti-Confederate sentiment. This judgment is more applicable to the Border and Mountain South, regions that were more fiercely divided over secession and war. In Deep South Mississippi, however, where unionism was less prevalent, conditions caused by the war—but not necessarily born out of patriotic sentiments—nurtured collective violence.

Historian Harry Ward notes that this phenomenon had precedents in the American Revolution, when bandits like the aforementioned Cowboys and Skinners operated "between the lines" of the war's patriot and loyalist sides to pillage civilians. Much like the occupied South's "no-man's land," the Revolution's contested spaces experienced anarchic conditions that fostered criminality. Despite bandits' partisan claims, their activities were often driven by self-interest and group loyalties that fed their desire to loot. Eric Hobsbawm explains that bandits are "symptoms of crisis and tension in their society—of famine, pestilence, war or anything else that disrupts it," and for this reason such groups "abounded in periods of disorder, war or its aftermath." This is what happened in Civil War Mississippi, where deserters' banditry demonstrated the limits of the hearth-and-home thesis as applied to Confederate soldiers.[17]

Deserters in Mississippi terrorized citizens throughout the state during the war. An August 1863 Confederate report claimed that "the number of absentees, stragglers, and deserters from our army scattered over the State is . . . alarmingly great." In May 1864, authorities concluded that "many thousands of deserters, and absentees from the army banded together throughout Mississippi perpetrating outrages." Alarmed at these developments, Mississippi senator James Phelan told Jefferson Davis: "[O]ur state literally swarms with deserters. In my own county . . . they appeared at the polls in the late election in armed bodies and defied arrest." Harvey Walter reported similar circumstances in northern Mississippi. "[T]he country is swarming with deserters, and without a force of regular troops I fear little can be done to break up these clans of tories," he wrote. Walter estimated that the number of rampaging deserters was "not less than 7,000." In 1864, General Leonidas Polk detached companies throughout Mississippi to quell the evils perpetrated by "a very large number of deserters from all the armies of the Confederacy," who organized into "formidable bands" and declared open "hostility to the Government." By the winter of 1865, the state had become a "deserters home" in which men were caught "roaming the country as jayhawkers, cotton-stealers and runners, [and] marauders, jeopardizing alike the discipline of the army and the safety of the citizen."[18]

Quantifying the exact number of deserters in the Confederacy is a near impossible task due to the incomplete nature of the available records. The most recent scholarly estimate puts the total number of white Mississippians who served in the Confederate armies at 94,414. The only official number of deserters in Mississippi comes from an 1870 report submitted to Congress that estimated them at 11,660, or 12 percent of the total number of

Mississippians who fought in Confederate armies. Certainly, this number was a small percentage of the larger whole, and it has led some historians to downplay the ways marauding deserters influenced public perception about national loyalty. Yet, as Mark Weitz notes, amid chaotic wartime conditions, deserters had power beyond their numbers. Contemporaries consistently remarked on the negative effects desertion had on wartime morale.[19] The actual number of deserters in Mississippi is less important than the psychological effect they had on the state's population.

Perry County sheriff G. W. Bradley understood all too well the impact that rampaging deserters had on civilian morale. "[T]he conditions of things in this county" necessitated "some relief," he warned Governor Clark. Bradley reported that deserters swarmed through the southeastern Piney Woods area, hindering his ability to collect taxes and even threatening his life. The deserters were "in formidable gangs [and] doing mischief . . . burning & destroying the property of all loyal citizens such as will not sympathize with them." Confederate cavalry had been detailed to Perry County to apprehend the deserters, but the cavalry, Bradley wrote, "prowl through the county frolicking and stealing too much," and proved mostly ineffectual at rounding up the deserters. "I will venture to say that there are more deserters in this county today than was here when the Cavalry came here," Bradley noted. The deserters had already murdered several citizens who piloted the cavalry, and there seemed to be no means for quelling the violence.[20]

Other counties in the Piney Woods faced similar problems. In January 1864, residents of Smith, Jones, and Jasper Counties demanded that Clark stop what they suspected were more than three thousand deserters running wild in the vicinity. "There is reason to believe that they get ammunition on the Coast of this state; that they are compelling good & true men to leave Jones County." The deserters also plundered at will. "Unless a strong force is soon sent for our protection many or all of us will be plundered of our moveable property," the petitioners concluded. Smith County was particularly "infested with deserters of the worst class" who regularly held "Union or peace meetings" and threatened to kill anyone "who dares speak out against them."[21]

The Piney Woods deserters defy easy categorization. Were they "disloyal" Confederates? Did they desert to defend hearth and home? The answer to the former is debatable, while the answer to the latter in many cases seems to be "no." Regardless of the deserters' motivation, witnesses described their behavior in nationalistic terms. The Piney Woods deserters destroyed the property of "loyal citizens" and made "Union speeches." Such accusations were born out of the same circulating nationalist discourse that led other

Mississippians to swear the Union oath as a means to other ends, whatever their actual national feelings.

Protective nationalists fostered this wartime environment by judging all behavior through a nationalist lens. This approach led ardent Confederates to make no distinctions between objective unionism, behavior that harmed the Confederacy and, by extension, aided the Union even if it was not intended to do so, and subjective unionism, in which people explicitly professed unionism as motivating their anti-Confederate behavior. If historians embrace all vaguely anti-Confederate behavior as objective unionism, concluding that because someone harmed the Confederacy he was necessarily a "unionist," they risk inflating the number of actual subjective unionists. This approach places them back into the "weak" or "strong" Confederate camps and obscures a wider range of loyalties that likely influenced deserters' actions. This approach also risks overemphasizing the power and reach of the Confederate state by assuming that Mississippians consistently tailored their behavior to reflect the influence of that state and its nationalistic goals, a conclusion not always supported by the evidence.

In the case of Mississippi deserters, the language of nationalism may conceal as much as it exposes. The most famous of the Piney Woods deserters were the Jones County–based Knight Company, led by Newton Knight and part of the "Free State of Jones," which was falsely rumored to have seceded from the Confederacy. The Knight Company operated out of an anti-Confederate ideology born out of a prewar opposition to secession and resentment over the Conscription Act. Researcher Ed Payne has also discovered that 201 Mississippians from the Piney Woods region enlisted in the Union's First and Second New Orleans Infantry. Still, the majority of the Piney Woods military-age men did not join the Union army, and the famous Knight Company remained in Jones County, where they clashed with Confederate cavalry in what historian Victoria Bynum calls an "inner civil war."[22] The Free State of Jones is one of the few documented cases in which Confederate authorities' charges of unionism rang true. The Jones County deserters' unionist leanings were widely known among Rebel authorities (although they still referred to the Knight Company as "lawless banditti" and "outlaws").[23] Beyond the Jones County unionists, however, Confederates often used the "unionist" charge to disparage marauding deserters throughout the state. These injections of multiple meanings into the outlaw label, however, may have obscured the very real and widespread existence of war-induced banditry that had less to do with national affiliations and more to do with base opportunism.

As the war turned Mississippi into a fractured society beset by the break-down of law and order, deserters plundered and citizens accused them of treason. In December 1863, for example, "an organized band of bold thieves consisting chiefly of deserters from the army" stole some thirty to forty thousand dollars' worth of freight from Mobile and Ohio Railroad cars in northern Mississippi. Earlier that spring, deserters in Choctaw County were "executing their malignant designs on good and loyal citizens" in the neigh-borhood of Bankston. The deserters burned houses, destroyed corn cribs and cotton bins, and attacked and robbed "loyal citizens" in their homes and along public highways. The Macon *Beacon* reported in April 1864 that Smith County and adjacent counties were "crowded with deserters and disaf-fected persons," who were "deserting and banding together for the purpose of thieving and pillaging the loyal citizens of the country." They forced citizens who failed to endorse their "many acts of villainy" to choose either exile or assassination.[24] Witnesses claimed that the deserters made "loyal" citizens targets of their outrages, and, by extension, suggested that deserters were "disloyal" Confederates.

In Decatur, Newton County, a man who at one time "made a good sol-dier" became upset when the army confiscated his horse. In retaliation, he led a band of deserters who took control of the neighborhood. The group included men who had apparently "made faithful soldiers for three years." They hid out in the swamps to avoid capture by the militia, and many local women aided these renegades by blowing trumpets to alert them of danger. The deserters killed one local man and savagely beat five others. A witness to the mayhem claimed that the army should "send them to Vicksburg for they are all Union and oppose the Confederate Government." Simpson County experienced similar problems when deserters "burned up two gin houses & one bridge across the river." By early 1865, "deserters and lawless men" had gained control of the Simpson County courts and vowed revenge after the provost guard shot fifty-six-year-old farmer James Rogers. Two of Rogers's sons, one of whom was likely Abel A. Rogers, a former member of Company A, Thirty-Ninth Infantry Simpson County Greys, were among the desert-ers who threatened to kill any Rebel soldiers who dared enter the county. According to Simpson resident Richard Cooper, Confederate army person-nel could not trust many people in the neighborhood who "on account of their relationship to deserters were of questionable loyalty."[25] Although the Simpson County case may seem like a clear-cut case of unionist deserters in revolt, the distinction between anti-Confederate behavior and opportunistic collective violence could blur in wartime conditions that fostered the latter.

The fact that Newton and Simpson County civilians aided deserters in their resistance to conscription does suggest that opposition to Confederate policies—if not outright unionism—influenced such behavior. This collusion between deserters and civilians, however, led one witness to conflate the two motivations by claiming that "they are all Union and oppose the Confederate Government." Yet, the breakdown of law enforcement and social order further encouraged deserters' pillaging and violence, which in turn accelerated the collapse of civil authority. This phenomenon was especially evident in Simpson County, where deserters gained control of the courts. In the Simpson case, the killing of James Rogers appeared to have aroused familial, as opposed to national, allegiances, which resulted in retaliatory threats against intruding Confederate soldiers. Nonetheless, witness Richard Cooper stated that the deserters' civilian accomplices were of "questionable loyalty," suggesting that they were disloyal by association. Another witness's claim that the courts had been taken over by "deserters and lawless men," however, suggests that some civilians recognized that the line between patriotically motivated chaos and the pursuit of "damaging means to pursue ends that would be unavailable or forbidden to them under other circumstances" was blurring.

Circuit court judge Robert Hudson, who witnessed the social breakdown of Mississippi's interior during the war, understood how the distinction between "deserters and lawless men" was perhaps too fine. Although he concluded that wartime Mississippi had become rife with "disloyal" people, he connected this alleged treason to the collapse of civil authority across the state. Hudson's complaints about deserters echoed reports of other witnesses. "The state is now under the tacit rule of deserters, thieves, and disloyal men and women," he warned Davis in March 1864. "Open-day and midnight robbery is practiced every day and night . . . by deserters, pretended soldiers, and soldiers with their commands," the judge continued; "privates steal and officers refuse to give the property when identified by the citizens and even punish the citizens for making claim to it." He claimed that many men had deserted multiple times without punishment and spent their time engaging in "gaming parties, drunkenness, marrying [sic], horse-racing, and stealing." Rather than claiming that these men deserted to protect hearth and home, Hudson observed that "they are not only absent from the army, but are *a great curse to home and the communities where they prowl*—and should the Yankees visit the interior, they will be joined as guides, informants & plunderers by the last one of them" (my emphasis). While he assured Davis that he was "no alarmist," he nonetheless warned that "Mississippi is almost a Sodom and Gomorrah ... and the day of our salvation, if neglected for a day, is forever gone."²⁶

Hudson made similar reports to Governor Clark, and although he continued to use the language of nationalism to call deserters "disloyal," he also connected the collapse of civil law to the explosion of criminal behavior among deserters who became a "curse" to hearth and home. "By the laws of this state it is made the imperative duty of all sheriffs, members of Boards of Police, Justices of the Peace and all other County officers to arrest and send to the army all deserters & evading conscripts in their respective counties," he told Clark. The problem for Hudson was that law enforcement officers were utterly derelict in their duties to arrest deserters, who were "killing or outraging the persons & property of good citizens." Hudson observed how the breakdown of law and order enabled deserters to commit opportunistic collective violence, with little regard for the sanctity of hearth and home. He also understood how kin networks and local ties supported the collective aspect of their behavior. The root of the problem regarding "the remissness" of civil county officers was that "their nearest neighbors, and often their own sons are deserters, with whom they meet, and sometimes feed & entertain without attempting to arrest, or even to reprimand them," he wrote.²⁷ Yet even as Hudson recognized how micro loyalties and social dissolution enabled deserters to wreak havoc, he also viewed their behavior as stemming from disloyalty to the Confederacy. He equated objective with subjective unionism and warned that the problem was spreading.

Hudson believed that the natural inclination for deserters was to join up with the Yankees. In late May 1864, he heard from Yazoo County sheriff William Mangum that the miscreants had spread from the interior to the Union-occupied Delta. "I am truly sorry to know that the counties of Leake, Attala, Neshoba, Winston & other counties are now and have been for the last six months emptying their filthy, base, disloyal, deserting, stealing, murdering population into Yazoo," Hudson told Mangum. He characterized the deserters as motivated by a rough mixture of delinquency and disloyalty. "They pretend to go there [at Union lines] to get corn to live on, but their real object is to avoid our army, steal, plunder, and be with the Yankees," Hudson warned, adding that "I know many of them, and know them to be a base, vile & worthless set, who never made a good or honest living anywhere."²⁸ Hudson identified some of the men by name, revealing how kin ties could become gang loyalties in the right conditions.

The deserters whom Hudson identified ran in family and neighborhood groups. Thomas, Reuban, and William Barrett of Neshoba County, and John and Samuel Adcock of Leake County, deserted from Mississippi regiments raised in their neighborhoods. Members of the Waller, Breazeale, Mooney, and Scott families of Neshoba and Leake Counties were also among the group. Amid the precarious wartime conditions, these family and neighborhood bonds became gang loyalties that enabled collective violence. Hudson recognized this but also put a nationalist spin on their criminality. "They are abolitionists, spies, deserters, liars, thieves, murderers and every thing foul & damnable," he wrote.[29] While likely subconsciously on Hudson's part, his comment nonetheless encapsulated how war degraded the social order and caused ostensibly partisan actors to act violently without necessarily partisan designs. The deserters went from "abolitionists," "spies," and "deserters," all terms indicating disloyalty to the Confederacy, into the criminal realm of "liars," "thieves," and "murderers." Hudson recognized how criminal behavior flourished in the right conditions, and he equated common criminality with treasonous behavior.

Much like Hudson, Captain Wirt Thompson of the Twenty-Fourth Mississippi Infantry recognized deserters' overt criminality but still framed their behavior in nationalist terms. Following an 1864 leave of absence spent in southeastern Greene County, Thompson wrote:

> Previous to starting to Mississippi I was aware of the presence of large numbers of deserters and conscripts in that section of the State, but until I arrived in the country I did not know that they were in organized bodies and committing depredations and deeds of violence, bloodshed, and outlawry, and that there was no force in the country to contend against them or to defend the loyal portion of the citizens from their savage caprices and brutal whims.

By 1864, the deserters controlled several swaths of southeastern Mississippi, and civilians lived in fear of these outlaws' wrath. The gangs exiled some dissenters and murdered other citizens in their own homes. The deserters also targeted conscription officers like Captain John Bradford, whom they spared from the noose but banished from Greene County. On the same day, the deserters also captured the area's tax-in-kind funds and forced a local resident to distribute the money to local families. "I was told that they boast of fighting for the Union," Thompson wrote, claiming that they had "frequent and uninterrupted communication" with the Yankees on Ship Island.[30] Although they terrorized many residents, the deserters' distributing of money to local families suggests collusion between some civilians and the renegades. Yet, even if divisions between local families had nationalist origins, the deserters' behavior indicated that gang loyalties, exacerbated by the chaotic circumstances, had pushed Greene County's war beyond partisan boundaries. Civilians likely chose to side with, or resisted, the deserters in a battle for wartime spoils. This internal battle eclipsed a conflict that may have originated in divisions between pro- and anti-Confederate sympathizers. Thompson, framing the events according to the nationalist paradigm, thought that unionism motivated the deserters, but their actions suggest banditry fueled by opportunistic conditions.

Greene County became a bandit-ruled ministate that pitted neighbor against neighbor. Residents feared leaving their homes. Some eavesdropped on their neighbors' houses by night and reported to the outlaws by day. The deserters burned bridges and ferryboats, and attacked passersby from swamps and roadside thickets. They also pillaged horses, wagons, guns, and whiskey from civilians and beat, murdered, or exiled those who resisted. The deserters' collective discipline amazed Thompson, who described how "deserters from every army and from every State" had "colonels, majors, captains, and lieutenants" and claimed to be "not less than a thousand strong in organized bodies, besides what others are outsiders and disloyal citizens."[31] Amid the vacuum of lawlessness, the deserters' group loyalties allowed them to commit organized banditry. Whatever their reasons for abandoning the army, their actions suggest the influence of self-interest inflamed by the possible spoils of war rather than a desire to protect hearth and home.

Mississippi's Gulf Coast also suffered from war-induced privations. The Confederate government saw little strategic value in the state's coastline and had abandoned it to the Federals by 1862. Gulf Coast Mississippians protested this abandonment. Hancock County resident Freeman Jones warned Governor Pettus that the removal of home guards from the coast would "lead to open rebellion at home." By the end of 1862, eight months after the Union captured New Orleans, scarcities of corn and bread drove citizens to travel to far-off Mobile to buy high-priced goods. In January 1863, a Pascagoula resident told Pettus that "famine is inevitable and will drive the poor people to the Yankees & invite them to come and protect them from starvation." That spring, the *Weekly Mississippian* alerted the governor that coastal residents faced "the giant skeleton of Famine." Desperate conditions combined with the absence of civil and military authority to spur banditry in coastal counties. An 1863 report noted that deserters "infest the coast." A year later, one Confederate officer claimed that with the state's seacoast "within the lines of the enemy," Confederate sympathizers were "being murdered and driven from the country by deserters from our army" who held "communication with the enemy off of Ship Island."[32] The Confederate government's abandonment of the Gulf Coast resulted in a worsening of the region's social conditions, which, when combined with the Union presence, fueled Confederate deserters' destructive behavior.

By 1863, especially after the fall of Vicksburg, witnesses' tendency to associate deserters' pillaging with either objective or subjective unionism waned. Mississippians became more inclined to view deserters as a criminal element that needed to be squelched. For its part, the Confederate government proved largely unable to apprehend or stop the outlaws. As the war reached its midpoint, witnesses across the state increasingly commented on deserters' criminality but eschewed connecting such behavior to alleged anti-Confederate feelings.

In March 1863, for example, Pettus authorized Lieutenant Colonel W. L. Lowry to round up "certain marauding bands now infesting the counties of Tishomingo, Tippah and Marshall" who had organized "for the purpose of seizing and confiscating . . . the goods . . . of the citizens of said counties." Similarly, witness H. Winslow reported that the counties west of Columbus were "filled with deserters and robbers, who are devastating the country of horses and mules." Particularly onerous was a gang led by a Captain Bobo, who claimed war department authority to plunder. "In many cases, these men of Bobo's have taken the cotton and supplies of people, and themselves sold it upon the lines for their own uses and benefit," Winslow noted. Another gang, led by a Monroe County farmer and former sergeant in the Fourteenth Mississippi Infantry named W. F. English, stole $900 from a citizen and generally preyed upon "the unprotected families of soldiers." Calhoun County farm laborer James Cartright, "a notorious robber and spy" formerly of the Fourth Mississippi Infantry, commanded another gang of thieves. In Yazoo County, a partisan ranger described conscript commander Samuel Dyer's regiment as "deserters" and "conscripts." These men were also "professional thieves and robbers" and "a terror to the citizens and a disgrace to the Confederate army." In northern Mississippi, Colonel George Hodge explained that after deserting with a portion of his command, a Captain Reson "had established himself and inaugurated a system of private plunder ostensibly against the common enemy, but too often without regard to the sentiments of the owners of property." Further, Reson consistently urged friends still in the army to join his band, "luring them by promises of brigandage and free quarters."[33] Witnesses variously described these gangs as "marauding," a "terror," "robbers," and "thieves" who were attracted to "brigandage." Although deserters never entirely escaped the "disloyal" tag, civilians and military authorities more often emphasized their criminality, and that they posed a direct threat to Mississippi neighborhoods.

These outlaws terrified civilians. Tishomingo County residents complained of being "surrounded on two sides at least by a population in part disloyal & mixed with Bushwhackers & deserters, ready at any time ... to pounce upon us & commit the worst acts of depredation & violence." Likewise, a Franklin County resident told Clark of "deserters from this section who have committed many depredations in this county from their familiar acquaintance with the roads and paths so as to escape the vigilance of the regular pickets and scouts." Betty Beaumont witnessed "much lawlessness," which caused people to live "in constant fear of losing their little possessions." She feared traveling the Natchez countryside, where "lawless bands calling themselves soldiers" were "prowling around ready to rob and even murder." These "bushwhackers or pretended Confederate soldiers," Beaumont noted, "infested all the roads and made everything unsafe." In early 1864, Louisa Lovell contemplated shipping her valuables out of Natchez, which was beset with arsonists and thieves. "Everybody is robbed and plundered without mercy," she told her husband; "some desperadoes set fire to Melrose [Plantation] about a week ago."[34] Such roving "desperadoes" were more often than not Confederate deserters who took advantage of the breakdown of law enforcement to engage in opportunistic collective violence, especially armed robbery.

In July 1864, for example, Confederate cavalrymen in Covington County arrested "quite a number of deserters & outlaws who had banded together" under the veneer of organizing for the service. In fact, these deserters organized "really for bad purposes," which included taking "revenge on all good & loyal citizens." Eliza Sively reported that authorities in Hinds County had arrested one Bob Carpender "for stealing Mrs. Washington's cotton and selling it to the Yanks." Carpender was also charged with "desertion and highway robbery" before he bribed a guard and escaped. On her way to Memphis in August 1863, Caroline Seabury met a Mississippi family hiding on a river island after being plundered by "a band of Southern guerillas," deserters from Chalmers's army, who "robbed them in broad daylight of all the money & clothing they could find." The family had known the robbers for years, and the thieves were outraged to find a Union oath among the family's possessions. While partisan divides seemed to motivate the deserters to plunder their neighbors, they did not find the Union oath until *after* they began ransacking the family's possessions. Hence, the gang took advantage of the chaotic wartime conditions to steal *for themselves,* not to act on the Confederacy's behalf. The family's alleged unionism provided an easy justification for plunder, but soldiers-turned-bandits hardly needed such an excuse. Samuel Agnew recognized how the wartime conditions turned former soldiers into criminals. When two soldiers robbed a neighbor walking home at night, Agnew remarked that "a good many of our soldiers are becoming lawless. Some of them are to be almost as much feared as the Yankees."[35] With the breakdown of law and order, the line between partisanship and opportunistic violence often vanished. Mississippi's deserters could not reasonably claim to be simultaneously plundering and protecting hearth and home, and civilians knew it.

Deserters often invoked Confederate military authority in the service of gang interests that bore little tangible connections to any kind of service to the nation. Beaumont's observation that these men were "pretend Confederate soldiers" was quite apt, since they used military authority as a means to advance criminal ends. During the winter of 1864, for example, Bolivar County citizens complained to Governor Clark about deserter gangs, "knaves all," who invaded citizens' homes brandishing falsified papers supposedly signed by Confederate general Stephen D. Lee. "Their game is robbery," the citizens wrote; "they take mules—horses—provisions—anything they lay their hands on, robbing everybody of any money they can find." In one particular incident, acting like "anything else but the soldier," the gang, led by a Captain Price, arrested and handcuffed local men and ransacked their houses while insulting onlooking women. "Somebody is to blame," the civilian victims fumed; "we don't think this the way to conquer a place, on the contrary, we believe it to be the opposite."[36] By claiming military authority to rob for their own personal gain, the deserters threatened civilians who believed that such abuse of authority was "no way to conquer" the hearts and minds of those on the home front. It was difficult to accept the military as a force for the greater national good when soldiers invoked it to terrorize hearths and homes.

Marauding deserters in other parts of the state similarly cloaked their behavior under the banner of military authority. Stationed in Marshall County, cavalry scout R. H. Bowers complained to Captain Thomas Henderson about "stragglers from almost every cavalry command we have, who profess to be scouts, but who rob persons, steal horses, trade in cotton & do everything else except what duty requires & what a true Confederate soldier would do." Carrying confiscation papers forged with General Pemberton's signature, the deserters robbed civilians and federal cotton buyers, and then they sold the stolen cotton in Memphis, pocketing the profits. They also stole horses from civilians, and, on one occasion, they even took Bowers's own mount. In another instance, they threatened to torch a woman's house if she did not give up her cash. "Is there no way to protect the citizens from such lawless bands?" Bowers wondered. "[T]hey should be made to suffer for their acts but I have no way of bringing them to justice." Henderson told General Pemberton that "the high-way robbers of whom Bowers writes, are mostly deserters from *our* army & *pretend* to act under your authority." Bowers begged the general to authorize partisan rangers to snuff out the "terrible annoyance."[37] These deserters' criminal behavior earned them tags like "knaves," "lawless bands," and "high-way robbers." Bowers's inability to protect the citizenry spoke to a major weakness in the state's capacity to enforce national loyalty in its soldiery and defend civilians within its borders. The army was not sufficient a nationalist symbol to stave off the influence of deserters' gang loyalties and their self-interested drive to plunder.

Gang loyalties were precisely the kind of micro allegiances that influenced a group of deserters/horse thieves near Pontotoc County. In March 1864, Samuel Agnew attended the magistrate trial of one of the alleged thieves, Pontotoc native Napoleon Bonaparte Bolen. One day in March, a group of men that included John Chisholm and John Watkins confronted a traveling minister named Randall and searched him under suspicion that he was a spy. While the men soon let Randall go, his horse went missing. A search crew eventually found the horse—and Bolen—concealed in a thicket on the property of one William H. Gober. When arrested, Bolen initially identified himself as "Armstrong" and denied stealing the horse. Later, when threatened with the noose, he admitted to obtaining it from a group of thieves that included John Watkins of Chickasaw County and John Chisholm of Itawamba County, the two men who had initially harassed Randall. The gang of thieves also included Luther Privet of Pontotoc County, William H. Gober and Littleton Wages of Tippah County, and Lafayette Bolen, a native of Saint Clair County, Alabama, and likely a relative of Napoleon's since both men were born in Alabama. While the coerced nature of Napoleon Bolen's testimony cautions against taking it as irrefutable evidence of his guilt, the circumstances of his arrest, combined with the horse thieves' local connections, suggest that he was in some way associated with the gang.[38]

Besides being caught with the horse, Bolen, as Agnew noted, "did not feel safe" in jail without a guard, suggesting he may have feared the gang's reprisal for his fingering them in the theft. Bolen's initial assumption of an alias also indicated that he might have had something to hide. In addition to these circumstances, Bolen and the horse thieves shared local connections. Excepting Lafayette Bolen, they all lived in the cluster of northeastern counties near the Tennessee border, and they all served in the following Mississippi regiments: the Thirty-First Infantry, Twelfth Cavalry, Seventh Cavalry, Eighteenth Cavalry, and First Infantry. Lafayette Bolen served in the Fifty-First Alabama Cavalry. Each of these regiments mustered out in, or near, their home counties. The men also came from similar socioeconomic backgrounds, either as small farmers or as farm laborers who owned little or no property, and none of them were slaveholders save John Watkins, whose father owned fourteen slaves. Given these local ties, the men likely associated with each other before the war, and these same ties persisted as they deserted and operated as a criminal gang. For his part, Napoleon Bolen may have betrayed the gang when threatened with hanging, but self-interest need not dispel the influence of past group allegiances.[39]

So who were Mississippi's deserters? A chart demonstrating the socioeconomic and county-level data of Mississippi deserters (located in appendix B) reveals that they differed little in background from average Confederate soldiers. Out of 177 known Mississippi deserters, 123 appear in the 1860 census. Only 14 of the 123 (11.4 percent) owned slaves or came from slaveholding families. A dozen of these slave owners, 86 percent, owned ten slaves or fewer. The remainder, 109 deserters (89 percent), did not own slaves at all. In addition, out of the sample of 123, 35 of them (28.5 percent) owned less than $1,000 worth of real estate, while 61 (49.6 percent) owned no real estate. Only 27 deserters (22 percent) owned or came from families that owned $1,000 or more in real estate. The value of deserters' personal estates was slightly more spread out: 66 deserters (54 percent) owned personal estates worth less than $1,000, while 31 deserters (25 percent) held no personal estate at all. Meanwhile, 26 deserters (21 percent) had a personal estate valued at $1,000 or more. The majority of deserters, 89.4 percent, were either farmers or farm laborers. Thirty of them (24 percent) were poor whites; 59 of the 123 (48 percent) were plain folk. A single deserter fell into the category of middling or large farmer, and a mere 4 of them were planters or from planter families. Thus, the majority of the Mississippi deserters were either poor whites or plain folk who worked in agriculture.[40]

These deserters were, in fact, quite normal, and representative of the average Mississippi soldier, a fact reflected in their social and economic backgrounds. A majority of them were family men, and their average age was twenty-six. Of the sample of 123, 76 men (62 percent) were married, 75 (61 percent) were heads of household, and 68 (55 percent) had children.

These figures correspond with conclusions reached by Larry Logue in his random sampling of 1,010 Mississippi soldiers. He finds that 77 percent were either farmers or other agricultural workers, compared to 89.4 percent of my sampled deserters. The average soldier's age in Logue's sample was 25.6, matching the deserters' average age of 26. Furthermore, 61.2 percent were heads of household, equaling the 61 percent of deserters who were heads of household. Logue includes slaves with Mississippi soldiers' personal property; thus, his sample does not specify the percentage of slaveholders versus non-slaveholders. Aaron Marrs, however, finds that most South Carolina deserters, like those in Mississippi, were non-slaveholders. Joseph Glatthaar shows that the majority of men in the Army of Northern Virginia, 62.8 percent, did not own slaves. The percentage of Mississippi deserters who were non-slaveholders was higher, at 89 percent, revealing that deserters represented the average Confederate soldier in most respects, but they did have a lower percentage of slave ownership.[41]

Mississippi deserters reflected the socioeconomic status of the average Confederate soldier and were also a microcosm of antebellum Southern society in general.[42] Although most were poor, suggesting that they may have been inclined to pillage when circumstances allowed, they were also mostly married men with children. They were therefore fully enmeshed in the normal social order before the war, which suggests that it was the war-induced breakdown of that order that drove them to banditry. Why then, did these normal Confederate soldiers resort to collective violence when many others did not? Charles Tilly notes that there is no explanation for why some people perform "self-serving damage," since such motivations reside in the individual psyche. Nonetheless, it is possible to identify the conditions that fuel opportunism, which include the combination of interpersonal relations like group loyalties in conjunction with pertinent environmental conditions.[43]

Beyond the deserters' shared socioeconomic backgrounds, the census information presented in appendix B also reveals geographic links that further indicate the presence of prewar local attachments. First, they rarely deserted alone. Sources providing deserters' names almost always listed two or more men at one time, often those who hailed from the same county, the same neighborhoods, and served in the same company or regiment mustered out of those counties and neighborhoods. The chart in appendix B has been organized alphabetically by county to show these connections. Sociologist Peter Bearman finds that "solidarity in homogenous companies," combined with "local county society," created a "localist identity" that influenced Confederate soldiers to desert. He shows that men who deserted in clusters all came from the same neighborhoods, in communities with spatially close households. Bearman concludes that "old localisms" that were "nurtured within the Confederate army" influenced deserters more than their collective identity as soldiers, causing them to pursue ends like desertion that were different from expectations of soldiers as dedicated to military cause and comrades.[44] Although I argue that Bearman's conclusion, that localism was stronger than Confederate nationalism, is questionable, the importance he places on local attachments is illuminating and reflects the data on Mississippi deserters. It underscores why their decisions were not necessarily connected to nationalism.

The prevalence of these local attachments helps in part to explain deserters' ability to commit organized collective violence under wartime conditions. These group ties were already in place, but the war's circumstances severed them from their traditional social moorings, thereby rendering them vulnerable to thriving in conditions suitable to group activity but bereft of the normal constraints that limited the collective propensity toward deviant behavior.

Desertion, however, was not the only conduit through which banditry flourished in Civil War Mississippi. Joining partisan ranger units—officially sanctioned guerrillas whom the government commissioned to operate near their homes and to turn over captured weapons and other goods to army quartermasters in exchange for payment—allowed men to stay in their home territory while still ostensibly serving the Confederacy. As the Confederate army contracted toward Vicksburg in 1863 with the Federals in pursuit, Mississippians flocked to these companies, claiming that they could better defend their state if free to navigate the back roads and swamps and ambush Union soldiers. As army-sanctioned guerrillas, partisan rangers played a role in the larger guerrilla conflict that wracked the Confederate home front. Quite often, however, the independence of partisan service, coupled with conditions in the state, drove ranger groups to banditry.[45]

Reporting from Grenada, Mississippi, Brigadier General M. Jeff Thompson recognized how the partisan ranger policy facilitated criminality. He claimed that partisan ranger corps did not understand "the true object of the act of Congress or the true material with which success is to be gained." According to Thompson, a pioneer spirit should guide partisan rangers to "brave the hardships and dangers of the frontier to better their condition." It was the bravery of "the mountaineer and the explorer" that rangers should emulate, "not the bravery that dares the halter to steal a horse, or your knife, to rob your pocket." He concluded that those "most anxious" to join ranger outfits "have been induced to believe that they are to be a band of licensed robbers, and are not the men to care whether it be friend or foe they rob."[46] As Thompson recognized, much like the roving deserter bands, some partisan rangers operated as organized banditti and were a direct threat to Mississippians on the home front. They chose their targets indiscriminately: whether their victims held Union or Confederate loyalties did not factor into rangers' decisions to rob these people. National allegiances likewise had little bearing on the rangers' personal decisions to rob. Banditry, not nationalism, motivated these looters.

Partisan units sometimes exploited civilians' trust in them as protectors in order to rob those civilians. Betty Beaumont described how groups of men "professing to be home guards" entered civilians' homes on "familiar footing" by promising the residents protection. Entering people's dwellings, however, allowed these "pretend patriots" to discreetly steal jewelry and other items "whenever a convenient opportunity occurred." In one instance a "general" came into Beaumont's house and asked her husband to see one of her rings for "close inspection." After a lengthy conversation, the general discretely departed with the ring. "[W]hile conversing with their entertainers about the outrages of the Federals and condemning the rapacity of the speculators ... these home protectors were constantly on the alert to take every advantage possible in the way of enriching themselves," Beaumont remarked.[47] Her language was telling: she used the phrase "home protectors" ironically to protest the actions of partisan units who invoked military authority to pilfer, rather than protect, Southern homes.

Other reports supported Beaumont's claims that partisan rangers had theft on their agendas. In early 1863, a Hancock County resident complained to Governor Pettus that "three to four hundred ... conscripts and deserters," most of whom "were members of [Major Abner C.] Steed's Partisan Rangers," had disbanded in the area. Although some fled to Union lines, others emptied into nearby Marion County's swamps, from which they raided Hancock County "in small parties, pillaging and plundering private property." During the summer of 1864, Monroe County resident M. A. Banks told Governor Clark that while he disliked speaking of soldiers "in any other way than in their praise," there were some troops "organized under orders from your Excellency" who were "playing but a small part of the true and gentlemanly soldier." A ranger company under a Captain Little had ransacked Banks's home multiple times and stolen whiskey from his young son. Claiming the authority to destroy illegal distilleries, the men instead spared only those distilleries whose owners gave the rangers a sufficient amount of spirits. Banks implored Clark to "disband them and let them go into the regular service." Echoing Banks, Colonel William Falkner described ranger companies who plundered civilians as a "great nuisance." These ranger squads "are not serving their country, but are making fortunes for themselves by taking property from what they call Tories." The bands may have claimed to rob from "Tories," a common name for unionists and other disloyal Confederates, but, as other witnesses observed, roving gangs seldom pillaged along partisan lines. More than likely, describing their victims as "Tories" was a rhetorical strategy employed to give the impression that they operated in Confederate service when, in fact, self-interest drove them to plunder.[48]

Like the roving deserter gangs, these partisan rangers pillaged rather than protected the home front. Group loyalties fueled individual self-interest in men who took advantage of wartime conditions in a distinctly nonpartisan manner. As Falkner recognized, these men were certainly not "serving their country," even when in army units ostensibly formed to do so. The Hancock County witness's observation that Steed's partisan rangers included many deserters reveals an overlap between the two groups, suggesting that ranger service allowed deserters to continue their looting of the home front under the veneer of military service, while still avoiding the regular army. Confederate authorities' inability to stop such behavior attests to the state's infrastructural weaknesses regarding enforcement of national loyalty via army service.

Although the Civil War in Mississippi offered deserters and detached military companies the opportunity to plunder, not all soldiers resorted to opportunistic collective violence. Some, through desertion, shirking, absenteeism, and transfer requests, revealed the other ways in which multiple loyalties carried on into the war and continued to motivate individuals. By negotiating their loyalty layers amid expectations from Confederate partisans that they demonstrate a total protective nationalist devotion to the Southern war effort, white Mississippians sometimes used the military as a conduit through which they expressed loyalties other than nationalism.

Not all deserters, for example, turned to pillaging. Thomas Harris joined Louisiana and Mississippi companies, got the soldier's bounty, and then deserted, "attaching himself to another regiment, again securing bounty." Harris had evidently "practiced this trick several times" before getting caught and executed by firing squad. Harris used military service as an opportunity for self-enrichment, although at an obviously high cost. Four self-proclaimed Mississippi Union men from the state's northern counties, who associated with unionist John Aughey, ended up in the Tupelo prison for refusing to swear the Confederate oath and enlist. After being tried by court-martial and condemned to death, they finally took the oath and enlisted in order to "desert the first favorable opportunity and escape to the Federal lines." One of the men, Monroe County farmer Delevan Morgan, deserted from the First Mississippi Infantry and, along with the others, reached Union lines at Memphis.[49] For these men, Union allegiances ironically drove them to enlist in the Confederate army. Their circumstances underscore the need to resist the urge to automatically equate military service with Confederate loyalty.

Soldiers, however, could cause trouble even when they did not formally desert. Ardent Confederates thought that shirking and absenteeism, problems in large part facilitated by soldiers' close proximity to their homes, were detrimental to the war effort. In December 1862, Brigadier General James Z. George, commanding state troops at Grenada, warned Pettus that "desertions, or getting home without leave are of almost daily occurrence." That same month, Colonel Richard Harrison told the governor that it was "well known in Military Circles, that at least one half the fighting strength of that portion of the Army under Gen. Pemberton, composed of troops from this State, is now, and have been [sic] for months, at home." Harrison urged the state legislature to give sheriffs the power to arrest absentees and return them to their commands. "Nothing is wanting to strengthen this corps, to double its present force but to get these stragglers into the ranks," Harrison concluded; "it is not too late to save the country." A Copiah County citizen likewise complained that his neighborhood was rife with "several stragglers from the army that ought to be in their country's service." Many of these men were on expired furloughs or had not returned to service after being hospitalized after the Battle of Corinth. Like Harrison, this observer implored Pettus to address this "evil," which robbed the army of morale. "The more that remain in this state & the longer they stay the more the army becomes demoralized," he wrote.[50] According to these Confederates, soldiers' proximity to their homes tempted them to neglect their duty to country. Such sentiments reflected their recognition that home and nation were separate sectors and that national service should be the men's top priority.

Confederate officials ran into similar problems with Mississippians who served in partisan ranger units, state troops, and militia units.[51] Many officers believed that men who joined these organizations were at least objectively, if not subjectively, harming the Rebel cause because they joined such close-to-home outfits in order to avoid serving in the regular army. Colonel Isham Harris believed as much, telling Davis that parties in northern Mississippi claimed the War Department's authority to raise commands, but instead "raise little squads, report to no general, do no good, yet keep the men they claim out of the regular service." General Joseph Johnson similarly told Davis that "many persons in Georgia, Alabama, and Mississippi are recruiting for cavalry, ostensibly under authority of the War Department," but many "never completed their companies, having no other object than to keep themselves and a few friends out of service." Johnson noted that these groups depleted the ranks of the regular army "by keeping men from entering it, enticing soldiers to desert, and harboring deserters."[52] Military officers recognized that men who enlisted in these outfits often did so to remain at home while ostensibly serving the nation.

In southwestern Mississippi, men organized state commands near Union-occupied areas. Responding to the War Department's sanctioning of these units on the grounds that there was "no other way of securing to the country the service of these men living in the enemy's lines," Colonel Andrew Kellar complained that these companies were often "a refuge to deserters" and thus a major irritation to regular soldiers and civilians. "I know not a single organization of this kind which is reliable or which is attached to regular service," he wrote to General Braxton Bragg, entreating: "Is there no way to secure their service to the country under Confederate authority?" When conscripts responded enthusiastically to Governor Clark's November 1864 call for six-month state volunteers, General W. L. Brandon warned that "this organization will undoubtedly be a weak one, for the reason that the men who were rushing into it were those who had skulked the service from the beginning of the war" and used state service to continue shirking duty.[53] Many Mississippians joined state units to fulfill the Confederate government's demand that they fight for the nation, but doing so allowed them to remain at home, which they viewed as distinct from the nation and the regular army that served it.

In January 1864, Brigadier General James A. Chalmers reiterated this point, telling Clark that he would no longer accept conscripts in state companies. He acknowledged that there were "some good men among these companies" but thought that "the great majority are simply seeking some hiding place from conscription, and never will do any service as cavalry, or while they remain so close to their homes." Chalmers concluded that "the best interest of the service requires that they should be conscripted and put in the infantry." Colonel James Drane made a similar point. "I find many able bodied men loitering about under the pretense of raising Cavalry Companies," he told Pettus; "there are probably 12 dozen attempted to be raised where one exceeds and the conscript law is evaded by young men attaching themselves to these half formed *and never to be finished Companies*" (emphasis in original). Furthermore, Drane believed that the existence of these companies did not benefit the Southern war effort. "There are now in this county several hundred able bodied men subject to conscription," he wrote; "our cavalry is less ifficient [*sic*] for the very reason that men go into it to evade hard service and danger and half their time are at home."[54]

While generally stopping short of calling them disloyal, Confederate military authorities viewed shirkers as neglecting their duties to the war effort and identified the source of this neglect as the men's proximity to their homes. In this way, authorities suggested that home and nation were distinct spheres and that shirkers cared more about staying at the former than serving the latter. This may have been the case with conscripts in particular. Kenneth Noe finds that later-enlisting Confederates—many of whom were conscripts—were less motivated by nationalism than 1861 volunteers, but proved effective soldiers once they did enter the service.[55] Although this point may seem contradictory, many Mississippians who evaded regular military service did not do so out of disloyalty to the Confederacy; rather, they voiced concerns *unrelated* to nationalism. Local allegiances that predated the war motivated them to seek service in home units or to request an army discharge, but they couched these requests in nationalist language in order to sway Confederate authorities who demanded unflinching devotion to the war effort.

Stephanie McCurry identifies a version of this rhetorical strategy in which men wishing to guard slaves and other personal property often masked their intentions by voicing a desire to protect soldiers' wives.[56] This rhetoric allowed citizens to negotiate what the Confederate state expected from them in terms of national sacrifice, and Mississippians used it to balance the state's new wartime demands with prewar attachments that continued to influence their behavior. The state wanted Mississippians to place nationalism over all other loyalties as a means of achieving Confederate independence. Thus, those citizens who petitioned the state to be relieved from military service in order to address local allegiances had to couch their claims in nationalist rhetoric. They therefore paid lip service to Confederate demands for total national devotion, often by claiming that they could better serve the nation at home than in the army. This is not to say that they simply lied about their desire to defend the national interest. Instead, they used nationalism as a medium of rhetorical exchange. To what extent they prioritized nationalism over other loyalties is impossible to deduct. Rather than providing evidence of weak or strong Confederate nationalism, this nationalist rhetoric shows how Mississippians accommodated multiple loyalties and how they dissociated home from nation. This rhetoric also reveals the limited powers of the Confederate state: although it could make Mississippians use the *language* of loyalty, it could not make them *act* totally loyally, at least in accordance with protective nationalism. The use of nationalism as rhetorical exchange revealed the perception of state power rather than state power itself.

Early on in the war, some Mississippians distinguished home from nation. In May 1861, a group of Yalobusha County men stated their willingness to form a military company, provided they could remain at home. The company, they insisted, "will not be composed of those who are desirous of skulking from their public duty, but who have private, and local duty, which they are unwilling to forego, unless public necessity require it." Save the major caveat of remaining homebound, the men claimed that they were otherwise "entirely willing" to serve where needed. A year later, D. J. Jernigan of Panola County thought that he could "be of more service to my country in the capacity of a Partisan Ranger than any other" and claimed that he would fight for up to three years if allowed "to return home at such times as we could be of no service to the government." The Yalobusha men separated "private" from "public" duties, emphasizing how local attachments were distinct from national issues. Nonetheless, they vowed to serve the "public necessity" if the state honored their private duties. Jernigan was a farmer who owned $5,000 in real estate and $30,000 in personal property.[57] He therefore had concrete material reasons for wanting to stay home. Nevertheless, Jernigan used a rhetorical strategy that became common among Mississippians seeking exemptions and deferrals by claiming that he could be "more of service to my country" at home.

Implicit in Jernigan's statement was that home and nation were *not* one and the same, a sentiment echoed by other Mississippians. C. W. Shiel of Lafayette County wanted a transfer from the Eighteenth Mississippi Regiment, stationed in Virginia, to work at his family's grist and saw mill in Oxford, Mississippi, which the Confederate government had pressed into its service. He claimed to the Secretary of War that since his father-in-law was too old and infirm to work the mill, "it would be to my interest and also to that of the government's to have one [engineer] there—moreover I would be with my family." Like Shiel, Dr. J. M. Greene of the Seventeenth Mississippi Regiment wanted a transfer back to his home in Chickasaw County to look after his widowed mother, who lived near an army hospital. "If I had a position there ... she could live with me," Greene wrote. Although he was aware that war was "no time for the obtrusion of individual hopes," he argued that if military service could "be made compatible with the discharge of sacred obligations to our aged parent, is it unreasonable that I should wish to associate the two?" Greene's desire to "associate" loyalty to his mother with loyalty to the cause reveals how multiple allegiances shaped his wartime decision making. He looked for common ground from which he could serve home and nation, different spheres that normally required separate duties. Shiel similarly looked for a way to "be with my family" while also serving a national cause that otherwise interfered with home attachments. Thus, both Shiel and Greene used nationalist language to defend local concerns.[58]

Such distinctions are important because they point to a broader trend among Mississippians who sought military exemptions. They did not say that home equaled nation. In fact, they had to convince the state that even though the two spheres were distinct, they were still capable of serving both honorably, and that national duty need not be sacrificed on the altar of localism. As in the cases of oath swearing and the contraband trade, Mississippians who wished to act on multiple loyalties had to convince Confederate authorities operating under the protective nationalist ideal either that their behavior did not conflict with their national loyalty or that it actually served the Confederate cause.

The Fifth Regiment, Mississippi State Troops, tried to make this case when they requested "a release from service indefinitely," citing the Union army's "brooding destruction" of the state as the reason they should be sent home to harvest crops. They assured Pettus that they were still committed to the "Holy Cause," arguing: "[O]ur service at home . . . would . . . be of far greater advantage . . . to our country than the duty we now perform." Mississippians fighting out of state made similar points. Joseph Jayne, serving in the Forty-Eighth Mississippi Regiment in Lee's army, asked Davis for a leave of absence or an assignment near his Washington County, Mississippi, home in order to look after family and finances. "I . . . am willing to lose all if necessary," he wrote, "but I see no imminent danger impending over this army." Davis thought that Jayne, being "extensively and favorably known in the region where he resides," might help conscript men into the regular army. "Few men would more attract recruits and I fear unless some influence is brought to bear, that the new conscripts will join almost exclusively the Companies serving near to their homes," Davis told Lee.[59] Davis supported Jayne's transfer not because he believed that Jayne could better defend the nation back in Mississippi; rather, he ironically thought that Jayne could conscript men into the national army who, like him, preferred to stay at home.

In February 1864, Isaac Jordan of the Fortieth Mississippi Infantry asked Secretary Seddon for a transfer from Mobile back to his home in Leake County, Mississippi, to stop the Federals from "laying devastation." If transferred to Mississippi, Jordon insisted that he could "render service more destructive to the Cause of the enemy in that position than the one I now hold, and [be] equally beneficial to the Cause of my own Country." Jordan also likely wanted to protect his large family, whose $1,500 in real estate and $5,000 in property stood in the Federals' path. In a similar vein, officers of the Twelfth Mississippi Regiment, who hailed from the Mississippi Delta, asked Governor Clark to transfer them to that region, where they "could render efficient service to the State" and stop "the deprivations of the enemy" as a cavalry regiment. Two of these men, Robert Patterson and J. Lewis Vaughan, lived and owned property in Lawrence and Claiborne Counties, respectively, which Union troops could raid via the Big Black and Pearl Rivers.[60] By claiming that they could render "efficient service to the State," they draped worries about their property's safety in patriotic rhetoric. Jordan and the Twelfth Regiment officers claimed that, in their cases, national and local interests coincided. That the interests of home and nation could occasionally coincide, however, was not the same thing as them being synonymous with each other. Jordan and the officers never claimed as much. Instead, they demonstrated how national allegiance always existed in tandem with other loyalties. In claiming that they could serve the nation better at home, they tried to harmonize what they and Confederate authorities considered to be otherwise separate sectors.

Mississippi civilians also used the language of national sacrifice as a form of rhetorical exchange in their appeals to Confederate authorities to release men from military duty in the name of local interests. In October 1862, a group of Panola County citizens petitioned Secretary of War George Randolph for the release of Dr. James Leach from the First Mississippi Cavalry, "our only chance for a physician." They ended the petition with nationalistic language: "In the din of passing events we would arrest your attention and ask your sympathies for the suffering families of those who are sacrificing their lives upon their country's altar." Women in Neshoba County, who claimed to be suffering from "sickness without the least hope of getting a physician or even a dose of medicine," used similar language to appeal for Dr. James Abercrombie's release. They assured Randolph that Abercrombie would "attend to his profession for the good of his neighbors" and "practice gratis for the familys [sic] of poor volunteers that are not able to pay." Carroll County citizens who wanted Dr. L. N. Ely spared from conscription told the secretary that Ely was "the only Physician ... to whom the poor & needy can apply for medical aid." They also employed patriotic rhetoric, asserting that Ely was "capable of doing much more good in this present sphere than performing the active duties of the soldier."[61]

These petitioners chose their language carefully, claiming that doctors could better aid the families of "poor volunteers" by working on the home front rather than in the army. Maybe these petitioners believed that doctors could serve the nation better at home, but trying to ascertain the veracity of such statements misses their broader significance. These petitioners distinguished the home sphere from the national one but used nationalistic language as a medium through which to accommodate local and national loyalties in their negotiations with Confederate authorities who prioritized nationalism above all other allegiances.

In addition to physicians, Mississippians requested the discharge of other skilled tradesmen such as blacksmiths, teachers, overseers, shoemakers, and tanners. These groups were eligible for exemption following an October 11, 1862, amendment to the original Exemption Act passed in April of that year, although physicians required more than five years of medical practice to qualify.[62] Civilians took advantage of the Exemption Act to bring men back to their neighborhoods to provide what they deemed essential services, and they insisted that those men could serve their country better at home than in the army. Historians have debated whether military exemption helped or hindered the Confederate war effort.[63] I am less concerned with taking sides in that debate than I am with identifying what citizens' requests for exemptions reveal about the influence of multiple loyalties in Mississippi. Whether or not exemptions hurt the war effort, many Confederate authorities *thought* that they did, and this fact had important implications for how citizens petitioned the state in wartime.

In January 1864, Newton County citizens wanted shoemaker S. R. Castles out of the Fifty-Sixth Mississippi Regiment. They claimed that their community "very much needed" his services but assured Secretary Seddon that they would "rather add ten thousand to, than diminish one single individual from, the army" and therefore "weaken the army by this detail." To get around this conundrum, they claimed that Castles was "unfit for Military service due to a foot wound and a severe cut" on his arm "which prevents his handling his gun as he should." Citizens in Neshoba County similarly claimed to recognize the need for "placing in the Army every available soldier," but they nonetheless wanted shoemaker Joseph Ingram released from the Twenty-Sixth Mississippi Regiment because he would be "greatly useful" to his community. For added effect, the petitioners noted that Ingram had a sick father at home and had lost five brothers to the war, whose families were now "greatly destitute and dependent and without his aid." Finally, while observing that Ingram was "still . . . devoted to our cause," they insisted that his health was in rapid decline and that "he cannot long make a soldier."[64] These citizens were aware of Confederate officials' belief that exempting men from military service harmed the war effort. Therefore, they claimed that Castles and Ingram could serve the nation better at home. To further justify their concern for local attachments, they added that Castles was too injured and Ingram was too sick to fight, points that allegedly neutralized any damage their removal from the army might cause. The sincerity of their statements notwithstanding, these petitioners' use of nationalist discourse underscores how they tried to justify their local concerns to Confederate officials who thought that such concerns should be subordinated to the greater war effort.

Mississippians flooded the secretary of war's office with similar requests for exemptions. They attempted to justify local allegiances with nationalist rhetoric in hopes of securing soldiers' release. In the winter of 1863, James Duff of Pontotoc County tried to get his son, John, a tanner, discharged from the Twenty-Third Mississippi Regiment. Duff explained to General Reuben Davis that Pontotoc County needed tanned leather to make shoes for "our families" and "our soldier friends in the war." Duff argued that his son would "do more good for his country in the tan yard than in the war." Duff also added that John's leg had been crippled from birth and that consequently he could only perform "the active duties of a soldier" with "great pane [sic]." Residents of Monroe County made a similar pitch to secure shoemaker Francis Isaiah's discharge from the Twenty-Fourth Mississippi Regiment, claiming that Isaiah's skills were "much and greatly needed" throughout the county. Isaiah was on furlough, and the petitioners insisted that he "was not yet sufficiently restored physically to return to his command, perhaps never will be." With this in mind, they concluded that Isaiah would be "of infinitely more service and benefit to the Confederacy if permitted to remain at home and follow his occupation as shoe & boot maker than he possibly can be . . . in the army as a soldier."[65] By claiming that removing men from the army would actually *help* the Confederate war effort, citizens tried to assuage Confederate officials' suspicions that Mississippians were not sacrificing all to ensure national victory.

Confederate nationalists certainly held such suspicions. Civilians' consistent claim that men were better able to serve the nation at home than in the army suggests that there was no assumption on behalf of Confederate officials that home was synonymous with nation. Higher-ups expected men to serve in the military first, because the armies were fighting for national independence. While home-front issues were important, some suspected rampant abuse of the exemption laws. Judge Hudson complained about exempted men—especially artisans—using "their freedom from the service to speculate" while making "themselves and their trades engines of oppression to all classes, especially to the poor." He suggested ending or curtailing the exemption laws, arguing that "there are plenty of old men and women to teach our schools . . . plenty of old physicians to do our practice . . . plenty of old men and negroes to do our tanning, shoemaking, blacksmithing, &c." Richard Archer echoed Hudson's concerns, telling Pettus that artisans "are exempted . . . because it is supposed they will not be needed" when, in fact, they were. "Behind this shield of age and exemption for useful trade," he wrote, "nearly all tanners, mechanics etc. are extortioners to a grievous extent."[66]

No Mississippian raged against exemption more than Albert Gallatin Brown. In his December 1863 speech to Congress, Brown proposed repealing the exemption laws, "the fruitful source of untold mischief to the army," which "decimated the ranks, bestowed favors on . . . the least meritorious, and sowed the seeds of discontent . . . among the brave men who . . . have stood by their country." Brown scoffed at the laws' supposed benefits. "The plausible pretexts under which these laws were passed, and by which it is now proposed to maintain them, is that the exempts and persons furnishing substitutes would be profitably employed in producing food, clothing, and other necessary supplies for the army, and for home consumption," he stated. Yet he saw no evidence to back up these assertions. "They have reaped when they have not sown, consumed when they have not produced," he stated, railing against the "able-bodied men, capable of bearing arms" who instead loitered in the streets, hotels, theaters and railroad cars.[67] Much like the internal debate within Confederate Mississippi over the swearing of loyalty oaths and trading with the Union—acts that might be construed as either loyal or disloyal depending on the observer—debates over the merits of military exemptions hinged on whether or not individuals embraced protective nationalism. Brown certainly did, and his frustration over what he thought was Mississippians' failure to demonstrate unwavering national loyalty reflected a larger anger among protective nationalists over the Confederate state's inability to instill and enforce total loyalty in its citizenry.

Through their continued concerns with local attachments, many Mississippians thwarted protective nationalists' goal of enforcing total nationalism.

Nonetheless, that civilians consistently claimed that releasing men from service would *benefit* the war effort demonstrated their need to feign observance of protective nationalist ideals. Wilkinson County residents, for example, argued that tailor John Duncan should be spared from conscription because he was "a very poor man" with a "helpless family," but they also claimed that he was "indispensable to carrying out the manufacturing of clothing by the Ladies for the Companies from this county." Widow Eliza Scott appealed for her son Rutilius's release from the army, claiming that the "horrible war" had rendered her "almost childless and disconsolate" and left her without overseers or an estate administrator. She reassured Secretary Randolph that she felt "the deepest interest in the Cause" and claimed that Rutilius "can better serve his country at home ... on the unattended farms & in the management of business now ... than he possibly can ... in camp." Residents of Jefferson County petitioned for the release Dr. H. Loomis on the basis that he "cant [sic] be as useful placed in any post in the army as he can be useful if left at home to take care of the familys [sic] of those absent."[68]

These petitioners' letters to Confederate officials underscore the importance they placed on loyalties distinct from nationalism. They tried to cancel out negative consequences of soldiers' exemptions by claiming that men could serve the nation better at home than in the army, but they also tried to placate protective nationalists' expectations of total national devotion. As these petitions reveal, the influence of micro loyalties shows that for all of its expanded infrastructural strength, the Confederate nation-state was not strong enough to achieve its major goal of enforcing total national loyalty among the citizenry. The state could make people use the language of nationalism, but it could not always translate that rhetoric into action.

The case of Madison County native Benjamin Gafford shows just how far some were willing to go to justify a soldier's release from the army. On Christmas Eve, 1862, Madison County citizens wrote to General Earl Van Dorn to request that the furloughed Gafford be permanently released from service because he was "of quite a delicate constitution" and would "not be able long to stand the exposure of a military campaign." Two doctors asserted that Gafford had a "chronic" and "permanent" case of tonsillitis, while a group of women attested that Gafford was "infirm" and "often for weeks unable to work at his trade." Despite these health issues, the petitioners claimed that Gafford was a skilled coffin maker and mechanic, the only one "left within our reach that can make a decent coffin," and he also joined a "company of Guerrillas." After the War Department denied the initial requests for Gafford's release, Madison County resident W. Davis Jr. insisted that because he was sick on furlough, Gafford could not return to the army because "his health is so precarious." Nevertheless, Davis also claimed that Gafford was an indispensable blacksmith, wagon maker, and gristmill operator. For good measure, Davis reminded military authorities that Gafford's family was "entirely dependent on him for support." Thus, Madison County petitioners claimed that a man too sick for the army, whose illness kept him from working for weeks at a time, was nonetheless an able member of a guerrilla company whose skills as a coffin maker, mechanic, blacksmith, wagon maker, gristmill operator, and family provider made him an indispensable neighborhood asset.[69]

Gafford doubtless had some mechanical ability, as the 1860 census lists him as a carriage maker. Further, as a middle-class owner of $2,000 worth of real estate and $4,500 of personal property—including one slave—Gafford may have had some influence that drove his neighbors to present an impressive number of excuses to absolve him from service.[70] While it is impossible to know for sure why Madison County citizens wanted him kept out of the army, their petitions reveal much about the Confederate state's effectiveness at enforcing national loyalty. If Gafford truly was such a skilled and indispensable tradesman, then Madison County citizens' concerns with local attachments guaranteed their inability to live up to protective nationalist ideals. Even if they were telling tales in their claims about Gafford, their willingness to lie tacitly demonstrated how they viewed protective nationalism not as an ideal to strive toward but as an impractical demand. If they lied, they did so in order to get a man out of the army, and they knew that Confederate officials believed that such an action damaged the war effort. Either way, the demands of protective nationalism proved difficult to enact in any concrete way in Mississippi.

The Civil War in Mississippi created new conditions that shaped people's reactions according to established loyalties. Even the Confederate military, as a symbol of national unity, was not strong enough to supersede the influence of these other attachments. Military defeat, Union occupation, economic collapse, and the breakdown of law and order facilitated opportunistic collective violence among Confederate deserters, whose localized group attachments underlay their indiscriminate pillaging of the Mississippi home front. These deserters' socioeconomic backgrounds reflected that of the average Confederate soldier. Most were poor, and a majority were married heads of household, suggesting that their antisocial behavior was a product of altered wartime conditions. This behavior suggests clear limits to the scholarship that contends that Confederate soldiers fought or deserted for the same reason: to defend hearth and home from Union invasion and war-induced privations.

In Mississippi, thousands of deserters pillaged rather than protected the home front, thereby becoming a major element in the *cause of*, rather than the *solution to*, wartime deprivations. Their banditry suggests that the local was no more sacred than the national was. Although these deserters were a small percentage of the Mississippi soldiers who fought in the Confederate armies, their negative impact was real and widespread. Further, as Confederate soldiers, their actions also demonstrated the limited capacity of the army to serve as a nationalizing institution.

Mississippi soldiers who viewed military service as a means to address localized micro loyalties also underscore the army's limitations as a nationalizing symbol. Shirking and absenteeism, and Confederate observers' subsequent attribution of men's proximity to home as the root of those problems, reveal that soldiers and authorities alike often did not view home interests as synonymous with national ones. This point is also born out in soldiers' requests to serve in home guards and partisan ranger units out of a desire to address local concerns. They used the rhetorical strategy of connecting home with nation in letters to Confederate authorities as a means to assuage the worries of higher-ups, who were inclined to think that citizens prioritized local allegiances at the nation's expense. Mississippi civilians similarly invoked patriotic rhetoric to attend to local interests. They assured authorities that soldiers could "serve the nation better at home" because the exigencies of the home front led them to make choices according to personal, familial, and neighborhood loyalties. In many instances, soldiers and civilians alike demonstrated that the army and the Confederate nation-state in general did not necessarily temper the influence of loyalty layers even in a wartime atmosphere.

Just as the Civil War transformed the antebellum loyalties of Mississippi deserters by creating new gang affiliations that expanded beyond Union or Confederate partisanship, the war's exigencies also had a major impact on another group of loyalties. Mississippi's slaves and slaveholders learned that the war would forever alter the traditional notions of loyalty that long undergirded the vastly unequal relationship between master and servant. How the conflict changed the master-slave relationship had profound consequences that shaped the state's sociopolitical trajectory well into the twentieth century.

CHAPTER FIVE

"I BELIEVE THAT 'THE INSTITUTION' IS EXTINCT"

Loyalty in the Master-Slave Relationship

IN LATE OCTOBER 1860, NATCHEZ PLANTER GEORGE SARGENT TOLD HIS son that "the negroes are prophesying freedom for themselves" from Abraham Lincoln's election. "[M]y own servants have asked me about it as having been told so by others." This sentiment did not abate after Mississippi seceded from the Union. "The Slaves have in many places been persuaded that they are to obtain their Freedom when Lincoln is elected," he told a friend; "there has been no outbreak anywhere but the news has spread among them over the whole Country." Sargent noted that preventing any possible slave "outbreak" required a "Master's presence" to "reduce them to subjection." Recalling her childhood as a Mississippi slave, Susan Snow described a wartime incident when she sang a song to her mistress that she had heard the older slaves sing only in private. She sang about how Union general John Pope "Called a Union band, [To] Make de Rebels un'erstan', To leave de lan', Submit to Abraham." In response, Snow's mistress "grabbed up de broom an' laid it on me. She made *me* submit." Snow did not think that singing the song was wrong, but she had heard from her mother that Lincoln "was a' tryin' to free de niggers an' my mammy says she want to be free."[1]

Sargent's insistence that his slaves required a "Master's presence" to subject them for believing that a political event directly affected their lives, and Snow's description of how her mistress violently "made *me* submit," underscore how the Civil War in Mississippi broadened the long-simmering conflict between slaves and slaveholders over the master-slave relationship. The reinforcement of black servility was at the heart of this relationship. Slaveholders insisted that because slaves were property, not citizens, they could be loyal *only* to their masters. To Sargent, the idea that blacks desired freedom after Lincoln's election meant that they would no longer be under white control, that they would not be forced to demonstrate fealty to the master class. This ideology of white racial mastery also led Snow's mistress to insist that Snow should submit not to Jefferson Davis, Lincoln's presidential rival, but to *her*. This was a crucial distinction. The Civil War in Mississippi unleashed a new front in the internal conflict between masters who fought to enforce black servile loyalty, and slaves who fought to separate themselves from their masters' authority.

This chapter focuses on the internal war between Mississippi slaves and slaveholders that had simmered during the antebellum era but was stoked by secession and the Union army's arrival in 1862. Confronted with slave escapes to Union lines, many Mississippi slaveholders tried to mask slaves' obvious disloyalty to their masters by attributing flight to the deluded beliefs of the enslaved that the Federals genuinely cared for their well-being. Slaves took advantage of the Union army's arrival to resist slaveholders' authority and act on loyalties to self, family, neighborhood, and nation. In doing so, they embraced multiple conceptions of freedom.

For Mississippi's enslaved people, the term "freedom" constituted both a general state that meant release from bondage and an individualized conception that differed according to people's lived experiences. As Chandra Manning writes, "Emancipation itself was not enslaved people's longed-for destination but rather one important—indeed crucial—step in the journey from slavery to freedom."[2] Foremost, of course, freedom for black Mississippians meant freedom from slavery, but once they broke free from their masters' control, the loyalty layers that they forged before the war played a direct role in shaping how they viewed freedom in a wartime/postemancipation South. In addition to freedom from slavery, black Mississippians realized the lived experience of freedom by carving out spaces for individual loyalties on their own terms. Many slaves fled their masters, but even those who did not flee nonetheless contested white dominance from within their households. Other slaves aided and joined the Union army as part of their more personal struggle against the established racial order. Black visions of freedom were intrinsically tied to a negative concept: their desire to escape white racial authority. Beyond this broader goal, however, freedom as a lived experience meant different things to different black Mississippians.

Slaves' chattel status before the war constrained the ways they could act on their loyalty layers. Stephanie McCurry notes how the Confederacy excluded blacks from citizenship and participation in the political community, expecting them to serve the cause out of racially based subservience, not out of patriotic fidelity. This major distinction made black Mississippians' experience of wartime loyalty distinct and separate from that of white Mississippians in a society that was stratified along lines of slavery and freedom. Slaves were to be loyal not to the government, but to their *owners* who were citizens of that government. In a March 1861 letter to his brother, A. F. Burton of Lauderdale County referenced the latter point: "The people of the South do not consider negroes their equals as do the Black Republicans of the North. That is the only question now to be considered, is negro equality." Burton may have been wrong about most Republicans' commitment to black equality, but his thoughts on the issue within the South underscored how white Mississippians refused to sanction any allegiances among blacks beyond loyalty to the master class. If black people were equal to whites, then they could not be perpetually loyal slaves, and they would thereby undermine the very ideological foundation of the Confederacy.[3]

This view was a continuation from antebellum Southern law that regarded masters as the "absolute others" to whom slaves were "bound . . . by ties of subjection to a particular master, owing obedience and allegiance exclusively to him." The Confederacy was an attempt to found an independent nation based on slaveholders' rights to maintain and perpetuate that relationship. Elizabeth Duquette notes that the trope of the "loyal slave" symbolized "a fundamental commitment to an organization of power" that was "predicated on racial hierarchies and principles," which discriminated loyalty along racial lines. Most crucially, those hierarchies existed between individuals, between slaves and slaveholders. In this racialized demarcation of allegiances, white loyalty was never servile because it was "predicated on an attachment to an abstraction, like a cause or an ideal, not a person." Black loyalty, by contrast, was *entirely* servile: it could be defined only as loyalty to a person, the slaveholder. Whereas white Mississippians could espouse allegiance to a cause like nationalism, the concept of the loyal slave "metonymically situated black Americans within the nation, figuring black equality as continued servility." Thus, Burton's disgust at the idea of Republicans unleashing "negro equality" upon Mississippi was rooted not just in the thought of slavery's abolition but also in the fear of the abolishment of continued black servility. In this potential new reality, blacks would no longer be "within the nation" as servile subjects but would instead be equal citizens who shaped the nation's social and political trajectory. With this fear in mind, white Mississippians intended to enforce black servility even after emancipation.[4]

Black Mississippians resisted the threat of continued servility during the Civil War and its immediate aftermath. Their behavior, however, was not always political in terms of explicit, targeted rebellion against a state, defined as institutions that "claim absolute authority within their borders" and have "a monopoly on legitimate violence, the definition of right and wrong, control of the distribution of resources, and . . . power over life and death." McCurry argues that, by resisting the Confederacy, slaves engaged in political acts despite their exclusion from the polity and that these acts forced the Confederate state to "concede slave men's membership in the body politic" in order to "counter slaves' treasonous activity with state violence." This conclusion reveals how the Confederate government came to view slaves as threats to the state but says less about how slaves themselves viewed their relationship to the state.[5]

Along with exploring slaves' own actions, comparing how different groups of Southern whites interpreted blacks' wartime behavior allows historians to better illuminate slaves' views on these matters. Doing so highlights how whites upheld the ideal of black servile loyalty and how blacks tried to escape from it. Examining whites' attitudes about slaves' actions also underscores that many white Southerners did not come to recognize slaves as political agents in the way whites understood the concept. Losing sight of the ways white Southerners strove to maintain the racial hierarchy during, and after, the war severs the Confederacy from its historical moorings and thereby underemphasizes the threads of continuity that connected it to the antebellum and the postwar South.

Agents of the Confederate government, using nationalist language while fighting a war against another political state, eventually interpreted slaves' behavior as disloyal to the nation. Mississippi slaveholders, however, labeled slaves as disloyal to their masters. Slaveholders therefore fought to maintain the racial hegemony that undergirded the Confederate cause but the enforcement of which began at the local level. This distinction is critical because it reveals the internal war in which slaves resisted masters' roles as intermediaries between them and the state, and masters defined slaves not as enemies of the state but as enemies of the racial hierarchy.[6]

Slaveholders' insistence that slaves owed allegiance solely to their masters often put the Confederate government in conflict with planters when the latter group argued that the state should limit its impressment of slave labor based on respect for private property rights. So crucial was the concept of servile loyalty to Mississippi's white master class that their struggle to maintain it outlasted the Confederacy. After the Civil War, white Mississippians, faced with the specter of racial equality and the reactionary desire to maintain local control, intimidated freed people in an attempt to reassert white racial mastery over blacks. In this respect, the brief period historians refer to as "Presidential Reconstruction" saw a continuation of the internal war that blacks and whites waged before, and during, Mississippi's Civil War. Although the Confederacy lost its bid for national independence, the war between blacks and whites over black servility continued, and it directly shaped the trajectory of Mississippi's socioeconomic and political culture well into the twentieth century.[7]

In light of slaveholders' attempts to uphold the racial hierarchy, black Mississippians saw freedom in terms that went beyond mere allegiance to a political state. In addition to macro loyalty to a nation, freedom for black people meant the ability to openly, and without coercion, act on micro loyalties to self, family, and community, thereby constructing lives as autonomous individuals unmolested by white authority. Black Mississippians embraced these loyalties regardless of whether or not a political state sanctioned or condemned their behavior. This is not to say that they did not understand the connection between freedom and the nation-state. Even before the Union army entered Mississippi, as George Sargent discovered, slaves believed that Lincoln's election portended their liberation. They viewed potential Union invasion as an attack on slavery that legitimized the claiming of their own freedom. Yet, their conceptions of freedom did not always reflect a distinctly nationalist inclination to ingratiate themselves to a US government that often refused to fully acknowledge their desires. Nor did black Mississippians embrace a singular, broad collective goal in terms of what they expected to gain from being free.

Identifying what Southern blacks wanted from their lived experience of freedom after emancipation has been a major focus of Civil War and Reconstruction scholarship. Historians like Steven Hahn and others view Southern slaves as the most consistent members of America's working class in the nineteenth and twentieth centuries. They argue that through their rebellion during the Civil War, slaves began developing a collective, working-class identity as a landless peasantry. After emancipation, this collective identity coalesced into a shared vision as a rural proletariat who associated freedom with land ownership and racial solidarity.[8] In tying freedom to land ownership, however, rural slaves ensured that even when emancipated, they could not achieve the status of a free landed peasantry unless the Union government redistributed planters' lands, a step that the federal government was not prepared to take.

Other scholars, such as Eric Foner and Leon Litwack, accept the existence of a collective, African American working-class identity, but they also identify a parallel goal that freed people embraced within the realm of formal politics, in which they "identified fully with the new nation-state" and demanded equal citizenship rights in return for their loyalty.[9] Still other historians assert that freed people wanted families, farms, schools, full citizenship, and equal rights.[10] In other words, in emancipation's wake, black Southerners wanted multiple things, each of which reflected different aspects of freedom on a day-to-day basis. While often agreeing that African Americans wanted land and political equality, different historians have emphasized one or the other, depending on whether they focus on rural freed people or urban property holders. These differences in emphasis, however, indirectly reflect how freed people wanted many things, which scholars have often overlooked in efforts to identify a collective African American identity. Eschewing attempts to locate a collective slave identity allows historians to, per Alex Lichtenstein's suggestion, "link the particular experiences of the emancipated with the larger structural constraints that shaped the world in which they struggled to make freedom meaningful."[11]

The racial hierarchy was the largest of all these constraints. In Civil War Mississippi, slaves shared a mutual desire to escape white racial dominance. As Lynda Morgan writes, freed people's visions of freedom "were grounded in the experience of slavery and the role of labor in human society," a labor that the white master class appropriated under the aegis of proslavery racism. For Mississippi's slaves, however, bondage was not ideological but "unique and visceral," and it shaped their response to a postemancipation South. In this sense, race was a "unifying ideal" for slaves in which they embraced an African American identity born in response to the forced servility of human bondage. This transformation grew out of a process in which slaves, recognizing that whites viewed black people as chattel, responded by constructing an identity based on their shared membership in a group whose skin color made their interests diametrically opposed to the interests of their masters.[12] Although slaves embraced a collective identity in terms of their shared opposition to the racial hierarchy that equated blackness with servility, once they escaped white mastery, they embraced multiple conceptions of freedom as a lived experience. For black Mississippians, loyalty layers served as both the means and the ends in their quest to live out free existences. The ability to hold other allegiances—to self, family, community, and nation—held a special significance for them. Unlike whites, their existence as chattel mean that, in theory, they could be loyal only to their masters.

Enslaved African Americans developed domestic arrangements and kin networks that "formed the social basis of developing Afro-American communities, which prepared slaves to deal with legal freedom." Family networks provided slaves with companionship and functioned as a survival mechanism through the forging of personal attachments that bound individuals together, creating strong identities through shared loyalties. Beyond the family, slave neighborhoods, encompassing the terrain of enjoining plantations, gave slaves the opportunity to develop interpersonal relations at communal functions. The very existence of these micro loyalties to self, family, and acquaintances undermined whites' claims that, as servants, blacks were to be loyal to their masters alone. Family and neighborhood networks created not one black identity but multiple individual identities, forged through interpersonal relations among individual people. During the Civil War, Mississippi's slaves used the lines of communication and personal relationships formed in neighborhoods to discern the war's aims and prospects, contest white authority, and chart paths to freedom.[13]

Recognizing why slaves in Civil War Mississippi sought to act on multiple loyalties allows historians to, as Walter Johnson suggests, move beyond viewing everyday slave agency as "the antidote to the indignities of exploitation."[14] This is not to deny the tradition of slave resistance, which historians have exhaustively documented.[15] Johnson, however, cautions against equating every aspect of slaves' lives, such as family formations, with resistance to slavery itself, because doing so reduces them to mere reflections of their servile condition. Instead, he suggests that historians view slaves' ideas and actions as "shaped by the material conditions of their enslavement" but also as "insistently transcendent—productive of new, creative, vibrant, and sustaining forms of human being, commonality, and, ultimately, solidarity." Considering Johnson's suggestions helps to explain how slaves' forging of micro loyalties in the antebellum period motivated them to resist the master class's authority during the Civil War. Black Mississippians embraced bonds in slavery that undergirded lives in freedom, unfettered from the stifling servility of the racial hierarchy. Slaves' loyalty layers did not intrinsically constitute resistance; rather, they facilitated it. These attachments sustained black identities under slavery and enabled freed people to envision how they would *live* as free people.[16]

Understanding how multiple allegiances drove blacks to resist white authority during the Civil War requires an awareness of how the master-slave relationship facilitated such attachments among slaves while simultaneously reinforcing masters' supremacy. Christopher Morris recommends studying this relationship through the lens of articulation theory, in which a dominant group with specific interests (slaveholders) tries to make another group (slaves) carry out those interests. Through the articulation process, separate interests indirectly converged, resulting in benefits to masters and servants that still preserved the dominance of the master class. For example, although slaves gained mutual support and love from marriage, masters sanctioned slave marriages on the basis that they mitigated temptations to abscond and encouraged work and discipline through mutual company. Likewise, slaveholders' permitting slaves to keep personal garden plots provided slaves with a measure of independence, but masters viewed garden plots as a cost-neutral way of supplementing slave diets. Masters' sanctioning of property ownership gave slaves a measure of autonomy but also fostered discipline. Slaveholders allowed slaves to hire themselves out, providing servants with a form of semifreedom via distance from their owners, but they also pocketed a portion of slaves' earnings.[17] Thus, slaves derived some benefits from masters' actions, but this resulted from the slaveholders' acting in their own self-interest. Masters benefited from slaves' responses to circumscribed freedoms, but this was because slaves acted in *their* interests, not because they acquiesced to the master's desire to maintain dominance.

Articulation necessarily fostered personal attachments within slave families and communities, but because these loyalties emerged in part through slaveholders' desire to uphold the racial hierarchy, the articulation process created conflict between the two parties. Both achieved a measure of control over slaves' lives, but both wanted *total* control. Morris notes, however, that total control eluded both parties because the "periodic conflict between individual masters and slaves" attacked the power of individual masters, but the personal nature of such conflict prevented it from escalating into the kind of organized uprisings that would have struck at the system of slavery itself, which bolstered articulation.[18] In Mississippi, the Civil War changed this status quo by providing the means through which slaves contested the racial hierarchy in numerous individual ways that, taken together, constituted a broader collective assault on the slave system. Faced with escaping the ideology of forced servile loyalty that underlay slavery, slaves did not try to reverse the racial hierarchy; they tried to escape from it. They took advantage of the chaos of war to undermine the master class, and the micro loyalties they had forged under slavery shaped the multiple conceptions of freedom that they formulated. Mississippi's slaves, therefore, demonstrated solidarity in their resistance to servile loyalty but multiplicity in how they experienced the freedom that such resistance brought.

When war erupted, Mississippi whites' fears of servile disloyalty heightened. The state had seceded and joined the Confederacy to protect slavery from perceived Northern threats, but white Mississippians understood that slaves themselves posed an internal threat to the institution and the racial hierarchy that bolstered it. Fears of slave insurrections, a perennial concern of white Mississippians, spiked during the secession crisis. Confederate authorities identified several planned rebellions, but none materialized on the scale whites alleged. Historians note that white fears of slave revolts underscore the perilously vulnerable nature of slaveholders' sense of mastery over blacks. For white Mississippians, fears of slave uprisings threatened not only physical danger but also a reversal of the racial hierarchy, wherein slaves appropriated physical coercion to dominate their masters.[19]

The best-known cases of alleged insurrection occurred in Adams County in 1861. That summer, white vigilance committees arrested, tortured, and executed dozens of slaves in Natchez and the nearby Second Creek plantations for supposedly plotting to burn the city down, murder white men, and ravage white women. In late September 1861, Adams County resident Louisa Lovell described an environment where "no one is safe." Vigilance committees and home guards were "constantly on the alert arresting and confining suspected individuals," some of whom were hanged. By October, news of the plot had spread south to Wilkinson County. Woodville resident Sophia Hunt Hughes told her sister of "a formidable insurrection" in Adams County: "27 have been hung. . . . [I]t is kept very still not to be in the papers, the investigation is still going on." That investigation resulted in confessions elicited through torture. The limited evidence for these "plots," therefore, came from white inquisitors' recordings of the events, leading historians to debate whether the Adams County conspiracies were real or products of white delusions.[20]

Although insurrection panics likely reflected white fears (as opposed to black actions), they continued to erupt throughout the course of the Civil War in Mississippi. In January 1861, Jackson resident N. H. Boyd informed her cousin that "there were 2 negroes to be hung here Friday," one for killing his overseer and the other for stealing. Many came to "witness the execution." In early August of that year, with most of the white men gone into the army, Ophelia Howe of Harrison County worried that "there is an immense number of negroes in Harrison county and this parish and I think for the safety of the country, their masters should by all means stay with them." Similarly, a Tippah County resident warned Governor Pettus of "the possibility of an insurrection of the black population," who allegedly planned to poison and attack local whites. In June 1861, John Kirkland told his daughter that the slaves were working "smoothly," and that he had "never seen negroes more obedient" or "better satisfied." He attributed this supposed harmony to local whites who treated slaves as mildly "as can be done consistent with their conditions of master and slave." Nonetheless, Kirkland revealed the underlying fear inherent in such a relationship by adding that "the patroll [*sic*] are very strict and are out 2 or 3 times a week." Whites could not afford to be too careful even when slaves appeared to be "satisfied."[21]

The idea that otherwise contented peons might revolt at the first available opportunity weighed heavily on whites, who already had to worry about a potential Yankee invasion of the Magnolia State. In the summer of 1861, General C. H. Dahlgren reported that the white population of Yazoo and Holmes Counties "fear an insurrection." He warned that "vigilance should characterize the people at home, otherwise the negroes will go to the Yankees, and perhaps do damage at home."[22] In these cases, the "damage" that slaves might do specifically referred to personal, bodily attacks against whites. Such attacks epitomized the direct reversal of the master-slave relationship, since maintaining the racial hierarchy rested on the threat of coercive violence through the lash or other means.

State authorities made it clear that slave revolts signaled the reversal of the racial hierarchy and tacitly admitted that whites might lose the authority to enforce servile loyalty in their human chattel. In his November 1863 address to the state legislature, Governor Pettus warned that the Union army was enlisting slaves as "tools of our subjugation" and described how "marauding bands of these freed negroes" were "desolating" neighborhoods and murdering white citizens. Pettus's successor, Charles Clark, reiterated these themes later that month when he warned that the Yankees were "inciting our slaves to insurrection" by raising black regiments "to fight against their masters." Like Pettus, Clark described slaves as disloyal servants by emphasizing that they were incited to fight against their masters, not against the Confederate state, even as soldiers in the Union army. He cautioned that Union victory would bring "the immediate emancipation of your slaves and the elevation of the black race to a position of equality, aye, of superiority, that will make them your masters and rulers," thereby reversing the Southern racial hierarchy and putting whites in the servile position. Both governors used the language of submission to indicate how slave revolts threatened not just whites' physical safety but also their status as the master class.[23]

White Mississippians' ability to maintain effective physical control over slaves was central to upholding the veneer of slave "loyalty" that undergirded the racial hierarchy in Mississippi. During the war, the Confederacy's need to fill its armies left whites on the home front, especially women, open to what they thought were vengeful slaves who would refuse to work or, worse, attack their owners.[24] In September 1862, an amendment to the original April 1862

Conscription Act raised the draft age from thirty-five to forty-five, drawing even more white men into the ranks.[25] In response, whites implored Confederate officials to release relatives and overseers from the army to remedy the problem of slave control.

For whites left on the home front, the lack of overseers was a terrifying prospect. In the fall of 1862, Macon resident E. A. Dowling wanted Secretary of War George Randolph to release her son Joseph from the army to oversee eighty neighborhood slaves. That same month, Socky Davis, of Lowndes County, pleaded for her son's release because she was unable to "manage her negroes and give direction to their labor." Neshoba County residents Clary and Sarah Donald, who owned twenty slaves, wanted their overseer discharged "to take charge and manage said negroes." In February 1863, Columbus resident Julia Cox asked Jefferson Davis to release her son to manage her "large and very unruly family of servants" who had become "uncontrollable and unprofitable." Abigail Jones, of Jasper County, similarly appealed to Davis for her son's discharge so that she and her daughters would have someone to "govern, direct and control the thirty five negroes upon our plantation." These petitions were among scores that Mississippians wrote to Confederate authorities. They revealed a widespread concern that, without proper enforcement of black servility, slaves were an inherent threat to the whites in their midst. These particular letters did not detail what slaves had *done*, but the absence of overseers justified, in slaveholders' minds, concerns that slaves *would do* something.[26]

A large number of these petitions followed the enactment of the infamous Twenty Negro Law of October 11, 1862, which authorized owners of twenty or more slaves, or one white man per plantation, to be exempted from military service for the purpose of slave control. The law was controversial throughout the Confederacy, as it appeared to favor wealthy planters at the expense of poorer soldiers. Nonetheless, the law attempted to address what slaveholders felt were legitimate fears of slave revolts.[27]

Calls to draw overseers from the army stemmed from concerns that slaves would attack whites, especially women, who remained on the plantations. In early 1863, Claiborne County resident Lititia Adams implored Pettus to "consider also the helpless women and children . . . deprived of their natural protector, and left wholly at the mercy of the blacks." Bolivar County native Frank Yaden similarly asked Secretary Randolph to be discharged from the First Mississippi Cavalry to hold off "[t]he Hydra head of insurrection" that "has already made its appearance but was met promptly by the few citizens who were left to contend with it." Yaden was concerned that his family was "exposed to the insults" of their slaves and noted that a neighbor had several slaves "severely punished" for making "gross propositions to her." As Yaden noted, fears that slaves would assault white women were especially potent. In November 1863, Chickasaw County residents Charity and Rachel Buchanan implored Secretary of War James Seddon to release Rachel's husband from the army to control more than forty slaves on two plantations who "have lately manifested a disposition to commit acts of insubordination." The petitioners feared that without "a suitable white man" to control the slaves, "some great bodily injury will be inflicted upon them by said negroes."[28] Mississippi's slaveholders placed a high priority on maintaining mastery over their servants, believing that failure to do so invited mortal threats.

Fear of violence at the hands of slaves lifted the veil of complacency from white Mississippians who had grown accustomed to the veneer of servile loyalty from blacks. A Franklin County resident warned Clark that further conscription of white men would "increase the temptation to the slaves, and the danger to the families left at home." O. J. M. Holladay of Lauderdale County claimed that several slaves had "made a plot to arm themselves and steal all the horses they could and fight their way to Vicksburg." Holladay also noted that a slave "laid his hands" on two sleeping white women and claimed that sexual assault by slaves was "common." Echoing Holladay's accusation, Lettie Vick Downs reported that after "another raid from the negroes . . . one of them had committed rape on a young lady." Historians, however, should use caution when interpreting such reports. Emancipation unleashed a long-held fear of the supposed sexual threat that black males, free from white male control, posed to white women's virtue.[29] Nonetheless, these reports do reveal that Mississippi slaveholders interpreted black freedom in terms of the reversal of the master-slave relationship. In their minds, disloyal slaves did not just want freedom for themselves; they wanted the freedom to *dominate* their masters. The absence of any nonmilitary organized incidents of black retaliatory violence against whites in Mississippi, however, suggests that such fears were products of white paranoia. Yet, if slaves did not want to reverse the racial hierarchy, they nevertheless wanted to escape from it.[30]

One of the ways they did this was by running away to Union lines in large numbers, thereby physically separating themselves from their owners. In doing so, they continued a long antebellum tradition in which slaves fled plantations and farms, either temporarily by lying out for days, weeks, or even months, or by going north to permanently escape their bondage.[31] Antebellum slave flight both facilitated and strengthened micro loyalties among individuals. Often, runaway slaves lay out in their own neighborhoods, or moved between adjoining plantations to visit kin. They also absconded back to neighborhoods where they had previously resided to reunite with friends and family. Beyond kin ties, runaways forged networks with people they met in their journeys, using any information gleaned from these meetings to aid their goals as fugitives. Runaway slaves also acted on self-loyalty. As one historian notes, planters recognized that "the runaway slave epitomized alienation from bondage" because "the slave's theft was of his person." Runaway slaves shared personality traits like "self-confidence, self-assurance, self-possession, determination, and self-reliance." The key word in these traits was "self." Mack Henderson, a former Warren County slave who ran away in 1863 and then joined the Union army, put it succinctly when he stated, "the reason I ran away to the Yankees . . . is because I wanted to be free."[32] By effectively stealing themselves, runaways asserted their own interests and rejected the servile deference that masters expected from them. By running off, slaves both acted on, and continually forged, micro loyalties. Collectively, these attachments made running off a major form of resistance to white authority that carried into the Civil War.[33]

As soon as the Union army arrived, white Mississippians reported slaves' flights to federal lines.[34] In July 1862, the Confederate provost marshal at Natchez observed "a great disposition" among "insubordinate" blacks "to run away and go to the Federals." A Panola County resident similarly observed that slaves near the Union's Memphis lines and along the Mississippi River "have in great numbers run off." He believed that "there is danger of the whole negro population of the South becoming greatly demoralized if the war continues another year, certainly wherever their army goes." After the Second Battle of Corinth, a partisan ranger noted that "negroes from the South part of the state" were "making their way to the Federal lines." John Miller, of Pontotoc County, found it difficult to move slaves from the Yankees' path because "many of them run away." He added that "all the negroes are waiting for the arrival of the Yankees & will leave en masse," and that "hundreds have gone from Tippah & all from Tishomingo." By early January 1863, a Confederate cavalryman observed that the number of slaves running to Union lines was "increasing beyond convenience." Warren County planter Charles Whitmore noted that on the day Vicksburg fell to the Union, "nearly all negroes [are] missing. They have left without cause in a regular stampede."[35] As the war progressed and the Federals overran the state, slaves' flight only accelerated.

Enslaved people in Mississippi used their feet to resist white authority by removing themselves from their masters' presence. After the Federals established themselves at Vicksburg, Jackson resident William Thomson thought that "probably nine-tenths of the negroes between Big Black and Pearl river have been run off, sold, or gone to the Yankees." Washington County planter Jona Pearce told Secretary Seddon that Confederate attempts to steer slaves from the Union path would cause "a stampede of all the balance, who would take every mule with them to the Yankees." Stationed in Meridian in early 1864, William Sively informed his mother that "a great many negroes" there had fled to Union lines, adding that "it is thought that ten thousand is a low estimate." A month later, Sophia Hughes complained to her brother that "so many negroes ran off to the Yanks, and each one takes a mule or horse that they are very scarce & very high [priced]." The Canton *American Citizen* described how black Union cavalrymen convinced the local slaves to "bid farewell to Dixie, and accept Yankee freedom." The paper estimated that "nine-tenths" of the city's slaves had gone off with the black troops. After a visit from Union soldiers, planter James Maury proclaimed that "it is amazing with what intuitive familiarity the negroes recognized the moment of deliverance."[36] For Mississippi's slaves, the arrival of the Union army was the catalyst through which "deliverance" came via the chance to flee their owners' authority. Slaveholders, in turn, reacted with anger, exasperation, and betrayal at what they considered slaves' brazen displays of disloyalty.

Perhaps more than anything else, slaves' failure to show the expected due deference infuriated slaveholders. In November 1863, for example, William Dameron reported that his brother's slaves had planned "for a general stampede" and that they were "more trouble than they are worth, all of them." Dameron voiced a common refrain among white Mississippians, that disloyal slaves were ungrateful and too troublesome to deal with. At one point, Eliza Sively claimed that her slaves were "very well satisfied, though they all may go." A week later, she again wrote that her slaves were still "very well satisfied though they may leave at any time." Many slaveholders struggled to come to terms with the fact that "satisfied" slaves nonetheless did not seem to want to stick around. In the late summer of 1861, Louisa Lovell told her husband that "those miserable abolitionists" would be shocked at "such manifestations of devotion and affection on the part of the poor maltreated slave, whose heart, according to them, is only the abode of hatred and revenge against their masters." Northerners, she insisted, "know nothing of the bond that unites the master & servant, of its tenderness and love on the one side, and its pride of duty and attachment on the other." Two years later, however, Lovell felt betrayed when some of her slaves fled to Union lines and others planned to follow suit. "I never want to live in the South anymore & call upon a darky again," she fumed; "I have been cured lately of all love for that race, in most of cases they have displayed such want of affection, such ingratitude. . . . I suppose we must prepare to become our own servants."[37]

Lovell was genuinely shocked at the "ingratitude" of slaves who refused to display the expected "duty and attachment" to their masters. She and other slaveholders voiced betrayal over their slaves' flight to Union lines. Their anger, in turn, reveals how they considered the servile loyalty that bonded master and slave to be *essential* to the maintenance of slavery as an institution. By running off, slaves, by contrast, demonstrated how freedom for themselves necessitated resistance to white expectations of servility. Whites' demands of servile loyalty directly influenced slaves' decisions to act on self-loyalty. Slaves knew that masters expected their unquestioned devotion, and they often feigned loyalty as part of a general preparation to run off when the moment was right.

As the war dragged on, slaveholders repeatedly interpreted slaves' decisions to stay or run off as evidence of either loyalty or betrayal. Panola County planter Everard Baker noted that while many slaves had run off, "mine so far have showed their good sense & stood true to mine & their interests." Given the paternalism of the master-slave relationship, Baker thought that obedient slaves recognized the reciprocal interests of both. Confederate officer Harvey Walter suspected that his slaves might flee but still felt betrayed when they did. "They talked against the Yankees & I never suspected any of them going away so soon," he told his sister. Despite his slaves' assurance that they would stay, "they all deceived me very well for I was shocked," he wrote. "I have learned a great deal about my servants since they left, I will never trust another darkie." Living near the Vicksburg lines, Elizabeth Ingraham had "reason to think that hands will all leave." She described a still-remaining slave named Elsie as "still true" and "faithful," while Nancy, who fled, was "not true." Adams County resident Kate Foster noted how slaves were "flocking to the enemy in town," although none of hers had gone. "I hope they will all prove faithful to the end," she wrote.[38]

In addition to viewing runaway slaves as disloyal and those who remained as "faithful to the end," whites often claimed that slaves' misguided desires for freedom actually fueled disloyalty to their masters. They demonstrated the "fatal self-deception" of slaveholding paternalism, which stemmed from masters' attempts to justify the exploitation inherent in human bondage.[39] For example, Susan Miller believed that her deluded slaves had forgotten their subservient place when Union troops marched through northern Pontotoc

County. "They seem to be intoxicated with the idea of careless freedom held out to them," she told her son. Miller insisted that slaves did not know where their interests lay:

> The negroes generally are in exuberant spirits, & my private opinion is that the most of them will be ready to go [with Union troops] without compulsion. There is something so alluring in the idea of freedom & equality with their masters. Many of them will go from curiosity & a desire to attest the novelty of change. As I look at ours singing, dancing, & whistling, so free from the heart-ache & hardship of us who own them, I can but pity them, for the unhappy charge that will so soon come over them, when they forsake the home God has so kindly given them. But let them go.

For Miller, slaves had to be "intoxicated" in order to want "equality with their masters." She believed that curious slaves merely wanted "the novelty of change" as opposed to actual freedom. Such delusions would backfire, she insisted, because in betraying their masters, they forsook the benevolence of white protection.[40]

Other slaveholders similarly concluded that slaves were delusional, if not stupid, to forsake their masters' benevolence in pursuit of freedom. Exasperated over her fleeing slaves' "bad conduct," Emilie McKinley, of Warren County, proclaimed that "negroes are creatures you cannot convince but in some ways like children. It is useless to argue with them." William Nelson told his mother that slaves in Holly Springs only ran because "the Yankees resorted to the artifice of lying to them, to frighten them away, when all other efforts had failed." Kate Foster called runaway slaves "poor deluded creatures" who would "find out too late who are their best friends, Master or Massa." Natchez resident Elizabeth Brown likewise derided runaways as "poor deluded fellows" who "ought to have known better than to leave home." Many white Mississippians chafed at such brazen disloyalty from their servants. As Foster demonstrated, slaveholders intent on upholding the racial hierarchy believed that slaves desired the authority of one "Master," the Federals, or another "Massa," the slaveholder. They loathed the idea that slaves might show fealty to neither and actually desired autonomy. For runaway slaves, taking the first step toward freedom entailed separation from the authority of the master class.[41]

Whereas slaveholders expressed outrage over the disloyalty of slaves who ran to Union lines, they also feared that slaves would physically assault their masters within the household. Whites well understood that bodily attacks by slaves symbolized blacks' rejection of white mastery at the most visceral level. Eliza Sively's slave, Bill, whom she considered capable of violently assaulting her and her family, escaped before she could sell him off to Texas. "No doubt Bill will do us all the injury he can if he gets out here, which he will be certain [*sic*] to do," she wrote, looking upon his visit "with fear and trembling." Yazoo County planter Robert Shotwell noted that several of his slaves "would not be controlled" and "would no doubt shoulder the musket [for the Union] willingly and be dangerous negroes in that capacity" if Vicksburg fell. Especially worrisome for Shotwell was his blacksmith, whom he described as "a dangerous negro if he should rebel & I understand swears he will not be taken off." Shotwell emphasized these slaves' "dangerous" proclivities, believing that they were already inclined toward violence against whites. Putting them in the Union army, therefore, would only further license, in their eyes, these violent tendencies.[42]

In another incident of suspected slave violence, Warren County resident Tully Gibson left for Virginia accompanied by her young son and two "demoralized" slaves. Shortly after her departure, Gibson's correspondence with friends ceased, leading her neighbor, Emilie McKinley, to suspect that "her servants may have murdered her for her money." Lettie Vick Downs, also of Warren County, feared that "a negro raid were on their way up the creek killing every white person as they came." She believed that the "lawless creatures" were mere tools of the Union army. "How can a Union with a people who instigate a race that have been raised and cared for as children to rise and slay their owners in cold blood, ever be tolerated?" Downs attributed the slaves' behavior to servile disloyalty. Whether or not the events she described actually occurred, her choice of language, that slaves rose up against their "owners" (not against the Confederacy), indicates how slaveholders first feared an internal war in which servants violently betrayed their masters. In the eyes of Mississippi's master class, reversing the racial hierarchy would transform their lives in the worst possible way by turning masters into slaves and vice versa.[43]

Slaveholders' fears of slave assaults were not entirely unwarranted. The antebellum period saw a "persistence of violence on the plantation," which was "spontaneous" and primarily directed against whites, including owners, their family members, and overseers. Indeed, year after year, in nearly every Southern state, slaves were indicted for assaulting and sometimes killing whites. The particular restraints of American slavery, especially the swift and merciless white responses to perceived organized slave revolts, facilitated individual slave resistance against masters even as it discouraged collective revolts. Occasionally, individual Mississippi slaves attacked their masters during the war. They appropriated violence, the method the master class used to enforce servile loyalty in slaves, to reject that servility.[44]

In May 1863, Kezziah, the slave of Emilie McKinley's friend Ellen Batchelor, "attacked her mistress," saying: "You have had me beat enough." When Batchelor's neighbor tried to intervene, Kezziah "raised her shovel on them and told them to leave." Yet, she also refused to run to Union lines, saying that "she wasn't going to leave her property." In attacking Batchelor, Kezziah took part in the wartime phenomenon in which, as Thavolia Glymph writes, mistresses and slaves fought over slaves' right to "be free and live fuller lives" within plantation households. In assaulting her mistress, Kezziah rejected the servile allegiance that was expected of slaves. Freedom for Kezziah meant the ability to act on self-loyalty, by owning property and staying at her home while living free of Batchelor's authority. A month later, McKinley wrote that after her neighbor, Mr. McGaughey, left his wife alone in the house, "his negroes came to the house to whip Mrs. McG." A white boarder tried to fight them off but to no avail, then pleaded for help from federal soldiers, who captured the slaves but then quickly released them. The slaves then returned and "whipped him and made him call them *Master* and *Mistress*." These slaves appropriated the master's lash to demonstrate their rejection of white authority. The day after Christmas, 1864, William Sykes, of Winona, wrote that "the other day a neighbour undertook to correct a negroe [*sic*], was knocked down with an axe and nearly killed. The negroe mounted his horse and left."[45] Slaves who assaulted their owners rejected the master-slave relationship and its underlying premise that blacks owed allegiance only to their masters. Instead, they acted on self-loyalty by literally using their bodies to assert their freedom from white dominance.

Mississippi's enslaved people, however, did not have to run away or attack their owners in order to be labeled disloyal. Masters' expectations of servile loyalty shaped the creation of slaves' micro allegiances through the articulation process; thus, many slaves acted in their own interest by staying behind and appropriating spaces for themselves within the confines of ostensibly white control, actions that slaveholders denounced as indicating servant betrayal.[46] In the spring of 1863, for example, a *Daily Mississippian* correspondent in Jackson chafed at the sight of "well dressed negroes . . . striding along the pavement, smoking cigars, talking and swearing, loud and deep, and perfectly oblivious of the proximity of Caucasion [*sic*] blood." The writer believed that freed slaves' refusal to observe the racial hierarchy through public deference necessitated "personal chastisement" from whites to keep servants "under proper restraint." That summer, "a negro man in . . . Sunday clothes" walked into an Adams County church and wanted to be seated with the white congregants. The congregation was "astounded" by the "impudent scamp" and demanded that he sit in the servants' section. Louisa Lovell fumed at the sight of "well dressed troupes of little proud niggers . . . going to school," and "the noisy, insolent, black girls & women" who dressed "so gaily & fashionably," thereby making Natchez a "disgusting Yankee & negro town." "How disgruntled it makes one feel, to see these creatures, as set up, out of their place," she wrote; "I believe that '*the* institution' is extinct."[47] For Lovell, slavery's extinction was not just a product of Lincoln's legal decree: she and other whites defined it via blacks' appropriation of white space. In so doing, slaves defied their expected roles as loyal servants by securing space in the masters' realms.[48]

In addition to occupying white-dominated spaces, slaves asserted their rights by refusing to work. Work was central to the lives of slaves in the Deep South. While enduring working lives that were constantly subject to the authority of masters and overseers, they attempted to exert some control over their work through day-to-day acts of resistance. So intertwined did work become with black Mississippians' identities that their ideas about a postemancipation future "were grounded in the experience of slavery and the role of labor in human society."[49] Nevertheless, work could not facilitate free bodies if those bodies were subject to white people's lashes, so slaves rebelled in their work.

Slaves feigned illness, pretended to misunderstand orders, slowed their pace, and "accidentally" broke tools. These forms of "silent sabotage" allowed slaves to act on self-loyalty, even if in highly circumscribed ways. Scholars observe that slaves' labor "represented an accommodation to the coercive power of their owners," which slaves tried to limit, drawing distinctions "between the time and services they 'owed' the master and the time and rewards they could claim for themselves." Prior to the Civil War, white Southerners, acting with the support of the federal government, managed to maintain the slave system despite slaves' day-to-day resistance. Once the war began, however, those same everyday actions against slavery combined with the pressure of Union arms to bring down the system. With so many white men fighting in the Confederate armies, whites left on the home front could not easily enforce slave discipline. In this context, slaves took the opportunity to refuse to work and otherwise demonstrate to whites that they had lost the "loyalty" of their black servants.[50]

Frustrated slaveholders complained constantly about slaves shirking their laboring duties. In early 1863, a concerned citizen informed Governor Pettus that conscription left few overseers to "enforce negro labor." This was problematic, since "the negroes are poor managers and naturally indolent at best." Later that year, former governor William McWillie petitioned Secretary of War Seddon for the release of overseers from the army. "[W]e have great apprehension that unless details are made for some overseers . . . our whole system of slave labor will be a failure," he warned. McWillie also appealed for the release of his own overseer to make his slaves work: "now that the [white] men are all gone it is very doubtful how long they will continue in a state of subordination." In a letter to General Reuben Davis, A. M. Alexander of Monroe City wanted her son's release from military service because, after two years without an overseer, her farm was "very much out of repair." Of course, her farm was "out of repair" because her slaves refused to work. Residents of Yalobusha County petitioned Secretary Randolph on behalf of a planter who wanted his son out of the army to control "a quantity of slaves doing nothing for the want of an overseer." Slaveholders emphasized the need for overseers to "enforce" slave labor by keeping slaves in "subjection." By refusing to work, slaves took advantage of a wartime environment that limited whites' ability to enforce black servility. They therefore rejected their masters' authority and, by extension, as McWillie recognized, attacked the "whole system of slave labor."[51]

The war's disruptions gave slaves the opportunity to stop working without fear of white retaliation. Planter Charles Whitmore noted that after Vicksburg fell, the few slaves that remained were "of no use." In November 1863, he had "six or seven 'servants' with me yet, who do a dogged & unwilling graceless service. . . . [T]hey have not earned their meat & bread since July." Whitmore hoped to convince his remaining slaves that "freedom does not consist in lazy, idle imprudence, but in stout attention to the duties of life." That spring, Loulie Feemster of Monroe County told her husband that "the negroes are as free as the white people, if you want one to do anything you have to ask them very kindly." William Nelson feared that with slaves not working, "the fatigue of household work" would tax his mother's and brother's "health and Patience." Aside from being angry over the loss of slave labor, slaveholders were angry over their inability to *enforce* that labor. For them, the inability to command servile loyalty in slaves signaled the collapse of the racial hierarchy itself, hence Feemster's angry observation that "the negroes are as free as the white people."[52]

Losing slave labor was bad enough, but the loss of white mastery really aroused slaveholders' ire. When Elizabeth Brown awoke on a mid-January morning in 1863, she noticed that "the servants had not done their work, and that did not preserve the equanimity of my temper." That spring, Elizabeth Ingraham complained that "the negroes are as idle as darkies only can be; nearly four weeks since 'their vacation began,' as Elsie calls it, and not a stroke of work." One wet nurse refused to work without pay, while others only milked cows for themselves. "They . . . go when they please, and do as they please; no one interferes," Ingraham griped. Molly Vaughn of Coffeeville, Mississippi, told her sister that her "impudent" slave, Sam, did not want to hire out, and threatened to run to the Yankees if forced to do so. Louisa Lovell complained that "the darkies do no work nowadays, except for themselves." After her cook ran off, she was forced to employ a neighbor's servant, and one of her slaves was "making money" in town. "The scamp always waves to me whenever I meet him," Lovell fumed; "the nigger is decidedly all bon ton now."[53] Slaves refused to work for their masters knowing that, in many cases, masters could no longer *compel* them to work. Slaveholders feared that if they lost control over the terms of black labor, the racial hierarchy would become obsolete. Even if they could negotiate terms of work with slaves, such negotiation gave blacks a measure of say in their labor and therefore contradicted the very idea of white racial mastery.

Sometimes, slaveholders found it downright painful to acknowledge their loss of mastery. In 1864, for example, Madison County civil authorities threatened a widow, Sarah Garrett, with jail time and a $1,500 fine for allowing three of her slaves, a barber and two draymen, "to go at large and trade as freemen." Petitioners supporting Garrett claimed that she "was, of necessity, to make them at all profitable, compelled to permit them to hire themselves." Because her slaves had become "demoralized & difficult of management," Garrett, in her "helpless state," chose to let them hire out rather than "permit them to go at large . . . without any restraint or control being exercised over them." Such language assumed Garrett's authority to "permit" her slaves to hire out, but her acquiescence to their demands suggests that she actually contracted with them. Garrett's slaves asserted their freedom to work on their own terms, threatening to flee unless she "permitted" them to hire out. They therefore undermined the master-slave relationship by invoking their rights to negotiate for compensated labor. Because work had for so long defined slaves' lives, being able to control their own work schedule signaled a very real freedom.[54]

For Garrett's slaves, freedom meant the right to negotiate their work, thereby acting in their own self-interest rather than on forced loyalty to their masters. Elizabeth Ingraham's slave, Elsie, similarly negotiated her work with her mistress, and Ingraham found it hard to accept her loss of mastery. Elsie had consistently resisted her husband, Jack's, requests to leave with him and their children, which Ingraham construed as Elsie's being "strictly honest and true, a rare thing in a black." In fact, Elsie began working on her own time and split the housework between herself and Ingraham, who began paying Elsie a twelve-dollar monthly wage plus food for her children. Moreover, Elsie told Jack that if he would "get her a home and a way of getting her a living," she would leave Ingraham. Until then, however, she did not want to associate with runaway field hands who were "only niggers" and "the commonest set of people."[55]

Ingraham's claim notwithstanding, Elsie stayed out of self-loyalty and family ties that she had forged in bondage, not out of loyalty to her mistress. Like Sarah Garrett's slaves, Elsie could have run away. But her vision of freedom differed from that of those who fled. Indeed, Elsie did not share an identity with runaway field hands, whom she dismissed as stemming from a lower class than herself. For runaways, freedom meant literal separation from their masters, but Elsie, like Garrett's slaves, envisioned freedom as control of her own labor and a home of her own. In her examination of Elsie's case, Noralee Frankel notes that because "their accommodations were often roomier and better furnished with more cast-off pieces from whites," domestic slaves like Elsie faced greater material losses by running off than did field hands. These distinctions reinforce how, beyond the common goal of escaping servile loyalty, freedom meant different things for different Mississippi slaves under different conditions.[56]

In addition to demanding the right to work on their own terms, slaves outright stole from whites. Because whites earned their wealth through black labor, slaves had long believed that they shared in the ownership of whites' property. For enslaved people, "stealing was not considered theft, merely appropriating their due." Alex Lichtenstein observes that because theft "represented the slave's insistence on receiving his or her due from the master" in terms of the "the right to products of labor," theft by slaves was "part of the sustained struggle between master and slave to define the perimeters of power." When slaves stole from whites, they did not just take material goods; they also flouted slaveholders' claims to the right to control every aspect of slaves' lives and, in the process, undermined slaveholders' perceived authority.[57]

As wartime circumstances eroded slaveholders' control, slaves took advantage of their expanded freedom to openly steal from whites. In 1864, Samuel Agnew described slaves holding "big parties" where each attendant paid "a hank of thread" to participate. "These parties explain the stolen thread, wheat and chickens which have been missed in the neighborhood," Agnew wrote, calling the slaves "verily great rascals." Elizabeth Brown berated "impudent niggers" who stole her wood, calling them "vile creatures who think themselves equal to whites." In one incident, she scolded an "impudent colored lady" for stealing, but "got insolence in return, & afterwards had more impudence from others." Warren County resident Ellen Batchelor accused her slave, Mary, of stealing clothing and jewelry. Mary admitted to taking the items but refused to return them because Batchelor "abused her." Elizabeth Ingraham complained that her fineries went missing to the slave cabins by servants who had "stolen to their very hearts [sic] content," and were therefore "well supplied" with muslin shirts, gold watches, and other like items. State judge Robert Hudson complained that "Lincoln's negro equality scheme" would only fuel blacks' "thieving propensities," and griped that there were "not . . . enough penitentiaries made to hold the convicted negro thieves." By taking slaveholders' property, slaves by extension undermined white claims to mastery. As a Union official noted after talking to runaway slaves at the Holly Springs contraband camp, "they do not consider it dishonest to take from their masters."[58] By accusing thieving slaves of thinking themselves "equal to whites," slaveholders recognized that the act of stealing from masters, especially in the context of wartime conditions that already limited whites' ability to enforce black servility, undermined the racial hierarchy by signaling the loss of white mastery. After all, "loyal" servants did not steal.

Property rights were especially crucial in terms of how urban slaves viewed freedom as a daily lived experience. As previously noted, historians have argued that rural slaves shared a collective, peasant class consciousness forged through their common fieldwork, which in turn led them to embrace freedom as the right to own and work Southern lands. Because the majority of Southern slaves worked in rural rather than urban environments, scholars have tended to associate a rural proletariat identity with the general pre- and postemancipation black experience.[59] Although I argue that there was no collective, working-class black identity among all Mississippi slaves, it is true that many rural slaves in the state envisioned freedom in the form of land ownership. Unlike urban slaves, rural slaves had primarily worked on farms and plantations, and this experience led them to associate freedom with the right to own and work the land on which they had for so long toiled. This was the case for freed people sent to work on the Davis Bend plantations, including those owned by Jefferson Davis and his brother Joseph, located thirty miles south of Vicksburg. In November 1864, Union officials designated Davis Bend a "home farm" where blacks could live and work the land. The government provided black workers with tools, animals, and seeds. By early 1865, roughly 1,750 former slaves worked the Bend in small collectives on separate plots.[60]

Freed people at Davis Bend, however, did not just want to lease and work the land; they wanted to own it. Union military chaplain James Hawley judged Davis Bend a "grand success" in which blacks farmed, sold their products, and kept their money, none of which "passed through the hands of white people." Colonel Samuel Thomas, recognizing how blacks desired to own the land where they worked "separate and apart from the white citizens of the state" and from their former owners, recommended to Major General Oliver Howard that several of the plantations be set aside for at least three years for the freed people's use.[61] Many newly freed rural slaves did indeed view freedom in terms of land ownership, but Mississippi's urban slaves had different conceptions of freedom, even as they shared with rural slaves a desire to escape white dominance and the servile loyalty it imposed.

Although both urban and rural Mississippi slaves owned personal property (private property that was movable), urban slaves more closely identified freedom in terms of personal property such as livestock, wagons, carriages, cash, produce, and prepared foods and goods rather than immovable land.[62] This association of freedom with personal property stemmed from the nature of urban slaves' work, which historians have argued placed these slaves in "a middle ground between slavery and freedom" by providing them with opportunities to hire out as well as labor in workshops and factories, where they could earn wages and work for periods of time apart from their masters. In contrast to rural slaves, whose vision of freedom via land ownership often tied them to a fixed location and made them reliant on subsistence agriculture, urban slaves were more mobile, working a variety of different jobs in cities and towns that were not tied to land. These slaves' presence in urban commercial hubs also integrated them more fully into the marketplace, where they bought and sold goods on a daily basis. The combined mobility of their work and their daily experience with city commerce, therefore, made urban slaves less attached to land as a symbol of freedom. After the war, former urban slaves stood a better chance of getting their property back from a federal government that paid out claims to personal property while refusing to redistribute land.[63]

Mississippi's freed people associated personal property with freedom in their postwar claims to the Southern Claims Commission (SCC). Nearly all of the former slaves who applied to the commission to receive payment for property taken by the Union army had lived and worked in Mississippi's cities and towns. Just as the contraband trade demonstrated how prewar commerce continued along familiar commercial channels even as the United States split into two distinct political entities, urban slaves demonstrated the continuity that connected the antebellum and postwar eras by linking their property ownership as bondspeople to their status as freed people. Like white Mississippians who filed claims, black people had to prove sufficiently their loyalty to the Union during the war. Owning property had provided urban slaves with a modicum of freedom before the war. As a result, property ownership defined their vision of freedom in a postemancipation South. The language freed people used to demonstrate their allegiance to federal authorities marks a crucial rhetorical intersection where notions of loyalty and property, freedom and servility, continuity and change all collided to reveal how the Civil War was both a significant break from, as well as a continuation of, the Southern past. More than just political loyalty was at stake in the claims process: for newly freed urban slaves, the right to consolidate their personal property constituted a declaration of self-loyalty in defiance of the forced servility under which they had labored for so long. For their part, the SCC took extra consideration of how slaves had served the Union during the war. After all, before emancipation, slaves owed their servile loyalty to slaveholders alone, not to any government. By aiding the Union war effort, however, they demonstrated a capacity to be loyal to a nation-state and expected compensation for their allegiance.[64]

In the postwar period, former slaves expressed Union loyalty because the Union granted them legal freedom. Of course, postwar property claims were inextricably bound up with declarations of allegiance, as any claimant desiring compensation *had* to claim that they were loyal, whether they were or not. Although assertions of loyalty in claims should not be taken at face value, they are important because they reveal how nationalism was always bound up with other allegiances. In this respect, former slave claimants shared similarities with white claimants, as both groups engaged in a process of affirming national loyalty in order to achieve personal ends. This process began during the war itself. Just as white Mississippians swore the Union oath in order to visit relations behind the lines, secure food and supplies, do business in Union-held areas, and avoid Confederate conscription, and just as contraband traders had to affirm Union loyalty to exchange goods at federal lines, black and white Mississippians who submitted claims did so in part out of self-interest.

Slavery, however, remained the major difference between black and white claimants. Whereas white claimants' affirmations of loyalty centered on preserving the Union, black claimants linked their interpretation of the war to their status as slaves. As Susanna Michele Lee writes, "[f]ormer slaves identified their loyal sympathies as a self-evident consequence of their enslavement."[65] In this respect, former slaves understood the war in terms of emancipation, not preservation of the Union. As a result, their claims to loyalty were inseparable from their experiences as enslaved people. Trying to gauge their "true" national feelings based on these claims misses the broader significance of how such constrained declarations of loyalty reveal the influence of multiple allegiances on individuals during and after the war.

Former urban slaves did not submit claims merely to voice their loyalty to the government: they made them because they wanted restitution for confiscated property. Freedom as a lived experience, as opposed to freedom as a legal abstract, meant the right to own personal property.[66] They had experienced this partial freedom before emancipation, but true freedom came when they could act in their own self-interest by earning wages and owning property free from slaveholders' authority. Many former urban slaves undoubtedly felt loyalty to the United States, but by couching their desires for property reparation in declarations of Union loyalty, they also acted on micro loyalties by making such statements as a means to personal ends.

George Winter, a former slave in Canton, Madison County, claimed twenty-four head of hogs and five hundred bushels of corn. "My sympathies were on the side of Union because I believed if they whipped [the Confederates] I should be free," he stated, although he had protested the army's taking of his property in 1864. Before the war, Winter "made a good deal of money" working odd jobs in town and "was in the habit of having property of his own." The commission's report acknowledged that Canton slaves often owned property. Jackson slave Martha Patton claimed livestock taken by Sherman's army. Patton's mistress permitted her to hire herself out for washing and sewing, and allowed her to "keep a table with Refreshments & Eatables" during fairs and other public events where she "made considerable money." With obvious pride, Patton noted: "I made the property and controlled it and everybody knew it was mine." Like Winter, she asked the army to spare her property, to no avail, and insisted that she "never assisted the Rebels in any way." Another Jackson slave, Maria Carter, claimed two horses and two wagons. Like Patton, she hired herself as a washerwoman and also "made some money" owning and operating an "eating stand" at the railroad depot, paying her mistress ten dollars of her earnings every month. Carter said that she "never lived much" with her owners and, fearing reenslavement by the Confederates, ran to Union lines to secure "the freedom of myself and my family."[67] These freed people associated personal property ownership with freedom because working and owning property before the war gave them tangible freedom in the form of limited independence from their masters' authority. For Carter especially, the Union army enforced the freedom she had already claimed for herself by running off. Beyond being free in the legal sense, *living* free for Carter meant the right to get back the property she had amassed on her own.

The influence of former urban slaves' loyalty layers ensured that their declarations of Union allegiance to the SCC were always intertwined with self-interest. Indeed, some explicitly argued that, in exchange for their loyalty, the government should reciprocate with property compensation. Natchez slave Richard Dorsey, a drayman who had "hired his time for fifteen years of his master," claimed over $1,200 in horses and riding supplies. During the war, he had used his dray service to haul commissary stores and cotton for the Union army without pay, claiming that he "always sympathized with the Union cause." Dorsey and other slaves were glad that the federal presence in Natchez had negated slaveholders' authority. "Colored men had no public reputation for loyalty—the white people knew that they all desired the success of the Union forces." But Dorsey also appreciated how Union occupation gave him the opportunity to get "all the business I wanted" and make money "right fast." Nelson Findley, a slave blacksmith in Woodville, Wilkinson County, claimed $355 in horses, which he had accumulated, alongside "a good deal of money & purchased stock," by purchasing and selling horses "as if I was free." Findley said that he was "for the Union cause" and followed the army hoping to get his horses back, only to end up working as a blacksmith and a fireman on Union transport boats. He deemed recompense for his lost property as just payment for his work for the Union during the war.[68] Dorsey and Findley recognized that the federal government made them legally free by undermining slaveholders' authority. Thus, they willingly aided the Union. In exchange for their service, however, they wanted payment for their impressed property. For them, loyalty to the nation was contingent on that nation's guaranteeing protection for property rights. For Dorsey and Findley, self-interest defined freedom in tandem with macro loyalty to the Union.

Other urban Mississippi slaves echoed Dorsey's and Findley's positions, suggesting that their loyalty to the Union was, in part, contingent on the expectation that the federal government would respect their rights to private property. In this respect, they ironically shared similarities with Mississippi planters who protested Confederate impressments of their slaves based on the idea that a nation worthy of their loyalty should respect the rights of property owners. Henry Banks, a slave carriage and hack driver in Vicksburg, claimed $1,000 in a carriage and horses. He explained that he had hired himself out for years and "got up considerable property when the war came on." When Union soldiers confiscated his hack and horses, Banks protested but ultimately affirmed that he was "as a loyal man," because if the Yankees prevailed, "we [slaves] could go where, when, & how we pleased, and our children would no longer be sold." Yet, it was precisely concerns about freedom of choice that lay behind Banks's anger over the loss of his property. During the war, he claimed that he "could have made Twenty dollars a day clear of expense," because cotton buyers "spent money like water" and Union soldiers "would pay anything you asked, and we asked all we thought we could get." Banks estimated that he "lost not less than Five Hundred Dollars."[69] He rooted his complaints about federal impressments in the claim that without his hack and horse, he was losing money, and that he deserved just compensation. Much like Mississippi planters who complained about Confederate impressments of slaves, Banks believed that in exchange for his loyalty, the federal government should respect his property rights.

A nation that respected property rights was equally important to Severin Boudreaux of Pascagoula. He was atypical for a Mississippi slave, being a mixed-race member of the state's small, French-descended, Gulf Coast Creole population.[70] Boudreaux was born to a free father and a slave mother, and he "was practically a free man" who "acted for himself, acquired property, and was to all intents and purposes his own master." He claimed over $6,000 to replace nearly two hundred head of cattle lost to Union forces. Boudreaux affirmed that while he did not serve either side during the war, he was "always in favor of the United States." This sympathy notwithstanding, he angrily told the claims interviewer, "I want you to put down that since the war ended I have suffered a great deal till now; because the United States government took all I had." Two witnesses testified on Boudreaux's behalf that Creoles were "generally good Union people" with some "exceptions among the white creoles" but "hardly any among the colored." After a long investigation, the commission approved his claim, concluding that Creole slaves often led "lives of independence" and pursued business "as they pleased." Like Henry Banks, Boudreaux said that he supported the Union but argued that a government bent on verifying his loyalty should respect his property rights. Although he was not typical of Mississippi slaves, Boudreaux shared with other urban slaves the view that, alongside the legally free status granted by the federal government, self-interest via property ownership was essential to how they experienced freedom on a daily basis.[71]

The fact that Mississippi slaves acted on loyalty layers does not negate the fact that nationalism was one of the loyalties that drove their wartime behavior. Even Severin Boudreaux, who lived in relative independence due to an absent mistress, was still ineligible to vote, and white Creoles considered him racially inferior. This underscored how even the most "free" of Mississippi slaves were still under the heel of white authority. Many slaves therefore considered the Union to be a powerful symbol of their newfound freedom. After all, Union armies helped to undermine the authority of slaveholders. Slaves aided the Union cause by hauling goods for federal troops and working as laborers, while others worked to escape and undermine slaveholders' mastery by fighting for the Union as spies and soldiers.

Slaves throughout the state offered Union officials valuable intelligence on Confederate plans and troop movements. "I find the Yankees keep well-posted through negroes . . . who run as couriers to them, taking by-paths through the swamp," observed a Mississippi cavalry officer. In 1862, a Union officer stationed in Corinth told a colonel to protect slaves who brought "important information concerning the enemy." During the Vicksburg campaign, an Iowa regiment colonel informed General John Rawlins that "bright and intelligent" slaves provided "a great deal of information in regard to the Condition of affairs at Vicksburg." One of the slaves had worked on Confederate artillery and knew "the position & numbers of almost every gun from Vicksburg down to Warrenton." In September 1864, Jack, a Hinds County slave, described how he went "thrgh [sic] the woods & cane brakes [and] swam Big Black River" to reach Union lines at Vicksburg, where he told the Federals that Lieutenant General Nathan Bedford Forrest was stalking the Pearl River "with six (6) thousand cavly & right smart of artillery." Union officials recognized the military value of runaway slaves' local knowledge.[72]

Mississippi slaveholders chafed at slaves' colluding with the Federals. "Oh! Deliver me from the 'citizens of African descent,'" Louisa Lovell wrote; "they are all alike ungrateful and treacherous, every servant is a spy upon us, & everything we do or say is reported to the Yankees." In one such example, Pike County resident S. N. Gilman implored jailers in Jackson not to release his runaway slave, Henry Banks. Gilman claimed that Banks had become "dangerous to the community" and would run to the enemy, "to whom his services would at this time be invaluable" due to his "perfect knowledge of this part of the state." Confederate spy M. Carrigan told General John Pemberton that a friend had given him a slave woman who was "more trouble than all the rest of the negroes in the neighborhood. She is a spy for the Yankees." Carrigan said that his friend "wanted me to bring her into the swamp and kill her," noting that "he would have killed her himself but is so closely watched that no opportunity has presented itself."[73] Slaves betrayed their expected servile loyalty to slaveholders by spying for the Federals, knowing full well that Union victory would undermine slaveholders' authority. The master class, in turn, reacted with outrage at such "ungrateful" servant betrayal. They understood that by aiding the Union, slaves were undermining the Confederate war effort, but, more importantly, they believed that slaves were also fighting to reverse the master-slave relationship.

Beyond spying for the Union, black Mississippians also fought in its armies. Most accounts credit Mississippi with providing roughly seventeen thousand black troops, 21 percent of the state's black men between the eligible fighting ages of eighteen and forty-five. In his recent study of Civil War Mississippi, Timothy Smith expands this estimate to twenty-five thousand to thirty thousand black Union troops by including regiments raised in Mississippi but credited to other states, and regiments raised outside of the state but consisting of black Mississippians. Most of these troops served garrison duty in the occupied parts of the state, although the regiment raised at the Corinth contraband camp took part in the Battle of Brice's Crossroads in June 1864, and the Fifty-Fourth US Colored Infantry earned accolades for their fighting at Milliken's Bend in June 1863.[74]

White Mississippians refused to accept the idea of black soldiers. Elizabeth Brown, for example, was "very much alarmed" when more Union cavalry marched through Natchez. "I thought they were armed men (I cannot call them Soldiers) of African *descent*," she wrote, but was relieved that "they were [white] Yankees, because of the two evils I think I would rather have the latter." Brown distinguished black soldiers from "Yankees," because if blacks were soldiers for the Union cause, then they rejected unconditionally loyalty to Mississippi's white master class, a true "evil" in Brown's eyes. When William Sively heard of black Union raiders in Hinds and Madison Counties, he told his sister that "*a* negro will never get any quarter from me." The war's most infamous "no quarter" instance came in April 1864, when Confederates under General Nathan Bedford Forrest massacred surrendered black troops at Fort Pillow, Tennessee. Referencing the massacre, black soldiers in northern Mississippi "shook their fists" at white civilians and "told them they were going to show Forrest that they were his rulers." Samuel Agnew later described how Forrest returned to Mississippi with Union prisoners, including black soldiers. "The most of the negroes were shot, our men being so much incensed that they shoot them wherever they see them," he wrote; "it is certain that a great many negroes have been killed."[75]

White Mississippians' "no quarter" approach to black Union troops was merely one facet of the broader personal conflict in which they tried to reassert mastery over blacks. In 1863, Union general James Wadsworth toured the Mississippi Valley to assess the status of blacks in the region. Even though many slaves had fled to Union lines, he expressed worry over "the efforts that are made to restore them to slavery" and predicted that postwar Mississippi would be host to "a sort of war between freedom and slavery." Wadsworth believed that if white Mississippians accepted emancipation as "a fixed fact," the Federals could withdraw from the state. Yet, one planter told him that "we are ready to give up the name of 'slavery,' we care nothing about the name, but we must have a certain control over these people." In light of such sentiments from whites, Wadsworth advocated that the government divide plantations out among black families and arm blacks for protection, but admitted that such efforts required "very complicated machinery for the Govt. to manage it."[76] Wadsworth proved prophetic. Even after Confederate surrender, "a sort of war between freedom and slavery" waged on, but it was the same conflict between slaves and slaveholders that had flared during the antebellum period and escalated during the Civil War. As black people struggled to realize their visions of freedom in postwar Mississippi, the master class fought to maintain the racial hierarchy. The federal army found itself the de facto—if not entirely dedicated—mediator between these two factions.

In the waning months of the war, as Confederate defeat seemed all but certain, former slaves found that despite emancipation, former slaveholders were determined to maintain white dominance. Black Mississippians chose different paths to freedom, with some choosing to flee from, and others to work as paid laborers for, their old masters. Nevertheless, they demanded that whites recognize that freedom signaled the end of the master-slave relationship and its attendant expectations of black servile loyalty. Confederate defeat eventually deprived white Mississippians of a slaveholding republic, but black freedom threatened to divest them of the personal power they had long wielded over servants at the most intimate level. They therefore refused to drop the coercive methods used to enforce black servility and uphold the racial hierarchy.

In October 1864, for example, Nat Green, the slave of Thomas Jones of DeSoto County, considered fleeing until Jones offered to pay him wages if he stayed to work. Green worked for Jones until May 1865 but "never received any pay whatsoever." When Green demanded his wages, Jones threatened his life, after which Green fled to Union lines. Betsey Robinson, of Panola County, testified that she had worked for her master well into 1865 because "he never gave me any information in regard to My being free. I left him because My self and Children were suffering for food and clothing." Before fleeing, Robinson demanded payment from her master for "part of the years labor," which he refused. In a particularly violent incident, Harriet Kilgore stated that in December 1865, when she refused to work due to a backache, her master, Landon Kilgore, beat her; she said: "I thought that I was free and would do nothing he told me too." Kilgore stripped her and flogged her with "a stake used to hold up th [*sic*] side boards of a waggon Box" and threatened death if she reported the beating. Harriet fled to federal authorities the next day, claiming that "the white people in my neighborhood tell all the Colored ones that they are not free but are slaves and I did not know that I was free till you told me so today." In these cases, slaveholders denied slaves the freedom that the law had granted to them, and used the same coercive methods that characterized the master-slave relationship to enforce postemancipation black servility. What mattered to them was not the semantics of racial control but the ability to maintain it.[77]

Freed people expected their former masters to honor the right to act on micro loyalties to self and family. When whites refused, some blacks protested with their feet. When Madison County planter A. Murdock contracted with two of his former slaves to leave their jobs in Vicksburg and work for him, the men instead took their families from his plantation and returned to the city. They encouraged others to take advantage of Vicksburg wages that paid sixty dollars per month. Murdock's former slaves told the Federals that he was "whipping them badly," to which Murdock claimed that he only did so "when actually Necessary" to "enforce necessary obedience and discipline on the farm." Murdock's former slaves acted in their own and their family's interests by removing their kin from his authority and seeking their own employment in Vicksburg. In doing so, they also rejected his demands for continued obedience. As Sharon Ann Holt writes, "because family loyalties survived despite the depredations of white hegemony, whenever African Americans displayed the power of their family ties, they were simultaneously mocking the vanity of white tyranny."[78]

The former master class did not take kindly to this mocking of their authority. When a Marshall County freedman named Dabney was repeatedly punched and caned by the son and mother of his former master, he fled to

Union authorities. Dabney believed that his employer wanted to drive him from the premises "so as to keep the crop for his own use and benefit." Based on this testimony, federal authorities fined Dabney's employer and forced him to pay Dabney his share of wages. In November 1865, several of Carroll County planter Joseph Stanley's former slaves testified to Union authorities that after they refused to work in the afternoon, Stanley tried to whip them, beat one woman over the head with a hoe, and then shot at them when they fled the premises. A federal peace officer informed Stanley that if he wanted the freedmen to work for him, "perhaps it will be best not to whip them."[79] In these cases, freed people either attempted to separate themselves from their former owners or invoked federal authority to claim the wages owed them as free workers. Well aware of whites' intentions to uphold the master-slave relationship by enforcing servile loyalty, black Mississippians resisted this effort by attempting to live out their conceptions of freedom and calling on federal authorities to protect their new rights.

Federal authorities were certainly aware of the continuing racial conflict. In July 1865, chaplain James Hawley observed that the common feeling among planters was that "the Freed men should remain on the plantations . . . 'as they always had done'" (emphasis in original). Planters, he noted, were most concerned with "1. How to control the negro. 2. How to work him hard enough. 3. How to pay him with the least possible expense. . . . [T]hey could not endure the thot [sic] of giving up the blessed privilege of 'licking a nigger.'" Black Mississippians recognized that whatever federal law said, the first line of struggle continued to be with the former slaveholders. As Hawley recognized, "the rough barbarism of war has torn off the veil that covered the radical barbarism of Slavery."[80] For Union officials, the war against the Confederacy had overshadowed the internal war between black and white Mississippians, a war that freed people continued to wage against the "radical barbarism" that threatened to diminish their freedom by denying their right to express loyalty to anyone but Mississippi's white master class.

By mid-1865, federal authorities recognized that racial conflict in Mississippi was intensifying. They agreed that black rights needed to be enforced but argued over what measures the government should take to do so. An August 1865 Freedmen's Bureau circular reminded whites that "Emancipation is a fact" and chastised them for "abuses of Freedmen of the gravest character." While it admitted that blacks were "universally suspicious of white men and especially of former slave-holders," the circular warned that only "kindness and fair dealing" could minimize racial conflict. A month earlier, cavalry officer H. R. Brinkerhoff reported on planters' efforts to return freed people "peremptorily to their '*masters*'" by denying them fair treatment as workers. "There is already a secret, Rebel, anti-emigration Pro-slavery Party formed or forming in this State," he noted, who were laboring "for a restoration of the old system of slavery . . . or some manner of involuntary servitude." Brinkerhoff indicated a thread of continuity between the antebellum, wartime, and postwar periods. By using words like "masters," "slavery," and "Rebel," he detailed how Mississippi whites planned to bridge these periods through the continued upholding of the racial hierarchy.[81]

The Civil War in Mississippi escalated the internal conflict between slaves and slaveholders that had simmered during the antebellum era but intensified when the Union army arrived in the state. Slaveholders insisted that their slaves only express an unconditional servile loyalty to their masters, which was the basis of the master-slave relationship. Slaves rejected this servility by acting on micro loyalties to self, family, and community. These loyalty layers, forged under slavery, were both the means and the ends in slaves' struggle for freedom. They enabled enslaved people to construct realized lives despite being under slaveholders' dominance, and they informed the multiple conceptions of freedom that individual people formulated during and after the war. Rather than displaying a collective, rural proletarian identity that envisioned freedom within the constructs of a separate black nation, Mississippi slaves embraced many different visions of what freedom entailed.

The various ways that slaves rejected their masters' authority during the war were all methods that they had employed during the antebellum era and reflected individual slaves' interpretations of freedom. Recognizing the opportunity provided by the encroachment of Union forces in Mississippi, many slaves ran off to federal lines, demonstrating that for them, freedom from white mastery meant physical separation from their owners. Slaves who did not run off nonetheless appropriated spaces for themselves within the realm of white control. Some chose to work according to their own schedules, while others chose not to work at all. Because work had been so central to slaves' lives, many envisioned freedom as controlling their own labor. Some slaves even appropriated the violent coercion whites used to enforce servility in blacks by physically attacking their owners, using their bodies to assert their autonomy in their masters' presence. Because their work lives centered on agriculture, rural slaves saw freedom in land ownership. By contrast, Mississippi's urban slaves, whose masters frequently permitted them to hire out, hold property, and even run small businesses, saw freedom in property rights and wage work. Some slaves experienced freedom by spying for, or fighting in, the Union army. By aiding the Union's fight against the Confederacy, slaves by extension rejected slaveholders' racially based mastery, the ideology that the Confederacy was founded to protect. Although freedom meant different things for different black Mississippians, they shared a common desire to separate themselves from white dominance, thereby gaining the right to openly act on loyalties to self, family, community, and nation free from the racial hierarchy.

Mississippi slaveholders interpreted slaves' wartime behavior as disloyalty to the master class, not as treason against the Confederate government. As the intermediaries between slaves and the state, they understood that slaves were waging an internal war against the racial hierarchy. As the primary enforcers of white mastery, slaveholders believed that if they lost the ability to enforce black servility, then the racial hierarchy would be reversed. This distinction matters because it reveals a critical continuity between the antebellum, wartime, and postwar eras. Because the vast majority of interactions between blacks and whites took place at the local level, the collapse of the Confederate government did not signal an end to the racial hierarchy that was its cornerstone. The right of whites to exercise total dominance over blacks, justified by the idea that slaves, as such, were expected to express unconditional loyalty to their masters, had been the underlying principle of Southern race relations during the antebellum period. Protecting this right was the central goal of the Confederate cause, but the ideal of white mastery transcended the Confederacy and continued to guide white Mississippians' actions in the postwar period precisely because it was a consistent theme of Southern history.

"ALLEGIANCE AND PROTECTION ARE AND MUST BE RECIPROCAL"

The Aftermath of War in Mississippi

IN AN 1866 SPEECH TO A DESOTO COUNTY GRAND JURY, MISSISSIPPI LAW-yer James Trotter reflected on the Civil War and what the South should expect now that it was over. "We made a sacrifice of upward of 4,000,000, slaves[,] a *peace-offering* upon the altar of the Union," he stated. Mississippi now had "every motive to be true and loyal" to the federal government, he continued, and, in return for this loyalty, Mississippians reserved the right to "assert the rightful jurisdiction of our State and enforce our own municipal codes." Trotter added that although state laws regarding "the labor and the conduct of our late slaves" were not "entirely satisfactory" to federal au-thorities, he hoped that they would allow Mississippi to "enjoy the protection which our allegiance challenges. For allegiance and protection are and must be reciprocal." Writing to his wife in August 1865, James Alcorn similarly advocated Southern loyalty in exchange for racial control. He advocated letting blacks testify in court and vote because "political equality does not imply by any means social equality." Black political behavior, he wrote, could be circumscribed, noting that "his [the freedman's] testimony may be made to go to his credibility, & his suffrage may be based upon his property.[1]

Trotter's and Alcorn's statements outlined how white Mississippians justi-fied renouncing Confederate loyalty in exchange for the right to enforce the racial hierarchy at the local level. Alcorn, Mississippi's most prominent Old Whig scalawag, recognized the reality of emancipation, and he knew that black people would demand political rights. To deal with this reality, he pro-posed granting limited black suffrage while still quelling their vote numbers enough to keep whites in control of state government.[2] Thus, after the Civil War, white Mississippians were determined to uphold white racial dominance based on the underlying ideology of black servility. Their attempt to do so, and freed people's resistance to such an attempt, was the most significant of the continuities that linked Mississippi's antebellum, Civil War, and postwar periods.

By the spring of 1865, the Confederacy was nearing total collapse, and Mississippi in particular was in shambles. As civil law ceased to function, deserters infested nearly every county in the state, plundering at will. The state's Confederate legislature had its last meetings in February and March, although it existed as a government in name only, being unable to aid or assist its citizenry or pass any enforceable laws. Following Robert E. Lee's surrender to Ulysses S. Grant at Appomattox Court House on April 9, 1865, and Joseph Johnson's surrender to William T. Sherman on April 26, Richard Taylor's forces at Mobile remained the only significant Confederate army east of the Mississippi. When Taylor finally surrendered his command of the Department of Alabama, Mississippi, and East Louisiana to Union general Richard Springs Canby on May 4, official Confederate military activities in Mississippi ended. Governor Charles Clark and the Mississippi state legislature made a final defiant stand in Jackson on May 20, authorizing themselves to negotiate postwar peace settlements with federal authorities. A few days later, however, Union officials arrested Clark and sent him to Fort Pulaski, Georgia, where he remained until receiving pardon several weeks later.[3]

In June 1865, President Andrew Johnson appointed William L. Sharkey provisional governor of Mississippi. A longtime admirer of Henry Clay, Sharkey was an old-line conservative Whig who had opposed secession in 1861 and had even conferred with Union officers during the war about plans for eventual Reconstruction. In August 1865, Sharkey called a constitutional convention in Jackson, which eventually voted to abolish slavery and establish a new constitution. It also scheduled elections for state and local officials for October. Despite his conservative unionism, Sharkey balked at securing political rights for the freed people. He argued against federal military intervention on behalf of freed people's rights, insisting that these issues should be tackled by the reconstruction convention and the state legislature. Federal military officials, however, disagreed. Although President Johnson had vaguely stated that the military was to "aid" but not "interfere" with the provisional government's affairs, the 1865 Act of Congress establishing the Freedmen's Bureau placed it under the control of the War Department, thereby empowering the military, in the eyes of many federal officers, to help freed people in any way it saw fit.[4]

The Federals' suspicion that the provisional government, and, indeed, the entire white population refused to accept the realities of emancipation was well founded. In October 1865, voters elected former Confederate general Benjamin G. Humphreys governor and packed the state legislature with erstwhile Confederates. This body immediately passed a group of laws collectively known as the Black Code. James Currie writes that "there is a quantum jump . . . between emancipation and equality," and Mississippi at that time was "unwilling to consider seriously any proposition by which black men and whites would legally become equals." The Black Code prevented most blacks from renting or leasing rural lands, denied them the right to own firearms, required that they display difficult-to-acquire licenses to hold a variety of jobs, and forced them to document that they were not vagrants by providing written evidence of having a home. The code also contained vagrancy laws under which "suspicious" blacks could be arrested, fined, and "hired out" to their former masters if they could not pay the fine.[5] Lest there be any confusion that the antebellum ideology of black servile loyalty underlay this code, one of its provisions stated:

All the penal and criminal laws now in force in this State, defining offences and describing the mode of punishment for crimes and misdemeanors committed by slaves, free negroes, or mulattoes . . . are hereby re-enacted, and declared to be in full force and effect, against freedmen, free negroes and mulattoes, except so far as the mode and manner of trial and punishment have been changed or altered by law.[6]

The newly elected legislature demonstrated how the state's white population continued its struggle to uphold the racial hierarchy. Not coincidentally, their resolve intensified amid rumors throughout 1865 that armed blacks in the South would rebel against whites, and that the federal government would confiscate white-owned land or the freed people would simply seize the land for themselves. Many whites expected the insurrection to come to a head during the Christmas season. Stephen Nissenbaum notes that African Americans had long associated Christmas with "a symbolic inversion of the social hierarchy—with grand gestures of paternalist generosity by the white patrons who had always governed their lives." Masters acted in their own self-interest by giving slaves gifts and leisure time during the holidays, hoping that doing so would dissuade rebellious behavior in the coming year. Nonetheless, slaves took advantage of these paternalistically granted holiday "freedoms" by moving in unconstrained fashion around the planters' homes and symbolically mocking white authority through popular revelry, which included dancing while dressed in the style of their gentry patrons. In 1865, however, white Mississippians feared that freed slaves had new white patrons, the federal army, who would give them the ultimate Christmas gift: reversal of the racial hierarchy. Thus, the Christmas insurrection scare thrived on the same fears exhibited by white Mississippians during the war, namely that disloyal blacks would rise up in violent rebellion to reverse the racial hierarchy.[7]

In order to prevent this supposed Christmas rebellion, white Mississippians violently intensified their efforts to reassert racial dominance. This was part of a general pattern throughout the former Confederate South, where, as Kidada Williams writes, "the violence that white southerners had used to subjugate enslaved and free blacks before and during the Civil War continued and intensified after emancipation."[8] White Mississippians believed that acknowledging the reality of emancipation did not entail accepting social equality. Just as they had used coercive violence to enforce black servility under slavery, they also used it to control black people's access to land, employment, firearms, suffrage, and the courts, and to restrict their freedoms of speech and assembly.

Whites used unsubstantiated fears of black uprisings to justify violence. White fears and paranoia of black revolts had thrived in the South before and during the war, but, as Mark Wahlgren Summers observes, "the war's conclusion only intensified the tendency to accept misinformation." He notes that "desperation breeds the most outlandish hopes," and, for white Southerners bent on enforcing black servile loyalty, "the wildest rumors were welcome, when they promised a revolution in events." The maintenance of black servile loyalty constituted just such a "revolution in events." Rumors of a Christmas uprising were rooted in a kernel of truth. Desirous of economic independence, many freed people believed that a redistribution of land was coming at the end of the planting season, and they held off from signing new work contracts until 1866. Further, to accommodate daytime work schedules and to avoid white retaliation, freed people gathered at night to hold fraternal assemblies and discuss politics. Whites saw in these after-hours gatherings evidence of conspiracies. In the final months of 1865, Summers notes, "white southerners expected the worst, even without evidence"; then again, evidence for them was unnecessary anyway, since "only by the severest of subordination could one race keep the other from striving to dominate." Rumors of a black Christmas uprising further justified, in whites' eyes, the need for racial coercions.[9]

Mississippi state officials stoked fears of a coming holiday insurrection in the fall of 1865. In October, for example, Governor Sharkey warned

Freedmen's Bureau commissioner Oliver Howard that blacks expected "a distribution of property this winter" and that "a general revolt is contemplated in case the property is not divided." Sharkey demanded that black people be disarmed and arrested for idleness and called for the removal of all black federal troops from the state. He included a letter from a concerned Holmes County citizen who claimed that the freed people were planning to "rise and do a great deal of harm to the country." Federal officials like Colonel Samuel Thomas were often skeptical of such claims. "People who talk so much of insurrection, and idleness, and vagrancy among the freedmen, have an ulterior motive," he told Howard; "if they can once get free of all control, they know they can do as they please with the negro." Thomas even noted that, privately, Sharkey admitted that "all fears of an insurrection were unfounded."[10] By painting the freed people as a threat to public safety, Mississippi whites hoped to remove all federal protection for black people from the state, thereby making it easier for them to circumscribe black freedoms.

Rumors of an impending black insurrection continued to swirl around the state. Noxubee County citizens told President Johnson that the freed people expected to "get our lands Homes mules Horses Corn &&c &c by Christmas," adding that if the government did not redistribute these things, blacks intended to "fight & kill off the white population & get what they want by force." Natchez militia captain William Martin warned Sharkey that freed people would "never again work for white men." Martin recommended disarming blacks, insisting that "[s]uch a Servile population—So numerous so disaffected, So misinformed, so ignorant & withall [sic] so vicious Can not be held in check very Easily."[11] Both of these reports claimed that blacks intended to revolt if they did not receive whites' land and property, but Martin's language was especially telling. In casting freed people as an inherently "servile" population, he by extension justified retaliatory crackdowns to enforce black people's "proper" place as a group who should demonstrate unconditional loyalty to their once-and-forever white masters.

Federal authorities recognized that the rumors of a black Christmas insurrection corresponded with increasing white violence against freed people. In late November, Pike County–based Captain James Mathews told Major George Reynolds that "daily murders" were being perpetrated by "Militia or black cavalry . . . who seem to have special fears of an insurrection" and were "particularly adapted to hunting, flogging and killing colored people." Mathews believed that circulating reports of black insurrection was "a mere subterfuge by which to justify the most foul and bloody murders . . . upon a race that is unarmed and unable even to defend themselves." He asked for more federal troops, noting that whites were always the first aggressors and that blacks were "defenceless in the eyes of the law, and before tribunals whose prejudices are as old as the laws themselves."[12] Mathews understood that whites spread rumors of a black uprising to justify the continued sub-jugation of freed people and recognized that the violence of 1865 was a continuation of the long-running racial struggle in which whites, driven by old "prejudices," tried to enforce servile loyalty in blacks.

In response to Mathews's plea for more manpower to prevent the abuse of freed people, Captain Adam Kemper first advised him to judge whether the civil authorities showed "good faith" in restoring the functions of gov-ernment, or whether they wanted to use government "as an instrument for oppressing the Freedmen and reducing them to their old condition of slav-ery." That Mississippi whites seemed intent on the latter was born out in the way planters continued to use coercive methods to dominate their "disloyal" workers.[13] In late November, for example, freedman George Lanier agreed to work for a Mr. Rusell, of Yalobusha County, in exchange for monthly pork rations. After Rusell refused to give Lanier the pork, however, Lanier threatened to complain to the Freedmen's Bureau, to which Rusell responded, "the Buzzards would pick his Bones Yet." When Lanier refused to back down, Rusell had him hunted down, arrested, and forced to sign a year's labor con-tract with his former master. That same month, freedmen William Head and Nelson Porter began building on land they had rented outside of Jackson, when several whites told them to leave under threat of being shot. After Head and Porter ignored the threats, they found a card attached to a stake on their land that read, "I think you had better leave here." A few days later, the state legislature passed the law forbidding blacks to rent rural lands.[14] Such instances of white abuse against freed people continued to erupt amid rumors of the impending Christmas revolt, the supposed existence of which white Mississippians used to justify their violent reassertion of mastery.

Black Mississippians protested against this abuse, well aware that it stemmed from whites' desire to uphold the racial hierarchy. Yet, beyond their desire to be free from white dominance, freed people expressed different objectives for their postemancipation lives, depending on their particular circumstances. A November 1865 resolution passed by African Americans in Vicksburg, for example, demanded that black people be permitted to vote, own property, and be paid fair wages. "All we ask is justice," they stated; "remove legal disability, give us the rights of citizens in law, and then no special legislation is needed for the colored man more than the white. The only difficulty of the new order of things, arises from a desire to evade, rather than grant justice." These urban freed people called for political and social equality with whites. They espoused a vision of freedom based on equal citizenship under the law, and they protested whites' desire to uphold the same racial hierarchy that had defined the antebellum social order despite the "new order of things."[15]

In early December, a group of freed people from Port Gibson expressed similar sentiments to Governor Humphreys. "Mississippi has abolished—slavery," they wrote; "does She mean it or is it a policy for The present[?] we fear from the late acts of the legislature that she will not treat us as free." They maintained that rumors of black insurrection were a "falsehood" and denied any desire to become masters over whites. "Now we are free [what] would we rise for. . . . [W]e do not want our rights by murdering." They did not want to reverse the racial hierarchy, but these freed people emphatically wanted to escape from it. They cited the Black Code's provisions that gave white employers total control over their labor, including the right to hunt black workers if they fled, as slavery in all but name. "We are [too] well acquainted with the yelping of bloodhounds and the tareing of our fellow servents To pisces when we were slaves and now we are free. . . . [A]ll we ask is justice and to be treated like humane beings."[16] In contrast to the Vicksburg petitioners, who advanced specific legal reforms geared toward achieving political and social equality with whites, the Port Gibson writers demanded basic human rights. The Vicksburg petitioners' specific, grammatical calls for legal reforms suggest that they were likely former urban slaves or free blacks before the war, groups who displayed a greater level of education and formal political engagement than did rural slaves.[17] By contrast, the Port Gibson freed peoples' ungrammatical prose, and their complaints about how their current status resembled the conditions of slavery, suggest that they were likely less educated former field hands. Their immediate experiences as plantation slaves informed their vision of freedom as the right not to be treated as forced labor, whereas the Vicksburg petitioners viewed freedom in terms of specific legal rights. Both groups denounced white racial dominance, but they shared different visions of what constituted freedom in postwar Mississippi.

Although they recognized the injustices perpetrated against freed people, federal authorities still found it difficult to prevent such abuse. In late November, Major Thomas Wood, commander of the Department of Mississippi, flatly stated to Governor Humphreys that the Black Code was "enacted for the protection of slavery" and that any disarmament of freed people should be done only after the "full consultation and understanding between the civil and military authorities." Major George Reynolds agreed. "The old code of Miss may have made it unlawful for free negroes to carry arms but these laws were passed in the interests of slavery and its protection," he wrote; "such a thing as an 'insurrection' among the Freedmen is entirely improbable and could only be brought about by an attempt to reduce them to their former position." Governor Humphreys, however, refused to rescind the law disarming freed people. If freed people knew that they could rely on federal forces for protection, he reasoned, they would revolt.[18] Major Wood nonetheless refused to abide by Humphreys's order and requested clarification from Washington as to whether blacks should be disarmed. Secretary of War Edwin Stanton eventually confirmed to Wood that decisions regarding disarmament of any persons in Mississippi fell to the military authorities in the state. Nevertheless, Wood never officially declared the disarmament law null and void, and although one circuit court in the state found the law unconstitutional, enforcement of the court's decision was largely nonexistent. Wood preferred to deal with cases of abuse toward blacks on an individual basis to avoid mass violence and promote goodwill between the races, but he lacked the manpower to effectively curb abuses throughout the state.[19]

After all the rumors and all the fear, Christmas Day came and went without incident. No property was redistributed, and no blacks rose up against whites. The so-called Christmas rebellion had a very real significance, however, because it underscored how the struggle between blacks and whites over the racial hierarchy continued even after the Civil War and emancipation. At stake was the notion of loyalty, which group would still be masters, and which group would still be loyal servants.

This struggle continued via the competing micro loyalties of blacks and whites, as both groups sought opposing goals in their efforts to define what constituted freedom. By spreading rumors of rebellion, white Mississippians acted on a shared racial loyalty that reinforced their commitment to maintaining black servility in the face of freed people's demands for civil rights. Although black Mississippians did not violently revolt, they spread rumors of impending land redistribution in order to petition the government into action, demanding the right to openly act in their own self-interest. Thus, the real conflict underlying the Christmas rebellion was not between blacks who wanted to revolt and whites who feared such a revolt; rather, the conflict stemmed from the long-simmering tension between whites who demanded that blacks remain loyal to the old master class, and black people who wanted the right to act on their own loyalties. By calling for land redistribution, blacks by extension called for the ability to hold attachments to self, family, neighborhood, and nation free from white dominance. This black political mobilization spurred a strong white backlash that undermined Presidential Reconstruction, challenged former slaveholders' authority, and brought to the forefront issues of equality that Republican congressional radicals would advocate in 1867.[20]

The persistence of both white paranoia and black political mobilization underlines how the influence of multiple loyalties in Mississippi bridged the antebellum, Civil War, and postwar periods with threads of continuity despite the very real ruptures of war and emancipation. Long-standing racial loyalties united white Mississippians in a way Confederate protective nationalism never could, and the importance blacks placed on their own multiple allegiances drove their continued opposition to white reassertions of racial dominance.[21] That the stifling of black freedoms continued after the Christmas rebellion failed to materialize only validated freed people's belief that their struggle against the racial hierarchy did not end with emancipation and Confederate defeat. Their difficulties in this struggle were compounded by federal authorities who were sympathetic to blacks' plight but lacked the manpower, and often the patience and will, to effectively curb abuse against the freedmen.

Freed people protested federal refusal to protect their rights as "a desertion by the government" and argued that if left to the whims of "their old masters ... to secure ... their rights & privileges," they would "receive nothing but oppression and ill treatment," making their condition "worse than it was in the days of slavery." Although he recognized that the state was coming under the control of "overpowered but not unconquered Rebels" who aimed to "drive out the thieving Yankees and shoot the niggers," state Freedmen's Bureau commissioner Samuel Thomas chafed at blacks' refusal "to settle down as contented laborers," calling them "children" who "can appreciate nothing that does not secure for them some immediate advantage. The lessons we have been taking in political economy during the last year are lost upon them."[22]

Like Thomas, other federal officials recognized how black Mississippians faced resistance from recalcitrant whites but nonetheless expected them to work for their former masters. US cavalry corps commander Edward Hatch lamented that freed people were "becoming more and more demoralized" despite the army's best efforts to "enjoin industry and quiet." While he acknowledged some white abuse of black workers, Hatch complained that "the slightest friction of the home harness is enough to drive them into vagabondism" and expressed the belief that blacks were "determined not to work." Hatch thought the army incapable of remedying this problem. "As Federal Soldiers we can neither recognize Slavery nor its equivalent, and are left helpless lookers on while the broken ship and crazed crew are drifting on the rocks together."[23] Hatch's statement summarized a general feeling among federal officials that even with the Confederacy in ashes, they were unable to quell the ongoing conflict between black and white Mississippians. The feeling that the military was a helpless onlooker to a racial struggle that threatened to heave the state into social chaos underscored how local loyalties maintained a persistent influence on blacks and whites.

What emerged during Mississippi's postwar era was not, as some historians argue, merely a reemergent Confederate nationalism in the form of the Lost Cause.[24] Such a conclusion conflates localized micro loyalties with macro national allegiance. Rather, racial loyalties, in the form of whites' desire to uphold black servility and blacks' desire to reject that servility and assert their rights to act on multiple allegiances free from white control, continued to shape sociopolitical conflicts in the state. As Christopher Waldrep notes, the racial hierarchy defined how white Mississippians interpreted the legacy of the war. To them, "the Civil War . . . did not mean they could no longer whip blacks. Emancipation did not mean that whites could not force their former slaves to work." The fact that most of the postwar occupation troops in the state were black, and the virulence with which whites demanded their removal, only underscored how the internal racial war continued to rage. Whites viewed black troops as the embodiment of the racial hierarchy's reversal: the living symbol of armed servants now determined to dominate their old masters.[25] The federal government's ultimate failure to understand the depth of this racial animosity and enforce black equal rights in the South, and the political triumph of the white "Redemption" movement in the late 1870s, has led scholars to describe Reconstruction as a "splendid failure" and an "unfinished revolution."[26]

The failure of Reconstruction, however, reflected in large part the depth with which the master-servant relationship, characterized by black loyalty enforced by the white lash, defined life in the antebellum and postwar South. Additionally, federal authorities' insistence that freed people should work contentedly for their old masters revealed a reluctance to recognize how black Mississippians understood freedom as the right to escape from white dominance and act on their own multiple allegiances. If blacks believed that freedom entailed rejecting the federal government's demand that they submit to white authority, then so be it. Although historians rightly point out that the Civil War created an expanded and powerful federal state, like the similarly expanded wartime Confederate state, it was not powerful enough to dispel the influence of micro loyalties in either white or black Mississippians. One of Reconstruction's biggest failures was federal authorities' inability to recognize the importance that such long-entrenched racial conflict played in shaping black and white Mississippians' responses to national events.

EPILOGUE

THIS BOOK HAS USED MISSISSIPPI FROM 1860 TO 1865 AS A CASE STUDY to reexamine the nature of Confederate loyalty during the Civil War. Rather than focusing on the war's outcome, it has examined the war as a process during which multiple loyalties influenced people's actions. Historians have viewed white Southerners' wartime behavior in terms of their degree of national commitment to the Confederacy. Although such studies use impressive evidence and sophisticated methodologies, these competing arguments have nonetheless become deadlocked into viewing Confederate nationalism as weak or strong. To bypass this deadlock, this book demonstrates how multiple, coexisting loyalty layers influenced Mississippians' actions in ways that were often unconnected to their nationalist views. This approach helps makes sense of how the mass accusations of disloyalty in wartime Mississippi were not evidence of widespread unionism or eventual support for Republican Party policies. Rather, this alleged disloyalty revealed how the Confederate state, operating on the ideological framework of protective nationalism, was limited in its ability to directly influence the everyday behavior of its citizens.

Mississippi's Confederate boosters promoted a total protective nationalism in which the Confederacy would be economically self-sufficient and its citizens would work toward the goal of achieving national independence from the North. This nationalist vision fused citizens' interests with those of the state, viewing them as component parts working on behalf of the greater national machine. The wartime environment, however, tested the limits of protective nationalism by limiting citizens' ability to act as simple "traitors" or "patriots." By engaging in behavior such as swearing the Union oath, trading with the Union army, spying, and deserting from the Confederate army, Mississippians revealed how loyalty layers, in accordance with specific wartime circumstances, shaped their behavior. Moreover, the expectations of servile racial loyalty that underlie the master-slave relationship stoked a long-raging

internal war between slaves who resisted servile loyalty and sought different avenues of freedom, and the slaveholders who tried to maintain white
dominance.

The reality of war and occupation in Civil War Mississippi necessitates
an approach that looks beyond attempts to measure the intensity of people's
allegiance to a national state. Although nationalism was indeed one loyalty
among the many that guided Mississippians' behavior, it could not supersede
other allegiances. When the Union army brought war to the state, Mississippians found it difficult to ignore long-held loyalties merely to acquiesce to
protective nationalists' demands for unyielding dedication to the cause. Just
as Confederate authorities remained suspicious of Mississippians' loyalties,
so too did Union officials find it difficult to discern national allegiances from
other motives. In cities like Vicksburg, where the Federals made declarations
of loyalty a prerequisite for Mississippians wishing to engage in basic daily
activities, they recognized that such declarations were inherently suspicious
because Mississippians made them in part with the goal of monetary gain.
Like Confederate officials, however, federal authorities maintained a wartime
protective nationalist vision that left little room for other loyalties. They
struggled to define individuals as simply loyal or treasonous, a process they
continued after the war when assessing Mississippians' claims to the Southern
Claims Commission.

Confederate and Union authorities' attempts to implement protective
nationalism in Mississippi proved incompatible with loyalty layers that had
not changed since the prewar period. What *did* change was protective nationalists' creation of a wartime atmosphere that infused partisan implications
into previously nonpolitical behavior, a process that turned many facets of
people's daily lives into possible gauges of patriotism. During the war, both
the Union and Confederate states expanded in terms of their infrastructural
reach into citizens' lives. Although the justification for such expansion was
to compel and enforce national allegiance among the populace, neither state
fully succeeded in this goal, revealing the limits of their expanded powers.
Mississippians themselves stymied both governments' attempts to end antebellum continuities in order to affect desired wartime changes.

The Civil War in Mississippi also revealed the continued influence of
other local allegiances when it expanded the long-raging antebellum struggle
between slaves and slaveholders over the master-slave relationship. Even
in the immediate days after Lincoln's election, slaves understood that the
coming conflict portended their freedom by offering escape from white
authority. Slaveholders insisted that slaves show unconditional servile loyalty

to their masters, as this forced allegiance was at the heart of the master-slave relationship. During the antebellum period, however, the articulation process facilitated slaves' ability to forge multiple loyalty layers to self, family, kinfolk, and neighborhood. These allegiances not only undermined slaveholders' demand that slaves show fealty only to the white master class but also formed the basis of slaves' individual identities, based around the idea that freedom meant the right to escape from white mastery. Although slaves shared a collective ideal of escaping from the racial hierarchy, they nonetheless embraced multiple conceptions of freedom as a lived experience.

As slaves rejected their masters' authority throughout the course of the war, slaveholders responded by attempting to reassert mastery. They maintained that blacks could only be loyal to the master class. Their claims that slaves were being disloyal to their masters, not to the Confederate government, underscored how a separate, internal war between slaves and slaveholders raged amid the larger war between the Union and the Confederacy. Even as emancipation became a fact midway through the conflict, whites only intensified their efforts to maintain racial control over blacks. The continuation of the internal war over racial hierarchy provided a common link between the antebellum, wartime, and postwar periods. Although the Confederacy was founded on the right to Southern white supremacy over a black servile class, the desire to uphold the racial hierarchy outlasted the Confederacy and defined sociopolitical relations in Reconstruction-era Mississippi precisely because it was a defining theme of Southern history. White Mississippians' paranoia over the alleged Christmas rebellion demonstrated the persistence with which whites and blacks continued to struggle over the master-slave relationship, even with slavery abolished.

When Mississippi Fire-Eater Albert Gallatin Brown stood before the Confederate Congress in 1863 and called for "a more earnest and ardent patriotism" as the cure for the Confederacy's flagging morale, he operated under the flawed assumption that any single loyalty could be "all-pervading." Brown proposed expanding government power in order to enforce his vision of patriotism. Thus, if men did not want to fight, the state would conscript them to fight; if citizens refused to give up supplies to the army, the army would take those supplies; if private industry would not devote its production to the Confederate cause, the government would force it to do so. Even in instances when the Confederacy could compel citizens to do these things, however, it could not make them *want* to do them. It was in this most crucial respect that the Confederate state did not succeed according to its expectations in Mississippi. This is not to say that Confederate nationalism was "weak" or that it "failed": surely, the Confederacy's impressive military mobilization and the ferocity with which its armies fought through four years of war indicates that loyalty to the Confederacy existed. Rather, this study has been concerned with how multiple human loyalties existed in tandem with nationalism, and how protective nationalists like Brown could never hope to make their vision into reality.

James A. Seddon was Confederate secretary of war from November 21, 1862, to February 5, 1865. Among his tasks were delineating the often contradictory rules regarding the persistent contraband trade between the lines in Mississippi. National Archives. Series: Mathew Brady Photographs of Civil War–Era Personalities and Scenes, 1921–1940; Record Group 111: Records of the Office of the Chief Signal Officer, 1860–1985.

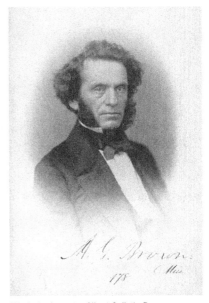

Mississippi senator Albert Gallatin Brown, arch-protective nationalist who demanded total commitment to the Confederate cause. Library of Congress Prints and Photographs Division, Washington, DC, at http://hdl.loc.gov/loc.pnp/ pp.print. From *McClees' Gallery of Photographic Portraits of the Senators, Representatives, and Delegates of the Thirty-Fifth Congress* (Washington, DC: McClees and Beck, 1859), 178.

Jefferson Davis, planter, US senator from Mississippi, and the first and only president of the Confederate States of America. National Archives. Series: Mathew Brady Photographs of Civil War–Era Personalities and Scenes, 1921–1940; Record Group 111: Records of the Office of the Chief Signal Officer, 1860–1985.

Brierfield, the plantation home of Jefferson Davis on the former Davis Bend (now Davis Island). Freed people occupied Davis's former plantation lands after the war. Library of Congress Prints and Photographs Division, Washington, DC, at http://hdl.loc.gov/loc.pnp/pp.print. From Mississippi History Now, at http://mshistorynow.mdah.state.ms.us/.

The Big Black River crossing into Vicksburg was the site of illicit trading between Mississippians and Union forces. Library of Congress Prints and Photographs Division, Washington, DC, at http://hdl.loc.gov/loc.pnp/pp.print. From Hirst D. Milhollen and Donald H. Mugridge, comp., Civil War Photographs, 1861–1865 (Washington, DC: Library of Congress, 1977), no. 0675. Photograph by William Reddish Pywell.

Confederate dead in front of Fort Robinette, Corinth, Mississippi, 1862. The war in Mississippi destroyed bodies and treasure and had left much of the state in ruins by 1865. Library of Congress Prints and Photographs Division, Washington, DC, at http://hdl.loc.gov/loc.pnp/pp.print. Photograph by Nicholas Brown.

Private Henry Augustus Moore of Company F, Fifteenth Mississippi Infantry Regiment. He holds an artillery short sword and features a sign that reads "Jeff Davis and the South!" In first year of war, a nationalist fervor engulfed military-aged Mississippians, and many were willing to die to secure Southern independence. Library of Congress Prints and Photographs Division, Washington, DC, at http://hdl.loc.gov/loc.pnp/pp.print.

Confederate Mississippi currency note, fifty dollars. Confederate Collection, P&W 25116, Boston Athenaeum, at http://catalog.bostonathenaeum.org/vwebv/holdingsInfo?bibId=482305.

A native of Jones County, Mississippi, Newton Knight led a unionist guerrilla uprising against Confederate forces and established the Free State of Jones in the southeastern Piney Woods region. Herman Welborn Collection via the Mississippi Historical Society, at http://mshistorynow.mdah.state.ms.us/articles/309/ newton-knight-and-the-legend-of-the-free-state-of -jones. The photograph is in the public domain.

The Union provost marshal's house in occupied Vicksburg, guarded by black soldiers. Library of Congress Prints and Photographs Division, Washington, DC, at http://hdl.loc.gov/loc.pnp/ pp.print.

Union general William Tecumseh Sherman tested the limits of Mississippians' loyalties by forcing them to take an oath of allegiance to the United States in exchange for the right to conduct business, preserve property, and travel in Union-occupied cities. Library of Congress Prints and Photographs Division, Washington, DC, at http://hdl.loc.gov/loc.pnp/pp.print.

Vicksburg, Warren County, Mississippi, photographed between 1861 and 1865. The "Gibraltar of the Confederacy" became a site where everyday commercial and social interactions became tests for national loyalties. Library of Congress, Prints and Photographs Division, Washington, DC, at http://hdl.loc.gov/loc.pnp/pp.print.

Street view of Vicksburg taken during the war. Living and working in Union-occupied Vicksburg meant negotiating national loyalties with personal attachments. Library of Congress Prints and Photographs Division, Washington, DC, at http://hdl.loc.gov/loc.pnp/pp.print.

Soldiers of the Sixty-Fourth Colored Infantry Regiment stand in formation in their camp at Palmyra Bend, Warren County, Mississippi. In the foreground are stacked rifles. Few things horrified white Mississippians more than "disloyal" servants rising up against their masters as members of the Union army. Library of Congress Prints and Photographs Division, Washington, DC, at http://hdl.loc.gov/loc.pnp/pp.print.

The oath of allegiance of Montgomery Withers Boyd of Jackson, Mississippi, May 25, 1865. The decision to take the Union oath proved a major point of contention when it came to discerning Mississippians' loyalty during the Civil War. M. W. Boyd Collection, Special Collections, University of Mississippi Libraries, at http://purl.oclc.org/umarchives/MUM00042/.

Unionist, senator, postwar governor, and vociferous critic of Jefferson Davis, James Lusk Alcorn made a fortune trading with the Union during the war. When the conflict ceased, he served as Republican governor of Mississippi in 1870–1871. Library of Congress Prints and Photographs Division, Washington, DC, at http://www.loc.gov/pictures/item/brh2003000417/PP/.

John Hill Aughey, Mississippi unionist who earned the wrath of his Confederate neighbors. *Documenting the American South*, University of North Carolina at Chapel Hill. This work is the property of the University of North Carolina at Chapel Hill. It may be used freely by individuals for research, teaching, and personal use.

John J. Pettus was a dyed-in-the-wool Fire-Eater who served as governor of Mississippi from 1859 to 1863. He fielded many a wartime letter from Mississippians seeking aid. Mississippi Department of Archives and History via Wikipedia. The photograph is in the public domain.

Charles Clark succeeded John Pettus as governor of Mississippi and served from 1863 to 1865. During his tenure, he witnessed the social and economic collapse of his state. Mississippi Department of Archives and History via Wikipedia. The photograph is in the public domain.

General John C. Pemberton (here photographed after the war) commanded the Confederate army at Vicksburg. Library of Congress Prints and Photographs Division, Washington, DC, at http://www.loc.gov/pictures/item/96514378/.

The February 2, 1861, issue of *Harper's Weekly* depicted Mississippi's seceding delegation in Congress. Pictured left to right at the top are Reuben Davis, Senator Jefferson Davis, and Otho R. Singleton. Pictured left to right at the bottom are Lucius Quintus Cincinnatus Lamar, William Barksdale, and John J. McRae. In the center is Senator Albert Gallatin Brown. *Harper's Weekly*, January 10, 1863, at http://www.sonofthesouth.net/leefoundation/civil-war-feb-1861/mississippi-seceding-delegation.htm. The image is in the public domain.

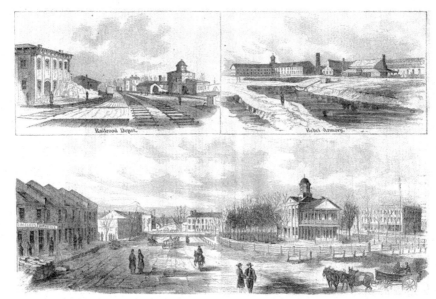

The city of Holly Springs, located in Marshall County, Mississippi, was a major site of illicit trade between Mississippi civilians and the Union army. This sketch appeared in the January 10, 1863, issue of *Harper's Weekly*. It depicts the city center as well as the railroad depot and Confederate armory. *Harper's Weekly*, January 10, 1863, at http://www.sonofthesouth.net/leefoundation/civil-war/1863/january/holly-springs-mississippi.htm. The image, sketched by A. Simplot, is in the public domain.

APPENDICES

APPENDIX A

List of Declared Vicksburg unionists who appeared in the 1860 census, alphabetized by name.

Source: Lists of Union or Loyal Men in and around Vicksburg, entry 370, box 3, Record Group 366, Records of Civil War Special Agencies of the Treasury Department, Second Special Agency Records, Vicksburg District, National Archives and Records Administration.

Name	County	City/Town	Occupation	Age in 1860	Real Estate	Personal Estate	Birth	Slaves
Ackerman, F.	Warren	Vicksburg	Butcher	30	None	None	Germany	None
Ball, Lewis	Pontotoc	New Albany	Brigman, MS Bottom	39	$5,000	$13,352	1821, SC	None
Baszinsky, Joseph	Warren	Vicksburg	Merchant	35	None	$10,000	1825, Poland	None
Baum, Frederick	Warren	Vicksburg	Horticulture/Nursery	53	$10,000	$15,000	1807, Germany	None
Baum, J.F.	Warren	Vicksburg	Grocery (Fruit Store)	32	$5,000	$8,000	1828, Germany	None
Baum, Philip	Warren	Vicksburg	Horticulture/Nursery	19	None	None	1841, MS	None
Billgerry, Joseph	Warren	Vicksburg	Brewer (Beer)	33	None	None	1827, France	None
Bitterman, Jacob	Warren	Vicksburg	Engineer	40	None	None	1820, PA	1
Bland, John C.	Warren	Vicksburg	Sheriff	38	$7,500	$7,000	1822, VA	8
Botto, Joseph	Warren	Vicksburg	Merchant (Grocery)	36	None	None	1824, Italy	NA
Bowie, Aquilla	Warren	Vicksburg	Farmer	47	$3,000	$800	1813, MD	2
Brantley, William M.	Warren	Vicksburg	Shoemaker	38	$800	None	1822, AL	None
Brening, L.	Warren	Vicksburg	Boarding	37	$5,000	None	1823, Germany	None
Brown, Michael	Warren	Vicksburg	Plasterer	40	$2,500	$1,000	1820, OH	1
Brown, S.B.	Warren	Vicksburg	Furniture	48	$12,000	$3,000	1812, NY	None
Brown, William J.P.	Warren	Vicksburg	Barkeeper	27	None	None	1833, Germany	None
Burwell, A.	Warren	Vicksburg	Lawyer	49	$25,000	$20,000	1811, VA	12
Butler, Joseph	Warren	Vicksburg	Butcher	42	$2,000	$10,000	1818, Nova Scotia	6
Camp, John (T.)	Tishomingo	Corinth	Wagon/Farm Laborer	39	None	$100	1821, MS	None
Cathel, James	Warren	Vicksburg	Planter	62	$5,000	$25,000	1798, GA	20

Name	County	City/Town	Occupation	Age in 1860	Real Estate	Personal Estate	Birth	Slaves
Cathel, Jonathan	Warren	Vicksburg	Farmer	21	None	None	1839, MS	None
Chapin, James	Warren	Vicksburg	Merchant	35	$9,000	$35,000	1825, NY	None
Cohen, Moses	Warren	Vicksburg	Merchant	44	$3,000	$9,000	1816, Poland	None
Coker, John	Warren	Vicksburg	Laborer	27	None	$135	1833, MS	None
Coleman, Julius	Milam, TX	Cameron	Merchant	31	None	$10,000	1829, Germany	None
Curlee, William M.	Warren	Vicksburg	Stone Clerk	33	$1,500	$1,200	1827, SC	None
Dailey, William	Yazoo	Yazoo City	Laborer (Stone)	24	None	None	1836, Ireland	None
Deschinger, Godhard	Claiborne	Port Gibson	Shoemaker	24	None	None	1836, NY	None
Deschinger, Henry	Claiborne	Port Gibson	B.Smith	20	None	None	1840, MS	None
Downing, Jacob	Warren	Vicksburg	Engineer	48	$2,000	$500	1812, PA	1
Ellis, Andrew	Warren	Vicksburg	Laborer	60	None	None	1800, Germany	None
Farmer, John W.	Warren	Vicksburg	Bricklayer	30	$2,000	$2,000	1830, OH	1
Finney, Thomas J.	Warren	Vicksburg	Merchant	48	$50,000	$50,000	1812, NC	45
Fisher, John	Warren	Vicksburg	Coffee House	28	$2,000	None	1832, MD	None
Fletcher, John	Warren	Vicksburg	Carpenter	43	$2,500	None	1817, TN	None
Flinn, Martin	Warren	Vicksburg	Watchman	50	None	None	1810, Ireland	None
Francis, Charles	Warren	Vicksburg	Shoemaker	40	$1,000	$8,000	1820, NY	None
Freeman, Lewis C.	Warren	Vicksburg	Merchant	28	None	$8,000	1832, NY	None
Gallagher, James	Warren	Vicksburg	Coffee House	26	$4,000	$1,000	1834, Ireland	None
Geary, James	Warren	Vicksburg	Laborer	39	$1,500	None	1821, Ireland	None

Name	County	City/Town	Occupation	Age in 1860	Real Estate	Personal Estate	Birth	Slaves
Gilman, Martin	Warren	Vicksburg	Physiciary	39	None	$3,500	1821, NY	3
Gizell, Jacob	Warren	Vicksburg	Baker	25	None	None	1835, Germany	None
Gomez, (Gomes) M.	Warren	Vicksburg	Cabinet Maker	40	None	None	1820, Portugal	None
Green, Duff	Warren	Vicksburg	Corn Merchant	36	$500	$43,700	1824, VA	6
Hafer, Michael	Warren	Vicksburg	Farmer	29	$600	None	1831, At Sea	None
Hampsey, Patrick	Warren	Vicksburg	Laborer	30	None	None	1830, Ireland	None
Haney, Martin	Warren	Vicksburg	None	38	None	None	1822, OH	None
Hawkins, George	Warren	Vicksburg	Gunsmith	45	None	$400	1815, IN	None
Henry, Robert W.	Warren	Vicksburg	Grocery	35	None	$300	1825, Ireland	None
Hewitt, Lewis	Warren	Vicksburg	Carpenter	39	$3,000	None	1821, PA	None
Hoag, Lewis	Warren	Vicksburg	Watchmaker	29	$200	$1,000	1821, Germany	None
Hoffman, Louis	Warren	Vicksburg	Gunsmith	37	None	$4,000	1823, Germany	None
Hopkins, George F.	Warren	Vicksburg	None	27	None	None	1833, DE	None
Hopkins, William A.	Warren	Vicksburg	Preacher (Methodist)	52	$800	$700	1808, DE	None
Horrigan, Jeremiah	Warren	Vicksburg	Barkeeper	52	None	None	1808, Ireland	None
Horrigan, Michael	Warren	Vicksburg	Boarding	29	None	None	1831, Ireland	None
Hough, Robert	Warren	Vicksburg	Dairyman	40	$8,000	$500	1820, England	None
Houghton, L.S.	Warren	Vicksburg	Judge Probate	45	$1,800	$1,500	1815, NY	None
Jeter, John J.	Warren	Vicksburg	Horticulture/Nursery	35	$2,000	$2,000	1825, TN	1
Johnson, W.C.	Warren	Vicksburg	Shoemaker	42	None	$3,000	1818, NY	None

Name	County	City/Town	Occupation	Age in 1860	Real Estate	Personal Estate	Birth	Slaves
Johnston, John	Hinds	Jackson	Engineer	26	None	None	1834, TN	None
Jones, Walter,	Warren	Vicksburg	None	17	None	None	1843, MS	None
Just, George	Warren	Vicksburg	Coffee House	30	$2,000	$4,000	1830, Germany	None
Katzmeyer, John	Warren	Vicksburg	Laborer	39	None	None	1821, Germany	None
Katzmire, Jacob	Warren	Vicksburg	?	42	$3,000	$1,000	1818, Germany	None
Kearn, John	Warren	Vicksburg	Laborer	18	None	None	1842, Ireland	None
Keiser/Kiger Frederick	Warren	Vicksburg	Merchant	20	None	None	1840, Germany	None
King, James	Warren	Vicksburg	Shoe Store	34	None	$25,000	1826, Ireland	None
Klein, J.A.	Warren	Vicksburg	Saw Mills	48	$25,000	$35,000	1812, VA	8
Krause, Charles	Warren	Vicksburg	Tailor	32	None	None	1828, Germany	None
Kress George C.	Warren	Vicksburg	Tailor	35	None	$3,080	1825, France	None
Kuhn, Alex	Warren	Vicksburg	Laborer	26	None	None	1834, Germany	None
Kuner, Max	Warren	Vicksburg	Jeweller	35	$5,000	None	1825, Germany	1
Laughlin, John	Warren	Vicksburg	Laborer	44	$500	None	1816, Ireland	None
Lavenburg, Levi M.	Warren	Vicksburg	Clerk	33	None	None	1827, Poland	None
Lehman, Charles	Warren	Vicksburg	Clerk	17	None	None	1843, MS	None
Linn, Jno C.	Warren	Vicksburg	Trader	50	$600	$4,000	1810, OH	4
Linnley, James	Warren	Vicksburg	Marble Yard	26	None	None	1834, OH	None
Lip(s)key, Andrew	Warren	Vicksburg	None	28	None	None	1832, Germany	None
Loed/Loyd Fredrick	Warren	Vicksburg	Laborer	24	None	None	1836, MA	None

Name	County	City/Town	Occupation	Age in 1860	Real Estate	Personal Estate	Birth	Slaves
Lowenhaupt, J.	Warren	Vicksburg	Merchant	24	None	None	1836, Germany	None
Manning, George L.	Warren	Vicksburg	Farmer	63	None	None	1797, KY	None
Martin, G.H.	Warren	Vicksburg	Printer	24	None	None	1836, PA	None
McCave, Thomas	Warren	Vicksburg	Laborer	40	None	None	1820, Ireland	None
McManus, John	Warren	Vicksburg	Laborer	35	None	None	1825, Ireland	None
Metcalf, Henry	Warren	Vicksburg	Brickmaker	45	$3,000	$20,000	1815, KY	None
Meyer, Adam	Madison	Canton	Baker	29	None	None	Germany	None
Miller, Charles	Warren	Vicksburg	Shoemaker	30	None	$2,000	1830, Germany	None
Miller, Valentine	Warren	Vicksburg	Butcher	22	None	None	1838, Germany	None
Monteath, John	Warren	Vicksburg	Gunwright	47	$1,500	$500	1813, PA	None
Moone, Richard C.	Maybe: This Guy	MS	Laborer	28	None	None	1832, MS	None
Morris, Jacob	Warren	Vicksburg	Boarding	46	$20,000	$2,000	1814, Belgium	
Mullen, Alex	Warren	Vicksburg	Engineer	28	None	None	1832, Scotland	None
Murphy, Michael	Warren	Vicksburg	Laborer	50	$3,000	$1,500	1810, Ireland	5
Myers, Thomas J.	Warren	Vicksburg	Baker	28	None	None	1832, France	None
Mygatt, Alston	Warren	Vicksburg	Preacher	55	$6,000	$3,000	1805, NY	2
Myles, John D.	Warren	Vicksburg	Dentist	30	$1,500	$2,000	1830, MS	None
Noah, George	Warren	Vicksburg	Carpenter	27	None	None	1833, OH	None
North, Royal F.	Warren	Vicksburg	Merchant	29	None	$3,000	1831, IN	None
O'Malley, John	Warren	Vicksburg	Raftsman	38	$3,500	$2,500	1822, Ireland	2
Orris, Adam	Warren	Vicksburg	Laborer	45	None	None	1815, OH	None

Name	County	City/Town	Occupation	Age in 1860	Real Estate	Personal Estate	Birth	Slaves
Palmer, Angelo	Warren	Vicksburg	Clerk	45	None	None	1815, Italy	None
Palmer, John B.	Warren	Vicksburg	Grocery	41	None	None	1819, Italy	None
Patrick McClusky	Warren	Vicksburg	Levying	28	$3,000	$100	1832, Ireland	None
Phillips, John	Warren	Vicksburg	Machinist	20	None	None	1840, PA	None
Porterfield, John	Warren	Vicksburg	Merchant	40	$16,000	$30,000	1820, Ireland	4
Porterfield, Thomas	Warren	Vicksburg	None	35	None	None	1825, Ireland	None
Pyle, George N.	Warren	Vicksburg	Engineer/Laborer	60	None	None	1800, OH	None
Quincey Sherely	Warren	Vicksburg	None	12	None	None	1848, MS	None
Quinn, Thomas	Warren	Vicksburg	Laborer	23	None	None	1837, Ireland	None
Rectanus, George S.	Warren	Vicksburg	Music Teacher	53	None	None	1807, Germany	None
Rhobacher, John	Warren	Vicksburg	Merchant	48	None	None	1812, France	None
Richard Dohler	Copiah	NA	Saloon Keeper	34	$1,000	$1,000	1826, Germany	None
Rinach, Lewis	Warren	Vicksburg	Physician	29	None	$500	1831, Germany	None
Rodge, John	Warren	Vicksburg	Coffee House	25	$4,000	$2,000	1835, Italy	1
Royal, A.A.	Warren	Vicksburg	Horticulture/Nursery	35	$2,000	None	1825, TN	None
Royal, Richard D.	Warren	Vicksburg	Book Keeper	25	None	None	1835, TN	None
Ryan, Cornelius	Warren	Vicksburg	Engineer	50	$8,000	None	1810, Ireland	11
Ryan, John	Warren	Vicksburg	Printer	22	None	None	1838, OH	7
Sanguinetti, N.	Warren	Vicksburg	Grocery	26	None	None	1834, Geneva, Switz.	None
Schroder, Frederick	Warren	Vicksburg	Grocery	53	None	$1,500	1807, Germany	None

Name	County	City/Town	Occupation	Age in 1860	Real Estate	Personal Estate	Birth	Slaves
Shannon, M.	Warren	Vicksburg	Painter	33	$11,000	$25,000	1827, NJ	11
Shean, Patrick	Warren	Vicksburg	Farmer	30	$2,000	$300	1830, Ireland	None
Sheehan, Michael	Warren	Vicksburg	Laborer	32	None	None	1828, Ireland	None
Sherley, James	Warren	Vicksburg	Lawyer	65	$5,000	$25,000	1795, MA	14
Shuler, Lewis	Warren	Vicksburg	Grocery	51	$2,400	$800	1809, Germany	None
Skillman, Jacob	Warren	Vicksburg	Carpenter	65	None	$500	1795, MD	None
Smith, Frank A.	Warren	Vicksburg	Shoemaker	26	NA	NA	1834, Germany	None
Smith, George W.	Warren	Vicksburg	Printer	27	$1,000	None	1833, GA	None
Solomon Rothchild	Warren	Vicksburg	Clerk	21	None	None	1839, Germany	None
Strong, Charles W.	Warren	Vicksburg	Raftsman	30	$1,000	None	1830, CT	None
Strong, Seth R.	Warren	Vicksburg	Raftsman	45	None	None	1815, CT	None
Theobald, Geo. Peter	Warren	Vicksburg	Drayman	27	None	None	1833, Germany	None
Thomas, William E.	Warren	Vicksburg	Corn Merchant	40	None	None	1820, VT	2
Tift, Solomon	Hinds	Jackson	NA	50	$100,000	$10,000	1810, NY	1
Tillman, William	Warren	Vicksburg	Saddler	52	$8,000	$10,000	1808, Germany	4
Trainer, Owen	Warren	Vicksburg	Carpenter	35	$1,200	None	1825, Ireland	None
Tucker, Fielding	Warren	Vicksburg	Raftsman	33	$1,000	$1,500	1827, SC	2
Tucker, James	Warren	Vicksburg	Raftsman	23	None	$100	1837, AR	None
Vick, John W.	Warren	Vicksburg	Farmer	54	$125,000	$15,000	1806, MS	25
Volenger, William	Warren	Vicksburg	Shoemaker	30	None	None	1830, Europe	None

Name	County	City/Town	Occupation	Age in 1860	Real Estate	Personal Estate	Birth	Slaves
Walker, William B.	Warren	Vicksburg	Brickmaker	32	$900	None	1828, VA	None
Webb, Thomas B.	Warren	Vicksburg	Gun Wright	46	$600	None	1814, VA	None
Webster, Isaac	Warren	Vicksburg	Book Keeper	46	None	None	1814, VA	None
Wheeler, William S.	Warren	Vicksburg	Book Keeper	32	None	None	1828, NY	None
Williams, Jonathan	Warren	Vicksburg	Carpenter	29	$1,100	None	1831, TN	7
Wilson, Victor F.	Warren	Vicksburg	Merchant	45	$20,000	$54,000	1815, Ireland	24
Wilson, William D.	Warren	Vicksburg	Overseer	33	None	None	1827, VA	None
Winegar, W.	Warren	Vicksburg	Tailor	30	$1,000	None	1830, Switzerland	None
Winstin, Abraham	Warren	Vicksburg	Clothing	36	None	None	1824, Poland	None
Wixson, P.H.P.	Warren	Vicksburg	Merchant	22	$300	None	1838, IN	None

APPENDIX B

Mississippi Deserters[1]

Sources for Appendix B: Robert S. Hudson to William H. Mangum, May 24, 1864, in Silver, "The Breakdown of Morale," 106–7; Charles Clark Correspondence, boxes 949, 950, MDAH; John J. Pettus Correspondence, RG 27, volume 52, roll 1333, MDAH; "Shooting a Deserter," Weekly Courier (Natchez), May 14, 1862; "Thirty Dollars Reward," Republican (Woodville, MS), August 27, 1864; Substitution and Desertion Records, Receipts for Deserters from the Army Arrested by the Sheriff of Chickasaw County, 1863–1864, series 404, box 8372, MDAH; Glenn Robins, ed., "Inside the Mind of Johnny Reb: The Civil War Letters of John Cato," Journal of Mississippi History 64 (Spring 2002): 33–45; OR, ser. 1, vol. 26, 536; OR, ser. 1, vol. 49, 950; OR, ser. 1, vol. 30, pt. 2, 14; OR, ser. 1, vol. 49, pt. 1, 950; OR, ser. 1, vol. 32, pt. 3, 635; J. A. Bigger Diary, August 12, 1862, MUM00747, folder 4, box 1976.3, UMASC; Diary of Jason Niles, July 18, October 30, 1863, January 21, 1864, Documenting the American South; Samuel Andrew Agnew Diary, January 13, March 13, 14, 15, 16, 1864, Documenting the American South; John C. Pemberton Papers, entry P1101-131, folder 2, box 2, NARA; Deserters, Misc. Records, Manuscripts, 1861–1865, entry 183, folders 1502, 1507, 1740, 1839, 1990, boxes 15, 17, 18, 20, RG 109, NARA; Lists of Deserters and Refugees at New Orleans, December 22, 24, 26, 1863, UPMF, roll 26, NARA; Bynum, The Free State of Jones, 99–101; "The Deserters," Beacon (Macon, MS), May 13, May 20, 1864; A. H. Clark to Mother, January 18, 1863, Thomas Clark Collection, MUM01027, folder 1, box 1984.1, UMASC; J. B. Crawford Letters, 1863–1864, in George M. Street Collections, 1914–1982, MUM00349, box 20, UMASC; and Charles B. Allen to Parents, October 29, 1864, James and Charles B. Allen Papers, 1788–1869, microfilm, 01697, roll 1, SHC.

Name[1]	Army Service[2]	County[3]	City/Town[4]	Occupation	Age in 1860	Real Estate	Personal Estate	Birth	Slaves	Married	Head of Household	Father
William Lewis	Co. E, MS 5 Inf. Rgt	Attala	Tnship 14, Range 7	Pupil (father: Physician)	19	father: $2500	father: $8500	1841, MS	6	No	No	No
Thomas B. Hight	NA	Attala	Tnship 15, Range 7	Farmer	41	None	$50	1819, TN	None	Yes	Yes	Yes
John R. Ware	Co. C, MS 40 Inf. Rgt	Attala	Tnship 13, Range 6	None (father: Farmer)	17	father: None	father: $500	1843, AL	None	No	No	No
Jeff B. Reynolds	Co. D, MS 11 Cv. Rgt	Attala	Not in census									
James C. Shuler	Co. A, MS 15 Inf. Rgt	Attala	Tnship 14, Range 5	Pupil	17	None	None	1843, MS	None	No	No	No
Thomas H. Presley	Co. E, MS 27 Inf. Rgt	Attala	Tnship 14, Range 8	Farmer	28	$10,000	$6,000	1832, SC	5	Yes	Yes	Yes
Charles W. Miller	Co. C, MS 11 Cv. Rgt	Attala	Tnship 14, Range 5	Farmer	40	$12,000	$7,650	1820, NC	2	Yes	Yes	Yes

[1] Deserters' names came from a variety of different primary and secondary sources. These sources are listed at the beginning of this appendix.

[2] In instances when sources did not give the company and regimental information, I used the US Civil War Soldiers Records and Profiles and other references to match the county in which the individual lived to the respective companies that were raised out of that county. For individuals who did not appear in the census but did appear in the soldiers' listings, I matched their company with the county in which it was raised. All background information is from the 1860 US Census and Slave Schedules, Mississippi, and US Civil War Soldiers Records and Profiles, digital images, Ancestry. com, at http://www.ancestry.com/; H. Grady Howell, For Dixie Land I'll Take My Stand! A Muster Listing of All Known Mississippi Confederate Soldiers, Sailors, and Marines, 2 vols. (Madison, MS: Chickasaw Bayou Press, 1998); and Dunbar Rowland, Military History of Mississippi, 1803–1898: Taken from the Official and Statistical Register of the State of Mississippi, 1908 (Spartanburg, SC: Reprint Company, 1978).

[3] Deserters are organized alphabetically by county.

[4] When the census did not list the city, township, or town, I listed the individual's postal location to demonstrate geographic proximities.

Name[1]	Army Service[2]	County[3]	City/Town[4]	Occupation	Age in 1860	Real Estate	Personal Estate	Birth	Slaves	Married	Head of Household	Father
Joseph Burnet	Co. B. MS 4 Inf. Rgt	Attala	Tnship 15, Range 7	Farm Laborer	22	$400	None	1838, GA	None	No	No	No
James Brown	NA	Attala	Tnship 13, Range 9	Farmer	29	$2,000	$300	1831, AL	None	Yes	No	No
Wade H. Gordon	Co. G. MS 43 Inf. Rgt	Calhoun	Erin	Farmer	30	$400	$250	1830, AL	None	Yes	Yes	Yes
J. Owens	Co. F, MS 4 Inf. Rgt	Calhoun	Not in census									
William R. Easly	Co. I, MS 4 Inf. Rgt	Calhoun	Hopewell	Farm Laborer	19	None	None	1841, MS	None	No	No	No
Isaac J. Gordon	Co. K, MS 17 Inf. Rgt	Calhoun	Sarepta	Farm Laborer	19	None	None	1841, MS	None	No	No	No
Duclesion L. Downs	Co. D, MS 31 Inf. Rgt	Calhoun	Cherry Hill	Merchant	24	$900	$2,500	1836, AL	None	Yes	Yes	Yes
Micajah Harden	Co. D, MS 31 Inf. Rgt	Calhoun	Cherry Hill	Farmer	25	$800	$500	1835, AL	None	Yes	Yes	No
Milton A. Brown	Co. D, MS 31 Inf. Rgt	Calhoun	Hopewell	Farmer	31	$2,240	$7,650	1829, AL	None	Yes	Yes	Yes
Wesley Gable	NA	Calhoun	Benela	Farmer	37	None	$800	1823, SC	None	Yes	Yes	No
Clark Smith	Co. D, MS 31 Inf. Rgt	Calhoun	Not in census									
Benjamin A. Beasly	Co. C, MS 44 Inf. Rgt	Calhoun	Cherry Hill	Farm Laborer	19	None	None	1841, AL	None	No	No	No

Name[1]	Army Service[2]	County[3]	City/Town[4]	Occupation	Age in 1860	Real Estate	Personal Estate	Birth	Slaves	Married	Head of Household	Father
Julian Beasly	Co. D, MS 31 Inf. Rgt	Calhoun	Cherry Hill	Farm Laborer	30	None	None	1830, SC	None	No	No	No
John Beasly	Co. D, MS 31 Inf. Rgt	Calhoun	Cherry Hill	Farm Laborer	21	None	None	1839, AL	None	No	No	No
Howard Beasly	Co. D, MS 31 Inf. Rgt	Calhoun	Not in census									
Henry Steel	Co. F, MS 42 Inf. Rgt	Calhoun	Banner	Farmer	28	$300	$400	1832, AL	None	Yes	Yes	Yes
Thomas J. Cook	Co. F, MS 42 Inf. Rgt	Calhoun	Cherry Hill	Farm Laborer	24	None	$150	1836, AL	None	Yes	Yes	Yes
James Cartright	Co. I, MS 4 Inf. Rgt	Calhoun	Hopewell	Farm Laborer	18	None	None	1842 AL	None	No	No	No
John Booth	Co. F, MS 2 Cv. Rgt	Calhon or Tishomingo	NA	NA	NA	NA	NA	NA	NA			
John Barton	Co. F, MS 2 Cv. Rgt	Calhoun, Tishomingo, Marshall or Yalobusha	NA	NA	NA	NA	NA	NA	NA			
Jerry D. Rutlege	Co. E, MS 21 Inf. Rgt	Catahoula, LA	Black River	(father: E. King Agent)	23	father: $111,000	father: $3000	1837, MS	None	No	No	No
James G. Law	Co. G, MS 5 Inf. Rgt	Chickasaw	Division 1	Day Laborer	18	None	None	1842, GA	None	No	No	No

Name[1]	Army Service[2]	County[3]	City/Town[4]	Occupation	Age in 1860	Real Estate	Personal Estate	Birth	Slaves	Married	Head of Household	Father
F.G. H. Woods	Co. F, MS 10 Cv. Rgt	Chickasaw	Not in census									
William Tricky	NA	Chickasaw	Division 2	Farmer	29	None	$150	1831, SC	None	Yes	Yes	Yes
John Watkins	Co. I, MS 12 Cv. Rgt	Chickasaw	Division 1	None (father: Farmer)	18	None (father: $4170)	None (father: $1500)	1842, AL	14	No	No	No
Charles Howell	Co. F, MS 44 Inf. Rgt	Chickasaw	Not in census									
F.M. Gullett	Co. C, MS 31 Inf. Rgt	Chickasaw	Not in census									
W.P. Corner	Co. B, MS 2 Cv. Rgt	Chickasaw	Not in census									
F. Mcleod	Co. C, MS 31 Inf. Rgt	Chickasaw	Not in Census									
G.D. Byars	Co. E, MS 19 Cv. Rgt	Chickasaw	Not in Census									
Melmoth T. Wofford	Co. H, MS 33 Inf. Rgt	Choctaw	Tnship 21	Farmer	22	None	$429	1838, SC	None	Yes	Yes	Yes
Jasper Elliott	Co. G, MS 33 Inf. Rgt	Choctaw	Not in census									
John Starnes	Co. D, MS 8 Cv. Rgt	Choctaw	Not in census									

Name[1]	Army Service[2]	County[3]	City/Town[4]	Occupation	Age in 1860	Real Estate	Personal Estate	Birth	Slaves	Married	Head of Household	Father
Philip Starnes	Co. K, MS 15 Inf. Rgt	Choctaw	Tnship 20	Farm Laborer	16	None	None	1844, MS	None	No	No	No
M.K. Legget	Co. H, MS 31 Inf. Rgt	Choctaw	Not in census									
Samuel Late	Co. H, MS 31 Inf. Rgt	Choctaw	Not in census									
Amos Davis	Co. D, MS 15 Inf. Rgt	Choctaw	Tnship 20	Farm Laborer	16	None	None	1844, SC	None	No	No	No
William Bass	Co. H, MS 31 Inf. Rgt	Choctaw	Not in census									
Laban B. Self	Co. D, MS 43 Inf. Rgt	Choctaw	Not in census									
B.L. Beuvers	Co. B, MS 31 Inf. Rgt	Choctaw	Not in Census									
Peter Hix	Co. A, MS 46 Inf. Rgt	Clarke	Beaver Dam	Farmer	27	None	$200	1833, MS	None	Yes	Yes	Yes
Alex Laxton	Co. A, MS 14 Inf. Rgt	Clarke	Not in census									
Jesse R. Rodgers	Co. A, MS 37 Inf. Rgt	Clarke	De Soto	School Teacher	29	$2000	$1000	1831, MS	None	Yes	Yes	Yes
R.W. Langston	Co. G, MS 6 Inf. Rgt	Copiah	Not in census									

Name[1]	Army Service[2]	County[3]	City/Town[4]	Occupation	Age in 1860	Real Estate	Personal Estate	Birth	Slaves	Married	Head of Household	Father
J.J. Entriken	MS Brkhaven Lt. Art.	Copiah	NA	Farmer	30	$800	$400	1830, MS	None	Yes	No	Yes
R.W. Lesley	Co. A, MS 4 Cv. Bat	Copiah	Not in census									
Thomas Ates	Co. G, MS 7 Inf. Bat	Covington	Williamsburg	Farmer	32	$1,000	$500	1828, LA	None	Yes	Yes	Yes
Daniel Reddoch	Co. G, MS 7 Inf. Bat	Covington	Williamsburg	Farmer	28	$1,200	$1,500	1832, MS	None	Yes	Yes	Yes
Charles McCaa	Co. E, MS 7 Inf. Rgt	Franklin	Meadville	Farm Laborer	16	None	None	1844, MS	None	No	No	No
John W. McDaniel	Co. E, MS 7 Inf. Rgt	Franklin	Veto	None: (father: Farmer)	16	father: $265	father: $20,000	1844, MS	None	No	No	No
Rutillius K. Scott	Co. E, MS 7 Inf. Rgt	Franklin	Friendship	None: (mother: Farmer)	17	mother: $1000	mother: $2900	1843, MS	1	No	No	No
R.S. Brown	Co. A, MS Wlkn Inf	Franklin	Friendship	Farmer	22	$5,000	$2,000	1838, MS	2	Yes	Yes	Yes
Beer Gardner	NA	Franklin	Friendship	Pealing	39	None	$200	1821, Germany	None	No	No	No
E.J. Wofford	Co. F, MS 3 Inf. Rgt	Hancock	Not in census									
G.W. Hardin	Co. F, MS 3 Inf. Rgt	Hancock	Not in census									
John H. Hastings	NA	Harrison	Biloxi	Not in census								

Name[1]	Army Service[2]	County[3]	City/Town[4]	Occupation	Age in 1860	Real Estate	Personal Estate	Birth	Slaves	Married	Head of Household	Father
S.F. Denifson	NA	Harrison	Handsboro	Railroad Worker	Not in census							
D.B. Denifson	NA	Harrison	Handsboro	Railroad Worker	Not in census							
John O. Chisholm	Co. B, MS 1 Inf. Rgt	Itawamba	Smithville	Farm Laborer	20	None	None	1840, MS	None	No	No	No
John Dick	Co. A, MS 43 Inf. Rgt	Itawamba	Mooresville	Steam Mill Laborer	20	None	$75	1840, AL	None	Yes	Yes	Yes
James Ivy	Co. F, MS 42 Inf. Rgt	Itawamba	Bigby Fork	Farmer	24	None	$100	1836, AL	None	Yes	Yes	Yes
Obediah Parker	NA	Jasper	Not in census	Farmer								
Marian L. Parker	Co. D, MS 3 Inf. Rgt	Jasper	Garlandsville	Farmer	21	None	$175	1839, MS	None	Yes	Yes	Yes
Joseph Byrd	Co. K, MS 37 Inf. Rgt	Jasper	Holts	Mechanic	24	$600	$300	1836, MS	None	No	No	No
John R. Cousins	Co. K, MS 37 Inf. Rgt	Jasper	Not in census									
William McNeill	Co. D, MS 37 Inf. Rgt	Jasper	Buckley's Store	Mechanic	33	None	$500	1827, MS	None	Yes	Yes	Yes
Newton Knight	Co. F, MS 7 Inf. Bat	Jasper	Turnersville	Farmer	23	$800	$500	1837, MS	None	Yes	Yes	Yes

Name[1]	Army Service[2]	County[3]	City/Town[4]	Occupation	Age in 1860	Real Estate	Personal Estate	Birth	Slaves	Married	Head of Household	Father
Jeff M. Collins	Co. F, MS 7 Inf. Bat	Jasper	Turnersville	Day Laborer	17	None	None	1843, MS	None	No	No	No
Maddie P. Bush	Co. C, MS 7 Inf. Bat	Jones	Ellisville	Farmer	24	$200	$247	1836, GA	None	Yes	Yes	Yes
Tapley Bynum	Co. F, MS 7 Inf. Bat	Jones	Ellisville	Farmer	23	$200	$250	1837, MS	None	Yes	Yes	No
Jasper J. Collins	Co. H, MS 37 Inf. Rgt	Jones	Ellisville	Farmer	33	$2,000	$1,120	1827, MS	None	Yes	Yes	Yes
Alpheus Knight	Co. B, MS 7 Inf. Bat	Jones	Ellisville	None	17	father: $3,000	father: $8450	1843, MS	4	No	No	No
Benjamin F. Knight	Co. B, MS 7 Inf. Bat	Jones	Ellisville	Farmer	23	$600	$295	1837, MS	None	Yes	Yes	Yes
James M. Valentine	Co. NA, MS 7 Inf. Bat	Jones	Ellisville	Farmer	19	$150	$250	1841, MS	None	No	Yes	No
John H. Harper	Co. F, MS 16 Inf. Rgt	Jones	Ellisville	Farmer	30	$1,000	$200	1830, SC	None	No	No	No
Warren Waters	NA	Jones	Not in census									
Allen McCrory	Co.K, MS 43 Inf. Rgt	Kemper	NA	Farmer	20	None	None	1840, MS	None	No	No	No
William Jones	Co. I, MS 5 Inf. Rgt	Kemper	NA	Laborer	28	None	None	1832, GA	None	Yes	Yes	No

Name[1]	Army Service[2]	County[3]	City/Town[4]	Occupation	Age in 1860	Real Estate	Personal Estate	Birth	Slaves	Married	Head of Household	Father
John W. Sanderson	Co. I, MS 5 Inf. Rgt	Kemper	NA	Farmer	28	None	None	1832, AL	None	No	No	No
James M. Simmons	Co. A, MS 35 Inf. Rgt	Kemper	NA	Farmer	29	$2,600	$11,000	1831, SC	10	Yes	Yes	Yes
William Richardson	Co. K, MS 24 Inf. Rgt	Kemper	NA	Farmer	34	None	None	1826, TN	None	Yes	No	Yes
Jacob A.D. Williams	Co. F, MS 42 Inf. Rgt	Lafayette	Paris	Farmer	31	None	$200	1829, AL	None	Yes	Yes	Yes
James Colwell	Co. F, MS 42 Inf. Rgt	Lafayette	Paris	Laborer	19	None	None	1841, SC	None	No	No	No
S.P. Dodd	NA	Lafayette	Paris	Farmer	36	None	$500	1824, AL	None	Yes	Yes	No
L.A. Dixon	Co. C, MS 5 Inf. Rgt MM	Lauderdale	Not in census									
William Gable	NA	Lauderdale	Beat 3	Farmer	27	$560	$300	1833, MS	None	Yes	Yes	Yes
John Waits	Co I, MS 37 Inf. Rgt	Lauderdale	Centre Beat	Farmer	43	None	$300	1817, GA	None	Yes	Yes	Yes
W.G. Davis	Co. C, MS 5 Inf. Rgt	Lauderdale	Beat 3	Farmer	34	$650	$350	1826, GA	None	Yes	Yes	Yes
W.T. Moseley	Co. H, MS 8 Inf. Rgt	Lauderdale	Not in census									
T.M. Hart	Co. D, MS 7 Inf. Rgt	Lauderdale	Beat 5	Farmer	25	None	$1,200	1835, AL	4	Yes	Yes	Yes

Name[1]	Army Service[2]	County[3]	City/Town[4]	Occupation	Age in 1860	Real Estate	Personal Estate	Birth	Slaves	Married	Head of Household	Father
Marion Pierce	Co. H, MS 6 Inf. Rgt	Lawrence	Monticello	mother: Planter	14	mother: $10,000	mother: $30,000	1846, MS	28	No	No	No
Meeke M. Fortinberry	Co. D, MS 26 Inf. Rgt	Lawrence	Monticello	Farmer	34	$1,500	$1,500	1826, MS	None	Yes	Yes	Yes
James M. Case	MS Brkhaven Lt. Art.	Lawrence	Monticello	Farmer	25	$800	$150	1835, MS	None	Yes	Yes	Yes
John Ray	Co.F, MS 12 Cv. Rgt	Leake	Carthage	father: Farmer	12	father: $200	father: $600	1848, MS	None	No	No	No
Joseph C. Newsom	Co. B, MS 40 Inf. Rgt	Leake	Carthage	Farmer	27	$600	$500	1833, GA	None	Yes	Yes	Yes
Charles R. Waller	Co. D, MS 1 Lt. Art.	Leake	Carthage	Farmer	25	None	$200	1835, GA	None	Yes	Yes	Yes
Emmet R. Scott	Co. B, MS 40 Inf. Rgt	Leake	Carthage	father: Farmer	15	father: $2000	father: $7500	1845, MS	1	No	No	No
James Fredrick	Co. H, MS 33 Inf. Rgt	Leake	Carthage	Farmer	30	$500	$1,800	1830, AL	None	Yes	Yes	Yes
C.W. Mooney	Co. F, MS 33 Inf. Rgt	Leake	Carthage	Farmer	22	None	$200	1838, AL	None	Yes	Yes	No
Robert Moore	Co.F, MS 33 Inf. Rgt	Leake	Carthage	father: Farmer	15	father: $800	father: $369	1845, MS	None	No	No	No
Isham R. Jinning	Co. G, MS 40 Inf. Rgt	Leake or Winston	Not in census									

Name[1]	Army Service[2]	County[3]	City/Town[4]	Occupation	Age in 1860	Real Estate	Personal Estate	Birth	Slaves	Married	Head of Household	Father
Amos Rice	Co. K, MS 14 Inf. Rgt	Lowndes	Not in census									
W.N. Clarke	Co. F, MS 29 Inf. Rgt	Lowndes	Not in census									
Malberry W. Whatley	Co. E, MS 40 Inf. Rgt	Lowndes	Columbus	Overseer	24	None	None	1836, AL	None	No	No	No
John Loftin	Co. D/F, MS 7 Inf. Rt	Marion	Columbia	Farmer	16	None	None	1844, MS	None	No	No	No
T. W. Harris	NA	Marshall	Holly Springs	Not in Census								
Charles F. Smith	Co. H, MS 34 Inf. Rgt	Marshall	Holly Springs	Sawyer	22	None	None	1838, MS	None	No	No	No
Delevan H. Morgan	Co. B, MS 1 Inf. Rgt	Monroe	NA	Farmer	50	$3,050	$25,000	1810, NC	None	Yes	Yes	Yes
A.W. Parre	Co. K, MS 11 inf. Rgt	Monroe	Not in census									
W.F. English	Co. G, MS 14 Inf. Rgt	Monroe	Eastern Division	Farmer	28	None	$200	1832, AL	None	Yes	Yes	Yes
Thomas Barrett	Co. B, MS 5 Inf. Rgt	Neshoba	Tnship 12, Range 12	Farmer	45	$200	$310	1815, AL	None	Yes	Yes	Yes
Reuban Barrett	Co. F, MS 40 Inf. Rgt	Neshoba	Tnship 11, Range 13	Farmer	32	None	$100	1828, AL	None	No	Yes	Yes
William G. Barrett	Co. A, MS 33 Inf. Rgt	Neshoba	Tnship 10, Range 10	Farmer	27	None	$345	1833, AL	None	Yes	Yes	Yes

Name[1]	Army Service[2]	County[3]	City/Town[4]	Occupation	Age in 1860	Real Estate	Personal Estate	Birth	Slaves	Married	Head of Household	Father
William R. Waller	Co. G. MS 40 Inf. Rgt	Neshoba	Tnship 12, Range 10	Farmer	15	None	None	1845, GA	None	No	No	No
Theodore G. Coghlan	Co. G, MS 40 Inf. Rgt	Neshoba	Tnship 12, Range 10	Farmer	30	None	$364	1830, MS	None	Yes	Yes	Yes
Jasper N. Fielder	Co. I, MS 35 Inf. Rgt	Neshoba	Tnship 12, Range 13	Farmer	24	None	$250	1836, AL	None	Yes	Yes	Yes
William P. Blount	Co. F, MS 4 Inf. Rgt	Neshoba	Tnship 12, Range 10	Farmer	33	$800	$636	1827, AL	None	Yes	Yes	Yes
William Dyer	Co. G, MS 40 Inf. Rgt	Neshoba	Tnship 12, Range 10	Farmer	16	None	None	1844, AL	None	No	No	No
Jackson Breazeale	Co. G, MS 40 Inf. Rgt	Neshoba	Tnship 12, Range 10	Farmer	21	None	None	1839, MS	None	No	No	No
John W. Adcock	Co. G, MS 40 Inf. Rgt	Neshoba	Tnship 12, Range 10	Farmer	22	None	$100	1838, AL	None	Yes	Yes	No
Samuel Adcock	Co. G, MS 40 Inf. Rgt	Neshoba	Tnship 12, Range 10	Farmer	15	None	None	1845, MS	None	No	No	No
Bart S. Coughran	Co. E, MS 40 Inf. Rgt	Neshoba	Tnship 9, Range 13	Farmer	24	None	None	1836, GA	None	No	No	No
J.S. Seuker	NA	Neshoba	Philadelphia	Not in census								
James C. Harrington	Co. A, MS 4 Cv. Rgt	Newton	Union	Farmer	33	$720	$683	1827, NC	None	Yes	Yes	Yes
J.H. Pingleton	Co. A, MS 19 Inf. Rgt	Noxubee	Not in census									

Name[1]	Army Service[2]	County[3]	City/Town[4]	Occupation	Age in 1860	Real Estate	Personal Estate	Birth	Slaves	Married	Head of Household	Father
Ephraim Youngblood	Co. B, MS 31 Inf. Rgt	Oktibbeha	Starkville	Overseer	21	None	None	1839, AL	None	Yes	Yes	No
Thomas J. Warren	Co. F, MS 6 Cv. Rgt	Oktibbeha	Starkville	Farmer	32	$100	$500	1828, AL	None	Yes	Yes	Yes
Francis M. Philpot	Co. D, MS 2 Cv. Rgt	Panola	Not in census									
James H. Ates	Co. G, MS 7 Inf. Bat	Pike	Holmesville	Farmer	27	$150	$100	1833, LA	None	Yes	Yes	Yes
William A. Lesley	Co. G, MS 1 P. Rang	Pontotoc	Tallibenela	Farmer	30	$1,000	$563	1830, SC	None	Yes	Yes	Yes
J.W. Harris	Co. G, MS 2 Inf. Rgt	Pontotoc	Not in census									
Samuel W. Newell	Co. G, MS 2 Cv. Rgt	Pontotoc	Randolph	father: Farmer	15	father: $2160	father: $2365	1845, NC	3	No	No	No
James S. Furr	Co. G, MS 2 Cv. Rgt	Pontotoc	Not in census									
Napoleon B. Bolen	Co. F, MS 31 Inf. Rgt	Pontotoc	Birmingham	Farm Laborer	21	None	None	1839, AL	None	No	No	No
Luther A. Privet	NA	Pontotoc	Ellistown	Farmer	32	None	$380	1828, NC	None	Yes	Yes	Yes
John K. Holden	Co. G, MS 1 Inf. Rgt	Rankin	Brandon	Farmer	30	$2,400	$540	1830, LA	None	Yes	Yes	Yes
Archibald St. Clair	NA	Rankin	Not in census	Farmer								

Name[1]	Army Service[2]	County[3]	City/Town[4]	Occupation	Age in 1860	Real Estate	Personal Estate	Birth	Slaves	Married	Head of Household	Father
J.J. Bannelle	NA	Rankin	Not in census	Teacher								
J.S. Hath	Co. H. MS 20 Inf. Rgt	Scott	Not in census									
Jesse A. Brown	Co. A, MS 39 Inf. Rgt	Simpson	Beat 3	Farmer	30	$500	$370	1830, GA	None	Yes	Yes	Yes
Amos Davis	NA	Simpson	Beat 4	Farmer	33	$3,000	$15,448	1827, GA	13	Yes	Yes	Yes
John W. Gentry	Co. F, MS 14 Inf. Rgt	Smith	NA	Farmer	21	None	$100	1839, MS	None	No	No	No
John Hawkins	Co. D, MS 6 Inf. Rgt	Smith	NA	Farmer	34	$1,500	$1,100	1826, NC	None	Yes	Yes	Yes
Pleasant Q. Hawkins	Co. F, MS 16 Inf. Rgt	Smith	NA	Farmer	30	$400	$500	1830, NC	None	Yes	Yes	Yes
William E. Hawkins	Co. H. MS 37 Inf. Rgt	Smith	NA	Fireman to Engine	27	None	$250	1833, NC	None	Yes	Yes	Yes
A.E. Hawkins	Co. G, MS 6 Inf. Rgt	Smith	NA	Farmer	26	$477	$300	1834, NC	None	Yes	Yes	Yes
Daniel O. Bankston	Co. D, MS 13 Inf. Rgt	Smith	Smith	Farmer	24	None	$300	1836, MS	None	Yes	Yes	Yes
Lafayette Bolen	Co. E, AL 51 Cv. Rgt	St.Clair, AL	Tnships 14, 15	Farmer	27	$300	$250	1833, AL	None	Yes	Yes	Yes
Jasper Pettigrew	Co. B, MS 3 Inf. Rgt	Sunflower	Not in census									

Name[1]	Army Service[2]	County[3]	City/Town[4]	Occupation	Age in 1860	Real Estate	Personal Estate	Birth	Slaves	Married	Head of Household	Father
John B. Ray	Co. F, MS A.craft Cv.	Tippah	Northern Division	father: Minister	20	None	None	1840, SC	None	No	No	No
John M. Bishop	Co. H, MS 23 Inf. Rgt	Tippah	Not in census									
Will. Harrison Gober	Co. K, MS Hams Cv.	Tippah	Southern Subdivision	Farmer	39	$500	$822	1821, GA	None	Yes	Yes	Yes
Littleton Wages	Co. D, MS 18 Cv. Bt	Tippah	Southern Subdivision	Farmer	23	$250	$458	1837, SC	None	Yes	Yes	Yes
Samuel L. Allen	Co. H, MS 19 Inf. Rgt	Tippah	Southern Subdivision	Farm Laborer	25	None	$411	1835, MS-	None	Yes	Yes	Yes
John W. Tate	Co. E, MS 23 Inf. Rgt	Tippah	Southern Subdivision	Farmer	36	$1,000	$973	1824, SC	None	Yes	Yes	Yes
William W. Ballentine	Co. H, MS 34 Inf. Rgt	Tippah	Southern Subdivision	Farmer	21	$500	$435	1839, TN	None	Yes	Yes	Yes
Andrew C. Vandiver	Co. E, MS 23 Inf. Rgt	Tippah	Southern Subdivision	Farmer	29	$500	$1,000	1831, TN	None	Yes	Yes	Yes
William Lindsey	Co. A, MS 23 Inf. Rgt	Tippah or Tishomingo	Not in census									
J.B. Hommry	Co. A, MS 23 Inf. Rgt	Tippah or Tishomingo	Not in census									
Richard Simmons	Co. B, MS 26 Inf. Rgt	Tishomingo	Not in census									

Name[1]	Army Service[2]	County[3]	City/Town[4]	Occupation	Age in 1860	Real Estate	Personal Estate	Birth	Slaves	Married	Head of Household	Father
Austin Hartin	Co. C, MS 7 Cv. Rgt	Tishomingo	Not in census									
Donald Street	Co. C, MS 26 Inf. Rgt	Tishomingo	Rienzi	Farmer	16	None	None	1844, NC	None	No	No	No
James Jordan	Co. G, MS 24 Inf. Rgt	Warren	Not in census									
Martin C. Parker	Co. E, MS J Davis Cv	Washington, AL	St. Stephens	Farmer	25	None	$335	1835, MS	None	Yes	Yes	Yes
H. Munzesheimer	Co. E, MS 21 Inf. Rgt	Wilkinson	Woodville	Not in census								
Richard A.J. Corey	Co. E, MS 21 Inf. Rgt	Wilkinson	Woodville	Farmer	20	None	$5,000	1840, MS	4	No	No	No
David A. Enlow	Co. D, MS 21 Inf. Rgt	Wilkinson	NA	Farmer	28	$400	$100	1832, MS	None	Yes	Yes	Yes
William McKinney	Co. E, MS 21 Inf. Rgt	Wilkinson	NA	Farmer	35	$1,200	$800	1825, SC	None	Yes	Yes	Yes
Benjamin C. Bass	Co. E, MS 21 Inf. Rgt	Wilkinson	NA	Farmer	46	$400	$200	1814, MS	None	Yes	Yes	Yes
James Tedder	Co. I, MS 3 Inf. Rgt	Yazoo	Not in census									

NOTES

INTRODUCTION

1. Jefferson Davis, speech at Jackson, Mississippi, December 26, 1862, in *The Papers of Jefferson Davis*, vol. 8, *1862*, ed. Lynda Lasswell Crist, Mary Seaton Dix, and Kenneth H. Williams (Baton Rouge: Louisiana State University Press, 1995), 565–79, quotations on 567, 574.

2. Ben Wynne, *Mississippi's Civil War: A Narrative History* (Macon, GA: Mercer University Press, 2006), 12.

3. Paul Quigley, *Shifting Grounds: Nationalism and the American South, 1848–1865* (New York: Oxford University Press, 2012), 11, 5–6.

4. See Wynne, *Mississippi's Civil War*; Timothy B. Smith, *Mississippi in the Civil War: The Home Front* (Jackson: University Press of Mississippi, 2010); Timothy B. Smith, *The Mississippi Secession Convention: Delegates and Deliberations in Politics and War, 1861–1865* (Jackson: University Press of Mississippi, 2014); and Michael B. Ballard, *The Civil War in Mississippi: Major Campaigns and Battles* (Jackson: University Press of Mississippi, 2011).

5. Andre M. Fleche, *The Revolution of 1861: The American Civil War in the Age of Nationalist Conflict* (Chapel Hill: University of North Carolina Press, 2011), 70.

6. Mark V. Wetherington, *Plain Folk's Fight: The Civil War and Reconstruction in Piney Woods Georgia* (Chapel Hill: University of North Carolina Press, 2005), 1–9; Andrew F. Lang, "'Upon the Altar of Our Country': Confederate Identity, Nationalism, and Morale in Harrison County, Texas, 1860–1865," *Civil War History* 55 (September 2009): 281–82; Brian S. Wills, "Shades of Nation: Confederate Loyalties in Southeastern Virginia," in *Inside the Confederate Nation: Essays in Honor of Emory M. Thomas*, ed. Lesley J. Gordon and John C. Inscoe (Baton Rouge: Louisiana State University Press, 2005), 60–61; Jacqueline Glass Campbell, *When Sherman Marched North from the Sea: Resistance on the Confederate Home Front* (Chapel Hill: University of North Carolina Press, 2003), 69–74; William A. Blair, *Virginia's Private War: Feeding Body and Soul in the Confederacy, 1861–1865* (New York: Oxford University Press, 1998), 144–46; and Aaron Sheehan-Dean, *Why Confederates Fought: Family and Nation in Civil War Virginia* (Chapel Hill: University of North Carolina Press, 2007), 146–47.

7. Gary W. Gallagher, *The Confederate War: How Popular Will, Nationalism, and Military Strategy Could Not Stave Off Defeat* (Cambridge, MA: Harvard University Press, 1997), 5–13; Gary W. Gallagher, *Becoming Confederates: Paths to New Loyalty* (Athens: University of Georgia Press, 2013); Joseph T. Glatthaar, *General Lee's Army: From Victory to Collapse*

(New York: Free Press, 2008), 316–17, 456; Keith S. Bohannon, "'Witness the Redemption of the Army': Reenlistments in the Confederate Army of Tennessee, January–March 1864," in Gordon and Inscoe, *Inside the Confederate Nation*, 111–14; Lisa Laskin, "'The Army Is Not Near So Much Demoralized as the Country Is': Soldiers in the Army of Northern Virginia and the Confederate Home Front," in *The View from the Ground: Experiences of Civil War Soldiers*, ed. Aaron Sheehan-Dean (Lexington: University Press of Kentucky, 2007), 91–92; Stephen V. Ash, *When the Yankees Came: Conflict and Chaos in the Occupied South, 1861–1865* (Chapel Hill: University of North Carolina Press, 1995), 72–75; Jason Phillips, *Diehard Rebels: The Confederate Culture of Invincibility* (Athens: University of Georgia Press, 2007), 2–5, 88; Peter S. Carmichael, *The Last Generation: Young Virginians in Peace, War, and Reunion* (Chapel Hill: University of North Carolina Press, 2005), 13–14; and Bradley R. Clampitt, *The Confederate Heartland: Military and Civilian Morale in the Western Confederacy* (Baton Rouge: Louisiana State University Press, 2011), 7–10, 13.

8. Ian Binnington, *Confederate Visions: Nationalism, Symbolism, and the Imagined South in the Civil War* (Charlottesville: University of Virginia Press, 2013); Michael T. Bernath, *Confederate Minds: The Struggle for Intellectual Independence in the Civil War South* (Chapel Hill: University of North Carolina Press, 2010), 1–2, 290; Robert E. Bonner, *Colors and Blood: Flag Passions of the Confederate South* (Princeton, NJ: Princeton University Press, 2002), 3–4; Anne S. Rubin, *A Shattered Nation: The Rise and Fall of the Confederacy, 1861–1868* (Chapel Hill: University of North Carolina Press, 2005), 12; and Drew Gilpin Faust, *The Creation of Confederate Nationalism: Ideology and Identity in the Civil War South* (Baton Rouge: Louisiana State University Press, 1988), 6–10.

9. William W. Freehling, *The South vs. the South: How Anti-Confederate Southerners Shaped the Course of the Civil War* (New York: Oxford University Press, 2001), 17–33, 47–85; Margaret Storey, *Loyalty and Loss: Alabama's Unionists in the Civil War and Reconstruction* (Baton Rouge: Louisiana State University Press, 2004), 20–26; Paul D. Escott, *After Secession: Jefferson Davis and the Failure of Confederate Nationalism* (Baton Rouge: Louisiana State University Press, 1978), 94–135; Georgia Lee Tatum, *Disloyalty in the Confederacy* (1934; repr., New York: AMS Press, 1970), 3–23; Victoria E. Bynum, *The Free State of Jones: Mississippi's Longest Civil War* (Chapel Hill: University of North Carolina Press, 2001), 98–104; William C. Davis, *Look Away! A History of the Confederate States of America* (New York: Free Press, 2002), 367; Mark A. Weitz, *More Damning Than Slaughter: Desertion in the Confederate Army* (Lincoln: University of Nebraska Press, 2005), vii–xix, 16–34; and David Williams, *Bitterly Divided: The South's Inner Civil War* (New York: New Press, 2008), 1–8, 109–71.

10. Thomas G. Dyer, *Secret Yankees: The Union Circle in Confederate Atlanta* (Baltimore: Johns Hopkins University Press, 1999), 4; Jonathan Dean Sarris, *A Separate Civil War: Communities in Conflict in the Mountain South* (Charlottesville: University of Virginia Press, 2006), 3; and Judkin Browning, *Shifting Loyalties: The Union Occupation of Eastern North Carolina* (Chapel Hill: University of North Carolina Press, 2011), 4. For other studies of the Border and Mountain South that emphasize how local attachments influenced national loyalty, see Michael Fellman, *Inside War: The Guerrilla Conflict in Missouri during the American Civil War* (New York: Oxford University Press, 1989), 47–65; Noel C. Fisher, *War at Every Door: Partisan Politics and Guerrilla Violence in East Tennessee, 1860–1869* (Chapel Hill: University of North Carolina Press, 1997), 62–63, 142–43; Martin Crawford, *Ashe County's Civil War: Community and Society in the Appalachian South* (Charlottesville: University of Virginia Press, 2001) 14, 52, 130; Robert Tracy McKenzie, *Lincolnites and Rebels: A Divided Town in the American Civil War* (Oxford: Oxford University Press, 2006),

124–40; and Barton Myers, *Executing Daniel Bright: Race, Loyalty, and Guerrilla Violence in a Coastal Carolina Community, 1861–1865* (Baton Rouge: Louisiana State University Press, 2009), 80, 127.

11. Gary W. Gallagher, "Disaffection, Persistence, and Nation: Some Directions in Recent Scholarship on the Confederacy," *Civil War History* 55 (September 2009): 352.

12. David M. Potter, "The Historian's Use of Nationalism and Vice-Versa," *American Historical Review* 67 (July 1962): 924–26; and Eric Hobsbawm, *Nations and Nationalism since 1780: Programme, Myth, Reality* (New York: Cambridge University Press, 1990), 11. See also Stephen Nathanson, *Patriotism, Morality, and Peace* (Lanham, MD: Rowman and Littlefield, 1993), 105–16; and Simon Keller, *The Limits of Loyalty* (Cambridge: Cambridge University Press, 2007), 21–22, 146.

13. James Connor, *The Sociology of Loyalty* (New York: Springer, 2007), 47.

14. Ibid., 47–49, quotation on 47; and Keller, *The Limits of Loyalty*, 13.

15. Matthew J. Hornsey and Jolanda Jetten, "Loyalty without Conformity: Tailoring Self-Perception as a Means of Balancing Belonging and Differentiation," *Self and Identity* 4 (January–March 2005): 83; Peter J. Burke and Jan E. Stets, *Identity Theory* (New York: Oxford University Press, 2009), 3; and George P. Fletcher, *Loyalty: An Essay on the Morality of Relationships* (New York: Oxford University Press, 2003), 17. Scholars in the various fields of the social sciences have struggled to define "identity," leading one sociologist to conclude that it is impossible to arrive at a single definition of the concept. Nevertheless, other scholars have provided definitions, which, despite their differences, tend to focus on the idea of identity as a marker of self, particularly in relation to others. Individuals' roles in society as neighbors, friends, spouses, siblings, parents, citizens, politicians, or soldiers cannot be separated from the person, institution, group, or ideal to which they profess allegiance. George Fletcher writes that the conception of "self" that constitutes identity "generates duties of loyalty toward the families, groups, and nations that enter into our self-definition." For more of the sociological literature on identity, see Karen A. Cerulo, "Identity Construction: New Issues, New Directions," *Annual Review of Sociology* 23 (1997): 385–409; Stephanie Lawler, *Identity: Sociological Perspectives* (Cambridge: Polity Press, 2008), 2; and Fletcher, *Loyalty*.

16. Wynne, *Mississippi's Civil War*, 181–95; and Mary Bobbitt Townsend, *Yankee Warhorse: A Biography of Major General Peter Osterhaus* (Columbia: University of Missouri Press, 2010), 190–98.

17. James C. Scott, *Domination and the Arts of Resistance: Hidden Transcripts* (New Haven, CT: Yale University Press, 1990), 1–5.

18. Nicholas Onuf and Peter Onuf, *Nations, Markets, and War: Modern History and the American Civil War* (Charlottesville: University of Virginia Press, 2006), 282, 318, 325.

19. Ernest Gellner, *Nations and Nationalism*, 2nd ed. (Oxford: Blackwell, 2006), 4, 6; and Montserrat Guibernau, *Nationalisms: The Nation-State and Nationalism in the Twentieth Century* (Cambridge: Polity Press, 1996), 58.

20. Onuf and Onuf, *Nations, Markets, and War*, 311, 331, 144–49; and Gellner, *Nations and Nationalism*, 6–7, 56.

21. Quigley, *Shifting Grounds*, 173, 200, 213.

22. Jefferson Davis, speech at Jackson, Mississippi, December 26, 1862, in Crist et al., *The Papers of Jefferson Davis*, 8:567.

23. See William A. Blair, *With Malice toward Some: Treason and Loyalty in the Civil War Era* (Chapel Hill: University of North Carolina Press, 2014).

24. For studies that argue that the Civil War created the modern American nation-state, see Emory Thomas, *The Confederacy as a Revolutionary Experience* (Columbia: University of South Carolina Press, 1971); Richard Franklin Bensel, *Yankee Leviathan: The Origins of Central State Authority in America, 1859–1877* (Cambridge: Cambridge University Press, 1990); Onuf and Onuf, *Nations, Markets, and War*; Melinda Lawson, *Patriot Fires: Forging a New American Nationalism in the Civil War North* (Lawrence: University Press of Kansas, 2002); Stephanie McCurry, *Confederate Reckoning: Power and Politics in the Civil War South* (Cambridge, MA: Harvard University Press, 2010), 153–56; and David Goldfield, *America Aflame: How the Civil War Created a Nation* (New York: Bloomsbury, 2011).

25. For more on the nature of state power, see William J. Novak, "The Myth of the 'Weak' American State," *American Historical Review* 113 (June 2008): 763. Novak defines infrastructural power as "the positive capacity of the state to 'penetrate civil society' and implement policies throughout a given territory." He argues that, historically, the infrastructural power of the United States—via national and state governments' roles in acquiring land, creating public infrastructure, building up national defense, increasing regulation of economic activity, and policing the citizenry—has always been strong, rendering untenable claims of a "weak" American state. Civil War historians have reached similar conclusions regarding the wartime Confederate state.

26. Albert Gallatin Brown, "State of the Country Speech in the Confederate Senate," December 24, 1863, in *Documenting the American South*, Digital Collection, The Southern Homefront, 1861–1865, University of North Carolina at Chapel Hill, 1999, at http://docsouth.unc.edu/imls/browna/browna.html, accessed September 24, 2009 (hereafter cited as *Documenting the American South*).

27. For studies that cast the Civil War as fitting within the greater nineteenth-century era of nationalist revolutions, see Fleche, *The Revolution of 1861*; and Quigley, *Shifting Grounds*.

28. Quigley, *Shifting Grounds*, 5.

CHAPTER ONE

1. Roxana Chapin Gerdine to Emily McKinstry Chapin, December 16, 1860, Roxana Chapin Gerdine Collection, Digital Collections, Civil War Archive, J. D. Williams Library, University of Mississippi, at http://clio.lib.olemiss.edu/cdm4/document.php?CISOROOT =/civil_war&CISOPTR=1654&REC=12, accessed December 5, 2011 (hereafter cited as UMDC); and US War Department, comp., *The War of the Rebellion: Official Records of the Union and Confederate Armies*, 128 vols. (Washington, DC: Government Printing Office, 1880–1901), ser. 4, vol. 1, 277 (hereafter cited as *OR*).

2. Westley F. Busbee Jr., *Mississippi: A History* (Wheeling, IL: Harlan Davidson, 2005), 89–90; Christopher J. Olsen, *Political Culture and Secession in Mississippi: Masculinity, Honor, and the Antiparty Tradition, 1830–1860* (New York: Oxford University Press, 2000); 17; and Wynne, *Mississippi's Civil War*, 3–7.

3. Adam Rothman, *Slave Country: American Expansion and the Origins of the Deep South* (Cambridge, MA: Harvard University Press, 2005), 38–45, 174, quotation on 45; and Busbee, *Mississippi: A History*, 74, 85.

4. Busbee, *Mississippi: A History*, 90–91; and Wynne, *Mississippi's Civil War*, 6–9. All factions in Southern politics used slavery as a political wedge issue, although the nullifiers exploited it to an exceptional degree. See William J. Cooper Jr., *The South and the Politics of Slavery, 1828–1856* (Baton Rouge: Louisiana State University Press, 1978).

5. William W. Freehling, *The Road to Disunion*, vol. 2, *Secessionists Triumphant, 1854–1861* (New York: Oxford University Press, 2007), 16; and William J. Cooper Jr., *Liberty and Slavery: Southern Politics to 1860* (1983; repr., Columbia: University of South Carolina Press, 2000), 38, 179. In 1850, Mississippi's free population totaled 295,718 (48.8 percent of the total) to a slave population of 309,874 (51.2 percent). In 1860, the free population was 353,899 (44.8 percent) compared to 436,631 (55.2 percent) enslaved. Wynne, *Mississippi's Civil War*, 13.

6. Busbee, *Mississippi: A History*, 120–25.

7. Ibid; and Bradley G. Bond, *Political Culture in the Nineteenth-Century South: Mississippi, 1830–1900* (Baton Rouge: Louisiana State University Press, 1995), 104–8.

8. Percy Lee Rainwater, *Mississippi: Storm Center of Secession, 1856–1861* (Baton Rouge: Otto Claitor, 1938), 42–47; and Wynne, *Mississippi's Civil War*, 15–20.

9. William L. Barney, *The Secessionist Impulse: Alabama and Mississippi in 1860* (Tuscaloosa: University of Alabama Press, 1974), 153, 174–77.

10. *Semi-Weekly Mississippian* (Jackson), October 5, 1860, quoted in Crist et al., *The Papers of Jefferson Davis*, 6:364–66.

11. John J. Pettus, Address to the State Legislature, *Journal of the House of Representatives of the State of Mississippi, Called Session, November 1860*, in *Mississippi in the Confederacy: As They Saw It*, ed. John K. Bettersworth (1961; repr., New York: Kraus Reprint Company, 1970), 1:22.

12. "Nullification," *Daily Evening Citizen* (Vicksburg), December 12, 1860; Edward Terry to Sister, December 15, 1860, Bullock and Hamilton Family Papers, 1757–1971, folder 32, 00101, Southern Historical Collection, Wilson Library, University of North Carolina at Chapel Hill (hereafter cited as SHC); Thomas Bailey to Mother, November 18, 1860, John Lancaster Bailey Papers, 1785–1874, folder 11, 00039, SHC; William L. Nugent to Nellie Smith Nugent, November 26, 1860, in William M. Cash and Lucy Somerville Howorth, eds., *My Dear Nellie: The Civil War Letters of William L. Nugent to Eleanor Smith Nugent* (Jackson: University Press of Mississippi, 1977), 136–39; and A. F. Burton to Family, January 14, 1861, Thomas W. Burton Papers, 1809–1921, folder 1, 04217-z, SHC.

13. Smith, *The Mississippi Secession Convention*, 13; and George Washington Sargent to George Sargent, December 5, 1860, George Washington Sargent to George Sargent, December 15, 1860, and George Washington Sargent to William Duncan, December 30, 1860, all in George Washington Sargent Papers, 1840–1900, folder 11, volume 11, 04025, SHC.

14. L. L. Walton to Granddaughter, November 21, 1860, James Lusk Alcorn and Family Papers, folder 1, Z/0317.00, Mississippi Department of Archives and History, Jackson, Mississippi (hereafter cited as MDAH); and Ruffin Thomson to William H. Thomson, undated, 1861, Ruffin Thomson Papers, folder 3, 03315, SHC.

15. "Correspondence of the Whig," *Daily Vicksburg Whig*, November 24, 1860; and "Disunion Carnival at Jackson," *Daily Vicksburg Whig*, November 28, 1860, in Percy Lee Rainwater Collection, 1929–1969, box 1, folder 18, Z/1112.000/S, MDAH.

16. Wynne, *Mississippi's Civil War*, 24–26; Barney, *The Secessionist Impulse*, 198–201; and Smith, *The Mississippi Secession Convention*, 77–80.

17. T. W. Compton to Alonzo Snyder, December 23, 1860, Alonzo Snyder Papers, box 11, folder 44, mss. 655, *Civil War: Context and Conflict*, Digital Collections, Louisiana State University Special Collections, Louisiana State University Libraries, Baton Rouge, at http://www.louisianadigitallibrary.org/cdm4/document.php?CISOROOT=/p15140co1110&CISOPTR=646 http://docsouth.unc.edu/imls/niles/niles.html, accessed December 20, 2011 (hereafter cited as *Civil War: Context and Conflict*).

18. David Grimsted, *American Mobbing, 1828–1861: Toward Civil War* (New York: Oxford University Press, 1998), 100–113, see also 114–78. On urban mobbing during the secession crisis, see Frank Towers, *The Urban South and the Coming of the Civil War* (Charlottesville: University of Virginia Press, 2004).

19. William W. Freehling, *The Road to Disunion: Secessionists at Bay, 1776–1854* (New York: Oxford University Press, 1990), 99; and Barney, *The Secessionist Impulse*, 177. On violence in the antebellum South, see Clement Eaton, "Mob Violence in the Old South," *Mississippi Valley Historical Review* 29 (December 1942): 351–70; Bertram Wyatt-Brown, *Honor and Violence in the Old South* (New York: Oxford University Press, 1986); and Edward L. Ayers, *Vengeance and Justice: Crime and Punishment in the Nineteenth-Century American South* (New York: Oxford University Press, 1984), 9–33. On the connection between slave patrols and political intimidation in the South, see Sally E. Hadden, *Slave Patrols: Law and Violence in Virginia and the Carolinas* (Cambridge, MA: Harvard University Press, 2001), 1–5, 167–200; Grimsted, *American Mobbing*, 85–135; John Hope Franklin, *The Militant South, 1800–1861* (1956; repr., Urbana: University of Illinois Press, 2002), 72–76; and Wyatt-Brown, *Honor and Violence*, 154–87.

20. Christopher Waldrep, *Roots of Disorder: Race and Criminal Justice in the American South, 1817–80* (Urbana: University of Illinois Press, 1998), 14–15, 21–22.

21. Betty Bentley Beaumont, *Twelve Years of My Life: An Autobiography* (Philadelphia: T. B. Peterson and Brothers, 1887), 105–6, 136, 157.

22. *Daily Evening Citizen* (Vicksburg), December 20, 1860; "A Female Abolitionist," *Daily Evening Citizen* (Vicksburg), December 18, 1860; and "A Natural Result of Abolition Aggression," *Daily Evening Citizen* (Vicksburg), December 20, 1860.

23. Stephen A. West, "Minute Men, Yeomen, and the Mobilization for Secession in the South Carolina Upcountry," *Journal of Southern History* 71 (February 2005): 91; and Barney, *The Secessionist Impulse*, 207–19. On South Carolina vigilance committees, see Steven A. Channing, *Crisis of Fear: Secession in South Carolina* (New York: W. W. Norton, 1974); for vigilance committees in Georgia, see Ayers, *Vengeance and Justice*, 141–50.

24. Barney, *The Secessionist Impulse*, 208–9; and John W. Wood, *Union and Secession in Mississippi* (Memphis: Saunders, Parish and Whitmore, 1863), 9.

25. John Hill Aughey, *Tupelo* (Lincoln, NE: State Journal Company, 1888), 30–31; Beaumont, *Twelve Years of My Life*, 168; and Randolph Roth, *American Homicide* (Cambridge, MA: Harvard University Press, 2009), 331.

26. Charles C. Bolton, *Poor Whites of the Antebellum South: Tenants and Laborers in Central North Carolina and Northeast Mississippi* (Durham, NC: Duke University Press, 1994), 125, 164; Barney, *The Secessionist Impulse*, 268–69; Wynne, *Mississippi's Civil War*, 27; and *Daily Vicksburg Whig*, December 25, 1860.

27. Olsen, *Political Culture and Secession*, 121–26; and Wood, *Union and Secession in Mississippi*, 40.

28. R. F. Crenshaw to Ella Austin, December 13, 1860, R. F. Crenshaw Letter, box 1997.1, folder 97–1, MUM01341, Archives and Special Collections, J. D. Williams Library, University of Mississippi, Oxford (hereafter cited as UMASC); "Glorious Result in Rankin," *Vicksburg Daily Whig*, December 27, 1860; and Aughey, *Tupelo*, 46.

29. Diary of Jason Niles, January 2, 1862, transcript of manuscript no. 950, *Documenting the American South*, at http://docsouth.unc.edu/imls/niles/niles.html, accessed August 5, 2009; and George Washington Sargent to Mr. Hethery, January 7, 1860, George Washington Sargent Papers, SHC.

30. Wood, *Union and Secession in Mississippi*, 27, 30; Wynne, *Mississippi's Civil War*, 28–31; and Smith, *The Mississippi Secession Convention*, 63–73.

31. *Proceedings of the Mississippi State Convention, Held January 7th to 26th, A.D. 1861* (Jackson: Power and Cadwallader, 1861), 15, *Documenting the American South*, at http://docsouth.unc.edu/imls/missconv/missconv.html, accessed January 23, 2012; "A Declaration of the Immediate Causes which Induce and Justify the Secession of the State of Mississippi from the Federal Union, 1861," *Proceedings of the Mississippi State Convention, Held January 7th to 26th, A.D. 1861* (Jackson: Power and Cadwallader, 1861), 47, *Documenting the American South*; and Smith, *The Mississippi Secession Convention*, 74–75.

32. John K. Bettersworth, *Confederate Mississippi: The People and Policies of a Cotton State in Wartime* (1943; repr., Philadelphia: Porcupine Press, 1978), 11; and Ballard, *The Civil War in Mississippi*, 4, 6.

33. Bettersworth, *Confederate Mississippi*, 11–12; Ballard, *The Civil War in Mississippi*, 4, 10–11; and Smith, *The Mississippi Secession Convention*, 174–86.

34. Thomas Bailey to Mother, February 16, 1861, April 28, 1861, John Lancaster Bailey Papers, 1785–1874, folder 11, 00039, SHC; Louisa T. Lovell to Joseph Lovell, January 27, 1861, Quitman Family Papers, 1784–1978, folder 105, series 1.2, 00616, SHC; and John Kirkland to William Otey, May 22, 1861, Wyche and Otey Family Papers, 1824–1936, folder 15, series 1.3, 01608, SHC.

35. N. H. Boyd to Eudora Hobbs, January 13, 1861, April 18, 1861, Hobbs Family Papers, *Intellectual Underpinnings of the American Civil War*, Digital Collections, Manuscripts Division, Special Collections Department, Mississippi State University Libraries, Starkville, at http://digital.library.msstate.edu/collections/document.php?CISOROOT=/ASERL&CISOPTR=83&REC=5, accessed January 22, 2012 (hereafter cited as *Underpinnings of the American Civil War*); Eliza Patterson to Anne Boyd Green, September 1, 1861, Hays-Ray-Webb Collection, *Underpinnings of the American Civil War*, at http://digital.library.msstate.edu/collections/document.php?CISOROOT=/ASERL&CISOPTR=69&REC=2, accessed December 10, 2011; Diary of Henry A. Garrett, March 25, 1861, in Bettersworth, *Mississippi in the Confederacy*, 1:46–47; and William C. Nelson to Elizabeth L. Cage, May 21, 1861, William Cowper Nelson Collection, UMDC, at http://clio.lib.olemiss.edu/cdm4/document.php?CISOROOT=/civil_war&CISOPTR=314&REC=3, accessed December 10, 2011.

36. *Vicksburg Sun*, November 12, 1860, quoted in Rainwater, *Storm Center of Secession*, 164; "The Possible Future of the South," *Natchez Daily Free Trader*, November 24, 1860, in Percy Lee Rainwater Collection, box 1, folder 18, MDAH; William Kirkland to Children, October 17, 1860, Wyche and Otey Family Papers, folder 14, SHC; and "January 1861," *Daily Vicksburg Whig*, December 28, 1860.

37. "The Secession of the State," *Weekly Panola (MS) Star*, January 17, 1861; "Remarks of W. P. Harris, of Hinds," *Proceedings of the Mississippi State Convention, Documenting the American South*; and H. Hobbs and Howel Hobbs to Eudora Hobbs, January 13, 1861, Howel Hobbs to Eudora Hobbs, January 23 1961, February 8, 1861, in Hobbs Family Papers, *Underpinnings of the American Civil War*, at http://digital.library.msstate.edu/collections/document.php?CISOROOT=/ASERL&CISOPTR=83&REC=5.

38. Francis Terry Leak Diary, January 27, March 7, February 26, March 28, 1861, Francis Terry Leak Papers, 1839–1865, folder 12, volume 6, 01095, SHC; Louisa T. Lovell to Joseph Lovell, January 27, 1861, Quitman Family Papers, SHC; Albert H. Clark to William C. McDonald, April 27, 1862, Clark Family Letters, UMDC, at http://clio.lib.olemiss.edu/cdm4/

document.php?CISOROOT=/civil_war&CISOPTR=22&REC=6, accessed December 10, 2011; and Thomas F. Burton to Brother, August 12, 1861, Bullock and Hamilton Family Papers, 1757–1971, folder 32, 00101, SHC.

39. "Inaugural Address of President Davis, February 18, 1861," *Proceedings of the Mississippi State Convention*, 120, *Documenting the American South*.

40. C. A. Howe to Daughter, August 2, 1861, Chiliab Smith Howe Papers, 1814–1899, folder 53, series 1.6, 03092, SHC; and Robert and Willie Hughes to Mary Adams, November 24, 1861, Hughes Family Papers, 1790–1910, folder 17, 02779, SHC. On the relationship between suffering and Confederate loyalty, see Quigley, *Shifting Grounds*, 171–213.

41. Beaumont, *Twelve Years of My Life*, 169; William L. Nugent to Nellie Smith Nugent, August 10, 1861, May 26, 1862, in Cash and Howorth, *My Dear Nellie*, 45, 77; and J. J. Little to Parents, June 28, 1861, August 9, 1861, J. J. Little Collection, UMDC, at http://clio.lib.olemiss .edu/cdm4/document.php?CISOROOT=/civil_war&CISOPTR=2183&REC=3, accessed December 10, 2011.

42. B. A. Terry to John J. Pettus, April 30, 1861, John J. Pettus Correspondence, roll 1812, volume 36, Record Group 27, MDAH; *Daily Evening Citizen* (Vicksburg), January 15, 1861; Louisa T. Lovell to Joseph Lovell, July 9, 1861, Quitman Family Papers, folder 106, SHA; and John Dickerson to John J. Pettus, May 18, 1861, John J. Pettus Correspondence, roll 2776, volume 37, Record Group 27, MDAH.

43. Henry Barnes to Julia Southall, May 20, 1861, Southall and Bowen Family Papers, 1833–1959, folder 6, 04135, SHC; and Diary of Jason Niles, January 2, 1862, *Documenting the American South*.

44. Thomas D. Cockrell and Michael B. Ballard, eds., *Chickasaw, a Mississippi Scout for the Union: The Civil War Memoir of Levi H. Naron* (Baton Rouge: Louisiana State University Press, 2005), 8–9, 12–21, quotations on 8, 18; and Aughey, *Tupelo*, 46–59, 65, 72–75, quotations on 46–47.

45. Hadden, *Slave Patrols*, 4, 167–203.

46. *Daily Evening Citizen* (Vicksburg), January 15, 1861; John T. Simmons to John J. Pettus, September 25, 1861, in Bettersworth, *Mississippi in the Confederacy*, 1:294; and O. J. Hood to John J. Pettus, June 19, 1861, in Bettersworth, *Mississippi in the Confederacy*, 1:293–94.

47. Roxana Chapin Gerdine to Emily McKinstry Chapin, March 21, 1862, Roxana Chapin Gerdine Collection, UMDC, at http://clio.lib.olemiss.edu/cdm4/document. php?CISOROOT=/civil_war&CISOPTR=1654&REC=12, accessed December 6, 2011; and How Hines to John J. Pettus, June 5, 1862, in Bettersworth, *Mississippi in the Confederacy*, 1:295.

CHAPTER TWO

1. "Mississippi and the War," *American Citizen* (Canton, MS), August 29, 1862; and "Cornelia," *The Concise Oxford Companion to Classical Literature*, ed. M. C. Howatson (Oxford: Oxford University Press, 1996), at http://www.oxfordreference.com/views/ ENTRY.html?subview=Main&entry=t9.e737, accessed February 14, 2011.

2. *Beacon* (Macon, MS), June 10, 1863.

3. Statement of James H. Harrington regarding James B. Wells, November 26, 1863, arrest papers of James B. Wells, November 26, 1863, nos. C871-1071, roll 88, Letters Received by the Confederate Secretary of War (hereafter cited as LRCSW), M-437, War Department

Collection of Confederate Records, Record Group 109, National Archives and Records Administration, Washington, DC, and College Park, Maryland (hereafter cited as NARA).

4. Elizabeth Duquette, *Loyal Subjects: Bonds of Nation, Race, and Allegiance in Nineteenth-Century America* (Piscataway, NJ: Rutgers University Press, 2010), 42.

5. For studies that argue that the Civil War created the modern American nation-state, see Bensel, *Yankee Leviathan*; Onuf and Onuf, *Nations, Markets, and War*; Lawson, *Patriot Fires*; and McCurry, *Confederate Reckoning*.

6. Wynne, *Mississippi's Civil War*, 63–71; Michael B. Ballard, *Vicksburg: The Campaign That Opened the Mississippi* (Chapel Hill: University of North Carolina Press, 2004), 422–31; Smith, *Mississippi in the Civil War*, 3, 120; and M. J. Blackwell to Margaret E. Blackwell, July 17, 1863, Margaret E. Blackwell Papers, folder 1, 04790-z, SHC.

7. Rubin, *A Shattered Nation*, 95–97.

8. Duquette, *Loyal Subjects*, 46.

9. Ash, *When the Yankees Came*, 44–45, 60–61; and Bertram Wyatt-Brown, *Southern Honor: Ethics and Behavior in the Old South* (Oxford: Oxford University Press, 1982), 33–34, 55–57.

10. Blair, *With Malice toward Some*, 139–41; Duquette, *Loyal Subjects*, 47; Harold Melvin Hyman, *Era of the Oath: Northern Loyalty Tests during the Civil War and Reconstruction* (Philadelphia: University of Pennsylvania Press, 1954), 35; and Richard Franklin Bensel, *The American Ballot Box in the Mid-Nineteenth Century* (New York: Cambridge University Press, 2004), 225–26.

11. "Conscience and the Confederacy; or, 'The Oath,' Morally and Practically Considered; A Sermon by the Rev. W. W. Lord," *Daily Southern Crisis* (Jackson), January 3, 1863.

12. William H. Thomson to Ruffin Thomson, undated, April 1863, Ruffin Thomson Papers, 1822–1889, folder 6, 03315, SHC; Eliza H. B. Sively to Jane Sively, undated, Jane Sively Letters, 1862–1867, folder 4, 01891-z, SHC; R. C. Webb to John J. Pettus, February 28, 1863, John J. Pettus Correspondence, roll 1446, volume 51, Record Group 27, MDAH; and William Dameron to Wife, November 15, 1863, Norton, Chilton, and Dameron Family Papers, 1760–1926, folder 8, series 1, 03264, SHC.

13. Edwin Miller to Mrs. H. R. Miller, March 29, 1863, Miller Family Papers, 1830–1864, MUM00297, folder 51, UMASC; W. C. Taylor to Thomas N. Wendal, March 4, 1863, Longstreet-Hinton Collection, 1841–1954, MUM00276, folder 4, UMASC; and Wyatt-Brown, *Southern Honor*, 112.

14. *OR*, ser. 4, vol. 2, 919.

15. "Oxford, Mississippi, Report from General Grant's Army Camp," MUM01249, box 1995.3, folder 95.2, UMASC; Jane Gibson to Jefferson Davis, November 9, 1864, in Crist et al., *The Papers of Jefferson Davis*, 11:150; and Gordon A. Cotton, ed., *From the Pen of a She-Rebel: The Civil War Diary of Emilie Riley McKinley* (Columbia: University of South Carolina Press, 2001), 26, 37, 64–65.

16. Suzanne L. Bunkers, ed., *The Diary of Caroline Seabury, 1854–1863* (Madison: University of Wisconsin Press, 1991), 103; Anna Pickens to Josie Howe, May 4, 1865, Chiliab Smith Howe Papers, 1814–1899, folder 53, series 1.6, 03092, SHC; Samuel Moore to Mary Moore, August 20, 1863, Samuel Blanche Moore Letters, Z/1800.000/F, MDAH; and James Lusk Alcorn to Wife, August 29, 1863, James Lusk Alcorn Papers, 1850–1949, folder 4, 00005-z, SHC.

17. Louisa T. Lovell to Joseph Lovell, December 5, 1862, February 7, 1864, March 8, 1864, Quitman Family Papers, 1784–1978, folders 110, 111, 112, series 1.2, 00616, SHC.

18. Cockrell and Ballard, *Chickasaw*, 53, 55; and Charles B. Allen to Parents, September 14, October 4, August 25, 1863, James and Charles B. Allen Papers, 1788–1869, microfilm, 01697, roll 1, SHC.

19. W. Maury Darst, ed., "The Vicksburg Diary of Mrs. Alfred Ingraham, May 2–June 13, 1863," *Journal of Mississippi History* 44 (February–November 1982): 174.

20. James Dick Hill to Jefferson Davis, March 23, 24, 1865, in Crist et al., *The Papers of Jefferson Davis*, 11:150.

21. W. L. Nugent to John J. Pettus, September 29, 1863, John J. Pettus Correspondence, reel 1446, volume 51, MDAH; Will Kirkland to Bettie Howard, December 12, 1864, Juanita Brown Collection, 1861–1864, MUM00048, box 1.18, folder 77-3, UMASC; Oaths and Safeguards of John Isenhood, John Herod, Henry Stam, and H. B. Watson, July 17, 1863, in Records of the Provost Marshal General (hereafter cited as RPMG), US Army Commands, Military Division of the Mississippi, Letters Recorded, Statements of Scouts, Misc. Papers, 1864–1865, Record Group 393, entry 2521, NARA; and US Bureau of the Census, Eighth Census of the United States, 1860, Schedule 1 (Free Inhabitants), Ancestry.com, at http://search.ancestry.com/search/db.aspx?dbid=7667, accessed April 7, 2011, records for Yazoo County, Mississippi, John Herod, Henry Stam, H. B. Watson, and J. M. Isenhood, digital images (hereafter US Census 1860).

22. "Archibald St. Clair, Joseph Byrd, Marion, Martin, Obadiah Parker, Barnet Brodnintza, Beer Gardner," in Lists of Persons Sent before the Union Provost Marshal at New Orleans, December 9, 22, 26, 1863, nos. 7207-7576, roll 26, Union Provost Marshal's File of Papers Relating to Two or More Civilians (hereafter cited as UPMF), M-416, War Department Collection of Confederate Records, Record Group 109, NARA; Statements Regarding W. H. Norberg and G. W. Andrews, October 21, 1863, roll 24, UPMF, NARA.

23. First, Second, and Third Statements of Thomas M. Sheppard, August 13, October 9, November 26, 1863, roll 88, LRCSW, NARA.

24. *OR*, ser. 1, vol. 39, pt. 2, 32.

25. Bettersworth, *Confederate Mississippi*, 241–43; and Busbee, *Mississippi: A History*, 133–34.

26. List of Civilians Who Took the Federal Oath on Steamers, February 1865, roll 52; List of Civilians on Ship Island, November 26, 1863, roll 25; "Henry Kirkwood, Mrs. Charles L. Gumbell," in Lists of Persons Sent before the Union Provost Marshal at New Orleans, December 9, 22, 1863, roll 26; and List of Refugees at New Orleans, December 24, 1863, all in UPMF, NARA.

27. Bettersworth, *Confederate Mississippi*, 241–42; Ella Lonn, *Foreigners in the Confederacy* (1940; repr., n.p.: Victor A. Lonn, 1968); Anne J. Bailey, *Invisible Southerners: Ethnicity in the Civil War* (Athens: University of Georgia Press, 2006), 1–10; and Susannah J. Ural, ed., *Civil War Citizens: Race, Ethnicity, and Identity in America's Bloodiest Conflict* (New York: New York University Press, 2010), 2–9.

28. Albert Gallatin Brown, December 24, 1863, "State of the Country Speech in the Confederate Senate," *Documenting the American South*, at http://docsouth.unc.edu/imls/browna/browna.html, accessed September 24, 2009; and "Enemies to the Southern Cause, from the Mississippian," *Weekly Panola (MS) Star*, July 9, 1862.

29. W. Cothran to John J. Pettus, November 15, 1862, John J. Pettus Correspondence, roll 2812, volume 50, MDAH; Resolution by Citizens of Preston to John J. Pettus, November 20, 1862, John J. Pettus Correspondence, roll 2812, volume 50, MDAH; John McAutis to John J. Pettus, April 10, 1863, John J. Pettus Correspondence, roll 1446, volume 51, MDAH; and

Statement of "Rebel Dragoon," February 23, 1864, Harry St. John Dixon Papers, 1855–1904, folder 5, 02375, SHC.

30. "An Appeal from the Ladies of Mississippi," *Weekly Mississippian* (Jackson), December 3, 1862; "What Shall We Do?" *Weekly Courier* (Natchez), March 4, 1863; Samuel Ward to John J. Pettus, November 23, 1862, John J. Pettus Correspondence, roll 1446, volume 50, MDAH; Edward Fontaine to John J. Pettus, January 11, 1862, John J. Pettus Correspondence, roll 1218, volume 48, MDAH; "Bread—Extortion," *Eastern Clarion* (Paulding, MS), May 2, 1862; and "Chief Commissary Office for Mississippi Circular," September 2, 1864, Norton, Chilton, and Dameron Family Papers, SHC.

31. "An Appeal to the Planters of the Country," *American Citizen* (Canton, MS), October 10, 1863; Francis Terry Leak Journal, May 5, 1862, Francis Terry Leak Papers, 1839–1865, folder 13, volume 7, 01095, SHC; "Submissionists," *Weekly Mississippian* (Jackson), April 8, 1863; *Beacon* (Macon, MS), November 4, 1863; Benjamin King to John J. Pettus, December 17, 1862, John J. Pettus Correspondence, roll 2812, volume 50, MDAH; and S. G. Miller to George Miller, October 31, 1862, Miller Family Papers, folder 40, UMASC.

32. "Speculators and Extortioners," *American Citizen* (Canton, MS), December 5, 1862; and Charles Whitmore to Joseph Lyon, February 15, 1864, Charles Whitmore Plantation Journal, microfilm, 02406, roll 1, SHC.

33. Arnoldus Brumby to Sarah C. Simpson, December 7, 1862, Simpson and Brumby Family Papers, 1847–1945, folder 2, subseries 1.1, 01408-z, SHC; William Delay to Charles Clark, November 27, December 21, 1863, Charles Clark Correspondence, series 768, box 949, volume 56, Record Group 27, MDAH; and I. W. C. Watson to Charles Clark, December 21, 1863, Charles Clark Correspondence, series 768, box 949, volume 56, Record Group 27, MDAH. On military confiscation, see Paul D. Escott, *Military Necessity: Civil-Military Relations in the Confederacy* (Westport, CT: Praeger, 2006), 25, 174; and Mark E. Neely Jr., *Southern Rights: Political Prisoners and the Myth of Confederate Constitutionalism* (Charlottesville: University of Virginia Press, 1999), 163–67.

34. Memorial of Joshua and Thomas Green to Jefferson Davis, July 26, 1862, roll 48, LRCSW, NARA.

35. Kenneth Radley, *Rebel Watchdog: The Confederate States Army Provost Guard* (Baton Rouge: Louisiana State University Press, 1989), 1.

36. R. L. Forrester to John B. Villepigue, July 30, 1862, John B. Villepigue to George W. Randolph, August 21, 1862, Samuel M. Hawkins to R. L. Forrester, June 28, 1862, Samuel M. Hawkins to George W. Randolph, August 9, 1862, Statement of E. S. Fisher, July 15, 1862, R. G. H. Kean to George W. Randolph, September 1, 1862, Arrest Papers of Samuel M. Hawkins, roll 52, LRCSW, NARA.

37. "Confederate Currency," *Weekly Mississippian* (Jackson), April 22, 1863; and "Refusing Confederate Money," *American Citizen* (Canton, MS), July 3, 1863.

38. Colin Edward Woodward, *Marching Masters: Slavery, Race, and the Confederate Army during the Civil War* (Charlottesville: University of Virginia Press, 2014), 55–79; and McCurry, *Confederate Reckoning*, 264, 276.

39. Lawrence N. Powell and Michael S. Wayne, "Self-Interest and the Decline of Confederate Nationalism," in *The Old South in the Crucible of War*, ed. Harry P. Owens and James J. Cooke (Jackson: University Press of Mississippi, 1983), 30; and McCurry, *Confederate Reckoning*, 285.

40. Woodward, *Marching Masters*, 60–68; and Bernard H. Nelson, "Confederate Slave Impressment Legislation, 1861–1865," *Journal of Negro History* 31 (October 1946): 396, 400,

402–3. On planters' response to slave impressment, see Harrison A. Trexler, "The Opposition of Planters to the Employment of Slaves as Laborers by the Confederacy," *Mississippi Valley Historical Review* 27 (September 1940): 211–24.

41. Richland Planters' Petition to John J. Pettus, March 23, 1863, John J. Pettus Correspondence, roll 1446, volume 51, MDAH; and Benjamin King to John J. Pettus, April 13, 1863, John J. Pettus Correspondence, roll 1446, volume 51, MDAH.

42. John C. Humphreys to John J. Pettus, March 4, 1863, Robert S. Hudson to John J. Pettus, March 1, 1863, F. Dillard to John J. Pettus, February 18, 1863, John J. Pettus Correspondence, MDAH; US Census 1860, records for Copiah County, Mississippi, F. Dillard, E. R. Brown, R. H. Taliaferro, and B. K. Hawkins; and Nelson, "Confederate Slave Impressment Legislation," 398, 400.

43. Thomas McCowen to John J. Pettus, March 4, 1863, John J. Pettus Correspondence, roll 1446, volume 51, MDAH. Jamie Amanda Martinez argues that individual Confederate states' ability to impress slaves was evidence of the effectiveness of increased government power via federalism in the Civil War South. She primarily interprets slaveholders' grudging willingness to supply slave labor to the government as evidence of their continued loyalty to the Confederacy, as opposed to a consideration of multiple loyalties in the face of a state that demanded unconditional devotion to the national cause. See Jaime Amanda Martinez, *Confederate Slave Impressment in the Upper South* (Chapel Hill: University of North Carolina Press, 2013).

44. Historians have identified Mississippi unionists according to variables of class, political preference, and geography. Opposition to secession and the Confederacy came from wealthy Delta slaveholders whose conservative Whig leanings precluded them from embracing a war that would stifle river trade and threaten the destruction of their plantations. Scholars also identify clusters of unionism in the southeast Piney Woods, in the state's central region, and in the hilly northeastern counties. These were relatively poor areas with low slaveholding density whose residents had little to gain from fighting a slaveholders' war. See Bettersworth, *Confederate Mississippi*, 8–9, 189–91; Mary Floyd Sumners, "Politics in Tishomingo County, 1836–1860," *Journal of Mississippi History* 2 (May 1966): 149–51; Barney, *The Secessionist Impulse*, 77–78; William T. Blain, "'Banner' Unionism in Mississippi: Choctaw County, 1861–1869," *Mississippi Quarterly* 2 (Spring 1976): 207–20; Bolton, *Poor Whites of the Antebellum South*, 85–119; Michael Shannon Mallard, "'Faithful Found among the Faithless': Popular Opposition to the Confederacy in Civil War Mississippi" (master's thesis, Mississippi State University, 2002); Bynum, *The Free State of Jones*, 47–69, 117–18; Victoria E. Bynum, *The Long Shadow of the Civil War: Southern Dissent and Its Legacies* (Chapel Hill: University of North Carolina Press, 2010), 1–5, 23, 31–32; and Smith, *Mississippi in the Civil War*, 127.

45. John K. Bettersworth, ed., "Mississippi Unionism: The Case of the Reverend James A. Lyon," *Journal of Mississippi History* 1 (October 1939): 40, 41–46, 49, quotations on 40, 42, 49.

46. "The Deserters," *Beacon* (Macon, MS), April 13, 1864; "From Noxubee Riflemen," *Beacon* (Macon, MS), April 20, 1864; US Census 1860, US Civil War Soldier Records and Profiles, Smith County, Mississippi, John, Pleasant Q., William E., and A. E. Hawkins, digital images; "Camp 20th Miss. Reg't. Near Canton, Miss., Oct. 20, 1863," *Beacon* (Macon, MS), November 11, 1863; US Census 1860, records for Lowndes County, Mississippi, Moses Jordon, digital images; David C. Glenn to Jefferson Davis, September 1, 1863, in Crist et al., *The Papers of Jefferson Davis*, 9:364–65; Wynne, *Mississippi's Civil War*, 125–26; Townsend, *Yankee Warhorse*, 194; and Smith, *Mississippi in the Civil War*, 47.

47. Cockrell and Ballard, *Chickasaw*, 8–9, 101, 105–6; W. W. Jackson to Major General C. C. Washburn, July 6, 1864, roll 39, UPMF, NARA; quotations in J. F. Riley and J. J. Williams to W. W. Jackson, May 5, 1864, roll 39, UPMF, NARA; Ballard, *The Civil War in Mississippi*, 276; and Richard Nelson Current, *Lincoln's Loyalists: Union Soldiers from the Confederacy* (Boston: Northeastern University Press, 1992), 103–6.

48. List of Prisoners and Refugees Arrested at Corinth, September 1, 1863, roll 23; Tri-Monthly Report of Union Refugees of Post of Jackson, TN, May 9, May 20, 1863, roll 17; Tri-Monthly Report of Union Refugees of Post of Jackson, TN, March 28, 1863, roll 15; List of Mississippians Who Came into Union Lines at New Orleans, December 1, 5, 26, 1863, roll 26; List of Mississippi Refugees at New Orleans, July 26, 1864, roll 39; List of Refugees at Fort Pike from Perry County, MS, May 12, 1864, roll 34; List of Oaths of Allegiances Administered to Persons Arriving at New Orleans by Way of Mississippi River, May 1865, roll 61, all in UPMF, NARA; US Census 1860, US Civil War Soldier Records and Profiles, records for Tishomingo County, Mississippi, William G. Douthet, digital images; List of Refugees from Ship Island, September 8, 1863, roll 24, UPMF, NARA; and Stephen V. Ash, "Poor Whites in the Occupied South, 1861–1865," *Journal of Southern History* 57 (February 1991): 47–48.

49. First Statement of James H. Carrington Regarding W. Cranford Whooten, November 25, 1863; Statement of B. F. Haller Regarding W. Cranford Whooten, Undated; Second Statement of James H. Carrington Regarding W. Cranford Whooten, November 25, 1863; W. Cranford Whooten to Jefferson Davis, November 10, 1863; Petition of Tishomingo County Citizens on Behalf of W. Cranford Whooten, November 28, 1863; Arrest Papers of W. Cranford Whooten, November 25, 1863; Statement of James H. Carrington regarding Eli Botts, November 25, 1863; Statement of B. F. Haller regarding Eli Botts, Undated; Statement of W. McGill regarding Eli Botts, Undated; L. Brown to S. H. Pope, July 12, 1863; Arrest Papers of Eli C. Botts, November 27, 1863; Statement of James H. Carrington regarding William Morris, November 25, 1863; Arrest Papers of William Morris, November 25, 1863, all in roll 88, LRCSW, NARA; US Census 1860, records for Holmes County, Mississippi, William L. Morris, digital image; and US Census 1860, US Civil War Soldier Records and Profiles, B. F. Morris.

50. Statement of W. L. Poindexter, October 28, 1863; C. H. Manship to General W. H. Jackson, August 13, 1863; Statement of W. H. Jackson, August 14, 1863; Solomon Tift to Brother, July 28, 1863; J. J. Fitzpatrick to Lieutenant Colonel L. W. Beasley, August 11, 1863; Statement of Solomon Tift, October 8, 1863; Solomon Tift to Mr. Hays, October 10, 1863; Statement of James H. Carrington, November 20, 1863; Arrest Papers of Solomon Tift, all in roll 88, LRCSW, NARA; and US Census 1860, records for Hinds County, Mississippi, S. Tift, digital image.

51. "Solomon Tift," in Lists of Union or Loyal Men in and around Vicksburg, entry 370, box 3, Record Group 366, Records of Civil War Special Agencies of the Treasury Department, Second Special Agency Records, Vicksburg District (hereafter cited as RCWSAT), NARA.

52. Fellman, *Inside War*, 52.

53. L. Welsh to Jefferson Davis, June 22, 1864; Statement of Daniel Ruggles, October 6, 1864; Statement of W. M. Pardner, July 6, 1864; Statement of Martha Emmaline Maness, January 4, 1864; Arrest Papers of Martha Emmaline Maness, May, 1863–July, 1864, all in roll 123, LRCSW, NARA; "Letter from Canton," *Daily Clarion* (Meridian, MS), June 9, 1864; and US Census 1860, records for Kemper County, Mississippi, July A. Clark, digital image.

54. Charles Allen to Parents, September 22, 1864, James and Charles B. Allen Papers, SHC.

55. Blair, *With Malice toward Some*, 36.

56. Franklin Fisk to C. D. Townsend, Statement Concerning the Disloyalty of W. B. Partee, Pfeifer, Hegewish, and Russel, December 5, 1863, roll 26, UPMF, NARA; General N. J. T. Dana, General Orders no. 82, November 22, 1864, Mahala P. Roach to Major General Dana, January 11, 1865, Papers Relating to the Banishment of Mrs. Eggleston, by General Dana, 1864, Eggleston-Roach Papers, 1792–1905, series 1, 832, Louisiana State University Special Collections, Hill Memorial Library, Baton Rouge (hereafter cited as LSU); and Letters from Confederate Soldiers in Vicksburg to Elizabeth Eggleston and Mahala P. Roach, 1862–1863, O. S. Holland to Elizabeth Eggleston, June 8, 1863, Roach and Eggleston Family Papers, 1825–1905, folders 2–3, series 1, 02614, SHC.

57. List of Civilian Prisoners in Natchez Military Prison, September 1–20, 1863, roll 23, UPMF, NARA; List of Citizen Prisoners Confined at Vicksburg, Mississippi, January 1–26, 1864, Record Group 393, entry 2521, RPMG, NARA; and Ash, *When the Yankees Came*, 59–60, 82–83.

58. W. E. Rogers to Major Tommey, August 30, 1864, Correspondence Received by the Assistant Special Agent, Memphis, January–December 1864, entry 223, box 1, RCWSAT, NARA; and Trade Store Permit Applications of Mina Concke, April 5, June 8, 1864, Charles Westel to R. S. Hart, January 13, 1864, Authority to Establish Trade Store Permits, Natchez, entries 291, 292, box 5, RCWSAT, NARA.

59. Ballard, *Vicksburg*, 1–8; and Christopher Morris, *Becoming Southern: The Evolution of a Way of Life, Warren County and Vicksburg, Mississippi, 1770–1860* (New York: Oxford University Press, 1995), 115–17.

60. Edwin L. Sabin, "Vicksburg, and After: Being the Experience of a Southern Merchant and Non-Combatant during the Sixties," *Sewanee Review* 15 (October 1907): 491–92, quotation on 485; Salmon P. Chase, *United States Treasury Department Rules Concerning Commercial Intercourse with and in States Declared in Insurrection, and the Collection of Abandoned and Captured Property* (Washington, DC: Government Printing Office, 1863), 16; James T. Currie, *Enclave: Vicksburg and Her Surrounding Plantations, 1863–1870* (Jackson: University Press of Mississippi, 1980), 25–26; and Vicksburg Court Cases of Cornelius Ryan, March 19, Thomas Purcell, March 25, Alexander Jeffrey, March 30, 1864, roll 30, UPMF, NARA.

61. Occupational categorizations are derived from Theodore Hershberg, Michael Katz, Stuart Blumin, Laurence Glasco, and Clyde Griffin, "Occupation and Ethnicity in Five Nineteenth-Century Cities: A Collaborative Inquiry," *Historical Methods Newsletter* 7 (June 1974): 179–87.

62. Lists of Union or Loyal Men in and around Vicksburg; US Census 1860, records for Warren, Hinds, and Claiborne Counties, Mississippi, and Sabine County, Texas, digital images.

63. Currie, *Enclave*, 15–18; and Trade Store Permits, 1863–1864, Vicksburg District, entry 369, box 3; Trade Store Permits, 1864, Natchez District, entries 291, 292, box 5; Authorities Granted for Trade Stores, Vicksburg, Mississippi, January 1864; Transcript of Record of Fees Received, January, February 1864, in Correspondence Received by the Assistant Treasury Agent, Vicksburg District, entry 360, box 2; Authorities Granted for the Purchase and Transport of Products, Vicksburg, Mississippi, November, January 1864, March, April 1865; Record of Authorities to Establish Supply Stores, Vicksburg, Mississippi, December

1864, March, April 1865; Record of Fees Received, Supply Stores, September 1864; Report of Clearances Given at the US Custom House, Vicksburg, Mississippi, November, December 1864, January, March 1865, all in Applications, Bonds and Authorities to Purchase and Transport Products, Districts in Mississippi, entry 382, box 5; no. 2 List of Union or Loyal Men in and around Vicksburg, all in RCWSAT, NARA.

64. No. 2 List of Union or Loyal Men in and around Vicksburg, RCWSAT, NARA; "Solomon Rothchild," in List of Union or Loyal Men in and around Vicksburg; Petition of Solomon Rothchild, September 14, 1864, Contracts and Affidavits to Establish Supply Stores, Etc. 1864, Office of the General Agent, entry 849, box 25, RCWSAT, NARA; "Alston Mygatt," in List of Union or Loyal Men in and Around Vicksburg; Trade Store Permit Application of Alston Mygatt, December 18, 1863, Trade Store Permits, Vicksburg District, 1863–1864, RCWSAT, NARA; and Plantation Lease of Alston Mygatt, November 24, 1864, Records on Renting and Leasing of Abandoned Property, 1864–1865, Records of the Mississippi Freedmen's Department ("Pre-Bureau Records") Office of the Assistant Commissioner, Records of the Bureau of Refugees, Freedmen, and Abandoned Lands, 1863–1865 (hereafter cited as RMFD), roll 3, M-1914, Record Group 105, NARA.

65. "Max Kuner," in List of Union or Loyal Men in and around Vicksburg; Trade Store Permit Application of Max Kuner, January 18, 1864, Trade Store Permits, Vicksburg District, 1863–1864, RCWSAT, NARA; Plantation Lease of Julia Glass, Max Kuner, Surety, December 27, 1864, roll 3, RMFD, NARA; Valentine Vogh to Vicksburg Provost Marshal, September 6, 1864, Correspondence Received by the Assistant Treasury Agent, Vicksburg District, box 2, entry 360, RCWSAT, NARA; US Census 1860, records for Warren County, Mississippi, Charles Francis, 923, digital image; Charles Francis to Vicksburg Provost Marshal, September 7, 1864, A. Mygatt, John Bland, W. J. Shuler and Duff Green to J. A. McCowell, December 26, 1863, Max Kuner to C. F. Calliot, September 8, 1864, T. C. Gatticut to Major General N. J. T. Dana, September 11, 1864, all in Correspondence Received by the Assistant Special Treasury Agent, NARA; and Morris, *Becoming Southern*, 118.

66. Statement of Murray Carter, June 13, 1864, Exhibit "B," Statement of M. Levy, May 19, 1864, Court Opinion, David Streat and C. C. Marsh, Signatories, undated, Vicksburg Court Case of M. Levy and Murray Carter, June 13, 1864, roll 35, UPMF, NARA.

67. "John W. Vick," in List of Union or Loyal Men in and around Vicksburg, RCWSAT, NARA; and Examination of John W. Vick, Claim of John W. Vick, May 31, 1872, Commission Remarks on Claim of John W. Vick, Southern Claims Commission (hereafter cited as SCC), Warren County, Mississippi, claim 14279, roll 21, digital images, Fold3.com, at http://www .fold3.com/, accessed November 29, 2011.

68. "James Cathell," in List of Union or Loyal Men in and around Vicksburg, RCWSAT, NARA; Statement of John W. Taylor, Claim of James Cathell, May 28, 1872, February 26, 1876, SCC, Warren County, Mississippi, claim 14197, roll 44, SCC; "Aquila Bowie," in List of Union or Loyal Men in and Around Vicksburg; and Claim of Aquila Bowie, June 17, 1871, claim 2602, roll 44, SCC.

69. George W. Fox to R. S. Hart, February 6, 1864, Oath of Allegiance of George W. Fox, February 19, 1864, Authority to Establish Trade Store Permits, Natchez, Statement of George W. Fox, Statement of Robert E. McClure, Statement of William Henderson, Claim of George W. Fox, June 21, 1871, SCC, Adams County, Mississippi, claim 2883, roll 003, SCC; Trade Store Permit Applications of Matthias D. Marks, April 7, June 9, 1864, Authority to Establish Trade Store Permits, Natchez; Statement of Matthias D. Marks, Statement of

Richard Sullivan, December 6, 1872, Claim of Matthias D. Marks, July 1, 1872, claim 14870, publication 1407, SCC.

70. Oath of Allegiance of Casey Mallory, January 30, 1864, Trade Store Permit Application of Casey Mallory, February 3, 1864, Casey Mallory to Judge Hart, January 30, 1864, Authority to Establish Trade Store Permits, Natchez, Statements of Abraham Scofield, William Shaw, R. E. McClure, William McGilvary, Cyrus Marsh, Statements of Casey Mallory, May 16, 1876, April 4, 1874, Report of Enos Richmond on the Claim of Casey Mallory, May 15, 1876, Summary Report on the Claim of Casey Mallory, December 5, 1877, Claim of Casey Mallory, October 21, 1872, claim 17132, roll 25, SCC.

CHAPTER THREE

1. "Natchez under Yankee Rule!," in Confederate Post Commissary Invoice and Discharge Book, 1862, Z/1661.000/F, MDAH.

2. Jacob Thompson to Jefferson Davis, December 23, 1863, In Crist et al., *The Papers of Jefferson Davis*, 10:123–24.

3. Ludwell H. Johnson, "Trading with the Union: The Evolution of Confederate Policy," *Virginia Magazine of History and Biography* 78 (July 1970): 310; Walter E. Pittman Jr., "Trading with the Devil: The Cotton Trade in Civil War Mississippi," *Journal of Confederate History* 2, no. 11 (1989): 140; Smith, *Mississippi in the Civil War*, 134; and *OR*, ser. 4, vol. 3, 282–83, 688; ser. 4, vol. 2, 585.

4. Black Mississippians also traded with Union forces and in the early part of the war were "contrabands" themselves. However, the Confederacy did not consider black people, slave or free, to be citizens, and expected them to serve the cause as servants, not as political agents. See McCurry, *Confederate Reckoning*, 20–24; and Davis, *Look Away!*, 130–62.

5. E. Merton Coulter, "Commercial Intercourse with the Confederacy in the Mississippi Valley, 1861–1865," *Mississippi Valley Historical Review* 5 (March 1919): 391–95; A. Sellew Roberts, "The Federal Government and Confederate Cotton," *American Historical Review* 32 (January 1927): 262, 274–75; Ludwell H. Johnson, "Contraband Trade during the Last Year of the Civil War," *Mississippi Valley Historical Review* 49 (March 1963): 639–42; Johnson, "Trading with the Union," 308–10; and Pittman, "Trading with the Devil," 139–42.

6. Thomas H. O'Connor, "Lincoln and the Cotton Trade," *Civil War History* 7 (March 1961): 21–25; and David G. Surdam, "Traders or Traitors: Northern Cotton Trading during the Civil War," *Business and Economic History* 28 (Winter 1999): 303, 310–11.

7. See George C. Rable, *Civil Wars: Women and the Crisis of Southern Nationalism* (Urbana: University of Illinois Press, 1989), 45, 50–51; LeeAnn Whites, *The Civil War as a Crisis in Gender, 1860–1890* (Athens: University of Georgia Press, 1995), 12–13; Drew Gilpin Faust, *Mothers of Invention: Women of the Slaveholding South in the American Civil War* (Chapel Hill: University of North Carolina Press, 1996), 81–82; and Victoria E. Ott, *Confederate Daughters: Coming of Age during the Civil War* (Carbondale: Southern Illinois University Press, 2008), 6, 37.

8. Faust, *The Creation of Confederate Nationalism*, 41–49.

9. On the economic aspects of protective nationalism as applied to the Confederacy, see Onuf and Onuf, *Nations, Markets, and War*, 324–33; and John Majewski, *Modernizing a Slave Economy: The Economic Vision of the Confederate Nation* (Chapel Hill: University of North Carolina Press, 2009), 3, 140–63.

10. James C. Cobb, *Away Down South: A History of Southern Identity* (Oxford: Oxford University Press, 2005), 7; Thomas, *The Confederacy as a Revolutionary Experience*; and Robert E. Bonner, *Mastering America: Southern Slaveholders and the Crisis of the American Nation* (New York: Cambridge University Press, 2009), 217–18.

11. Coulter, "Commercial Intercourse with the Confederacy," 377–95; Surdam, "Traders or Traitors," 302–3; and O'Connor, "Lincoln and the Cotton Trade," 20–29.

12. Coulter, "Commercial Intercourse with the Confederacy," 388; Johnson, "Contraband Trade," 637–38; and Bettersworth, *Confederate Mississippi*, 180.

13. Johnson, "Trading with the Union," 308–11.

14. E. Merton Coulter, "Effects of Secession upon the Commerce of the Mississippi Valley," *Mississippi Valley Historical Review* 3 (December 1916): 281–82; Johnson, "Trading with the Union," 310–17, 320–22; and *OR*, ser.1, vol. 17, pt. 2, 839–40.

15. E. S. Fisher to Charles Clark, February 14, 1865, Charles Clark Correspondence, series 768, box 950, volume 56, Record Group 27, MDAH.

16. Bettersworth, *Confederate Mississippi*, 174–78; and Smith, *Mississippi in the Civil War*, 134.

17. *OR*, ser.1, vol. 17, pt. 1, 532.

18. C. R. Barteau to Daniel Ruggles, February 12, 1863, John C. Pemberton Papers, MLR PI101, box 2, entry 131, War Department Collection of Confederate Records, Record Group 109, NARA; *OR*, ser. 1, vol. 52, pt. 2, 370–71; and Robert S. Hudson to Charles Clark, June 13, 1864, in James W. Silver, ed., "The Breakdown of Morale in Central Mississippi in 1864: Letters of Judge Robert S. Hudson," *Journal of Mississippi History* 16 (April 1964): 110. On Holly Springs, see Wynne, *Mississippi's Civil War*, 83–84.

19. R. M. Hool to L. D. Sandidge, January 20, 1863, John C. Pemberton Papers, NARA; "Caught at Their Tricks," *Weekly Panola (MS) Star*, July 30, 1862; and "A Crying Evil," *Daily Clarion* (Meridian, MS), June 9, 1864.

20. "Blockade Running," *Daily Mississippian* (Jackson), evening edition, April 22, 1863.

21. P. A. Willis to Sam Carey, December 3, 1863, Charles Nunnally Dean Jr. Memorial Collection, MUM00103, box 1, UMASC.

22. *OR*, ser. 1, vol. 31, pt. 3, 673; vol. 45, pt. 1, 9; and ser. 4, vol. 3, 646–48.

23. R. H. Bowers to Thomas Henderson, March 25, 1863, John C. Pemberton Papers, NARA; and Bunkers, *The Diary of Caroline Seabury*, 100.

24. Captain W. E. Montgomery to Charles Clark, November 25, 1863, Charles Clark Correspondence, box 949, MDAH; and Inaugural Address of Governor Charles Clark, *Journal of the House of Representatives of the State of Mississippi, December Session of 1862 and November Session of 1863*, 160, *Documenting the American South*, at http://docsouth.unc.edu/imls/msdec62/msdec62.html, accessed April 26, 2012.

25. *OR*, ser. 1, vol. 49, pt. 1, 950.

26. T. G. Braskings to Charles Clark, September 28, 1864, Charles Clark Correspondence, box 950, MDAH; *OR*, ser. 1, vol. 32, pt. 3, 634; Samuel Andrew Agnew Diary, November 26, 1863, *Documenting the American South*, at http://docsouth.unc.edu/imls/agnew/agnew.html, accessed August 20, 2009; and *OR*, ser. 4, vol. 2, 585.

27. J. D. B. DeBow to C. G. Memminger, April 9, 1864, "Report on the Condition of Government Cotton, Contiguous to the Mississippi and Its Tributaries," *Documenting the American South*, at http://docsouth.unc.edu/imls/cotton/cotton.html, accessed September 18, 2009; and M. Hairston to Niece, April 18, 1864, Wilson and Hairston Family Papers, 1751–1928, SHC.

28. *OR*, ser. 1, vol. 31, pt. 3, 693–94; vol. 39, 231–32; US Census 1860, records for Lowndes and Carroll Counties, Mississippi, T. C. Teasdale, Lewis Rawitch, and H. P. Atkins, digital images; and R. J. Morgan to Lieutenant General Leonidas Polk, April 30, 1864, Charles Clark Correspondence, box 949, MDAH.

29. *OR*, ser. 1, vol. 10, pt. 2, 451, 455, 515–16; W. C. Haywell to T. C. Tusser, February 9, 1863, S. W. Ferguson to J. J. Rund, February 15, 1863; S. W. Ferguson to J. J. Rund, February 17, 1863, all in John C. Pemberton Papers, NARA; US Census 1860, records for Bolivar County, Mississippi, R. O. Starke, D. W. Davis, digital images; and James Lewis to S. W. Tingman, February 19, 1863, John C. Pemberton Papers, NARA.

30. *OR*, ser. 1, vol. 31, pt. 3, 690.

31. Percy Lee Rainwater, ed., "Letters of James Lusk Alcorn," *Journal of Southern History* 3 (May 1937): 196–97.

32. James L. Alcorn to Wife, November 25, 1862, in Rainwater, "Letters of James Lusk Alcorn," 199–200; US Census 1860, records for Coahoma County, Mississippi, J. T. Pettit, B. A. Simms, Isaac Hull, John Miller, John Jones, and W. H. Atkinson, digital images.

33. James Lusk Alcorn Diary, March 5, 1863, in James Lusk Alcorn and Family Papers, Z/0317.000, series 1, box 1, MDAH. For more on Alcorn's politics, see Lilian A. Pereyra, *James Lusk Alcorn: Persistent Whig* (Baton Rouge: Louisiana State University Press, 1966).

34. James L. Alcorn to Wife, March 16, 1863, December 18, 1862, May 3, 1864, in Rainwater, "Letters of James Lusk Alcorn," 202, 204, 205.

35. Samuel Andrew Agnew Diary, October 21, November 12, 13, 1863, May 28, 1864, *Documenting the American South*.

36. Augustus Vaughn to Sallie Simpson, August 11, 1864, Augustus Vaughn to Richard Simpson, September 18, 1864, Simpson and Brumby Family Papers, 1847–1945, folder 2, subseries 1.1, 01408-z, SHC.

37. Eliza H. B. Sively to Jane Sively, April 30, 1864, Jane Sively Letters, 1862–1867, folder 3, 01891-z, SHC.

38. Eliza H. B. Sively to Jane Sively, January 21, April 10, April 19, May 16, 1864, Jane Sively Letters, folders 2–3, SHC.

39. Amanda Dougherty Worthington Diary, April 28, 1863, January 11–13, 1865, Amanda Dougherty Worthington Papers, 1819–1878, microfilm, 01931, SHC.

40. Louisa T. Lovell to Joseph Lovell, August 17, 1863, Louisa T. Lovell to W. S. Lovell, March 12, 1864, Louisa T. Lovell to Joseph Lovell, July 29, 1864, Quitman Family Papers, 1784–1978, folders 111–112, Sively00616, SHC.

41. Narcissa L. Black Diaries, May 12, 24, 26, 1862, microfilm, Z/1211, roll 36149, MDAH.

42. Narcissa L. Black Diaries, June 4, 1862, December 15, 1863, February 14, 1864, March 5, 1864, April 12, 1864, MDAH. For more on Black's wartime activities, see Mary Lohrenz, "Two Lives Intertwined on a Tennessee Plantation: Textile Production as Recorded in the Diary of Narcissa L. Erwin Black," *Southern Quarterly* 27 (Fall 1988): 72–93.

43. Beaumont, *Twelve Years of My Life*, 178, 183, quotation on 167.

44. Ibid, 233, 234.

45. Martha Craigin to Charles Clark, November 28, 1863, Charles Clark Correspondence, box 949, MDAH.

46. W. C. Falkner to John J. Pettus, February 13, 1863, John J. Pettus Correspondence, roll 1446, volume 51, Record Group 27, MDAH.

47. W. W. Bell to John J. Pettus, February 12, 1863, John J. Pettus Correspondence, MDAH.

48. *OR*, ser. 1, vol. 10, pt. 2, 279.

49. Robert S. Hudson to Charles Clark, June 13, 1864, in Silver, "The Breakdown of Morale," 110; "A Crying Evil," *Daily Clarion* (Meridian, MS), June 9, 1864; *OR*, ser. 1, vol. 39, pt. 1, 729; *Daily Clarion* (Meridian, MS), July 6, 1864; and *OR*, ser. 4, vol. 3, 282–83.

50. "Blockade Running," *Daily Clarion* (Meridian, MS), June 14, 1864.

51. Julia Southall to Emily Southall, November 5, 1863, Southall and Bowen Family Papers, 1833–1959, folder 10, 04135, SHC.

52. Elizabeth Fox-Genovese, *Within the Plantation Household: Black and White Women of the Old South* (Chapel Hill: University of North Carolina Press, 1988), 100–102, 194–95; Rable, *Civil Wars*, 2–8, 30–32; Brenda E. Stevenson, *Life in Black and White: Family and Community in the Slave South* (New York: Oxford University Press, 1996), 38; Faust, *Mothers of Invention*, 32; and Nancy Bercaw, *Gendered Freedoms: Race, Rights, and the Politics of Household in the Delta, 1861–1875* (Gainesville: University Press of Florida, 2003), 60–61.

53. Lisa Tendrich Frank, *The Civilian War: Confederate Women and Union Soldiers during Sherman's March* (Baton Rouge: Louisiana State University Press, 2015); 1–18; Rable, *Civil Wars*, 50–78; Faust, *Mothers of Invention*, 238–47; Laura F. Edwards, *Scarlett Doesn't Live Here Anymore: Southern Women in the Civil War Era* (Urbana: University of Illinois Press, 2000), 82–86; Jean V. Berlin, "Did Confederate Women Lose the War? Deprivation, Destruction, and Despair on the Home Front," in *The Collapse of the Confederacy*, ed. Mark Grimsley and Brooks D. Simpson (Lincoln: University of Nebraska Press, 2001), 173; Campbell, *When Sherman Marched North*, 71; and Ott, *Confederate Daughters*, 3–4, 6.

54. McCurry, *Confederate Reckoning*, 134–36, 148. For an earlier study of poor and yeoman women before and during the war, see Victoria E. Bynum, *Unruly Women: The Politics of Social and Sexual Control in the Old South* (Chapel Hill: University of North Carolina Press, 1992).

55. Monthly Report of Authorities Issued to Bring Products from Insurrectionary States, Etc., by Thomas H. Yeatman, Assistant Special Agent Treasury Department, December 1863–July 1864, Monthly Reports, Estimates, Returns, Etc. of the Assistant Special Agent, Memphis, 1863–1865, entry 226, box 1, Record Group 366, 2nd Special Agency Records, Treasury Papers (hereafter cited as SARTP), NARA; Charles Whitmore to Cousin Mary, January 29, 1864, Charles Whitmore Plantation Journal, microfilm, 02406, roll 1, SHC; John W. Wood to J. M. Lowery, March 18, 1864, Correspondence Received by the Assistant Special Agent, Memphis, 1864–1865, entry 223, box 1, SARTP, NARA; and US Census 1860, records for Lafayette County, Mississippi, Tabitha Ward, Susan Ward, digital images.

56. Eliza H. B. Sively to Jane Sively, May 28, 1864, Jane Sively Letters, SHC; and US Census 1860, records for Hinds County, Mississippi, S. Simons, J. Simons, H. Floren, M. Floren, digital images.

57. Arrest Papers of Eliza Agnes Herbert, March–May 1863, nos. 4622–4799, roll 17, UPMF, NARA.

58. Bill Cecil-Fronsman, *Common Whites: Class and Culture in Antebellum North Carolina* (Lexington: University Press of Kentucky, 1992), 144–45; Bynum, *The Free State of Jones*, 56–59; Edwards, *Scarlett Doesn't Live Here Anymore*, 37–39; Carl R. Osthaus, "The Work Ethic of the Plain Folk: Labor and Religion in the Old South," *Journal of Southern History* 70 (November 2004): 756; Jeff Forret, *Race Relations at the Margins: Slaves and Poor Whites in the Antebellum Southern Countryside* (Baton Rouge: Louisiana State University Press, 2006), 42; Wilma A. Dunaway, *Women, Work, and Family in the Antebellum Mountain South* (Cambridge: Cambridge University Press, 2008), 188–89, 195; and Jeff Robert Bremer,

"Frontier Capitalism: The Market Revolution in the Antebellum Lower Missouri River Valley, 1803–1860" (PhD diss., University of Kansas, 2006), 225–43.

59. Judith L. Van Buskirk, *Generous Enemies: Patriots and Loyalists in Revolutionary New York* (Philadelphia: University of Pennsylvania Press, 2002), 110–11, 121–22.

60. Beaumont, *Twelve Years of My Life*, 110–16.

61. *Daily Clarion* (Meridian, MS), June 14, 1864, July 6, 1864, and June 9, 1864.

62. William L. Nugent to Nellie Smith Nugent, September 25, 1863, in Cash and Howorth, *My Dear Nellie*, 136–38.

63. William L. Nugent to Nellie Smith Nugent, March 27, 1864, in Cash and Howorth, *My Dear Nellie*, 163–66.

64. T. J. Wharton to Jefferson Davis, April 16, 1864, in Bettersworth, *Mississippi in the Confederacy*, 1:307.

65. Barbara Cutter, *Domestic Devils, Battlefield Angels: The Radicalism of American Womanhood, 1830–1865* (DeKalb: Northern Illinois University Press, 2003), 8–10, 42, quotations on 9, 42. Claims by men like Nugent that independence from male guidance was a corrupting deviation from Southern gender norms did not consider that a significant population of unmarried Mississippi women of many classes and ethnic backgrounds led fulfilling, independent lives in cities like Natchez. See Joyce Linda Broussard, *Stepping Lively in Place: The Not-Married, Free Women of Civil-War-Era Natchez, Mississippi* (Athens: University of Georgia Press, 2016), 138–57.

66. Federal Picket Reports on Cotton, Memphis, 1863–1864, December 16, 17, 22, 30, 31, 1863, January 2, 8, 1864, entry 260, box 43, Record Group 366, SARTP, NARA; and US Census 1860 and US Civil War Soldiers Records and Profiles, records for Lafayette, DeSoto, Itawamba, Tippah, Panola, and Pontotoc Counties, Mississippi, Nancy Wiggins, Martha Griffis, Lucinda Herring, Mary Baily, Sarah J. Gossett, Sarah J. Boyd, Sallie A. Winn, and Susie C. Duke, digital images.

67. Sara Couper to James Maxwell Couper, October 30, 1862, Couper Family Papers, 1827–1955, microfilm, series 3, 00186-z, SHC.

68. W. M. Deason to Charles Clark, January 6, 1864; S. M. Hartley to Charles Clark, July 13, 1864; F. L. Martin to Charles Clark, July 15, 1864; Dr. J. R. Christian to Charles Clark, March 28, 1864; Charles Newman to Charles Clark, January 15, 1864, all in Charles Clark Correspondence, box 949, MDAH.

69. J. S. Reid to Unidentified Major, November 14, 1862, John C. Pemberton Papers, folder 7, box 1, NARA; F. T. Paine to Charles Clark, January 16, 1864, Charles Clark Correspondence, box 949, MDAH; B. B. Wilkinson to Charles Clark, December 12, 1863, Charles Clark Correspondence, MDAH; E. C. Cabell to James A. Seddon, December 24, 1862, nos. B 776–903, roll 84, Letters Received by the Confederate Secretary of War, LRCSW, NARA; W. A. Strong to Charles Clark, December 12, 1864, Charles Clark Correspondence, box 950, MDAH; Robert L. Kirk to Charles Clark, January 12, 1864, Charles Clark Correspondence, box 949, MDAH; and US Census 1860, records for Carroll and Chocktaw Counties, Mississippi, William A. Strong and Robert Kirk, digital images.

70. A. Q. Withers to Charles Clark, October 28, 1864, Charles Clark Correspondence, box 950, MDAH; "Capt. Albert Q. Withers," in Goodspeed Brothers, eds., *Biographical and Historical Memoirs of Mississippi* (1891; repr., Spartanburg, SC: Reprint Company, 1978): 2:1066–67; W. L. Dogan to John J. Pettus, February 11, 1863, John J. Pettus Correspondence, roll 2812, volume 50, MDAH; W. L. Dogan to Jefferson Davis, November 17, 1862, roll 89,

LRCSW, NARA; and US Census 1860, records for Shelby County, Tennessee, W. L. Dogan, digital image.

71. Thomas M. Truxes, *Defying Empire: Trading with the Enemy in Colonial New York* (New Haven, CT: Yale University Press, 2008), 1–8; and Van Buskirk, *Generous Enemies*, 107–13.

72. See Joseph H. Parks, "A Confederate Trade Center under Federal Occupation: Memphis, 1862 to 1865," *Journal of Southern History* 7 (August 1941): 289–314; and Robert A. Sigafoos, *Cotton Row to Beale Street: A Business History of Memphis* (Memphis: Memphis State University Press, 1979), 27–28, 40–44.

73. Bolivar County Citizens to Charles Clark, February 20, 1864, Charles Clark Correspondence, box 949, MDAH; M. D. Shelly to Charles Clark, September 28, 1864, Charles Clark Correspondence, box 950, MDAH; and J. Alexander Ventress to Charles Clark, February 6, 1864, Charles Clark Correspondence, box 949, MDAH.

74. Charles Clark to Major Saunders, October 24, 1864, Charles Clark Correspondence, box 950, MDAH; and *OR*, ser. 1, vol. 17, pt. 2, 839–40.

75. *OR*, ser. 4, vol. 2, 854–56.

76. *OR*, ser. 1, vol. 31, pt. 3, 833–35.

77. J. F. Riley and J. J. Williams to W. W. Jackson, May 5, 1864, roll 39, UPMF, NARA; Federal Picket Reports on Cotton, Memphis, 1863–1864, December 31, 1863, January 8, 15, 16, 1864, SARTP, NARA; and *OR*, ser. 1, vol. 39, pt. 1, 60–61, 22–23.

78. *OR*, Naval Records, ser. 1, vol. 25, 128.

79. *OR*, ser. 1, vol. 49, pt. 2, 179; and US Census 1860, records for Hinds County, Mississippi, A. H. Hardenstein, digital image.

80. Arrest Statement of Thomas B. Swan, October 4, 1863, roll 19, UPMF, NARA; and US Census 1860, records for DeSoto and Marshall Counties, Mississippi, George Barley, H. L. Barley, John D. Williams, and J. A. Blair, digital images.

81. William and Loretta Galbraith, eds., *A Lost Heroine of the Confederacy: The Diaries and Letters of Belle Edmondson* (Jackson: University of Mississippi Press, 1990), xiii–xxxi, 69–70, 82–83, 97, 113.

82. C. Shermin to Major General Earl Van Dorn, October 30, 1862, roll 73, LRCSW, NARA.

83. Charles B. Allen to Parents, October 4, 1863, September 11, 1864, October 15, undated, James and Charles B. Allen Papers, 1788–1869, microfilm, 01697, roll 1, SHC.

CHAPTER FOUR

1. US Census 1860, records for Claiborne County, Mississippi, R. T. Archer, digital image; Richard T. Archer to John J. Pettus, June 17, 1863, John J. Pettus Correspondence, roll 1333, volume 51, MDAH; and Harry M. Ward, *Between the Lines: Banditti of the American Revolution* (Westport, CT: Praeger, 2002), 19–20.

2. A. M. West to John J. Pettus, February 10, 1863, John J. Pettus Correspondence, roll 2812, volume 50, MDAH; US Census 1860, records for Holmes County, Mississippi, Tillman Lomax, digital images; and Bruce S. Allardice, *More Generals in Gray* (Baton Rouge: Louisiana State University Press, 1995), 233–34.

3. Sheehan-Dean, *Why Confederates Fought*, 1–2, quotations on 2. See also James M. McPherson, *For Cause and Comrades: Why Men Fought in the Civil War* (New York: Oxford

University Press, 1997), 95; Glatthaar, *General Lee's Army*, 33; Phillips, *Diehard Rebels*, 43; Chandra Manning, *What This Cruel War Was Over: Soldiers, Slavery, and the Civil War* (New York: Vintage Books, 2007), 138–39; and Blair, *Virginia's Private War*, 146.

4. Mark A. Weitz, *More Damning Than Slaughter: Desertion in the Confederate Army* (Lincoln: University of Nebraska Press, 2005), 5, xix, 210; and Escott, *After Secession*, xi, 140.

5. Clampitt, *The Confederate Heartland*, 9–13. On the Deep South, see also Campbell, *When Sherman Marched North*, 69, 72; and Rod Andrew Jr., "The Essential Nationalism of the People: Georgia's Confederate Congressional Election of 1863," in Gordon and Inscoe, *Inside the Confederate Nation*, 131, 143.

6. Ella Lonn, *Desertion during the Civil War* (Gloucester, MA: American Historical Association, 1928), 3; Weitz, *More Damning Than Slaughter*, xviii; and Robert M. Sandow, *Deserter Country: Civil War Opposition in the Pennsylvania Appalachians* (Bronx: Fordham University Press, 2009), 1–2, 8, quotation on 8. See also Peter S. Bearman, "Desertion as Localism: Army Unit Solidarity and Group Norms in the U.S. Civil War," *Social Forces* 70 (December 1991): 321–42; and Aaron W. Marrs, "Desertion and Loyalty in South Carolina, 1861–1865," *Civil War History* 50 (March 2004): 47–65.

7. Smith, *Mississippi in the Civil War*, 70–73, 90; and Davis, *Look Away!*, 285.

8. Wynne, *Mississippi's Civil War*, 139–41; and Smith, *Mississippi in the Civil War*, 115.

9. Wynne, *Mississippi's Civil War*, 137–39; and Smith, *Mississippi in the Civil War*, 38–49, 119.

10. Terry Whittington, "In the Shadow of Defeat: Tracking the Vicksburg Parolees," *Journal of Mississippi History* 4 (Winter 2002): 308–9, 311–13, 328; Diary of Jason Niles, July 21, 1863, transcript of manuscript no. 950, *Documenting the American South*, at http://docsouth.unc.edu/imls/niles/niles.html, accessed August 10, 2009; *OR*, ser. 4, vol. 3, 690; and Charles Clark, Message to the State Legislature, August 3, 1864, *Journal of the House of Representatives of the State of Mississippi, Called Session, at Macon, August 1864* (Meridian, MS: J. J. Shannon and Company, 1864), 9, *Documenting the American South*, at http://doc south.unc.edu/imls/msaug64/msaug64.html, accessed April 26, 2012.

11. Fellman, *Inside War*, 47–65; Fisher, *War at Every Door*, 62–63, 142–143; Sean Michael O'Brian, *Mountain Partisans: Guerrilla Warfare in the Southern Appalachians, 1861–1865* (Westport, CT: Praeger, 1999), xiii–xxiv; Daniel E. Sutherland, ed., *Guerrillas, Unionists, and Violence on the Confederate Home Front* (Fayetteville: University of Arkansas Press, 1999); John C. Inscoe and Gordon B. McKinney, *The Heart of Confederate Appalachia: Western North Carolina in the Civil War* (Chapel Hill: University of North Carolina Press, 2000), 105–38; Kenneth W. Noe, "Who Were the Bushwhackers? Age, Class, Kin, and Western Virginia's Confederate Guerrillas, 1861–1862," *Civil War History* 49 (March 2003): 5–26; Robert R. Mackey, *The Uncivil War: Irregular Warfare in the Upper South, 1861–1865* (Norman: University of Oklahoma Press, 2004), 3–23; McKenzie, *Lincolnites and Rebels*, 124–40; and Sarris, *A Separate Civil War*, 2–5, 69–80.

12. Fisher, *War at Every Door*, 61–62, 87–88; and Daniel E. Sutherland, *A Savage Conflict: The Decisive Role of Guerrillas in the American Civil War* (Chapel Hill: University of North Carolina Press, 2009), x, 125–26, 261.

13. Douglass C. North, John Joseph Wallis, and Barry R. Weingast, *Violence and Social Orders: A Conceptual Framework for Interpreting Recorded Human History* (New York: Cambridge University Press, 2009), 1–2.

14. Ash, *When the Yankees Came*, 99.

15. Charles Tilly, *The Politics of Collective Violence* (New York: Cambridge University Press, 2003), 131; Fellman, *Inside War*, xvi; and Roth, *American Homicide*, 19. For more on the connection between civil wars and crime, see Lisa Hultman, "Attacks on Civilians in Civil War: Targeting the Achilles Heel of Democratic Governments," *International Interactions* 38, no. 2 (2012): 164–81.

16. Keller, *The Limits of Loyalty*, 22; and Richard Stott, *Jolly Fellows: Male Milieus in Nineteenth-Century America* (Baltimore: Johns Hopkins University Press, 2009), 1, 57, 222–24.

17. Ward, *Between the Lines*, ix–xi, quotations on x, xi; Eric Hobsbawm, *Bandits*, rev. ed. (New York: New Press, 2000), 24, 40; William C. Davis, *A Way through the Wilderness: The Natchez Trace and the Civilization of the Southern Frontier* (New York: HarperCollins, 1995), 272–79; and Armstead L. Robinson, *Bitter Fruits of Bondage: The Demise of Slavery and the Collapse of the Confederacy, 1861–1865* (Charlottesville: University of Virginia Press, 2005), 195, 198. Robinson highlights the outbreak of social banditry in several Confederate states; see 195–99, 225–28, 233–35. Soldiers have been attracted to banditry because it appeals to unsettled young men as well as to men disillusioned with regimented army life. Mississippi already had a history of criminal gangs and highwaymen in its territorial days, especially along the storied Natchez Trace. The Civil War, however, saw an explosion of banditry among deserters. For an account of Civil War banditry in neighboring Louisiana, see Alexandre Barde, *The Vigilante Committees of the Attakapas: An Eyewitness Account of Banditry and Backlash in Southwestern Louisiana*, ed. David C. Edmonds and Dennis A. Gibson, trans. Henrietta Guilbeau Rogers (Lafayette, LA: Acadiana Press, 1981).

18. *OR*, ser. 1, vol. 24, pt. 3, 1044; ser. 1, vol. 39, pt. 2, 568; ser. 4, vol. 3, 707; ser. 1, vol. 39, pt. 1, 400; ser. 4, vol. 3, 976; ser. 1, vol. 32, pt. 3, 855–56; and ser. 1, vol. 49, pt. 1, 944.

19. Weitz, *More Damning Than Slaughter*, xvi–xvii; Ballard, *The Civil War in Mississippi*, 11; Bettersworth, *Confederate Mississippi*, 211–12; and Smith, *Mississippi in the Civil War*, 137. See also Wynne, *Mississippi's Civil War*, 138; and Lonn, *Desertion during the Civil War*, 75.

20. Sheriff G. W. Bradley to Charles Clark, February 8, 1864, Charles Clark Correspondence, series 768, box 949, volume 56, Record Group 27, MDAH.

21. Isaac Anderson et al. to Charles Clark, January 28, 1864, W. H. Quarles to Charles Clark, March 28, 1864, Charles Clark Correspondence, MDAH.

22. Bynum, *The Free State of Jones*, 99–101, 111; Bynum, *The Long Shadow of the Civil War*, 31–36; and Ed Payne, "Crossing the Rubicon of Loyalties: Piney Woods Enlistees in the Union 1st and 2nd New Orleans Infantry," *Renegade South: Histories of Unconventional Southerners* (blog), May 26, 2011, at http://renegadesouth.wordpress.com/2011/05/26/cross ing-the-rubicon-of-loyalties-piney-woods-enlistees-in-the-union-1st-and-2nd-north -orleans-infantry, accessed August 17, 2012.

23. *OR*, ser. 1, vol. 32, pt. 2, 688–89; and ser. 1, vol. 32, pt. 3, 633.

24. Milton Brown to Charles Clark, December 11, 1864, M. J. Wesson Bush to Charles Clark, March 26, 1864, Charles Clark Correspondence, MDAH; and *Beacon* (Macon, MS), April 13, 1864.

25. Hamilton Cooper to Charles Clark, December 26, 1864, Richard Cooper to Charles Clark, March 25, 1865, Charles Clark Correspondence, box 950, MDAH; and US Census 1860, records for Simpson County, Mississippi, James Rogers and Abel A. Rogers, and US Civil War Soldier Records and Profiles, A. A. Rogers, digital images.

26. Robert S. Hudson to Jefferson Davis, March 14, 1864, Robert S. Hudson to Charles Clark, October 26, 1864, in Silver, "The Breakdown of Morale," 102, 116.

27. Robert S. Hudson to Charles Clarke, May 2, 16, 1864, in Silver, "The Breakdown of Morale," 103–4.

28. Robert S. Hudson to William H. Mangum, May 24, 1864, in Silver, "The Breakdown of Morale," 106–7.

29. Ibid.; and US Census 1860, records for Neshoba and Leake Counties, Mississippi, Thomas, Reuban, and William G. Barrett, Samuel and John W. Adcock, William R. and Charles R. Waller, Jackson Breazeale, C. W. Mooney, and Emmet R. Scott, and US Civil War Soldier Records and Profiles, digital images.

30. *OR*, ser. 1, vol. 32, pt. 3, 711–12.

31. *OR*, ser. 1, vol. 32, pt. 3, 712.

32. Bettersworth, *Confederate Mississippi*, 241–43; Freeman Jones to John J. Pettus, December 24, 1862, E. Lewis to John J. Pettus, December 5, 1862, A. E. Lewis to John J. Pettus, January 18, 1863, John J. Pettus Correspondence, roll 2812, volume 50, MDAH; "Suffering on the Sea Coast of Mississippi," *Weekly Mississippian* (Jackson), April 8, 1863; *OR*, ser. 4, vol. 2, 782; and Officers of Third Mississippi Regiment to James A. Seddon, March 29, 1864, nos. H151-350, roll 129, LRCSW, NARA.

33. John J. Pettus to W. L. Lowry, March 17, 1863, John J. Pettus Correspondence, roll 1446, MDAH; *OR*, ser. 1, vol. 32, pt. 3, 635; US Census 1860, records for Monroe and Calhoun Counties, Mississippi, W. F. English, James Cartright, and US Civil War Soldier Records and Profiles, digital images; H. W. Thompson to Charles Clark, January 21, 1864, Charles Clark Correspondence, box 949, MDAH; and *OR*, ser. 1, vol. 39, pt. 2, 570.

34. Tishomingo Residents to Charles Clark, undated, Charles Clark Correspondence, box 950, MDAH; N. Cassedy to Charles Clark, September 12, 1864, Charles Clark Correspondence, MDAH; Beaumont, *Twelve Years of My Life*, 182, 208, 244; and Louisa T. Lovell to Joseph Lovell, February 26, 1864, Quitman Family Papers, 1784–1978, folder 112, series 1.2, 00616, SHC.

35. H. S. Van Eaton to Charles Clark, July 12, 1864, Charles Clark Correspondence, box 949, MDAH; Eliza H. B. Sively to Jane Sively, undated, Jane Sively Letters, 1862–1867, folder 4, 01891-z, SHC; Bunkers, *The Diary of Caroline Seabury*, 105–6; and Samuel Andrew Agnew Diary, January 21, 1864, *Documenting the American South*, at http://docsouth.unc.edu/imls/agnew/agnew.html, accessed September 13, 2009.

36. Bolivar County Citizens to Charles Clark, February 20, 1864, Charles Clark Correspondence, box 949, MDAH.

37. R. H. Bowers to Thomas Henderson, March 15, 1863, John C. Pemberton Papers, MLR PI101, folder 6, box 2, entry 131, War Department Collection of Confederate Records, RG 109, NARA; and Captain Henderson to John Pemberton, February 25, 1863, John C. Pemberton Papers, folder 3, NARA.

38. Samuel Andrew Agnew Diary, March 13, 14, 1864, *Documenting the American South*; and US Census 1860, records for Pontotoc, Chickasaw, Itawamba, and Tippah Counties, Mississippi, and Saint Clair County, Alabama, Napoleon B. Bolen, John Watkins, John Chisholm, Luther A. Privet, William H. Gober, Littleton Wages, and Lafayette Bolen, digital images.

39. Samuel Andrew Agnew Diary, March 13, 14, 1864, *Documenting the American South*; and US Civil War Soldier Records and Profiles, Napoleon B. Bolen, John Watkins, John Chisholm, Luther A. Privet, William H. Gober, Littleton Wages, and Lafayette Bolen, digital images.

40. My occupational classifications draw from Samuel C. Hyde Jr.'s definitions. Poor whites consisted of landless laborers and non-property-holding farmers. Plain folk were non-slaveholding farmers with land, as well as farmers owning one to five working slaves. Middling or larger farmers owned land and six to nine working slaves. Planters owned land and ten or more slaves. See Samuel C. Hyde Jr., "Plain Folk Reconsidered: Historiographical Ambiguity in Search of Definition," *Journal of Southern History* 71 (November 2005): 819.

41. Larry M. Logue, "Who Joined the Confederate Army? Soldiers, Civilians, and Communities in Mississippi," *Journal of Social History* 26 (Spring 1993): 614; Marrs, "Desertion and Loyalty in South Carolina," 53; and Joseph T. Glatthaar, *Soldiering in the Army of Northern Virginia: A Statistical Portrait of the Troops Who Served under Robert E. Lee* (Chapel Hill: University of North Carolina Press, 2011), 5–6.

42. Glatthaar, *Soldiering in the Army of Northern Virginia*, 5–6; James M. McPherson, *Battle Cry of Freedom: The Civil War Era* (New York: Ballantine, 1988), 614–15; and Frank L. Owsley, *Plain Folk of the Old South* (1949; repr., Chicago: Quadrangle, 1961), 7–10. For a review of the historiographical literature on common Southern whites, see Samuel C. Hyde Jr., "Plain Folk Yeomanry in the Antebellum South," in *A Companion to the American South*, ed. John B. Boles (Malden, MA: Blackwell, 2004), 139–55.

43. Tilly, *The Politics of Collective Violence*, 132, 7. Kenneth Noe identifies a similar thread of normalcy altered by wartime conditions in his study of Confederate bushwhackers in West Virginia, revealing that several bushwhackers were not society's dregs but "older and propertied men" who were "stable landowners" and therefore did not fit traditional assumptions about outlaws' backgrounds. See Noe, "Who Were the Bushwhackers?," 5–6.

44. Bearman, "Desertion as Localism," 337, 323, 340. Marrs finds similar neighborhood and household connections among South Carolina deserters, although, like Bearman, he concludes that local attachments were stronger than Confederate nationalism. See Marrs, "Desertion and Loyalty in South Carolina," 60–61.

45. Margaret E. Wagner, Gary W. Gallagher, and Paul Finkelman, eds., *The Library of Congress Civil War Desk Reference* (New York: Simon and Schuster, 2009), 447–49; and Sutherland, *A Savage Conflict*, 209–10.

46. *OR*, ser. 1, vol. 52, pt. 2, 325.

47. Beaumont, *Twelve Years of My Life*, 292–93.

48. Howard W. Wilkinson to John J. Pettus, January 1, 1863, John J. Pettus Correspondence, roll 2812, MDAH; M. A. Banks to Charles Clark, June 15, 1864, Charles Clark Correspondence, box 949, MDAH; W. C. Falkner to John J. Pettus, March 13, 1863, John J. Pettus Correspondence, roll 1446, volume 51, MDAH; and Davis, *Look Away!*, 259–63.

49. "Shooting a Deserter," *Weekly Courier* (Natchez), May 14, 1862; US Census 1860, records for Monroe County, Mississippi, Delevan H. Morgan, and US Civil War Soldier Records and Profiles, digital images; and Aughey, *Tupelo*, 289–94, quotation on 289.

50. J. Z. George to John J. Pettus, December 27, 1862; Richard Harrison to John J. Pettus, December 19, 1862; E. R. Brown to John J. Pettus, November 11, 1862, all in John J. Pettus Correspondence, roll 2812, MDAH.

51. Smith, *Mississippi in the Civil War*, 59–62.

52. *OR*, ser. 1, vol. 32, pt. 2, 602, 604.

53. *OR*, ser. 2, vol. 39, pt. 1, 728–29; ser. 4, vol. 3, 823–24.

54. *OR*, ser. 4, vol. 3, 8–9; and James Drane to John J. Pettus, August 21, 1863, John J. Pettus Correspondence, roll 133, volume 50, MDAH.

55. Kenneth W. Noe, *Reluctant Rebels: The Confederates Who Joined the Army after 1861* (Chapel Hill: University of North Carolina Press, 2010), 9–10, 208.

56. McCurry, *Confederate Reckoning*, 138–40, quotation on 139.

57. P. Randolph to Leroy Pope Walker, May 13, 1861, roll 2, LRCSW, NARA; D. J. Jernigan to George W. Randolph, June 28, 1862, roll 55, LRCSW, NARA; and US Census 1860, records for Panola County, Mississippi, D. J. Jernigan, digital image.

58. C. W. Shiel to James A. Seddon, December 3, 1862, roll 73, LRCSW, NARA; J. M. Greene to George W. Randolph, July 14, 1862, roll 48, LRCSW, NARA.

59. Petition by Fifth Regiment, Fourth Brigade, State Troops to John J. Pettus, February 21, 1863, John J. Pettus Correspondence, roll 1446, MDAH; and Joseph M. Jayne to Jefferson Davis, August 7, 1863, Jefferson Davis to Robert E. Lee, August 13, 1863, in Crist et al., *The Papers of Jefferson Davis*, 9:342.

60. I. H. C. Jordan to James A. Seddon, February 15, 1864, roll 131, LRCSW, NARA; Officers of Twelfth Mississippi Infantry to Charles Clark, January 31, 1864, roll 129, LRCSW, NARA; US Census 1860, records for Leake and Lawrence Counties, Mississippi, Isaac H. C. Jordan, Robert Patterson, and J. Lewis Vaughan, and US Civil War Soldiers Records and Profiles, digital images; and Smith, *Mississippi in the Civil War*, 78–79.

61. Panola County Citizens to George W. Randolph, October 9, 1862, roll 47, LRCSW, NARA; Neshoba County Women to George W. Randolph, August 24, 1862, roll 30, LRCSW, NARA; and Carroll County Citizens to George W. Randolph, August 25, 1862, roll 45, LRCSW, NARA.

62. William L. Shaw, "The Confederate Conscription and Exemption Acts," *American Journal of Legal History* 6 (October 1962): 368–405.

63. See David Herbert Donald, "Died of Democracy," in *Why the North Won the Civil War*, ed. David Herbert Donald (1960; repr., New York: Touchstone, 1996), 81–93; Richard E. Beringer, Herman Hattaway, Archer Jones, and William N. Still Jr., *Why the South Lost the Civil War* (Athens: University of Georgia Press, 1986), 203–36; Reid Mitchell, "The Perseverance of the Soldiers," in *Why the Confederacy Lost*, ed. Gabor S. Boritt (New York: Oxford University Press, 1992), 109–33; Gallagher, *The Confederate War*, 31–36; and Paul D. Escott, *The Confederacy: The Slaveholders' Failed Venture* (Santa Barbara, CA: Praeger, 2010), 43–65.

64. Newton County Citizens to James A. Seddon, January, 1864, roll 47, LRCSW, NARA; and Neshoba County Citizens to James A. Seddon, February 2, 1864, roll 131, LRCSW, NARA.

65. James Duff to Reuben Davis, February 11, 1863, roll 89, LRCSW, NARA; and Monroe County Citizens to James A. Seddon, February 9, 1864, roll 131, LRCSW, NARA.

66. *OR*, ser. 4, vol. 2, 857; and Richard T. Archer to John J. Pettus, December 10, 1862, John J. Pettus Correspondence, MDAH, roll 2812.

67. Albert Gallatin Brown, December 24, 1863, "State of the Country Speech in the Confederate Senate," *Documenting the American South*, at http://docsouth.unc.edu/imls/browna/browna.html, accessed September 24, 2009.

68. George H. Gordon to Jefferson Davis, January 27, 1863, roll 92; Eliza Scott to George W. Randolph, November 6, 1862, roll 109; William J. Gibson et al. to Jefferson Davis, May 20, 1862, roll 48, all in LRCSW, NARA.

69. Madison County Residents to Earl Van Dorn, December 24, 1862, roll 45; Madison County Women to Earl Van Dorn, December 24, 1862; W. Davis Jr. to O. R. Singleton, January 27, 1863, roll 89, all in LRCSW, NARA.

70. US Census 1860 and Slave Schedules, records for Madison County, Mississippi, B. S. W. Gafford, digital image.

CHAPTER FIVE

1. George Washington Sargent to George Sargent, October 30, 1860, George Washington Sargent to Mary Duncan, January 15, 1861, George Washington Sargent Papers, 1840–1900, folder 11, volume 11, 04025, SHC; and Susan Snow, *Born in Slavery: Slave Narratives from the Federal Writers' Project, 1936–1938*, vol. 9, *Mississippi Narratives*, American Memory, Manuscript Division, Library of Congress, Washington, DC, at http://memory.loc.gov/cgi-bin/ampage?collId=mesn&fileName=090/mesn090.db&recNum=138&itemLink=D? mesnbib:29:./temp/~ammem_1ajQ::, accessed June 6, 2012 (hereafter cited as *Mississippi Narratives*).

2. Chandra Manning, *Troubled Refuge: Struggling for Freedom in the Civil War* (New York: Alfred A. Knopf, 2016), 11.

3. McCurry, *Confederate Reckoning*, 20–24, 304; Davis, *Look Away!*, 130–62; and A. F. Burton to Thomas W. Burton, March 30, 1861, Thomas W. Burton Papers, 1809–1921, folder 1, 04217-z, SHC.

4. Eugene D. Genovese and Elizabeth Fox-Genovese, *Fatal Self-Deception: Slaveholding Paternalism in the Old South* (Cambridge: Cambridge University Press, 2011), 86; and McCurry, *Confederate Reckoning*, 304. For more on the absolute authority of slaveholders, see James Oakes, *Slavery and Freedom: An Interpretation of the Old South* (New York: Alfred A. Knopf, 1990), 4–8; Peter Kolchin, *American Slavery: 1619–1877* (New York: Hill and Wang, 1993), 111–27; and Duquette, *Loyal Subjects*, 141–42, quotations on 142.

5. Quigley, *Shifting Grounds*, 5–6; and McCurry, *Confederate Reckoning*, 306–9, quotations on 308. On slaves' behavior hampering the Confederate war effort, see also Robinson, *Bitter Fruits of Bondage*, 37–58, 163–89, 272–83; and Joseph T. Glatthaar, "Black Glory: The African-American Role in Union Victory," in Boritt, *Why the Confederacy Lost*, 133–63.

6. Waldrep, *Roots of Disorder*, 21–25.

7. On the importance whites continued to place on black submission after the Civil War in Mississippi and the South in general, see Vernon Lane Wharton, *The Negro in Mississippi, 1865–1890* (1947; repr., New York: Harper and Row, 1965), 80–96, 140–42; William C. Harris, *Presidential Reconstruction in Mississippi* (Baton Rouge: Louisiana State University Press, 1967), 79–140; Michael Perman, *Reunion without Compromise: The South and Reconstruction, 1865–1868* (New York: Cambridge University Press, 1973), 77–80, 90–94; James T. Currie, "From Slavery to Freedom in Mississippi's Legal System," *Journal of Negro History* 2 (Spring 1980): 112–25; Ronald L. F. Davis, *Good and Faithful Labor: From Slavery to Sharecropping in the Natchez District, 1860–1890* (Westport, CT: Greenwood Press, 1982), 1–19; Edward J. Blum, *Reforging the White Republic: Race, Religion, and American Nationalism, 1865–1898* (Baton Rouge: Louisiana State University Press, 2005), 3–7; Bruce Levine, *Confederate Emancipation: Southern Plans to Free and Arm Slaves during the Civil War* (New York: Oxford University Press, 2006), 155–64; and William A. Link and James J. Broomall, introduction to *Rethinking American Emancipation: Legacies of Slavery and the Quest for Black Freedom*, ed. William A. Link and James J. Broomall (New York: Cambridge University Press, 2016), 2–8.

8. Steven Hahn, *A Nation under Our Feet: Black Political Struggles in the Rural South from Slavery to the Great Migration* (Cambridge, MA: Harvard University Press, 2003), 10, 33, 26–41, 61, 64, 114, 6, quotations on 114, 6; Steven Hahn, *The Political Worlds of Slavery and Freedom* (Cambridge, MA: Harvard University Press, 2009), 55–115; Enrico dal Lago, "States of Rebellion: Civil War, Rural Unrest, and the Agrarian Question in the American South

and the Italian Mezzogiorno, 1861–1865," *Comparative Studies in Society and History* 47 (April 2005): 404, 412–13, 420; and Julie Saville, *The Work of Reconstruction: From Slave to Wage Laborer in South Carolina, 1860–1870* (New York: Cambridge University Press, 1996), 4. Other works that identify post–Civil War blacks as a rural proletariat include W. E. B. Du Bois, *Black Reconstruction in America, 1860–1880* (1935; reprint, New York: Frank Cass, 1966), 381–487; Barbara J. Fields, *Slavery and Freedom on the Middle Ground: Maryland during the Nineteenth Century* (New Haven, CT: Yale University Press, 1985), 190–91; Gerald David Jaynes, *Branches without Roots: Genesis of the Black Working Class in the American South, 1862–1882* (New York: Oxford University Press, 1986), 158–91; Joseph P. Reidy, *From Slavery to Agrarian Capitalism in the Cotton Plantation South: Central Georgia, 1800–1880* (Chapel Hill: University of North Carolina Press, 1992), 13, 136–242; and John C. Rodrigue, *Reconstruction in the Cane Fields: From Slavery to Free Labor in Louisiana's Sugar Parishes, 1862–1880* (Baton Rouge: Louisiana State University Press, 2001), 1–8.

9. Eric Foner, *The Story of American Freedom* (New York: W. W. Norton, 1998), 101–2, quotation on 102; see also Eric Foner, *Reconstruction: America's Unfinished Revolution, 1863–1877* (New York: Harper and Row, 1988), 102–19; and Leon F. Litwack, *Been in the Storm So Long: The Aftermath of Slavery* (New York: Alfred A. Knopf, 1979), 517.

10. Joel Williamson, *A Race for Order: Black-White Relations in the American South since Emancipation* (New York: Oxford University Press, 1986), 44; and John Spiller, "African Americans after the Civil War," *History Review* 65 (December 2009): 38.

11. Alex Lichtenstein, "Was the Emancipated Slave a Proletarian?," *Reviews in American History* 26 (March 1998): 135.

12. Lynda J. Morgan, *Known for My Work: African American Ethics from Slavery to Freedom* (Gainesville: University Press of Florida, 2016), 3–4; and Michael A. Gomez, *Exchanging Our Country Marks: The Transformation of African Identities in the Colonial and Antebellum South* (Chapel Hill: University of North Carolina Press, 1998), 219–20.

13. Herbert Gutman, *The Black Family in Slavery and Freedom, 1750–1925* (New York: Pantheon, 1976), 3, 8; John W. Blassingame, *The Slave Community: Plantation Life in the Antebellum South* (1972; reprint, New York: Oxford University Press, 1979), 149–91; and Anthony E. Kay, *Joining Places: Slave Neighborhoods in the Old South* (Chapel Hill: University of North Carolina Press, 2007), 4, 179.

14. Walter Johnson, "Agency: A Ghost Story," in *Slavery's Ghost: The Problem of Freedom in the Age of Emancipation*, by Richard Follett, Eric Foner, and Walter Johnson (Baltimore: Johns Hopkins University Press, 2011), 28.

15. The literature on slave resistance in the South is massive. For examples, see Herbert Aptheker, *American Negro Slave Revolts* (1943; repr., New York: International Publishers, 1993); David Williams, *I Freed Myself: African American Self-Emancipation* (New York: Cambridge University Press, 2014); Gerald W. Mullin, *Flight and Rebellion: Slave Resistance in Eighteenth-Century Virginia* (New York: Oxford University Press, 1974); Peter H. Wood, *Black Majority: Negroes in Colonial South Carolina from 1670 through the Stono Rebellion* (New York: W. W. Norton, 1974); Eugene D. Genovese, *Roll, Jordan, Roll: The World the Slaves Made* (New York: Pantheon, 1974); Leslie Howard Owens, *This Species of Property: Slave Life and Culture in the Old South* (New York: Oxford University Press, 1976); Vincent Harding, *There Is a River: The Black Struggle for Freedom in America* (New York: Harcourt, Brace and Company, 1981); Deborah Gray White, *Ar'n't I a Woman? Female Slaves in the Plantation South* (New York: W. W. Norton, 1985); James Oakes, "The Political Significance of Slave Resistance," *History Workshop* 22 (Autumn 1986): 89–107; Sylvia R. Frey, *Water*

from the Rock: Black Resistance in a Revolutionary Age (Princeton, NJ: Princeton University Press, 1991); Michael Mullin, *Africa in America: Slave Acculturation and Resistance in the American South and the British Caribbean, 1736–1831* (Urbana: University of Illinois Press, 1992); Philip D. Morgan, *Slave Counterpoint: Black Culture in the Eighteenth-Century Chesapeake and Lowcountry* (Chapel Hill: University of North Carolina Press, 1998); John Hope Franklin and Loren Schweninger, *Runaway Slaves: Rebels on the Plantation* (New York: Oxford University Press, 1999); William A. Link, *Roots of Secession: Slavery and Politics in Antebellum Virginia* (Chapel Hill: University of North Carolina Press, 2003); Stephanie M. H. Camp, *Closer to Freedom: Enslaved Women and Everyday Resistance in the Plantation South* (Chapel Hill: University of North Carolina Press, 2004); Albert J. Raboteau, *Slave Religion: The "Invisible Institution" in the Antebellum South* (New York: Oxford University Press, 2004); Jason R. Young, *Rituals of Resistance: African Atlantic Religion in Kongo and the Lowcountry South in the Era of Slavery* (Baton Rouge: Louisiana State University Press, 2007); Gabor S. Boritt and Scott Hancock, eds., *Slavery, Resistance, Freedom* (New York: Oxford University Press, 2007); Peter Charles Hoffer, *Cry Liberty: The Great Stono River Slave Rebellion of 1739* (New York: Oxford University Press, 2010); and Larry Eugene Rivers, *Rebels and Runaways: Slave Resistance in Nineteenth-Century Florida* (Urbana: University of Illinois Press, 2012).

16. Walter Johnson, "On Agency," *Journal of Social History* 37 (Autumn 2003): 115–16.

17. Christopher Morris, "The Articulation of Two Worlds: The Master-Slave Relationship Reconsidered," *Journal of American History* 85 (December 1998): 982–85; Kay, *Joining Places*, 62, 136; Blassingame, *The Slave Community*, 151–53; Loren Schweninger, *Black Property Owners in the South, 1790–1915* (Urbana: University of Illinois Press, 1990), 31–32, 54–56, 36; Jonathan D. Martin, *Divided Mastery: Slave Hiring in the American South* (Cambridge, MA: Harvard University Press, 2007), 72–138; and L. Diane Barnes, *Artisan Workers in the Upper South: Petersburg, Virginia, 1820–1865* (Baton Rouge: Louisiana State University Press, 2009), 4–5.

18. Morris, "The Articulation of Two Worlds," 1003.

19. George M. Fredrickson, *The Black Image in the White Mind: The Debate on Afro-American Character and Destiny, 1817–1914* (1971; repr., Middletown, CT: Wesleyan University Press, 1987), 52–53; Franklin and Schweninger, *Runaway Slaves*, 11–15; Laurence Shore, "Making Mississippi Safe for Slavery: The Insurrectionary Panic of 1835," in *Class, Conflict, and Consensus: Antebellum Southern Community Studies*, ed. Orville Burton and Robert McMath Jr. (Westport, CT: Greenwood Press, 1982), 96–127; Herbert Aptheker, "Notes on Slave Conspiracies in Confederate Mississippi," *Journal of Negro History* 29 (January 1944): 75–79; Philip D. Morgan, "Conspiracy Scares," *William and Mary Quarterly*, 3rd ser., 59 (January 2002): 166; Donald E. Reynolds, *Texas Terror: The Slave Insurrection Panic of 1860 and the Secession of the Lower South* (Baton Rouge: Louisiana State University Press, 2007), 1–28; and Walter Johnson, "The Future Store," in *The Chattel Principle: Internal Slave Trades in the Americas*, ed. Walter Johnson (New Haven, CT: Yale University Press, 2004), 6–7.

20. Louisa T. Lovell to Joseph Lovell, September 29, 1861, Quitman Family Papers, 1784–1978, folder 107, series 1.2, 00616, SHC; and Sophia Hunt Hughes to Jennie Hughes, October 15, 1861, Hughes Family Papers, 1790–1910, folder 17, 02779, SHC. For differing interpretations of the Adams County conspiracies, see Winthrop D. Jordan, *Tumult and Silence at Second Creek: An Inquiry into a Civil War Slave Conspiracy* (Baton Rouge: Louisiana State University Press, 1993); and Justin Behrend, "Rebellious Talk and Conspiratorial Plots:

The Making of a Slave Insurrection in Civil War Natchez," *Journal of Southern History* 77 (February 2011): 17–52.

21. N. H. Boyd to Eudora Hobbs, January 13, 1861, Hobbs Family Papers, *Underpinnings of the American Civil War*, at http://digital.library.msstate.edu/collections/document. php?CISOROOT=/ASERL&CISOPTR=83&REC=5, accessed January 22, 2012; Ophelia Howe to Ellen Howe, August 6, 1861, Chiliab Smith Howe Papers, 1814–1899, folder 53, series 1.6, 03092, SHC; D. D. Ranch to John J. Pettus, April 30, 1861, John J. Pettus Correspondence, roll 1812, volume 36, MDAH; and John Kirkland to Octavia Otey, June 16, 1861, Wyche and Otey Family Papers, 1824–1926, folder 15, series 1.3, 01608, SHC.

22. C. H. Dahlgren to Absalom West, July 16, 1861, Absalom West Collection, 1853–1870, MUM00782, box 1976.10, UMASC.

23. John J. Pettus, Address to Mississippi State Legislature, November 3, 1863, *Journal of the House of Representatives of the State of Mississippi, December Session of 1862 and November Session of 1863* (Jackson: Cooper and Kimble, 1864), 93, *Documenting the American South*, at http://docsouth.unc.edu/imls/msdec62/msdec62.html, accessed April 26, 2012; and Inaugural Address of Governor Charles Clark, November 16, 1863, *Journal of the House of Representatives of the State of Mississippi, December Session of 1862 and November Session of 1863*, 158–59, *Documenting the American South*.

24. Expectations of slave loyalty were central to white plantation mistresses' identity as household dependents. See Bercaw, *Gendered Freedoms*, 51–74; and Faust, *Mothers of Invention*, 53–79.

25. Shaw, "The Confederate Conscription and Exemption Acts," 376.

26. E. A. Dowling to George Randolph, October 19, 1862; Socky Davis, Petition to George Randolph, October 19, 1862; Clary and Sarah Donald to George Randolph, October 19, 1862, all roll 44, LRCSW, NARA; Julia A. Cox to Jefferson Davis, February 13, 1863, April 18, 1864, rolls 87, 123, LRCSW, NARA; and Abigail Jones to Jefferson Davis, October 25, 1862, roll 55, LRCSW, NARA.

27. Davis, *Look Away!*, 235–36.

28. Lititia A. Adams to John J. Pettus, March 28, 1863, John J. Pettus Correspondence, roll 1446, MDAH; Frank A. Yaden to George Randolph, April 23, 1862, roll 48, LRCSW, NARA; and Charity and Rachel Buchanan to James A. Seddon, November 6, 1863, roll 84, LRCSW, NARA.

29. Martha Hodes, *White Women, Black Men: Illicit Sex in the Nineteenth-Century South* (New Haven, CT: Yale University Press, 1997), 139–45.

30. N. Cassedy to Charles Clark, September 12, 1864, Charles Clark Correspondence, series 768, box 950, volume 56, Record Group 27, MDAH; O. J. M. Holladay to Charles Clark, August 19, 1864, Charles Clark Correspondence, box 949, MDAH; Journal of Lettie Vick Downs, September 7, 1863, Lettie Downs Collection, 1859, 1862–1866, 1972, Z1497, folder 1, MDAH; and Hannah Rosen, *Terror in the Heart of Freedom: Citizenship, Sexual Violence, and the Meaning of Race in the Postemancipation South* (Chapel Hill: University of North Carolina Press, 2009), 6–9, 44–49.

31. Franklin and Schweninger, *Runaway Slaves*, 97–296; Genovese, *Roll, Jordan, Roll*, 648–57; Kenneth M. Stampp, *The Peculiar Institution: Slavery in the Ante-Bellum South* (New York: Alfred A. Knopf, 1967), 109–24; Robinson, *Bitter Fruits of Bondage*, 178–80, 194–95; and Smith, *Mississippi in the Civil War*, 147–48.

32. Mack Henderson, *Mississippi Slave Narratives from the WPA Records*, MSGenWeb Special Projects, Library Project, at http://msgw.org/slaves/henderson-xslave.htm, accessed August 12, 2012.

33. Yael A. Sternhell, "Bodies in Motion and the Making of Emancipation," in Link and Broomall, *Rethinking American Emancipation*, 15–41; Kaye, *Joining Places*, 129–35; Calvin Schermerhorn, *Money over Mastery, Family over Freedom: Slavery in the Antebellum Upper South* (Baltimore: Johns Hopkins University Press, 2011), 45–48; Owens, *This Species of Property*, 81; Franklin and Schweninger, *Runaway Slaves*, 224; and Williams, *I Freed Myself*, 3–10.

34. Manning, *Troubled Refuge*, 111–25.

35. A. K. Farrar to John J. Pettus, July 17, 1862, in Bettersworth, *Mississippi in the Confederacy*, 1:235–36; P. B. Barringer to Brother, August 19, 1862, Daniel Moreau Barringer Papers, 1797–1873, folder 42, 03359, SHC; W. A. Hewitt to William L. Moses, John C. Pemberton Papers, MLR PI101, folder 7, box 1, entry 131, War Department Collection of Confederate Records, Record Group 109, NARA; John Miller to H. R. Miller, November 14, 1862, Miller Family Papers, 1830–1864, MUM00297, folder 45, UMASC; Pleasant Smith to J. Thompson, January 8, 1862, in Ira Berlin, Barbara J. Fields, Thavolia Glymph, Joseph P. Reidy, and Leslie S. Rowland, eds., *The Destruction of Slavery*, ser. 1, vol. 1, of *Freedom: A Documentary History of Emancipation, 1861–1867* (New York: Cambridge University Press, 1985), 300; and Charles Whitmore Diary, July 4, 1863, Charles Whitmore Plantation Journal, microfilm, 02406, roll 1, SHC.

36. William Thomson to Ruffin Thomson, September 10, 1863, Ruffin Thomson Papers, folder 3, 03315, SHC; Jona Pearce to James Seddon, November 3, 1863, in Berlin et al., *The Destruction of Slavery*, 775–76; William Sively to Jane Sively, March 18, 1864, Jane Sively Letters, 1862–1867, folder 2, 01891-z, SHC; Sophia Hunt Hughes to Brother, April 8, 1864, Hughes Family Papers, folder 21a; and James H. Maury to James J. Maury, September 28, 1863, in Bettersworth, *Mississippi in the Confederacy*, 1:241.

37. William Dameron to Wife, November 6, 1862, Norton, Chilton and Dameron Family Papers, 1760–1926, 1995, folder 8, series 1, 03264, SHC; Eliza H. B. Sively to Jane Sively, February 14, 26, 1864, Jane Sively Letters, folder 2, SHC; and Louisa Lovell to Joseph Lovell, July 28, 1861, August 17, 1863, Quitman Family Papers, folders 106, 111, SHC.

38. Everard Green Baker Diary, December 26, 1862, Everard Green Baker Papers, 1848–1876, folder 5, 00041, SHC; Harvey W. Walter to Sister, January 1, 1863, H. W. Walter Papers, box 2, folder 9, MUM0013, UMASC; Darst, "The Vicksburg Diary of Mrs. Alfred Ingraham," 165, 167; and Kate Foster Diary, July 16, 1863, Catherine (Kate) Foster Diary, 1863–1872, Z/0869.000, MDAH.

39. Genovese and Fox-Genovese, *Fatal Self-Deception*, 1–6; and Genovese, *Roll, Jordan, Roll*, 3–7.

40. S. G. Miller to George Miller, October 31, 1862, S. G. Miller to H. R. Miller, September 29 1862, Miller Family Papers, folders 38, 40, UMASC.

41. Cotton, *From the Pen of a She-Rebel*, 23–24; William C. Nelson to Maria C. Nelson, February 22, 1863, William Cowper Nelson Collection, UMDC, at http://clio.lib.olemiss.edu/cdm4/document.php?CISOROOT=/civil_war&CISOPTR=483&REC=2, accessed December 10, 2011; Kate Foster Diary, July 25, 1863, Catherine (Kate) Foster Diary, MDAH; and Elizabeth Christie Brown Diary, May 4, 1863, box 1996.1, MUM01330, UMASC.

42. Eliza H. B. Sively to Jane Sively, November 4, 27, 1863, January 1, 1864, Jane Sively Letters, 1862–1867, folders 1–2, 01891-z, SHC; and Robert Shotwell to T. B. Lamar, July 5, 1863, in Berlin et al., *The Destruction of Slavery*, 800–802.

43. Cotton, *From the Pen of a She-Rebel*, 29; and Journal of Lettie Vick Downs, August 28, 1863, Lettie Downs Collection, MDAH.

44. Franklin and Schweninger, *Runaway Slaves*, 77–78, quotations on 77; Kolchin, *American Slavery*, 159–64; and V. P. Franklin, *Black Self-Determination: A Cultural History of African-American Resistance* (Brooklyn: Lawrence Hill, 1984), 75.

45. Cotton, *From the Pen of a She-Rebel*, 12; and Thavolia Glymph, *Out of the House of Bondage: The Transformation of the Plantation Household* (New York: Cambridge University Press, 2008), 99–100. See also Renee K. Harrison, *Enslaved Women and the Art of Resistance in Antebellum America* (New York: Palgrave Macmillan, 2009), 86–93; Cotton, *From the Pen of a She-Rebel*, 24; and William Sykes to James Sykes, December 26, 1864, Rufus Ward Collection, UMDC, at http://digital.library.msstate.edu/collections/document. php?CISOROOT=/ASERL&CISOPTR=455&REC=13, accessed December 5, 2011.

46. Slaves had long attempted to make their own homes and spaces where they lived in bondage, as these places held deep emotional attachments. In doing so, they acted on a fundamental human need to experience a sense of territory and place, in which, according to Yi-Fu Tuan, "spaces are marked off and defended against intruders" and are transformed into places that are "centers of felt value" in which the feeling of security facilitates the lived experience of freedom on an individual's own terms. Places are characterized by the "meaning and experience" through which individuals seek to define their world. During the war, black Mississippians appropriated spaces in the midst of white control and infused them with personal meaning. See Noralee Frankel, *Freedom's Women: Black Women and Families in Civil War Era Mississippi* (Bloomington: Indiana University Press, 1999), 19–20; Yi-Fu Tuan, *Space and Place: The Perspective of Experience* (Minneapolis: University of Minnesota Press, 1977), 3–4, quotations on 4; and Tim Cresswell, *Place: A Short Introduction* (Malden, MA: Blackwell, 2004), 11.

47. *Daily Mississippian* (Jackson), April 15, 1863, in Bettersworth, *Mississippi in the Confederacy*, 1:238–39; Kate Foster Diary, July 28, 1863, Catherine (Kate) Foster Diary, MDAH; and Louisa Lovell to Joseph Lovell, February 26, October 20, 1864, Quitman Family Papers, folders 112–113, SHC.

48. For more discussion on how black Mississippians continued to contest public and private spaces during and after the Civil War, see Justin J. Behrend, *Reconstructing Democracy: Grassroots Black Politics in the Deep South after the Civil War* (Athens: University of Georgia Press, 2015); and Justin J. Behrend, "Black Political Mobilization and the Spatial Transformation of Natchez" (paper presented at the American Civil War and the Cities of the Slave South workshop, Calgary and Banff, Alberta, May 25–26, 2012).

49. Morgan, *Known for My Work*, 4.

50. Kolchin, *American Slavery*, 157; Owens, *This Species of Property*, 79; and Hahn, *A Nation under Our Feet*, 19–20. Mark Smith employs the term "Colored Peoples' Time" (CPT) to describe how blacks eschewed the authority of the clock and adopted "presentist and naturally defined notions of time" in order to repudiate the time-based labor demands of Southern agrarian capitalists. Through their consciously slowed work pace, black laborers "resisted planter-defined time during and after slavery." See Mark M. Smith, *Mastered by the Clock: Time, Slavery, and Freedom in the American South* (Chapel Hill: University of North Carolina Press, 1997), 130–52, quotations on 130; and Camp, *Closer to Freedom*, 2–3.

51. "A Well Wisher to the Confederacy" to John J. Pettus, April 2, 1863, John J. Pettus Correspondence, roll 1446, volume 51, MDAH; William McWillie to James Seddon, October 12, 1863, roll 83, LRCSW, NARA; William McWillie to Jefferson Davis, October 18, 1863, in Crist et al., *The Papers of Jefferson Davis*, 10:29; A. M. Alexander to Reuben Davis, January 15, 1863, roll 89, LRCSW, NARA; and Petition of Yalobusha County Citizens to George Randolph, October 9, 1862, roll 73, LRCSW, NARA.

52. Charles Whitmore Plantation Journal, July 4, November 25, 1863, SHC; Loulie Feemster to Alex W. Feemster, March 10, 1863, Oakley Papers, *Underpinnings of the American Civil War*, at http://digital.library.msstate.edu/collections/document.php?CISOROOT=/ASERL&CISOPTR=194&REC=5, accessed January 23, 2012; and William C. Nelson to Maria C. Nelson, March 12, 1863, William Cowper Nelson Collection, UMDC, at http://clio".lib.olemiss.edu/cdm4/document.php?CISOROOT=/civil_war&CISOPTR=488&REC=1, accessed December 10, 2011.

53. Elizabeth Christie Brown Diary, January 19, 1863, UMASC; Darst, "The Vicksburg Diary of Mrs. Alfred Ingraham," 172; Molly Vaughn to Sister, June 15, 1864, Wilson and Hairston Family Papers, 1751–1928, folder 10, 04134, SHC; and Louisa Lovell to Joseph Lovell, September 26, 1864, Quitman Family Papers, folder 113, SHC.

54. Rankin County Citizens to Charles Clark, October 6, 1864, Robert S. Hudson to Charles Clark, October 6, 1864, Charles Clark Correspondence, box 950, MDAH.

55. Darst, "The Vicksburg Diary of Mrs. Alfred Ingraham," 173–74.

56. Frankel, *Freedom's Women*, 21–22. On the importance of mother-child family relations among slaves, see Gutman, *The Black Family in Slavery and Freedom*; and Lynn Kennedy, *Born Southern: Childhood, Motherhood, and Social Networks in the Old South* (Baltimore: Johns Hopkins University Press, 2010).

57. Franklin and Schweninger, *Runaway Slaves*, 80; and Alex Lichtenstein, "'That Disposition to Theft, with Which They Have Been Branded': Moral Economy, Slave Management, and the Law," *Journal of Social History* 21 (Spring 1988): 413–40.

58. Samuel Andrew Agnew Diary, March 4, 1864, transcript of manuscript no. 923, *Documenting the American South*, at http://docsouth.unc.edu/imls/agnew/agnew.html, accessed August 20, 2009; Elizabeth Christie Brown Diary, August 9, 15, 1863, UMASC; Cotton, *From the Pen of a She-Rebel*, 42; Darst, "The Vicksburg Diary of Mrs. Alfred Ingraham," 168, 172, 177; Diary of Jason Niles, January 2, 1862, transcript of manuscript no. 950, *Documenting the American South*, at http://docsouth.unc.edu/imls/niles/niles.html, accessed August 5, 2009; and Testimony of John Eaton, General Superintendent of the Freedmen, Department of the Tennessee, April 29, 1863, 15, Letters Received by the Office of the Adjunct General, 1861–1870 (hereafter cited as LROAD), Preliminary and Final Reports, Transcripts of Proceedings and of Testimony Taken, and Other Records of the American Freedmen's Inquiry Commission, 1863–1864, roll 200, O-328, Record Group 94, NARA.

59. Exceptions to this conclusion include Michael Fitzgerald, *Urban Emancipation: Popular Politics in Reconstruction Mobile, 1860–1890* (Baton Rouge: Louisiana State University Press, 2002); and Schermerhorn, *Money over Mastery*.

60. Stephen V. Ash, *The Black Experience in the Civil War South* (Santa Barbara, CA: Praeger, 2010), 78; and Currie, *Enclave*, 83–95.

61. James Hawley to Samuel Thomas, January 10, 1866, Samuel Thomas to O. O. Howard, September 19, 1865, in Steven Hahn, Steven F. Miller, Susan E. O'Donovan, John C. Rodrigue, and Leslie S. Rowland, eds., *Land and Labor, 1865*, ser. 3, vol. 1, of *Freedom: A Documentary*

History of Emancipation, 1861–1867 (Chapel Hill: University of North Carolina Press, 2008), 742–45, 989–90.

62. The population of urban slaves represented a small 4.1 percent out of the total slave population of 3,953,760 living in the South in 1860; see Jane Riblett Wilkie, "The Black Urban Population of the Pre–Civil War South," *Phylon* 37 (Third Quarter 1976): 253; and Wagner et al., *The Library of Congress Civil War Desk Reference*, 70–71. On slave property ownership, see Philip D. Morgan, "The Ownership of Property by Slaves in the Mid-Nineteenth-Century Low Country," *Journal of Southern History* 49 (August 1983): 399–420; Schweninger, *Black Property Owners*; Ira Berlin and Philip D. Morgan, eds., *The Slaves' Economy: Independent Production by Slaves in the Americas* (London: Frank Cass, 1991); Betty Wood, *Women's Work, Men's Work: The Informal Slave Economies of Lowcountry Georgia* (Athens: University of Georgia Press, 1995); and Dylan Penningroth, *The Claims of Kinfolk: African American Property and Community in the Nineteenth-Century South* (Chapel Hill: University of North Carolina Press, 2003).

63. Whittington B. Johnson, *Black Savannah, 1788–1864* (Fayetteville: University of Arkansas Press, 1996), 86; Bobby L. Lovett, *The African-American History of Nashville, Tennessee, 1780–1930* (Fayetteville: University of Arkansas Press, 1999), 54; and Wilkie, "The Black Urban Population of the Pre–Civil War South," 262. The classic study of urban slavery and the quasi-freedom it provided is Richard C. Wade, *Slavery in the Cities: The South, 1820–1860* (New York: Oxford University Press, 1964). For studies focusing on slavery in specific Southern cities, which also emphasize the quasi-freedom of urban black life before, during, and after the Civil War, see John W. Blassingame, *Black New Orleans* (Chicago: University of Chicago Press, 1973); Wilbert L. Jenkins, *Seizing the New Day: African Americans in Post-Civil War Charleston* (Bloomington: Indiana University Press, 1998); Steven Elliott Tripp, *Yankee Town, Southern City: Race and Class Relations in Civil War Lynchburg* (New York: New York University Press, 1997); Midori Takagi, *"Rearing Wolves to Our Own Destruction": Slavery in Richmond, Virginia, 1782–1865* (Charlottesville: University of Virginia Press, 1999); and Richard Paul Fuke, *Imperfect Equality: African Americans and the Confines of White Racial Attitudes in Post-Emancipation Maryland* (Bronx: Fordham University Press, 1999).

64. Susanna Michele Lee, *Claiming the Union: Citizenship in the Post–Civil War South* (New York: Cambridge University Press, 2014), 90.

65. Ibid., 93.

66. On the importance slaves placed on personal property, see Dylan Penningroth, "Slavery, Freedom, and Social Claims to Property among African Americans in Liberty County, Georgia, 1850–1880," *Journal of American History* 84 (September 1997): 405–35.

67. Statement of George Winter, July 23, 1873, Statement of Samuel Brown, July 26, 1873, Commissioner's Remarks on George Winter, August 2, 1873, in Claim of George Winter, December 5, 1877, Madison County, Mississippi, claim 18415, RG 217, SCC; Statement of Martha Patton, October 24, 1874, Claim of Martha Patton, December 20, 1875, claim 16720, SCC; and Statement of Maria Carter, Statement of Louis Williams, March 9, 1875, Claim of Maria Carter, December 5, 1877, claim 11986, SCC.

68. Statement of Claims Commissioner for Richard Dorsey Claim, June 19, 1874, Statement of Richard Dorsey, Statement of James Hyman, September 25, 1873, Statement of James Hyman, September 25, 1873, Claim of Richard Dorsey, December, 1874, claim 4337, SCC; and Statement of Nelson Findley, Claim of Nelson Findley, December 20, 1875, claim 16219, SCC.

69. Statement of Henry Banks, June 24, 1873, Claim of Henry Banks, December, 1874, claim 14443, SCC.

70. Little has been written about Mississippi's Gulf Coast black and white Creole populations. For a general history of the region, with some discussion of its ethnic groups, see Cyril Edward Cain, ed., *Four Centuries on the Pascagoula*, 2 vols. (1953; repr., Spartanburg, SC: Reprint Company, 1983). On French and Spanish settlement in Mississippi, see Celest Ray, "European Mississippians," in *Ethnic Heritage in Mississippi: The Twentieth Century*, ed. Shana Walton and Barbara Carpenter (Jackson: University Press of Mississippi, 2012), 32–74. Another study that discusses the region's ethnic background is Edmond Boudreaux, *The Seafood Capital of the World: Biloxi's Maritime History* (Charleston, SC: History Press, 2011). On black Creoles in neighboring Louisiana, see Carl A. Brasseaux, Keith P. Fontenot, and Claude F. Oubre, *Creoles of Color in the Bayou Country* (Jackson: University Press of Mississippi, 1994).

71. Statement of Severin Boudreaux, Statement of Adolph Krebs, Statement of Alfred Henry, March 7, 1874, Claim Commissioner's Remarks Regarding Claim of Severin Boudreaux, March, 1874, Claim of Severin Boudreaux, December, 1874, claim 8644, SCC.

72. *OR*, ser. 1, vol. 31, pt. 3, 880; *OR*, ser. 1, vol. 17, pt. 2, 21; and Charles H. Abbott to John H. Rawlins, March 26, 1863, Affidavit of Jack, September 13, 1864, in Berlin et al., *The Destruction of Slavery*, 302–3, 325–26.

73. Louisa T. Lovell to Joseph Lovell, February 7, 1864, Quitman Family Papers, folder 112, SHC; S. N. Gilman to Jailer at Jackson, December 29, 1863, John J. Pettus Correspondence, roll 2812, MDAH; and M. Carrigan to John Pemberton, May 12, 1863, John C. Pemberton Papers, folder 2, box 6, NARA.

74. Gary W. Gallagher, *The Union War* (Cambridge, MA: Harvard University Press, 2011), 146n; and Smith, *Mississippi in the Civil War*, 153–55.

75. Elizabeth Christie Brown Diary, August 12, 1863, UMASC; William R. Sively to Jane Sively, December 9, 1863, Jane Sively Letters, folder 1, SHC; McPherson, *Battle Cry of Freedom*, 748; and Samuel Andrew Agnew Diary, June 11, 13, 1864, *Documenting the American South*. On Confederates' "no quarter" approach to black Union troops, see George S. Burkhardt, *Confederate Rage, Yankee Wrath: No Quarter in the Civil War* (Carbondale: Southern Illinois University Press, 2007); Gregory J. W. Urwin, ed., *Black Flag over Dixie: Racial Atrocities and Reprisals in the Civil War* (Carbondale: Southern Illinois University Press, 2004); Richard Slotkin, *No Quarter: The Battle of the Crater, 1864* (New York: Random House, 2009); and Kevin M. Levin, *Remembering the Battle of the Crater: War as Murder* (Lexington: University Press of Kentucky, 2012).

76. Testimony of General James Wadsworth, April 1863, 57, 69–70, roll 200, LROAD.

77. Affidavits of Nat Green, October 9, Betsey Robinson, August 3, Harriet Kilgore, December 4, 1865, in Hahn et al., *Land and Labor*, 326, 150, 168–69.

78. A. Murdock to Samuel Thomas, July 17, 1865, in Hahn et al., *Land and Labor*, 513–14; and Sharon Ann Holt, "Symbol, Memory, and Service: Resistance and Family Formation in Nineteenth-Century African America," in *Working toward Freedom: Slave Society and Domestic Economy in the American South*, ed. Larry E. Hudson Jr. (Rochester, NY: University of Rochester Press, 1994), 195.

79. Affidavit of Dabney, August 12, Affidavit of Henry Morris, November 16, 1865, in Hahn et al., *Land and Labor*, 585–86, 756–57.

80. James A. Hawley to Samuel Thomas, July 4, 1865, in Hahn et al., *Land and Labor*, 110, 113, 119.

81. Circular by the Mississippi Freedmen's Bureau Assistant Commissioner, August 4, H. R. Brinkerhoff to O. O. Howard, July 8, 1865, in Hahn et al., *Land and Labor*, 152–55, 617–19.

CONCLUSION

1. James F. Trotter Paper, 1866, 00930-z, SHC; and James L. Alcorn to Wife, August 26, 1865, James Lusk Alcorn Papers, 1850–1949, folder 4, 00005-z, SHC.

2. Foner, *Reconstruction*, 298.

3. Wynne, *Mississippi's Civil War*, 169–77.

4. Ibid., 180; and Harris, *Presidential Reconstruction in Mississippi*, 43, 61–62.

5. Wynne, *Mississippi's Civil War*, 180; Harris, *Presidential Reconstruction in Mississippi*, 121–40; and Currie, "From Slavery to Freedom in Mississippi's Legal System," 112–25, quotation on 112.

6. Currie, "From Slavery to Freedom in Mississippi's Legal System," 119.

7. Steven Hahn, "'Extravagant Expectations of Freedom': Rumour, Political Struggle, and the Christmas Insurrection Scare of 1865 in the American South," *Past and Present* 157 (November 1997): 122–23, 138–39; and Stephen Nissenbaum, *The Battle for Christmas: A Cultural History of America's Most Cherished Holiday* (New York: Vintage Books, 1996), 268, 279–97, quotation on 293.

8. Kidada E. Williams, *They Left Great Marks on Me: African American Testimonies of Racial Violence from Emancipation to World War I* (New York: New York University Press, 2012), 19, 4–5. For more on the pervasiveness of white on black violence in the Reconstruction South, see Allen W. Trelease, *White Terror: The Ku Klux Klan Conspiracy and Southern Reconstruction* (New York: Harper and Row, 1971); Mary Ellison, *The Black Experience: American Blacks since 1865* (London: B. T. Batsford, 1974); George Rable, *But There Was No Peace: The Role of Violence in the Politics of Reconstruction* (Athens: University of Georgia Press, 1984); Robert Shapiro, *White Violence and Black Response: From Reconstruction to Montgomery* (Amherst: University of Massachusetts Press, 1988); Donald G. Nieman, ed., *Black Freedom, White Violence: 1865–1900* (New York: Garland, 1994); Stetson Kennedy, *After Appomattox: How the South Won the War* (Gainesville: University Press of Florida, 1995); John C. Willis, *Forgotten Time: The Yazoo-Mississippi Delta after the Civil War* (Charlottesville: University of Virginia Press, 2000); and Rosen, *Terror in the Heart of Freedom*.

9. Mark Wahlgren Summers, *A Dangerous Stir: Fear, Paranoia, and the Making of Reconstruction* (Chapel Hill: University of North Carolina Press, 2009), 49–68, quotations on 50, 55.

10. William L. Sharkey to O. O. Howard, October 10, Samuel Thomas to O. O. Howard, November 2, 1865, in Hahn et al., *Land and Labor*, 814–15, 816–19.

11. F. Marion Shields to Andrew Johnson, October 25, William T. Martin to B. G. Humphreys, October 27, 1865, in Hahn et al., *Land and Labor*, 821–22, 823–24.

12. James H. Mathews to George D. Reynolds, November 27, 1865, in Hahn et al., *Land and Labor*, 850–52.

13. Adam Kemper to James H. Mathews, December 9, 1865, in Hahn et al., *Land and Labor*, 852.

14. Adam Kemper to James H. Mathews, December 9, 1865, Affidavit of George Lanier, November 25, 1865, Statement of William Head, November 21, 1865, in Hahn et al., *Land and Labor*, 852, 936–37, 722–23.

15. Resolutions of a Meeting of Colored Citizens of Vicksburg, October 30, 1865, in Hahn et al., *Land and Labor*, 817–18.

16. Claiborne County Mississippi Freed People to the Governor of Mississippi, December 3, 1865, in Hahn et al., *Land and Labor*, 856–57.

17. Paul D. Lack, "An Urban Slave Community: Little Rock, 1831–1862," *Arkansas Historical Quarterly* 41 (Autumn 1982): 271–72; Johnson, *Black Savannah*, 6, 162–68; and Takagi, *Rearing Wolves to Our Own Destruction*, 2–6, 146.

18. Thomas J. Wood to B. G. Humphreys, November 28, 1865, George D. Reynolds to Charles A. Gilchrist, November 20, 1865, Benjamin G. Humphreys to Thomas J. Wood, December 2, 1865, in Hahn et al., *Land and Labor*, 825–26, 829, 826–28.

19. Thomas J. Wood to William D. Whipple, December 3, 1865, Edwin M. Stanton to George H. Thomas, December 13, 1865, in Hahn et al., *Land and Labor*, 830–32; and Harris, *Presidential Reconstruction in Mississippi*, 147–48.

20. Dan T. Carter, "The Anatomy of Fear: The Christmas Day Insurrection Scare of 1865," *Journal of Southern History* 42 (August 1976): 364; Summers, *A Dangerous Stir*, 59; and Hahn, "Extravagant Expectations of Freedom," 123–26, 132, 158.

21. Hahn, "Extravagant Expectations of Freedom," 146; and Summers, *A Dangerous Stir*, 61–62, 66.

22. Samuel Thomas to O. O. Howard, December 13, 1865, Letters Sent, Records of the Assistant Commissioner for the State of Mississippi, Bureau of Refugees, Freedmen, and Abandoned Lands, 1865–1869, roll 1, M-826, Record Group 105, NARA.

23. Edward Hatch to W. D. Whipple, June 22, 1865, in Hahn et al., *Land and Labor*, 225–28.

24. See Charles Reagan Wilson, *Baptized in Blood: The Religion of the Lost Cause, 1865–1920* (Athens: University of Georgia Press, 1980); Rubin, *A Shattered Nation*, 141–201; and Anne Elizabeth Marshall, *Creating a Confederate Kentucky: The Lost Cause and Civil War Memory in a Border State* (Chapel Hill: University of North Carolina Press, 2010).

25. Christopher Waldrep, *Vicksburg's Long Shadow: The Civil War Legacy of Race and Remembrance* (Lanham, MD: Rowman and Littlefield, 2005), 67; and Townsend, *Yankee Warhorse*, 197–98. On differing interpretations of the Civil War's legacy, see also David W. Blight, *Race and Reunion: The Civil War in American Memory* (Cambridge, MA: Harvard University Press, 2001); and Bruce E. Baker, *What Reconstruction Meant: Historical Memory in the American South* (Charlottesville: University of Virginia Press, 2007).

26. Michael W. Fitzgerald, *Splendid Failure: Postwar Reconstruction in the American South* (Chicago: Ivan L. Dee, 2007); and Foner, *Reconstruction*.

BIBLIOGRAPHY

PRIMARY SOURCES: MANUSCRIPT COLLECTIONS

Louisiana State University Special Collections, Hill Memorial Library, Baton Rouge
Eggleston-Roach Papers

Mississippi Department of Archives and History, Jackson, Mississippi
Alcorn, James Lusk, Diary
Alcorn, James Lusk, and Family, Papers
Black, Narcissa L., Diaries
Clark, Charles, Correspondence and Papers, 1863–1865
Confederate Post Commissary Invoice and Discharge Book
Downs, Lettie, Collection
Foster, Catherine (Kate), Diary
Moore, Samuel Blanche, Letters
Pettus, John J., Correspondence and Papers, 1859–1863
Rainwater, Percy Lee, Collection
Substitution and Desertion Records, Receipts for Deserters from the Army Arrested by the
    Sheriff of Chickasaw County, 1863–1864

Archives and Special Collections, J. D. Williams Library, University of Mississippi,
    Oxford
Bigger, J. A., Diary
Brown, Elizabeth Christie, Diary
Brown, Juanita, Collection
Clark, Thomas, Collection
Crenshaw, R. F., Letter
Longstreet-Hinton Collection
Miller Family Papers
Nunnally Dean, Charles, Jr., Memorial Collection
Oxford, Mississippi, Report from General Grant's Army Camp, 1862
Street, George M., Collections
Walter, H. W., Papers
West, Absalom, Collection

Southern Historical Collection, University of North Carolina at Chapel Hill

Alcorn, James Lusk, Papers
Allen, James and Charles B., Papers
Bailey, John Lancaster, Papers
Baker, Everard Green, Papers
Barringer, Daniel Moreau, Papers
Blackwell, Margaret E., Papers
Bullock and Hamilton Family Papers
Burton, Thomas W., Papers
Couper Family Papers
Dixon, Harry St. John, Papers
Howe, Chiliab Smith, Papers
Hughes Family Papers
Leak, Francis Terry, Papers
Norton, Chilton, and Dameron Family Papers
Quitman Family Papers
Roach and Eggleston Family Papers
Sargent, George Washington, Papers
Simpson and Brumby Family Papers
Sively, Jane, Letters
Southall and Bowen Family Papers
Thomson, Ruffin, Papers
Trotter, James F., Paper
Whitmore, Charles, Plantation Journal
Wilson and Hairston Family Papers
Worthington, Amanda Dougherty, Papers
Wyche and Otey Family Papers

National Archives and Records Administration, Washington, DC, and College Park, Maryland

RG 94: Letters Received by the Office of the Adjunct General, 1861–1870, Preliminary and Final Reports, Transcripts of Proceedings and of Testimony Taken, and Other Records of the American Freedmen's Inquiry Commission, 1863–1864
RG 105: Records of the Mississippi Freedmen's Department ("Pre-Bureau Records"), Office of the Assistant Commissioner, Records of the Bureau of Refugees, Freedmen, and Abandoned Lands, 1863–1865, Letters Sent, Records of the Assistant Commissioner for the State of Mississippi, Bureau of Refugees, Freedmen, and Abandoned Lands
RG 109: War Department Collection of Confederate Records, Deserters, Misc. Records
Manuscripts, 1861–1865
Letters Received by the Confederate Secretary of War
Pemberton, John C., Papers
Union Provost Marshal's File of Papers Relating to Two or More Civilians
RG 366: Records of Civil War Special Agencies of the Treasury Department
Applications, Bonds, and Authorities to Purchase and Transport Products, Districts in Mississippi
Authority to Establish Trade Store Permits, Natchez
Contracts and Affidavits to Establish Supply Stores, Etc., 1864, Office of the General Agent

Correspondence Received by the Assistant Special Agent, Memphis
Correspondence Received by the Assistant Treasury Agent, Vicksburg District
Second Special Agency Records, Treasury Papers
Second Special Agency Records, Vicksburg District
Trade Store Permits, 1863–1864, Vicksburg District
Trade Store Permits, 1864, Natchez District
RG 393: Records of the US Army Continental Commands
Records of the Provost Marshal General

DIGITAL MANUSCRIPT COLLECTIONS

Civil War: Context and Conflict, Digital Collections, Louisiana State University Special
   Collections, Louisiana State University Libraries, Baton Rouge
Snyder, Alonzo, Papers

Intellectual Underpinnings of the American Civil War, Digital Collections, Manuscripts
   Division, Special Collections Department, Mississippi State University Libraries,
   Starkville
Hays-Ray-Webb Collection
Hobbs Family Papers
Oakley Papers

Documenting the American South, Digital Collection, The Southern Homefront,
   1861–1865, University of North Carolina at Chapel Hill
Agnew, Samuel Andrew, Diary
Niles, Jason, Diary
Brown, Albert Gallatin, "State of the Country" speech
DeBow, J. D. B., "Report on the Condition of Government Cotton, Contiguous to the
   Mississippi and Its Tributaries"
*Journal of the House of Representatives of the State of Mississippi, December Session of 1862
   and November Session of 1863*
*Journal of the House of Representatives of the State of Mississippi, Called Session, at Macon,
   August 1864*
Proceedings of the Mississippi State Convention, 1861

Digital Collections, Civil War Archive, J. D. Williams Library, University of Mississippi,
   Oxford
Clark Family Letters
Gerdine, Roxana Chapin, Collection
Little, J. J., Collection
Nelson, William Cowper, Collection
Ward, Rufus, Collection

DIGITAL DATABASES

Born in Slavery: Slave Narratives from the Federal Writers' Project, 1936–1938. American
   Memory. Manuscript Division, Library of Congress, Washington DC. At http://memo

ry.loc.gov/cgi-bin/ampage?collId=mesn&fileName=090/mesn090.db&recNum=138&i
temLink=D?mesnbib:29:./temp/~ammem_1ajQ.

Historical Data Systems Compilation. US Civil War Soldier Records and Profiles. Ancestry
.com. At http://search.ancestry.com/search/db.aspx?dbid=1555.

Mississippi Slave Narratives from the WPA Records. MSGenWeb Special Projects, Library
Project. At http://msgw.org/slaves/henderson-xslave.htm.

US Bureau of the Census. Eighth Census of the United States, 1860. Schedule 1 (Free
Inhabitants). Ancestry.com. At http://search.ancestry.com/search/db.aspx?dbid=7667.

———. Eighth Census of the United States, 1860. Slave Schedules. Ancestry.com. At http://
search.ancestry.com/search/db.aspx?dbid=7668.

US Southern Claims Commission. Approved Claims, 1871–1880: Mississippi, RG217,
National Archives and Records Administration, Civil War Collection, Southern
Claims Commission. Fold3.com. At http://www.fold3.com/title_473/southern_claims
_commission_approved_claims/.

———. Disallowed and Barred Claims, 1871–1880: Mississippi, RG 233, National Archives
and Records Administration, Civil War Collection, Southern Claims Commission.
Fold3.com. At http://www.fold3.com/title_12/southern_claims_commission/.

GOVERNMENT DOCUMENTS

Chase, Salmon P. *United States Treasury Department Rules Concerning Commercial
Intercourse with and in States Declared in Insurrection, and the Collection of Abandoned
and Captured Property.* Washington, DC: Government Printing Office, 1863.

US War Department. *The War of the Rebellion: A Compilation of the Official Records of the
Union and Confederate Armies.* 128 vols. Washington, DC: Government Printing Office,
1880–1891.

———. *The War of the Rebellion: A Compilation of the Official Records of the Union and
Confederate Navies.* 30 vols. Washington, DC: Government Printing Office, 1894–1922.

NEWSPAPERS

American Citizen (Canton, MS)
Beacon (Macon, MS)
Daily Clarion (Meridian, MS)
Daily Evening Citizen (Vicksburg)
Daily Mississippian (Jackson)
Daily Southern Crisis (Jackson)
Daily Vicksburg Whig
Eastern Clarion (Paulding, MS)
Natchez Daily Free Trader
Republican (Woodville, MS)
Semi-Weekly Mississippian (Jackson)
Vicksburg Sun
Weekly Courier (Natchez)
Weekly Mississippian (Jackson)
Weekly Panola (MS) Star

PUBLISHED PRIMARY SOURCES

Aughey, John Hill. *Tupelo*. Lincoln, NE: State Journal Company, 1888.

Barde, Alexandre. *The Vigilante Committees of the Attakapas: An Eyewitness Account of Banditry and Backlash in Southwestern Louisiana*. Edited by David C. Edmonds and Dennis A. Gibson. Translated by Henrietta Guilbeau Rogers. Lafayette, LA: Acadiana Press, 1981.

Beaumont, Betty Bentley. *Twelve Years of My Life: An Autobiography*. Philadelphia: T. B. Peterson and Brothers, 1887.

Berlin, Ira, Barbara J. Fields, Thavolia Glymph, Joseph P. Reidy, and Leslie S. Rowland, eds. *The Destruction of Slavery*. Ser. 1, vol. 1, of *Freedom: A Documentary History of Emancipation, 1861–1867*. New York: Cambridge University Press, 1985.

Bettersworth, John K., ed. *Mississippi in the Confederacy: As They Saw It*. 2 vols. 1961. Reprint, New York: Kraus Reprint Company, 1970.

———, ed. "Mississippi Unionism: The Case of the Reverend James A. Lyon." *Journal of Mississippi History* 1 (January 1939): 37–52.

Bunkers, Suzanne L., ed. *The Diary of Caroline Seabury, 1854–1863*. Madison: University of Wisconsin Press, 1991.

Cash, William M., and Lucy Somerville Howorth, eds. *My Dear Nellie: The Civil War Letters of William L. Nugent to Eleanor Smith Nugent*. Jackson: University Press of Mississippi, 1977.

Cockrell, Thomas D., and Michael B. Ballard, eds. *Chickasaw, a Mississippi Scout for the Union: The Civil War Memoir of Levi H. Naron*. Baton Rouge: Louisiana State University Press, 2005.

Cotton, Gordon A., ed. *From the Pen of a She-Rebel: The Civil War Diary of Emilie Riley McKinley*. Columbia: University of South Carolina Press, 2001.

Crist, Lynda Lasswell, Mary Seaton Dix, and Kenneth H. Williams, eds. *The Papers of Jefferson Davis*. 13 vols. to date. Baton Rouge: Louisiana State University Press, 1971–2012.

Darst, W. Maury, ed. "The Vicksburg Diary of Mrs. Alfred Ingraham, May 2–June 13, 1863." *Journal of Mississippi History* 44 (February–November 1982): 148–79.

Galbraith, William and Loretta, eds. *A Lost Heroine of the Confederacy: The Diaries and Letters of Belle Edmondson*. Jackson: University of Mississippi Press, 1990.

Hahn, Steven, Steven F. Miller, Susan E. O'Donovan, John C. Rodrigue, and Leslie S. Rowlan, eds. *Land and Labor, 1865*. Ser. 3, vol. 1, of *Freedom: A Documentary History of Emancipation, 1861–1867*. Chapel Hill: University of North Carolina Press, 2008.

Rainwater, Percy Lee, ed. "Letters of James Lusk Alcorn." *Journal of Southern History* 3 (May 1937): 196–209.

Robins, Glenn, ed. "Inside the Mind of Johnny Reb: The Civil War Letters of John Cato." *Journal of Mississippi History* 64 (Spring 2002): 33–45.

Sabin, Edwin L. "Vicksburg, and After: Being the Experience of a Southern Merchant and Non-Combatant during the Sixties." *Sewanee Review* 15 (October 1907): 485–96.

Silver, James W., ed. "The Breakdown of Morale in Central Mississippi in 1864: Letters of Judge Robert S. Hudson." *Journal of Mississippi History* 16 (April 1964): 99–120.

Wood, John W. *Union and Secession in Mississippi*. Memphis: Saunders, Parish and Whitmore, 1863.

SECONDARY SOURCES: BOOKS

Allardice, Bruce S. *More Generals in Gray*. Baton Rouge: Louisiana State University Press, 1995.

Andrew, Rod, Jr. "The Essential Nationalism of the People: Georgia's Confederate Congressional Election of 1863." In *Inside the Confederate Nation: Essays in Honor of Emory M. Thomas*, edited by Lesley J. Gordon and John C. Inscoe, 128–47. Baton Rouge: Louisiana State University Press, 2005.

Aptheker, Herbert. *American Negro Slave Revolts*. 1943. Reprint, New York: International Publishers, 1993.

Ash, Stephen V. *The Black Experience in the Civil War South*. Santa Barbara, CA: Praeger, 2010.

———. *When the Yankees Came: Conflict and Chaos in the Occupied South, 1861–1865*. Chapel Hill: University of North Carolina Press, 1995.

Ayers, Edward L. *Vengeance and Justice: Crime and Punishment in the Nineteenth-Century American South*. New York: Oxford University Press, 1984.

Bailey, Anne J. *Invisible Southerners: Ethnicity in the Civil War*. Athens: University of Georgia Press, 2006.

Baker, Bruce E. *What Reconstruction Meant: Historical Memory in the American South*. Charlottesville: University of Virginia Press, 2007.

Ballard, Michael B. *The Civil War in Mississippi: Major Campaigns and Battles*. Jackson: University Press of Mississippi, 2011.

———. *Vicksburg: The Campaign That Opened the Mississippi*. Chapel Hill: University of North Carolina Press, 2004.

Barnes, L. Diane. *Artisan Workers in the Upper South: Petersburg, Virginia, 1820–1865*. Baton Rouge: Louisiana State University Press, 2009.

Barney, William L. *The Secessionist Impulse: Alabama and Mississippi in 1860*. Tuscaloosa: University of Alabama Press, 1974.

Behrend, Justin J. *Reconstructing Democracy: Grassroots Black Politics in the Deep South after the Civil War*. Athens: University of Georgia Press, 2015.

Bensel, Richard Franklin. *The American Ballot Box in the Mid-Nineteenth Century*. New York: Cambridge University Press, 2004.

———. *Yankee Leviathan: The Origins of Central State Authority in America, 1859–1877*. Cambridge: Cambridge University Press, 1990.

Bercaw, Nancy. *Gendered Freedoms: Race, Rights, and the Politics of Household in the Delta,1861–1875*. Gainesville: University Press of Florida, 2003.

Beringer, Richard E., Herman Hattaway, Archer Jones, and William N. Still Jr. *Why the South Lost the Civil War*. Athens: University of Georgia Press, 1986.

Berlin, Ira, and Philip D. Morgan, eds. *The Slaves' Economy: Independent Production by Slaves in the Americas*. London: Frank Cass, 1991.

Berlin, Jean V. "Did Confederate Women Lose the War? Deprivation, Destruction, and Despair on the Home Front." In *The Collapse of the Confederacy*, edited by Mark Grimsley and Brooks D. Simpson, 168–94. Lincoln: University of Nebraska Press, 2001.

Bernath, Michael T. *Confederate Minds: The Struggle for Intellectual Independence in the Civil War South*. Chapel Hill: University of North Carolina Press, 2010.

Bettersworth, John K. *Confederate Mississippi: The People and Politics of a Cotton State in Wartime*. 1943. Reprint, Philadelphia: Porcupine Press, 1978.

Binnington, Ian. *Confederate Visions: Nationalism, Symbolism, and the Imagined South in the Civil War*. Charlottesville: University of Virginia Press, 2013.

Blair, William A. *Virginia's Private War: Feeding Body and Soul in the Confederacy, 1861–1865*. New York: Oxford University Press, 1998.

———. *With Malice toward Some: Treason and Loyalty in the Civil War Era*. Chapel Hill: University of North Carolina Press, 2014.

Blassingame, John W. *Black New Orleans*. Chicago: University of Chicago Press, 1973.

———. *The Slave Community: Plantation Life in the Antebellum South*. 1972. Reprint, New York: Oxford University Press, 1979.

Blauner, Bob. *Resisting McCarthyism: To Sign or Not to Sign California's Loyalty Oath*. Stanford, CA: Stanford University Press, 2009.

Blight, David W. *Race and Reunion: The Civil War in American Memory*. Cambridge, MA: Harvard University Press, 2001.

Blum, Edward J. *Reforging the White Republic: Race, Religion, and American Nationalism, 1865–1898*. Baton Rouge: Louisiana State University Press, 2005.

Bohannon, Keith S. "'Witness the Redemption of the Army': Reenlistments in the Confederate Army of Tennessee, January–March 1864." In *Inside the Confederate Nation: Essays in Honor of Emory M. Thomas*, edited by Lesley J. Gordon and John C. Inscoe, 111–28. Baton Rouge: Louisiana State University Press, 2005.

Bolton, Charles C. *Poor Whites of the Antebellum South: Tenants and Laborers in Central North Carolina and Northeast Mississippi*. Durham, NC: Duke University Press, 1994.

Bond, Bradley G. *Political Culture in the Nineteenth-Century South: Mississippi, 1830–1900*. Baton Rouge: Louisiana State University Press, 1995.

Bonner, Robert E. *Colors and Blood: Flag Passions of the Confederate South*. Princeton, NJ: Princeton University Press, 2002.

———. *Mastering America: Southern Slaveholders and the Crisis of the American Nation*. New York: Cambridge University Press, 2009.

Boritt, Gabor S., and Scott Hancock, eds. *Slavery, Resistance, Freedom*. New York: Oxford University Press, 2007.

Boudreaux, Edmond. *The Seafood Capital of the World: Biloxi's Maritime History*. Charleston, SC: History Press, 2011.

Brasseaux, Carl A., Keith P. Fontenot, and Claude F. Oubre. *Creoles of Color in the Bayou Country*. Jackson: University Press of Mississippi, 1994.

Broussard, Joyce Linda. *Stepping Lively in Place: The Not-Married, Free Women of Civil-War-Era Natchez, Mississippi*. Athens: University of Georgia Press, 2016.

Browning, Judkin. *Shifting Loyalties: The Union Occupation of Eastern North Carolina*. Chapel Hill: University of North Carolina Press, 2011.

Burke, Peter J., and Jan E. Stets. *Identity Theory*. New York: Oxford University Press, 2009.

Burkhardt, George S. *Confederate Rage, Yankee Wrath: No Quarter in the Civil War*. Carbondale: Southern Illinois University Press, 2007.

Busbee, Westley F., Jr. *Mississippi: A History*. Wheeling, IL: Harlan Davidson, 2005.

Bynum, Victoria E. *The Free State of Jones: Mississippi's Longest Civil War*. Chapel Hill: University of North Carolina Press, 2001.

———. *The Long Shadow of the Civil War: Southern Dissent and Its Legacies*. Chapel Hill: University of North Carolina Press, 2010.

———. *Unruly Women: The Politics of Social and Sexual Control in the Old South*. Chapel Hill: University of North Carolina Press, 1992.

Cain, Cyril Edward, ed. *Four Centuries on the Pascagoula*. 2 vols. 1953. Reprint, Spartanburg, SC: Reprint Company, 1983.

Camp, Stephanie H. M. *Closer to Freedom: Enslaved Women and Everyday Resistance in the Plantation South*. Chapel Hill: University of North Carolina Press, 2004.

Campbell, Jacqueline Glass. *When Sherman Marched North from the Sea: Resistance on the Confederate Home Front*. Chapel Hill: University of North Carolina Press, 2003.

Carmichael, Peter S. *The Last Generation: Young Virginians in Peace, War, and Reunion*. Chapel Hill: University of North Carolina Press, 2005.

Cecil-Fronsman, Bill. *Common Whites: Class and Culture in Antebellum North Carolina*. Lexington: University Press of Kentucky, 1992.

Channing, Steven A. *Crisis of Fear: Secession in South Carolina*. New York: W. W. Norton, 1974.

Clampitt, Bradley R. *The Confederate Heartland: Military and Civilian Morale in the Western Confederacy*. Baton Rouge: Louisiana State University Press, 2011.

Cobb, James C. *Away Down South: A History of Southern Identity*. Oxford: Oxford University Press, 2005.

Connor, James. *The Sociology of Loyalty*. New York: Springer, 2007.

Cooper, William J., Jr. *Liberty and Slavery: Southern Politics to 1860*. 1983. Reprint, Columbia: University of South Carolina Press, 2000.

———. *The South and the Politics of Slavery, 1828–1856*. Baton Rouge: Louisiana State University Press, 1978.

Crawford, Martin. *Ashe County's Civil War: Community and Society in the Appalachian South*. Charlottesville: University of Virginia Press, 2001.

Cresswell, Tim. *Place: A Short Introduction*. Malden, MA: Blackwell, 2004.

Current, Richard Nelson. *Lincoln's Loyalists: Union Soldiers from the Confederacy*. Boston: Northeastern University Press, 1992.

Currie, James T. *Enclave: Vicksburg and Her Surrounding Plantations, 1863–1870*. Jackson: University Press of Mississippi, 1980.

Cutter, Barbara. *Domestic Devils, Battlefield Angels: The Radicalism of American Womanhood, 1830–1865*. DeKalb: Northern Illinois University Press, 2003.

Davis, Ronald, L. F. *Good and Faithful Labor: From Slavery to Sharecropping in the Natchez District, 1860–1890*. Westport, CT: Greenwood Press, 1982.

Davis, William C. *Look Away! A History of the Confederate States of America*. New York: Free Press, 2002.

———. *A Way through the Wilderness: The Natchez Trace and the Civilization of the Southern Frontier*. New York: HarperCollins, 1995.

Donald, David Herbert. "Died of Democracy." In *Why the North Won the Civil War*, edited by David Herbert Donald, 81–92. 1960. Reprint, New York: Touchstone, 1996.

Du Bois, W. E. B. *Black Reconstruction in America, 1860–1880*. 1935. Reprint, New York: Frank Cass, 1966.

Dunaway, Wilma A. *Women, Work, and Family in the Antebellum Mountain South*. Cambridge: Cambridge University Press, 2008.

Duquette, Elizabeth. *Loyal Subjects: Bonds of Nation, Race, and Allegiance in Nineteenth-Century America*. Piscataway, NJ: Rutgers University Press, 2010.

Dyer, Thomas G. *Secret Yankees: The Union Circle in Confederate Atlanta*. Baltimore: Johns Hopkins University Press, 1999.

Edwards, Laura F. *Scarlett Doesn't Live Here Anymore: Southern Women in the Civil War Era.* Urbana: University of Illinois Press, 2000.

Ellison, Mary. *The Black Experience: American Blacks since 1865.* London: B. T. Batsford,1974.

Escott, Paul D. *After Secession: Jefferson Davis and the Failure of Confederate Nationalism.* Baton Rouge: Louisiana State University Press, 1978.

———. *The Confederacy: The Slaveholders' Failed Venture.* Santa Barbara, CA: Praeger, 2010.

———. *Military Necessity: Civil-Military Relations in the Confederacy.* Westport, CT: Praeger, 2006.

Faust, Drew Gilpin. *The Creation of Confederate Nationalism: Ideology and Identity in the Civil War South.* Baton Rouge: Louisiana State University Press, 1988.

———. *Mothers of Invention: Women of the Slaveholding South in the American Civil War.* Chapel Hill: University of North Carolina Press, 1996.

Fellman, Michael. *Inside War: The Guerrilla Conflict in Missouri during the American Civil War.* New York: Oxford University Press, 1989.

Fields, Barbara J. *Slavery and Freedom on the Middle Ground: Maryland during the Nineteenth Century.* New Haven, CT: Yale University Press, 1985.

Fisher, Noel C. *War at Every Door: Partisan Politics and Guerrilla Violence in East Tennessee, 1860–1869.* Chapel Hill: University of North Carolina Press, 1997.

Fitzgerald, Michael W. *Splendid Failure: Postwar Reconstruction in the American South.* Chicago: Ivan L. Dee, 2007.

———. *Urban Emancipation: Popular Politics in Reconstruction Mobile, 1860–1890.* Baton Rouge: Louisiana State University Press, 2002.

Fleche, Andre M. *The Revolution of 1861: The American Civil War in the Age of Nationalist Conflict.* Chapel Hill: University of North Carolina Press, 2011.

Fletcher, George P. *Loyalty: An Essay on the Morality of Relationships.* New York: Oxford University Press, 2003.

Foner, Eric. *Reconstruction: America's Unfinished Revolution, 1863–1877.* New York: Harper and Row, 1988.

———. *The Story of American Freedom.* New York: W. W. Norton, 1998.

Forret, Jeff. *Race Relations at the Margins: Slaves and Poor Whites in the Antebellum Southern Countryside.* Baton Rouge: Louisiana State University Press, 2006.

Fousek, John. *To Lead the Free World: American Nationalism and the Cultural Roots of the Cold War.* Chapel Hill: University of North Carolina Press, 2000.

Fox-Genovese, Elizabeth. *Within the Plantation Household: Black and White Women of the Old South.* Chapel Hill: University of North Carolina Press, 1988.

Frank, Lisa Tendrich. *The Civilian War: Confederate Women and Union Soldiers during Sherman's March.* Baton Rouge: Louisiana State University Press, 2015.

Frankel, Noralee. *Freedom's Women: Black Women and Families in Civil War Era Mississippi.* Bloomington: Indiana University Press, 1999.

Franklin, John Hope. *The Militant South, 1800–1861.* 1956. Reprint, Urbana: University of Illinois Press, 2002.

Franklin, John Hope, and Loren Schweninger. *Runaway Slaves: Rebels on the Plantation.* New York: Oxford University Press, 1999.

Franklin, V. P. *Black Self-Determination: A Cultural History of African-American Resistance.* Brooklyn: Lawrence Hill, 1984.

Fredrickson, George M. *The Black Image in the White Mind: The Debate on Afro-American Character and Destiny, 1817–1914*. 1971. Reprint, Middletown, CT: Wesleyan University Press, 1987.

Freehling, William W. *The Road to Disunion: Secessionists at Bay, 1776–1854*. New York: Oxford University Press, 1990.

———. *The Road to Disunion*. Vol. 2, *Secessionists Triumphant, 1854–1861*. New York: Oxford University Press, 2007.

———. *The South vs. the South: How Anti-Confederate Southerners Shaped the Course of the Civil War*. New York: Oxford University Press, 2001.

Frey, Sylvia R. *Water from the Rock: Black Resistance in a Revolutionary Age*. Princeton, NJ: Princeton University Press, 1991.

Fuke, Richard Paul. *Imperfect Equality: African Americans and the Confines of White Racial Attitudes in Post-Emancipation Maryland*. Bronx: Fordham University Press, 1999.

Gallagher, Gary W. *Becoming Confederates: Paths to New Loyalty*. Athens: University of Georgia Press, 2013.

———. *The Confederate War: How Popular Will, Nationalism, and Military Strategy Could Not Stave Off Defeat*. Cambridge, MA: Harvard University Press, 1997.

———. *The Union War*. Cambridge, MA: Harvard University Press, 2011.

Gellner, Ernest. *Nations and Nationalism*. 2nd ed. Oxford: Blackwell, 2006.

Genovese, Eugene D. *Roll, Jordan, Roll: The World the Slaves Made*. New York: Pantheon, 1974.

Genovese, Eugene D., and Elizabeth Fox-Genovese. *Fatal Self-Deception: Slaveholding Paternalism in the Old South*. Cambridge: Cambridge University Press, 2011.

Glatthaar, Joseph T. "Black Glory: The African-American Role in Union Victory." In *Why the Confederacy Lost*, edited by Gabor S. Boritt, 133–62. New York: Oxford University Press, 1992.

———. *General Lee's Army: From Victory to Collapse*. New York: Free Press, 2008.

———. *Soldiering in the Army of Northern Virginia: A Statistical Portrait of the Troops Who Served under Robert E. Lee*. Chapel Hill: University of North Carolina Press, 2011.

Glymph, Thavolia. *Out of the House of Bondage: The Transformation of the Plantation Household*. New York: Cambridge University Press, 2008.

Goldfield, David. *America Aflame: How the Civil War Created a Nation*. New York: Bloomsbury, 2011.

Gomez, Michael A. *Exchanging Our Country Marks: The Transformation of African Identities in the Colonial and Antebellum South*. Chapel Hill: University of North Carolina Press, 1998.

Goodspeed Brothers, eds. *Biographical and Historical Memoirs of Mississippi*. 2 vols. 1891. Reprint, Spartanburg, SC: Reprint Company, 1978.

Grimsted, David. *American Mobbing, 1828–1861: Toward Civil War*. New York: Oxford University Press, 1998.

Guibernau, Montserrat. *Nationalisms: The Nation-State and Nationalism in the Twentieth Century*. Cambridge: Polity Press, 1996.

Gutman, Herbert. *The Black Family in Slavery and Freedom, 1750–1925*. New York: Pantheon, 1976.

Hadden, Sally E. *Slave Patrols: Law and Violence in Virginia and the Carolinas*. Cambridge, MA: Harvard University Press, 2001.

Hahn, Steven. *A Nation under Our Feet: Black Political Struggles in the Rural South from Slavery to the Great Migration.* Cambridge, MA: Harvard University Press, 2003.

———. *The Political Worlds of Slavery and Freedom.* Cambridge, MA: Harvard University Press, 2009.

Harding, Vincent. *There Is a River: The Black Struggle for Freedom in America.* New York: Harcourt, Brace and Company, 1981.

Harris, William C. *Presidential Reconstruction in Mississippi.* Baton Rouge: Louisiana State University Press, 1967.

Harrison, Renee K. *Enslaved Women and the Art of Resistance in Antebellum America.* New York: Palgrave Macmillan, 2009.

Hobsbawm, Eric. *Bandits.* Rev. ed. New York: New Press, 2000.

———. *Nations and Nationalism since 1780: Programme, Myth, Reality.* New York: Cambridge University Press, 1990.

Hodes, Martha. *White Women, Black Men: Illicit Sex in the Nineteenth-Century South.* New Haven, CT: Yale University Press, 1997.

Hoffer, Peter Charles. *Cry Liberty: The Great Stono River Slave Rebellion of 1739.* New York: Oxford University Press, 2010.

Holt, Sharon Ann. "Symbol, Memory, and Service: Resistance and Family Formation in Nineteenth-Century African America." In *Working Toward Freedom: Slave Society and Domestic Economy in the American South,* edited by Larry E. Hudson Jr., 192–210. Rochester: University of Rochester Press, 1994.

Howell, H. Grady. *For Dixie Land I'll Take My Stand! A Muster Listing of All Known Mississippi Confederate Soldiers, Sailors, and Marines.* 2 vols. Madison, MS: Chickasaw Bayou Press, 1998.

Hoxie, Frederick E. *A Final Promise: The Campaign to Assimilate the Indians, 1880–1920.* Lincoln: University of Nebraska Press, 1984.

Hurt, R. Douglas. *Agriculture and the Confederacy: Policy, Productivity, and Power in the Civil War South.* Chapel Hill: University of North Carolina Press, 2015.

Hyde, Samuel C., Jr. "Plain Folk Yeomanry in the Antebellum South." In *A Companion to the American South,* edited by John B. Boles, 139–55. Malden, MA: Blackwell, 2004.

Hyman, Harold Melvin. *Era of the Oath: Northern Loyalty Tests during the Civil War and Reconstruction.* Philadelphia: University of Pennsylvania Press, 1954.

Inscoe, John C., and Gordon B. McKinney. *The Heart of Confederate Appalachia: Western North Carolina in the Civil War.* Chapel Hill: University of North Carolina Press, 2000.

Jaynes, Gerald David. *Branches without Roots: Genesis of the Black Working Class in the American South, 1862–1882.* New York: Oxford University Press, 1986.

Jenkins, Wilbert L. *Seizing the New Day: African Americans in Post–Civil War Charleston.* Bloomington: Indiana University Press, 1998.

Johnson, Walter. "Agency: A Ghost Story." In *Slavery's Ghost: The Problem of Freedom in the Age of Emancipation,* by Richard Follett, Eric Foner, and Walter Johnson, 8–30. Baltimore: Johns Hopkins University Press, 2011.

———. "The Future Store." In *The Chattel Principle: Internal Slave Trades in the Americas,* edited by Walter Johnson, 1–32. New Haven, CT: Yale University Press, 2004.

Johnson, Whittington B. *Black Savannah, 1788–1864.* Fayetteville: University of Arkansas Press, 1996.

Jordan, Winthrop D. *Tumult and Silence at Second Creek: An Inquiry into a Civil War Slave Conspiracy.* Baton Rouge: Louisiana State University Press, 1993.

Kay, Anthony E. *Joining Places: Slave Neighborhoods in the Old South*. Chapel Hill: University of North Carolina Press, 2007.

Keith, Jeanette. *Rich Man's War, Poor Man's Fight: Race, Class, and Power in the Rural South during the First World War*. Chapel Hill: University of North Carolina Press, 2004.

Keller, Simon. *The Limits of Loyalty*. Cambridge: Cambridge University Press, 2007.

Kennedy, Lynn. *Born Southern: Childhood, Motherhood, and Social Networks in the Old South*. Baltimore: Johns Hopkins University Press, 2010.

Kennedy, Stetson. *After Appomattox: How the South Won the War*. Gainesville: University Press of Florida, 1995.

Kolchin, Peter. *American Slavery: 1619–1877*. New York: Hill and Wang, 1993.

Laskin, Lisa. "'The Army Is Not Near So Much Demoralized as the Country Is': Soldiers in the Army of Northern Virginia and the Confederate Home Front." In *The View from the Ground: Experiences of Civil War Soldiers*, edited by Aaron Sheehan-Dean, 91–120. Lexington: University Press of Kentucky, 2007.

Lawler, Stephanie. *Identity: Sociological Perspectives*. Cambridge: Polity Press, 2008.

Lawson, Melinda. *Patriot Fires: Forging a New American Nationalism in the Civil War North*. Lawrence: University Press of Kansas, 2002.

Lee, Susanna Michele. *Claiming the Union: Citizenship in the Post–Civil War South*. New York: Cambridge University Press, 2014.

Levin, Kevin M. *Remembering the Battle of the Crater: War as Murder*. Lexington: University Press of Kentucky, 2012.

Levine, Bruce. *Confederate Emancipation: Southern Plans to Free and Arm Slaves during the Civil War*. New York: Oxford University Press, 2006.

Link, William A. *Roots of Secession: Slavery and Politics in Antebellum Virginia*. Chapel Hill: University of North Carolina Press, 2003.

Link, William A., and James J. Broomall. Introduction to *Rethinking American Emancipation: Legacies of Slavery and the Quest for Black Freedom*, edited by William A. Link and James J. Broomall, 1–14. Cambridge: Cambridge University Press, 2016.

———, eds. *Rethinking American Emancipation: Legacies of Slavery and the Quest for Black Freedom*. Cambridge: Cambridge University Press, 2016.

Litwack, Leon F. *Been in the Storm So Long: The Aftermath of Slavery*. New York: Alfred A. Knopf, 1979.

Lonn, Ella. *Desertion during the Civil War*. Gloucester, MA: American Historical Association, 1928.

———. *Foreigners in the Confederacy*. 1940. Reprint, n.p.: Victor A. Lonn, 1968.

Lovett, Bobby L. *The African-American History of Nashville, Tennessee, 1780–1930*. Fayetteville: University of Arkansas Press, 1999.

Mackey, Robert R. *The Uncivil War: Irregular Warfare in the Upper South, 1861–1865*. Norman: University of Oklahoma Press, 2004.

Majewski, John. *Modernizing a Slave Economy: The Economic Vision of the Confederate Nation*. Chapel Hill: University of North Carolina Press, 2009.

Manning, Chandra. *Troubled Refuge: Struggling for Freedom in the Civil War*. New York: Alfred A. Knopf, 2016.

———. *What This Cruel War Was Over: Soldiers, Slavery, and the Civil War*. New York: Vintage Books, 2007.

Marshall, Anne Elizabeth. *Creating a Confederate Kentucky: The Lost Cause and Civil War Memory in a Border State*. Chapel Hill: University of North Carolina Press, 2010.

Marszalek, John F. *Sherman: A Soldier's Passion for Order.* Carbondale: Southern Illinois University Press, 1993.

Martin, Jonathan D. *Divided Mastery: Slave Hiring in the American South.* Cambridge, MA: Harvard University Press, 2007.

Martinez, Jaime Amanda. *Confederate Slave Impressment in the Upper South.* Chapel Hill: University of North Carolina Press, 2013.

McCurry, Stephanie. *Confederate Reckoning: Power and Politics in the Civil War South.* Cambridge, MA: Harvard University Press, 2010.

McKenzie, Robert Tracy. *Lincolnites and Rebels: A Divided Town in the American Civil War.* Oxford: Oxford University Press, 2006.

McPherson, James M. *Battle Cry of Freedom: The Civil War Era.* New York: Ballantine, 1988.

———. *For Cause and Comrades: Why Men Fought in the Civil War.* New York: Oxford University Press, 1997.

Mitchell, Reid. "The Perseverance of the Soldiers." In *Why the Confederacy Lost*, edited by Gabor S. Boritt, 109–32. New York: Oxford University Press, 1992.

Morgan, Lynda J. *Known for My Work: African American Ethics from Slavery to Freedom.* Gainesville: University Press of Florida, 2016.

Morgan, Philip D. *Slave Counterpoint: Black Culture in the Eighteenth-Century Chesapeake and Lowcountry.* Chapel Hill: University of North Carolina Press, 1998.

Morris, Christopher. *Becoming Southern: The Evolution of a Way of Life, Warren County and Vicksburg, Mississippi, 1770–1860.* New York: Oxford University Press, 1995.

Muller, Eric L. *American Inquisition: The Hunt for Japanese American Disloyalty in World War II.* Chapel Hill: University of North Carolina Press, 2007.

Mullin, Gerald W. *Flight and Rebellion: Slave Resistance in Eighteenth-Century Virginia.* New York: Oxford University Press, 1974.

Mullin, Michael. *Africa in America: Slave Acculturation and Resistance in the American South and the British Caribbean, 1736–1831.* Urbana: University of Illinois Press, 1992.

Myers, Barton. *Executing Daniel Bright: Race, Loyalty, and Guerrilla Violence in a Coastal Carolina Community, 1861–1865.* Baton Rouge: Louisiana State University Press, 2009.

Nathanson, Stephen. *Patriotism, Morality, and Peace.* Lanham, MD: Rowman and Littlefield, 1993.

Neely, Mark E., Jr. *Southern Rights: Political Prisoners and the Myth of Confederate Constitutionalism.* Charlottesville: University of Virginia Press, 1999.

Nieman, Donald G., ed. *Black Freedom, White Violence: 1865–1900.* New York: Garland, 1994.

Nissenbaum, Stephen. *The Battle for Christmas: A Cultural History of America's Most Cherished Holiday.* New York: Vintage Books, 1996.

Noe, Kenneth W. *Reluctant Rebels: The Confederates Who Joined the Army after 1861.* Chapel Hill: University of North Carolina Press, 2010.

North, Douglass C., John Joseph Wallis, and Barry R. Weingast. *Violence and Social Orders: A Conceptual Framework for Interpreting Recorded Human History.* New York: Cambridge University Press, 2009.

Oakes, James. *Slavery and Freedom: An Interpretation of the Old South.* New York: Alfred A. Knopf, 1990.

O'Brian, Sean Michael. *Mountain Partisans: Guerrilla Warfare in the Southern Appalachians, 1861–1865.* Westport, CT: Praeger, 1999.

Olsen, Christopher J. *Political Culture and Secession in Mississippi: Masculinity, Honor, and the Antiparty Tradition, 1830–1860.* New York: Oxford University Press, 2000.

Onuf, Nicholas, and Peter Onuf. *Nations, Markets, and War: Modern History and the American Civil War*. Charlottesville: University of Virginia Press, 2006.

Ostler, Jeffrey. *The Plains Sioux and U.S. Colonialism from Lewis and Clark to Wounded Knee*. Cambridge: Cambridge University Press, 2004.

Ott, Victoria E. *Confederate Daughters: Coming of Age during the Civil War*. Carbondale: Southern Illinois University Press, 2008.

Owens, Leslie Howard. *This Species of Property: Slave Life and Culture in the Old South*. New York: Oxford University Press, 1976.

Owsley, Frank L. *Plain Folk of the Old South*. 1949. Reprint, Chicago: Quadrangle, 1961.

Penningroth, Dylan. *The Claims of Kinfolk: African American Property and Community in the Nineteenth-Century South*. Chapel Hill: University of North Carolina Press, 2003.

Pereyra, Lilian A. *James Lusk Alcorn: Persistent Whig*. Baton Rouge: Louisiana State University Press, 1966.

Perman, Michael. *Reunion without Compromise: The South and Reconstruction, 1865–1868*. New York: Cambridge University Press, 1973.

Phillips, Jason. *Diehard Rebels: The Confederate Culture of Invincibility*. Athens: University of Georgia Press, 2007.

Powell, Lawrence N., and Michael S. Wayne. "Self-Interest and the Decline of Confederate Nationalism." In *The Old South in the Crucible of War*, edited by Harry P. Owens and James J. Cooke, 29–45. Jackson: University Press of Mississippi, 1983.

Quigley, Paul. *Shifting Grounds: Nationalism and the American South, 1848–1865*. New York: Oxford University Press, 2012.

Rable, George C. *But There Was No Peace: The Role of Violence in the Politics of Reconstruction*. Athens: University of Georgia Press, 1984.

———. *Civil Wars: Women and the Crisis of Southern Nationalism*. Urbana: University of Illinois Press, 1989.

Raboteau, Albert J. *Slave Religion: The "Invisible Institution" in the Antebellum South*. New York: Oxford University Press, 2004.

Radley, Kenneth. *Rebel Watchdog: The Confederate States Army Provost Guard*. Baton Rouge: Louisiana State University Press, 1989.

Rainwater, Percy Lee. *Mississippi: Storm Center of Secession, 1856–1861*. Baton Rouge: Otto Claitor, 1938.

Ray, Celest. "European Mississippians." In *Ethnic Heritage in Mississippi: The Twentieth Century*, edited by Shana Walton and Barbara Carpenter, 32–74. Jackson: University Press of Mississippi, 2012.

Reidy, Joseph P. *From Slavery to Agrarian Capitalism in the Cotton Plantation South: Central Georgia, 1800–1880*. Chapel Hill: University of North Carolina Press, 1992.

Reynolds, Donald E. *Texas Terror: The Slave Insurrection Panic of 1860 and the Secession of the Lower South*. Baton Rouge: Louisiana State University Press, 2007.

Rivers, Larry Eugene. *Rebels and Runaways: Slave Resistance in Nineteenth-Century Florida*. Urbana: University of Illinois Press, 2012.

Robinson, Armstead L. *Bitter Fruits of Bondage: The Demise of Slavery and the Collapse of the Confederacy, 1861–1865*. Charlottesville: University of Virginia Press, 2005.

Rodrigue, John C. *Reconstruction in the Cane Fields: From Slavery to Free Labor in Louisiana's Sugar Parishes, 1862–1880*. Baton Rouge: Louisiana State University Press, 2001.

Rosen, Hannah. *Terror in the Heart of Freedom: Citizenship, Sexual Violence, and the Meaning of Race in the Postemancipation South*. Chapel Hill: University of North Carolina Press, 2009.

Roth, Randolph. *American Homicide*. Cambridge, MA: Harvard University Press, 2009.

Rothman, Adam. *Slave Country: American Expansion and the Origins of the Deep South*. Cambridge, MA: Harvard University Press, 2005.

Rowland, Dunbar. *Military History of Mississippi, 1803–1898: Taken from the Official and Statistical Register of the State of Mississippi, 1908*. Spartanburg, SC: Reprint Company, 1978.

Rubin, Anne S. *Shattered Nation: The Rise and Fall of the Confederacy, 1861–1868*. Chapel Hill: University of North Carolina Press, 2005.

Sandow, Robert M. *Deserter Country: Civil War Opposition in the Pennsylvania Appalachians*. Bronx: Fordham University Press, 2009.

Sarris, Jonathan Dean. *A Separate Civil War: Communities in Conflict in the Mountain South*. Charlottesville: University of Virginia Press, 2006.

Saville, Julie. *The Work of Reconstruction: From Slave to Wage Laborer in South Carolina, 1860–1870*. New York: Cambridge University Press, 1996.

Schermerhorn, Calvin. *Money over Mastery, Family over Freedom: Slavery in the Antebellum Upper South*. Baltimore: Johns Hopkins University Press, 2011.

Schweninger, Loren. *Black Property Owners in the South, 1790–1915*. Urbana: University of Illinois Press, 1990.

Scott, James C. *Domination and the Arts of Resistance: Hidden Transcripts*. New Haven, CT: Yale University Press, 1990.

Shapiro, Robert. *White Violence and Black Response: From Reconstruction to Montgomery*. Amherst: University of Massachusetts Press, 1988.

Sheehan-Dean, Aaron. *Why Confederates Fought: Family and Nation in Civil War Virginia*. Chapel Hill: University of North Carolina Press, 2007.

Shore, Laurence. "Making Mississippi Safe for Slavery: The Insurrectionary Panic of 1835." In *Class, Conflict, and Consensus: Antebellum Southern Community Studies*, edited by Orville Burton and Robert McMath Jr., 96–127. Westport, CT: Greenwood Press, 1982.

Sigafoos, Robert A. *Cotton Row to Beale Street: A Business History of Memphis*. Memphis: Memphis State University Press, 1979.

Slotkin, Richard. *No Quarter: The Battle of the Crater, 1864*. New York: Random House, 2009.

Smith, Mark M. *Mastered by the Clock: Time, Slavery, and Freedom in the American South*. Chapel Hill: University of North Carolina Press, 1997.

Smith, Timothy B. *Mississippi in the Civil War: The Home Front*. Jackson: University Press of Mississippi, 2010.

———. *The Mississippi Secession Convention: Delegates and Deliberations in Politics and War, 1861–1865*. Jackson: University Press of Mississippi, 2014.

Stampp, Kenneth M. *The Peculiar Institution: Slavery in the Ante-Bellum South*. New York: Alfred A. Knopf, 1967.

Sternhell, Yael A. "Bodies in Motion and the Making of Emancipation." In *Rethinking American Emancipation: Legacies of Slavery and the Quest for Black Freedom*, edited by William A. Link and James J. Broomall, 15–41. Cambridge: Cambridge University Press, 2016.

Stevenson, Brenda E. *Life in Black and White: Family and Community in the Slave South*. New York: Oxford University Press, 1996.

Storey, Margaret. *Loyalty and Loss: Alabama's Unionists in the Civil War and Reconstruction*. Baton Rouge: Louisiana State University Press, 2004.

Stott, Richard. *Jolly Fellows: Male Milieus in Nineteenth-Century America*. Baltimore: Johns Hopkins University Press, 2009.

Summers, Mark Wahlgren. *A Dangerous Stir: Fear, Paranoia, and the Making of Reconstruction*. Chapel Hill: University of North Carolina Press, 2009.

Sutherland, Daniel E., ed. *Guerrillas, Unionists, and Violence on the Confederate Home Front*. Fayetteville: University of Arkansas Press, 1999.

———. *A Savage Conflict: The Decisive Role of Guerrillas in the American Civil War*. Chapel Hill: University of North Carolina Press, 2009.

Takagi, Midori. *"Rearing Wolves to Our Own Destruction": Slavery in Richmond, Virginia, 1782–1865*. Charlottesville: University of Virginia Press, 1999.

Tatum, Georgia Lee. *Disloyalty in the Confederacy*. 1934. Reprint, New York: AMS Press, 1970.

Thomas, Emory. *The Confederacy as a Revolutionary Experience*. Columbia: University of South Carolina Press, 1971.

Tilly, Charles. *The Politics of Collective Violence*. New York: Cambridge University Press, 2003.

Tindall, George Brown, and David Emory Shi. *America: A Narrative History*. 7th ed. New York: W. W. Norton, 2007.

Towers, Frank. *The Urban South and the Coming of the Civil War*. Charlottesville: University of Virginia Press, 2004.

Townsend, Mary Bobbitt. *Yankee Warhorse: A Biography of Major General Peter Osterhaus*. Columbia: University of Missouri Press, 2010.

Trelease, Allen W. *White Terror: The Ku Klux Klan Conspiracy and Southern Reconstruction*. New York: Harper and Row, 1971.

Tripp, Steven Elliott. *Yankee Town, Southern City: Race and Class Relations in Civil War Lynchburg*. New York: New York University Press, 1997.

Truxes, Thomas M. *Defying Empire: Trading with the Enemy in Colonial New York*. New Haven, CT: Yale University Press, 2008.

Tuan, Yi-Fu. *Space and Place: The Perspective of Experience*. Minneapolis: University of Minnesota Press, 1977.

Ural, Susannah J., ed. *Civil War Citizens: Race, Ethnicity, and Identity in America's Bloodiest Conflict*. New York: New York University Press, 2010.

Urwin, Gregory J. W., ed. *Black Flag over Dixie: Racial Atrocities and Reprisals in the Civil War*. Carbondale: Southern Illinois University Press, 2004.

Van Buskirk, Judith L. *Generous Enemies: Patriots and Loyalists in Revolutionary New York*. Philadelphia: University of Pennsylvania Press, 2002.

Wade, Richard C. *Slavery in the Cities: The South, 1820–1860*. New York: Oxford University Press, 1964.

Wagner, Margaret E., Gary W. Gallagher, and Paul Finkelman, eds. *The Library of Congress Civil War Desk Reference*. New York: Simon and Schuster, 2009.

Waldrep, Christopher. *Roots of Disorder: Race and Criminal Justice in the American South, 1817–80*. Urbana: University of Illinois Press, 1998.

———. *Vicksburg's Long Shadow: The Civil War Legacy of Race and Remembrance*. Lanham, MD: Rowman and Littlefield, 2005.

Ward, Harry M. *Between the Lines: Banditti of the American Revolution*. Westport, CT: Praeger, 2002.

Weitz, Mark A. *More Damning Than Slaughter: Desertion in the Confederate Army*. Lincoln: University of Nebraska Press, 2005.

Wetherington, Mark V. *Plain Folk's Fight: The Civil War and Reconstruction in Piney Woods Georgia*. Chapel Hill: University of North Carolina Press, 2005.

Wharton, Vernon Lane. *The Negro in Mississippi, 1865–1890*. 1947. Reprint, New York: Harper and Row, 1965.

White, Deborah Gray. *Ar'n't I a Woman? Female Slaves in the Plantation South*. New York: W. W. Norton, 1985.

Whites, LeeAnn. *The Civil War as a Crisis in Gender, 1860–1890*. Athens: University of Georgia Press, 1995.

Williams, David. *Bitterly Divided: The South's Inner Civil War*. New York: New Press, 2008.

———. *I Freed Myself: African American Self-Emancipation*. Cambridge: Cambridge University Press, 2014.

Williams, Kidada E. *They Left Great Marks on Me: African American Testimonies of Racial Violence from Emancipation to World War I*. New York: New York University Press, 2012.

Williamson, Joel. *A Race for Order: Black-White Relations in the American South since Emancipation*. New York: Oxford University Press, 1986.

Willis, John C. *Forgotten Time: The Yazoo-Mississippi Delta after the Civil War*. Charlottesville: University of Virginia Press, 2000.

Wills, Brian S. "Shades of Nation: Confederate Loyalties in Southeastern Virginia." In *Inside the Confederate Nation: Essays in Honor of Emory Thomas*, edited by Leslie Gordon and John C. Inscoe, 59–78. Baton Rouge: Louisiana State University Press, 2005.

Wilson, Charles Reagan. *Baptized in Blood: The Religion of the Lost Cause, 1865–1920*. Athens: University of Georgia Press, 1980.

Wood, Betty. *Women's Work, Men's Work: The Informal Slave Economies of Lowcountry Georgia*. Athens: University of Georgia Press, 1995.

Wood, Peter H. *Black Majority: Negroes in Colonial South Carolina from 1670 through the Stono Rebellion*. New York: W. W. Norton, 1974.

Woodward, Colin Edward. *Marching Masters: Slavery, Race, and the Confederate Army during the Civil War*. Charlottesville: University of Virginia Press, 2014.

Wyatt-Brown, Bertram. *Honor and Violence in the Old South*. New York: Oxford University Press, 1986.

———. *Southern Honor: Ethics and Behavior in the Old South*. Oxford: Oxford University Press, 1982.

Wynne, Ben. *Mississippi's Civil War: A Narrative History*. Macon, GA: Mercer University Press, 2006.

Young, Jason R. *Rituals of Resistance: African Atlantic Religion in Kongo and the Lowcountry South in the Era of Slavery*. Baton Rouge: Louisiana State University Press, 2007.

SECONDARY SOURCES: JOURNAL ARTICLES

Aptheker, Herbert. "Notes on Slave Conspiracies in Confederate Mississippi." *Journal of Negro History* 29 (January 1944): 75–79.

Ash, Stephen V. "Poor Whites in the Occupied South, 1861–1865." *Journal of Southern History* 57 (February 1991): 39–62.

Bearman, Peter S. "Desertion as Localism: Army Unit Solidarity and Group Norms in the U.S. Civil War." *Social Forces* 70 (December 1991): 321–42.

Behrend, Justin. "Rebellious Talk and Conspiratorial Plots: The Making of a Slave Insurrection in Civil War Natchez." *Journal of Southern History* 77 (February 2011): 17–52.

Blain, William T. "'Banner' Unionism in Mississippi: Choctaw County, 1861–1869." *Mississippi Quarterly* 2 (Spring 1976): 207–20.

Carter, Dan T. "The Anatomy of Fear: The Christmas Day Insurrection Scare of 1865." *Journal of Southern History* 42 (August 1976): 345–64.

Cerulo, Karen A. "Identity Construction: New Issues, New Directions." *Annual Review of Sociology* 23 (1997): 385–409.

Coulter, E. Merton. "Commercial Intercourse with the Confederacy in the Mississippi Valley, 1861–1865." *Mississippi Valley Historical Review* 5 (March 1919): 377–95.

———. "Effects of Secession upon the Commerce of the Mississippi Valley." *Mississippi Valley Historical Review* 3 (December 1916): 275–300.

Currie, James T. "From Slavery to Freedom in Mississippi's Legal System." *Journal of Negro History* 2 (Spring 1980): 112–25.

Dal Lago, Enrico. "States of Rebellion: Civil War, Rural Unrest, and the Agrarian Question in the American South and the Italian Mezzogiorno, 1861–1865." *Comparative Studies in Society and History* 47 (April 2005): 403–32.

Eaton, Clement. "Mob Violence in the Old South." *Mississippi Valley Historical Review* 29 (December 1942): 351–70.

Gallagher, Gary W. "Disaffection, Persistence, and Nation: Some Directions in Recent Scholarship on the Confederacy." *Civil War History* 55 (September 2009): 329–53.

Hahn, Steven. "'Extravagant Expectations of Freedom': Rumour, Political Struggle, and the Christmas Insurrection Scare of 1865 in the American South." *Past and Present* 157 (November 1997): 122–58.

Hershberg, Theodore, Michael Katz, Stuart Blumin, Laurence Glasco, and Clyde Griffin. "Occupation and Ethnicity in Five Nineteenth-Century Cities: A Collaborative Inquiry." *Historical Methods Newsletter* 7 (June 1974): 174–216.

Hornsey, Matthew J., and Jolanda Jetten. "Loyalty without Conformity: Tailoring Self-Perception as a Means of Balancing Belonging and Differentiation." *Self and Identity* 4 (January–March 2005): 81–95.

Hultman, Lisa. "Attacks on Civilians in Civil War: Targeting the Achilles Heel of Democratic Governments." *International Interactions* 38, no. 2 (2012): 164–81.

Hyde, Samuel C., Jr. "Plain Folk Reconsidered: Historiographical Ambiguity in Search of Definition." *Journal of Southern History* 71 (November 2005): 803–30.

Johnson, Ludwell H. "Contraband Trade during the Last Year of the Civil War." *Mississippi Valley Historical Review* 49 (March 1963): 635–52.

———. "Trading with the Union: The Evolution of Confederate Policy." *Virginia Magazine of History and Biography* 78 (July 1970): 308–25.

Johnson, Walter. "On Agency." *Journal of Social History* 37 (Autumn 2003): 113–24.

Lack, Paul D. "An Urban Slave Community: Little Rock, 1831–1862." *Arkansas Historical Quarterly* 41 (Autumn 1982): 258–87.

Lang, Andrew F. "'Upon the Altar of Our Country': Confederate Identity, Nationalism, and Morale in Harrison County, Texas, 1860–1865." *Civil War History* 55 (September 2009): 278–306.

Lichtenstein, Alex. "'That Disposition to Theft, with Which They Have Been Branded': Moral Economy, Slave Management, and the Law." *Journal of Social History* 21 (Spring 1988): 413–40.

———. "Was the Emancipated Slave a Proletarian?" *Reviews in American History* 26 (March 1998): 124–45.

Logue, Larry M. "Who Joined the Confederate Army? Soldiers, Civilians, and Communities in Mississippi." *Journal of Social History* 26 (Spring 1993): 611–23.

Lohrenz, Mary. "Two Lives Intertwined on a Tennessee Plantation: Textile Production as Recorded in the Diary of Narcissa L. Erwin Black." *Southern Quarterly* 27 (Fall 1988): 72–93.

Marrs, Aaron W. "Desertion and Loyalty in South Carolina, 1861–1865." *Civil War History* 50 (March 2004): 47–65.

Morgan, Philip D. "Conspiracy Scares." *William and Mary Quarterly*, 3rd ser., 59 (January 2002): 159–66.

———. "The Ownership of Property by Slaves in the Mid-Nineteenth-Century Low Country." *Journal of Southern History* 49 (August 1983): 399–420.

Morris, Christopher. "The Articulation of Two Worlds: The Master-Slave Relationship Reconsidered." *Journal of American History* 85 (December 1998): 982–1007.

Nelson, Bernard H. "Confederate Slave Impressment Legislation, 1861–1865." *Journal of Negro History* 31 (October 1946): 392–410.

Noe, Kenneth W. "Who Were the Bushwhackers? Age, Class, Kin, and Western Virginia's Confederate Guerrillas, 1861–1862." *Civil War History* 49 (March 2003): 5–31.

Novak, William J. "The Myth of the 'Weak' American State." *American Historical Review* 113 (June 2008): 792–800.

Oakes, James. "The Political Significance of Slave Resistance." *History Workshop* 22 (Autumn 1986): 89–107.

O'Connor, Thomas H. "Lincoln and the Cotton Trade." *Civil War History* 7 (March 1961): 20–35.

Osthaus, Carl R. "The Work Ethic of the Plain Folk: Labor and Religion in the Old South." *Journal of Southern History* 70 (November 2004): 745–82.

Parks, Joseph H. "A Confederate Trade Center under Federal Occupation: Memphis, 1862 to 1865." *Journal of Southern History* 7 (August 1941): 289–314.

Penningroth, Dylan. "Slavery, Freedom, and Social Claims to Property among African Americans in Liberty County, Georgia, 1850–1880." *Journal of American History* 84 (September 1997): 405–35.

Pittman, Walter E., Jr. "Trading with the Devil: The Cotton Trade in Civil War Mississippi." *Journal of Confederate History* 2, no. 11 (1989): 132–42.

Potter, David M. "The Historian's Use of Nationalism and Vice-Versa." *American Historical Review* 67 (July 1962): 924–50.

Roberts, A. Sellew. "The Federal Government and Confederate Cotton." *American Historical Review* 32 (January 1927): 262–75.

Shaw, William L. "The Confederate Conscription and Exemption Acts." *American Journal of Legal History* 6 (October 1962): 368–405.

Spiller, John. "African Americans after the Civil War." *History Review* 65 (December 2009): 38–43.

Stremlau, Rose. "'To Domesticate and Civilize Wild Indians': Allotment and the Campaign to Reform Indian Families, 1875–1887." *Journal of Family History* 30 (July 2005): 265–86.

Sumners, Mary Floyd. "Politics in Tishomingo County, 1836–1860." *Journal of Mississippi History* 2 (May, 1966): 133–51.

Surdam, David G. "Traders or Traitors: Northern Cotton Trading during the Civil War." *Business and Economic History* 28 (Winter 1999): 301–12.

Trexler, Harrison A. "The Opposition of Planters to the Employment of Slaves as Laborers by the Confederacy." *Mississippi Valley Historical Review* 27 (September 1940): 211–24.

West, Stephen A. "Minute Men, Yeomen, and the Mobilization for Secession in the South Carolina Upcountry." *Journal of Southern History* 71 (February 2005): 75–104.

Whittington, Terry. "In the Shadow of Defeat: Tracking the Vicksburg Parolees." *Journal of Mississippi History* 4 (Winter 2002): 307–30.

Wilkie, Jane Riblett. "The Black Urban Population of the Pre–Civil War South." *Phylon* 37 (Third Quarter 1976): 250–62.

THESES AND DISSERTATIONS

Bremer, Jeff Robert. "Frontier Capitalism: The Market Revolution in the Antebellum Lower Missouri River Valley, 1803–1860." PhD diss., University of Kansas, 2006.

Mallard, Michael Shannon. "'Faithful Found among the Faithless': Popular Opposition to the Confederacy in Civil War Mississippi." Master's thesis, Mississippi State University, 2002.

BLOGS

Payne, Ed. "Crossing the Rubicon of Loyalties: Piney Woods Enlistees in the Union 1st and 2nd New Orleans Infantry." *Renegade South: Histories of Unconventional Southerners* (blog), May 26, 2011. At http://renegadesouth.wordpress.com/2011/05/26/crossing-the-rubicon-of-loyalties-piney-woods-enlistees-in-the-union-1st-and-2nd-north-orleans-infantry/.

CONFERENCE PAPERS

Behrend, Justin J. "Black Political Mobilization and the Spatial Transformation of Natchez." Paper presented at the American Civil War and the Cities of the Slave South workshop, Calgary and Banff, Alberta, May 25–26, 2012.

ONLINE REFERENCE WORKS

Howatson, M. C., ed. *The Concise Oxford Companion to Classical Literature.* Oxford: Oxford University Press, 1996. At http://www.oxfordreference.com/views/ENTRY.html ?subview=Main&entry=t9.e737.

INDEX

CPSIA information can be obtained
at www.ICGtesting.com
Printed in the USA
BVOW03*1210280817
492534BV00008B/2/P

9 781496 813961